EARLY CHILDHOOD EDUCATION AND CARE

Education at SAGE

SAGE is a leading international publisher of journals, books, and electronic media for academic, educational, and professional markets.

Our education publishing includes:

- accessible and comprehensive texts for aspiring education professionals and practitioners looking to further their careers through continuing professional development

- inspirational advice and guidance for the classroom

- authoritative state of the art reference from the leading authors in the field

Find out more at: **www.sagepub.co.uk/education**

EARLY CHILDHOOD EDUCATION AND CARE

An Introduction

Sheila Nutkins, Catriona McDonald and **Mary Stephen**

Los Angeles | London | New Delhi
Singapore | Washington DC

Los Angeles | London | New Delhi
Singapore | Washington DC

SAGE Publications Ltd
1 Oliver's Yard
55 City Road
London EC1Y 1SP

SAGE Publications Inc.
2455 Teller Road
Thousand Oaks, California 91320

SAGE Publications India Pvt Ltd
B 1/I 1 Mohan Cooperative Industrial Area
Mathura Road
New Delhi 110 044

SAGE Publications Asia-Pacific Pte Ltd
3 Church Street
#10-04 Samsung Hub
Singapore 049483

Commissioning editor: Jude Bowen
Assistant editor: Miriam Davey
Project manager/copyeditor: Sharon Cawood
Assistant production editor: Thea Watson
Proofreader: Rosemary Campbell
Indexer: Catriona Armit
Marketing manager: Catherine Slinn
Cover design: Wendy Scott
Typeset by: C&M Digitals (P) Ltd, Chennai, India
Printed in Great Britain by MPG Printgroup, UK

Library of Congress Control Number: 2012946208

British Library Cataloguing in Publication data

A catalogue record for this book is available from
the British Library

ISBN 978-1-4462-0711-6
ISBN 978-1-4462-0712-3 (pbk)

CONTENTS

ABOUT THE AUTHORS

Sheila Nutkins, Catriona McDonald and Mary Stephen are Teaching Fellows in the School of Education at the University of Aberdeen. They all support students on BEd (Hons), PGDE, BA Childhood Practice (BACP) undergraduate programmes and the Early Years Postgraduate Certificate in Education (EYPGCE). Catriona McDonald is the Programme Director for BACP and EYPGCE.

Sheila Nutkins taught in London as Deputy Head at St Paul's JMI in Primrose Hill, London NW1 and has lived and worked in Aberdeen since 1991. She developed course materials and taught in Further Education before joining the University in 2005.

Catriona McDonald trained as a primary teacher in Edinburgh and then completed the Froebel certificate. She taught in nursery classes in Scotland before going to Sweden with her husband where she lived for 20 years, working in primary and secondary schools there teaching English and music.

Mary Stephen completed her PGDE teaching qualification in Aberdeen after graduating with a BSc in Genetics and working in science research for five years. She taught in primary and particularly nursery (3–5) classes in north-east Scotland before working in Further Education on childcare and education courses and joined the University in 2008.

ACKNOWLEDGEMENTS

The authors would like to acknowledge the support provided by colleagues at the University of Aberdeen. The book stems largely from our development of the Early Years Postgraduate Certificate in 2009 which was funded by the Scottish Government. We were strongly supported in our initial bid and then the ongoing development by our then Head of School Myra Pearson. Others who deserve special thanks include Yvonne Yule and Alison Nicol for their valued expertise in ECEC over many years, Alan Paterson for sharing his expertise and photos regarding transient art and Liz Curtis for sharing her work on 'community walks'.

We especially want to acknowledge how much we have learned from all of our students and thank them for the materials some of them have allowed us to use.

We would like to thank Jude Bowen at SAGE for her very positive, encouraging assistance and we are all grateful to our long-suffering families.

PART 1

CHILD DEVELOPMENT AND LEARNING

Introduction

The purpose of this first part, and indeed the whole book, is to explore some particular and pertinent aspects of practice and provision drawing on new research evidence where possible, as well as returning to theories from decades ago that can still inform our practice today. The book is underpinned by our shared, firmly held belief that the early years of life from conception to age 8, and particularly the first three years, are crucial and influence the rest of an individual's life. Our continued personal study and research, as well as our learning from teaching both undergraduate students and professionals, has built this belief into a firm philosophy. This philosophy, which could broadly be described as learning (meaning knowledge and understanding, skills and informed attitudes) during the first years of life, is of paramount importance. Establishing a positive disposition towards learning in the early years is most important of all, and it is the responsibility of all adults involved with young children to work together to achieve this.

Here in Part 1, we explore some new understanding of development from conception to 3, revisit the importance of play, examine the importance of risk and highlight two specific approaches in 'Kodály' and 'transient art'. Throughout, we endeavour to explain some complex ideas, concepts and information as simply as possible. We try to show

how new research evidence, evidence from our own work with students and old and new theories can inform practice and provision in the 21st century. We hope we have given some practical suggestions in terms of how to examine practice and how to adapt or change practice, and a useful guide to further recommended reading at the end of each chapter is given to help in this process.

We will use the term Early Childhood Education and Care (abbreviated to the acronym ECEC) professionals when referring to 'the reader'. This is the terminology currently used in Europe to encompass all those who work (or are students) in the early years sector educating and caring for children aged 0–8. It is our intention that this book will be relevant to all students and practitioners within this sector as it is our belief that there is a specific body of knowledge pertinent to all ECEC professionals.

In this first part, we will explore:

- some recent research evidence with regard to cognitive development and language acquisition from conception to 3
- the critical nature of these first years of life in relation to later development, learning and outcomes
- our understanding of the importance of play; how play-based approaches to learning can and should be extended beyond pre-school; and the importance of risk taking as part of play opportunity and learning
- two creative approaches for adults engaged in the care and education of very young children.

The first chapter, 'Development from conception to 3 – new understanding', considers some of the more recent research that is informing our understanding of how the child develops. This is considered in terms of the impact on later development and learning and how this in turn might impact on practice and provision for 3–8-year-olds. The chapter explores some of the increasing body of evidence that emphasises the importance of very early years to later learning and outcomes. It examines some of the very recent research into cognitive development made possible by the use of MRI scanning. It seems an important point to pause, take stock and explore the new understanding developing from this information about the connection between cognitive development and language acquisition in particular, which supports the need for earlier intervention – the earlier the better. This new evidence needs to be considered by students and early childhood education and care professionals in terms of the possible impact on practice and provision of education and care for very young children.

Chapter 2, 'Play as active learning', builds on the understanding that the importance of play from birth to 5 and the difference between free play and structured play is understood and explores why play opportunities, which are still not consistently offered to children, are withdrawn too early. It looks at how a play-based approach to learning can and should be extended beyond pre-school and be seen as 'active learning' rather than 'just play', or a reward for when 'work' is finished. The reader is encouraged to explore their own experiences of play, drawing on a Swedish research paper, as a basis for understanding attitudes to play as learning. The quality of play provision and the role and nature of adult interaction in children's play is considered. In Scotland through the implementation of the Curriculum for Excellence, the aim is to smooth the transition between Nursery (3–5-year-olds) and Primary 1 (P1, first year of primary school, rising 6 years old) by adopting a play-based approach to learning and teaching in Primary 1. This part of the process began in earnest with the publication of the document *Building the Curriculum 2 – Active learning in the early years* (Scottish Government, 2007). The approach is very much along the lines of the Foundation Stage (DCSF, 2008), where the guidelines clearly call for well-planned play, both indoors and outdoors, as a key way in which to support young children's learning whilst providing enjoyment and challenge, and particularly the approach taken in Wales in recent years (Welsh Government, 2002). The play-based approach to learning is also being promoted and extended beyond 5 in many other countries including Australia (Northern Territory Government, 2012). Some suggest that this will merely move the transition and create a 'jump' from Primary 1 to Primary 2 (rising 7 years old). It is important, if this is to be avoided, that all ECEC professionals not only understand the place of play in the curriculum but that they are able to justify and defend the approach to others, particularly parents.

Chapter 3, 'Play and risk', continues the discussion in Chapter 2 by discussing the importance of outdoor play, risk awareness and management and the impact of risk aversion on children's access to and engagement with play opportunities. It considers how to create 'places of possibility' and why we should look at what happens elsewhere. It also considers a specific project and approach found in the Forest Schools initiative. The chapter explores the evidence that risk aversion is curtailing children's experiences and learning, the debate around the importance of risk taking in children's play, lives and learning and some opportunities to enable professionals to strike a better balance between protection and freedom. Evidence suggests that limited opportunities to take risks in childhood may have specific damaging effects in the long term, both in terms of physical and emotional health and well-being. This is the justification for looking closely at this issue in the chapter and looking for some ways for ECEC professionals to drive the dialogue and provide more and better opportunities for children in their care.

Chapter 4, 'Creative approaches to teaching and learning – Kodály', explores the use of the Kodály method of music education (a method devised by a Hungarian composer and used to teach children from babyhood in schools in Hungary). Before explaining the methodology involved in the Kodály approach, the question of creativity is examined and the importance of nurturing this in our children from the very beginning is established. The chapter draws on evidence and case studies from students on two post-graduate courses at the University of Aberdeen to examine the benefits to children of using the Kodály method. It looks at how Kodály impacts on learning across the curriculum, in particular in terms of language acquisition and how it can help establish and maintain quality interactions between professionals, parents and children. The benefits of training using Kodály methodology are promoted and ways in which the non-specialist can engage and adapt the basic underpinning principles to enhance practice are explored.

Chapter 5, 'Creative approaches to teaching and learning – transient art', explores the benefits of transient art projects (impermanent artwork such as playdough, finger paint, etc.) for children's learning across the curriculum. This chapter develops the discussion about the importance of nurturing creativity from birth which began in Chapter 4 through examination of just a few examples of this approach in action. This exploration of an approach that might encourage the use of imagination, independence and creativity, with examples, will be used as a basis for discussion. This will be set against the ideas of those who feel schools are killing creativity, such as Sir Ken Robinson, whose work has already been explored in Chapter 4; along with the artwork of those such as Andy Goldsworthy and the approach taken in other parts of the world such as Reggio Emilia, which is explored in Chapter 12.

This chapter will conclude by identifying the opportunities for learning how to learn that creative approaches, such as transient art and Kodály, can help establish. These approaches are suggested as ways to establish a sense of self-worth from which children can develop better dispositions towards learning. We feel it is vital that ECEC students and professionals in their continuing professional development have an understanding of their vital role in establishing a positive disposition towards learning that will impact on the child's ability to reach their full potential. The whole part should be viewed as a starting point for further study and discussion.

References

Department for Children, Schools and Families (DCSF) (2008) *Practice Guidance for the Early Years Foundation Stage.* Available at: https://www.education.gov.uk/publications/eOrderingDownload/eyfs_practiceguid_0026608.pdf (accessed 27.07.12).

Northern Territory Government (2012) *Play-based Learning.* Available at: http://www.det.nt.gov.au/__data/assets/pdf_file/0015/960/play-based_learning.pdf (accessed 24.07.12).

Scottish Government (2007) *Curriculum for Excellence: Building the Curriculum 2 – Active learning in the early years.* Edinburgh: Scottish Government. Available at: http://www.scotland.gov.uk/Resource/Doc/325191/0104856.pdf (accessed 27.07.12).

Welsh Government (2002) *Welsh Assembly Government Play Policy.* Available at: http://wales.gov.uk/docrepos/40382/40382313/childrenyoungpeople/403821/623995/play-policy.pdf (accessed 26.07.12).

CHAPTER 1

DEVELOPMENT FROM CONCEPTION TO 3 – NEW UNDERSTANDING

Keys ideas explored in this chapter

- new research evidence and current thinking that can inform ECEC practice
- the need for early years' practitioners to be secure in their understanding of normative development
- factors from conception and through the first months of life that may affect long-term development.

Valuable research from a number of disciplines including psychology, medicine and education now supports our understanding of the importance of factors in early development in relation to long-term outcomes for children. The Early Years Framework states: 'It is during our very earliest years and even pre-birth that a large part of the pattern of our future adult life is set' (Scottish Government, 2008: 1).

The development of non-invasive scanning techniques now enables medical researchers to monitor and analyse development and brain activity from conception and from birth (Goswami, 2008; Huotilainen, 2010). Researchers and academics in the fields of psychology and education continue to use this 'hard' evidence to theorise and develop understanding of how children develop and learn and how best adults can educate and care for them.

Trevarthen and Aitken (2001) identified that children exhibit the essential motivation for learning in the first months when they actively seek to engage in proto-conversation with a main carer. A proto-conversation is the interaction pattern between mothers (usually) and babies where the mother speaks when their baby stops babbling, or when the mother finishes the baby's 'conversations'. Babies begin to 'read' facial and vocal emotions and clearly favour their mother tongue. For an infant to survive and develop to their full potential, the caregiver must provide emotional attachment but also the opportunity for active engagement with the environment.

Normative development

All children undergo an orderly and predictable sequence of neurological development and physical growth considered as normative development. For example, physical development involves first lifting the head, then rolling over before sitting up unaided and then standing and walking. These are developmental 'milestones' that all children pass through in the same order. However, each child is unique and will pass these at different ages. There are milestones for all aspects of development and it is important for all ECEC professionals to be familiar with these. If you have not already done so, it is a good idea to start by studying the physical developmental milestones and then working through all aspects such as cognitive, social, etc. and then looking at how development in one area can impact on another. For example, development of the pincer grip (bringing the thumb and fore-finger together) around eight months enables the child to manipulate tools, providing greater independence and the ability to make marks. This has an impact on cognitive development (Bruce and Meggitt, 2006).

A knowledge of the expected developmental 'milestones' helps us in a number of ways, including:

- allowing us to expect a stage to be reached within a particular time span
- allowing us to identify potential problems and address these early – notice anything unusual, particularly any developmental delay
- allowing us to provide appropriate challenges and a suitably stimulating environment.

Development is the interplay between the unique genetic blueprint for each individual and the unique experiences each has from conception. Parents will naturally draw on their own experiences and, often, subconsciously follow the model laid down by their own parents. If a child has experienced a childhood lacking in affection, support and stimulation from adults, they may recall and replicate this model, which in turn may promote a cycle of deprivation. Alternatively, an adult may completely reject a bad model of parenting; for example, the child of an alcoholic who abstains from alcohol. Bruce (2004) highlights how early theorists such as Freud and Erikson suggested that an appropriately stimulating environment combined with stable relationships positively supports development. A wide body of current research confirms this.

The Tickell Review (2011) draws from international research to support what early years practitioners had already identified, namely that 'foundations laid in the first years of life, if weak, can have a detrimental impact on children's longer term development' (p. 2). It is important that ECEC professionals reflect on their own experiences from childhood and parenting, as well as professional experience, to determine the influences on their own practice. Ongoing critical self-evaluation against an understanding of normative development and influencing factors is key to developing good reflective practice and will allow ECEC professionals to intervene early to support the needs of each unique child.

REFLECTIVE ACTIVITY

A case study considering normative development

An only child, Edward is 4 years old and has been in nursery since he was 3. His mother is Thai and his father is British. Dad works full time and mum works evening shifts at a local supermarket. When Edward walks for any length of time, or runs, he does so on tiptoe, not on the heel and ball of his foot. The nursery team is becoming concerned as his physical development does not seem normal.

How would you approach the parents to address this problem and what suggestion would you offer?

Discuss with colleagues or other students and then see the response at the end of the chapter.

New understandings

Pre-natal development occurs during the 38 weeks from conception, between the point at which the egg is fertilised, and birth. It is difficult to comprehend that within 38 weeks one egg will develop into at least 100 trillion cells and become a unique human being. One third of a million babies emerge daily into the world ready to face a range of challenges.

Our understanding of child development continues to grow and research and study no longer rely on observations. Development can now be mapped using new technologies which allow us to gather images during gestation and from the functioning brain. Goswami (2008) identifies three techniques appropriate to studying brain activity in children:

1   Electroencephalography (EEG)
2   Functional magnetic resonance imaging (fMRI)
3   Functional near-infrared spectroscopy (fNIRS)

There are advantages and disadvantages with each technique. The advantage of using fNIRS is that a young child need not be exposed to the large chamber associated with fMRI. However, according to Goswami (2008), fNIRS does not, at present, offer temporal accuracy comparable to EEG, or spatial accuracy comparable to fMRI. To record foetal and neonatal cognitive abilities, Huotilainen (2010) has effectively developed the use of magnetoencephalography (MEG), a non-invasive technique which records the magnetic fields produced by the active neurons in the brain. This experimentation has identified that during the last trimester (the final stage of pregnancy) and the first months of life, both emotional recognition and language acquisition develop rapidly. Cognitive abilities start to develop prior to birth, and the newborn has advanced abilities related to processing emotional information and speech sounds so that the foundations of native language acquisition and social skills are firmly in place (Huotilainen, 2010).

It is interesting to consider what an 'infant' is at this point, or rather how 'infancy' is defined. The word infant is derived from the Latin 'infans' meaning unable to speak, covering the period from birth to 2 years. Even this term indicates how human development is closely linked to the ability to communicate. The infant may lack the ability to communicate verbally, but these research methods indicate that the building blocks for language are initiated during neonatal development. *In utero* growth and development can now be closely monitored. Understanding how these very early experiences may result in different responses to later experiences in young children and have repercussions throughout their life, could help parents and ECEC professionals support children better.

Brain development

The term 'tabula rasa' (blank slate) is the epistemological theory that individuals are born without built-in mental content and that their knowledge comes from experience. Huotilainen (2010), through her research, asserts that the neonatal brain is already a product of development, not 'tabula rasa' but a highly capable organ. The foetal brain *in utero* has high levels of plasticity and most neurons are present by the seventh month following conception (Rakic, 1995). At birth we have all our neurons. We do not need and do not grow any more but we do need to connect them up. The more connections there are, the better the brain will function. From six months to a year, the brain can make the most rapid neural connections and growth and this is facilitated by biochemicals generated by the intense social bond with the primary caregiver (Gerhardt, 2004).

Babies' brains develop as a consequence of their relationship with caregivers (Gerhardt, 2004; Szalavitz and Perry, 2011; Zeedyk, 2006). Forming and reinforcing connections between the brain cells or *neurons* are the key tasks of early brain development which is partly determined by the genetic code, but is then supported and influenced by relationships and the environment. Neurons make connections with others across the gap between them called the *synapse* in a process called *synaptogenesis*. Neurons that make successful connections remain, whilst the brain rids itself of those that are unsuccessful in another process called *synaptic pruning* (Doherty and Hughes, 2009). The brain develops in relation to the world, and once the key pathways are established, they remain and are carried into adulthood (Zeedyk, 2006). Early intervention should be interpreted as the 'earliest possible intervention' in order to establish the pathways that enable the child to learn and go on learning to reach their full potential. It would be wrong to suggest that *only* very early intervention will effect change as connections do continue to be made throughout life, as evidenced by the examination of Einstein's pickled brain by researchers in Canada. They found that the part of the brain involved in maths reasoning and visual-spatial thinking was 15 per cent larger than the brains of other men of comparable age (Gerhardt, 2004). We do however have clear evidence that earlier interventions are more effective.

We may have lost some of our intuitive survival skills over the millennia but a newborn baby has not. One area in the Highlands of Cameroon encourages their children to retain one of the early reflex actions. All newborns have the innate ability to take steps when a few days old but in our society this reflex action is lost and re-learned when the child starts to walk. The Cameroon mothers carry their children long distances in order to work and they need their children to be able to walk as early as possible. From about one month old, they encourage the children to 'make jump', which involves holding the children's arms, making them stand and bouncing them on their legs to strengthen the leg muscles and build and reinforce pathways within the brain. This reflex action has survived and does not need to be relearned so by 7 months most children are walking, not just with tentative baby steps, but surely and steadily. Children walking so early seems remarkable to us and demonstrates how neurological pathways are developed within the brain, creating synaptic connections.

Kotulak (1997) suggests that the principle 'if you don't use it, you lose it' is as true for cognitive skills as it is for muscle development. A newborn baby can swim at birth and some mothers allow their babies to swim unaided early on. Whilst it is not suggested that ECEC professionals throw babies into swimming pools or force them to walk, these examples suggest that neurological pathways can remain established and develop sooner given the necessary environment, rather than being 'pruned' out and then re-learned later.

The infant brain needs to form connections that will allow the child to survive; therefore the primary sensory systems need to be established first and these are the auditory, visual and motor systems. The areas of the brain dealing with higher-order association will mature later (Casey et al., 2005). Many pregnant women can recall a time when their baby seemed to be reacting to an auditory stimulus. This is frequently one that is musical or contains some type of melodic rhythm. The neonatal auditory system is capable of detecting small changes in frequency and has the potential to detect differences in the formant frequencies that separate vowels from each other (Dehaene-Lambertz and Baillet, 1998). This would indicate that neonates have the ability to note that some syllables follow one another whilst others do not; such skills are highly important for native language acquisition. ECEC professionals can support development through the use of singing, rhyme and rhythm (see Chapter 4 where the Kodály approach is discussed to promote language acquisition and support other developmental areas).

All babies are born with a range of mechanisms at their disposal to learn, but it is the adult's role to provide a range of suitable experiences. The plasticity of the immature human brain allows new pathways to develop through interactions with fellow humans. Researchers now believe that as much as 80 per cent of the basic brain architecture is 'wired' by the age of 3 (Kotulak, 1997).

This 'wiring' begins in the womb and is most rapid in the first months of life. The non-invasive research techniques discussed above have identified that children are building synaptic connections in the brain during the last trimester of pregnancy, linked to auditory development. The foetus will have listened to the mother's voice and other sounds whilst in the womb so that the infant at birth has already tuned into its mother's voice and therefore its native language. Newborn babies are programmed to search out human faces (Johnson et al., 1991), possibly an early survival technique; when a close bond is made, the chance of being cared for and protected will be higher. A baby is born as a learner and certainly does not wait to reach school to make a start!

Goswami (2008) has identified three types of learning:

1   Learning by imitation
2   The ability to connect cause and effect – explanation
3   Associative learning – analogy

Babies from birth to three days have been shown to be able to imitate gestures such as tongue protrusion and mouth opening after watching an adult carry out the same gestures (Meltzoff and Moore, 1983). This is despite the fact that a newborn does not even know what the object is that it is copying or comprehend that it has a face of its own! This ability to learn by imitation supports the development of social cognition. Developing social skills from an early age allows us to integrate into our culture. All human contact, whether it is with a parent, sibling or key worker, offers opportunities to imitate. Without such a close bond, this type of learning would not occur, as has been shown in children who have been isolated from human contact. Research into the impact on brain development and learning of the harrowing experiences of Romanian orphans constantly left, sometimes tied in their cots and unable to form any kind of relationship, shows 'a virtual black hole where their orbitofrontal cortex should be' (Chugani et al., 2001, cited in Gerhardt, 2004: 38). Within the Maori culture, siblings and children tend to care for younger children and this may offer better opportunities to learn through imitation as children are far more animated in how they talk and move (Barr and Hayne, 2003).

REFLECTIVE ACTIVITY

Where the opportunity arises, observe a young baby's interaction with a slightly older child and consider these interactions: the body language, how the child uses language and the response from the baby. Compare and contrast a similar interaction between an adult and a baby. How does the adult's behaviour change?

The majority of UK nurseries working with children aged 0–3 accommodate them in relation to their specific age, so all babies up to the age of 1 are in one area. Consider the activity above and how children interact. Consider whether it would be better to accommodate them in family groupings so children can learn from each other. Family groupings might offer children more challenge. This model will be discussed further in the section related to Swedish daycare but it is interesting to note that during our own research, students commented on this structure and how it had made them question the often rigid division into classes in school by age.

> I think … it is restrictive … I think children are social and learning is social and that it's so valuable for younger children to learn from older children and vice versa and having one age group together can really limit their experiences, their opportunities … (Primary 1 teacher reflecting back on her 0–3 placement)

CASE STUDY

Euan is 1 year old and has a baby gym with lots of equipment for developing fine motor skills, such as pushing buttons, turning etc. and he can predict cause/effect reactions there. He has imitated his parents and grandparents in operating this equipment and also 'tried' to learn by trial and error. He is also able to use learning by analogy and found, for example, the push buttons on the phone/TV remote control. At 1 year old, he was only interested in

(Continued)

(Continued)

pushing buttons to see what was happening. Now – at 20 months – he knows that the mobile phone is something that you talk on – and *imitates* a conversation when holding it to his ear – after pushing the buttons!

The case study of 'Euan' demonstrates the difference between imitation and analogy. Imitation is when the child has observed an action of another person and then copies the action, whereas analogy is something that the child has learned (perhaps by imitation or trial and error) and then can transfer to a new situation.

Young children demonstrate the ability to connect cause and effect. They constantly ask questions, and it is this questioning that supports the development of early memory. Young children also clearly have the ability to learn that certain events co-occur; this is referred to as associative learning. A baby makes the link that, 'if I cry someone will pick me up and soothe me and feed me'. This early example of associative learning is another basic survival technique.

Perris, Myers and Clifton (1990) demonstrated that six-month-old babies could retain memories of events for a very long time. Their research identified that at the age of 2 and a half, a child had retained a memory of a single event that occurred when they were six months old. Again, such child memory retention potentially has major implications for the carer. If a child has been subjected to a traumatic experience at an early age, this will be stored but the ability to actually retell this event later in life may not be possible, as the event could be buried deep in the child's memory.

External factors that affect the developing foetus

In utero, a foetus may be exposed to a range of damaging substances. These are referred to as 'teratogens' and include drugs, caffeine, alcohol and diseases such as genital herpes, mumps, rubella and HIV. Even expectant mothers who are aware and responsive to advice about dangers may expose the developing child to risks because of unknown factors beyond their control or even due to conflicting advice (Bing-Chen et al., 2010).

Drugs and alcohol can directly affect the developing foetal organs and restrict overall growth. When discussing drugs, we generally consider illegal substances; however certain long-term medications such as drugs for epilepsy do need to be administered and monitored during pregnancy. With continual improvement in medical intervention and increased survival rates of individuals with previously life-threatening conditions, there is an increase in the number of mothers with conditions that previously would have precluded them from giving birth. There may be a connection between emotional behavioural disorders or learning difficulties presented and factors such as mothers taking prescribed drugs, illegal drugs or excessive alcohol. This is an important factor for ECEC students and professionals to consider in terms of the impact on the development and learning of children in their care.

Hanson et al. (1976) studied women with severe chronic alcoholism and identified foetal alcohol syndrome (FAS). This presents as a range of physical and cognitive malformations in children. Their work was linked to that of Lemoine et al. (1968) who reported on a series of 127 offspring of chronic alcoholics from 69 different families, which noted:

- peculiar faces – smooth philtrum – the groove between the nose and the upper lip flattens
- considerable retardation of growth in height and weight
- increased malformation to organs such as the heart
- psychomotor disturbances – this means the development of skills that involve both mental and muscular activity does not progress normally and might present as lack of control over voluntary movements or bodily functions.

The authors identified that such children failed to thrive after birth. Similar patterns are observed in newborns exposed to harmful drugs, suggesting that withdrawal symptoms are occurring. Hanson et al. (1976) suggested that women should avoid consuming alcohol whilst pregnant and although many years have passed, unfortunately the consumption of alcohol, particularly in women, continues to rise.

In the first 12 weeks of foetal development, the central nervous system is established and an excessive intake of alcohol can be particularly damaging. In the last 30 years, consumption of alcohol has increased and the culture of binge drinking may contribute to FAS, particularly when women are unaware they are pregnant. Some factors related to FAS, particularly the impact on brain development during gestation, may explain the increase in a range of behavioural problems within care and education today. The effects can go beyond the physical and early impact during gestation to affect the mother and baby relationship or 'bonding' and long-term emotional development (Ostera et al., 1997).

What we see today are foetal alcohol spectrum disorders (FASD) ranging from mild learning difficulties through to birth defects. In the UK, it is estimated that 6,000 babies per year are born with FASD, with alcohol-related birth defects (ARBD) which may range from mild to severe, depending upon the amount of alcohol exposure and during which trimester the exposure occurred. It is possible that Attention Deficit Hyperactivity Disorder (ADHD) may be another effect of foetal alcohol exposure and research is ongoing into this (NOFAS, 2011).

FAS and FASD have been frequently under-diagnosed and under-reported. In Scotland, for example, there are more than 900 children (0–18) who have FAS with many more, possibly thousands of, children damaged in a more subtle way. The effects of FAS/FASD cannot be repaired and may result in adults with long-term learning difficulties and/or anti-social behaviour preventing them from gaining employment, or they may be involved in substance abuse or addiction. There are obvious long-term socio-economic effects. The immediate negative impact on a young child's ability to learn can have an adverse effect on life chances (Children in Scotland, 2011).

Stress is a 'condition' we have in our daily lives and pregnancy itself can be a stressful time for some women (DiPietro, 2004). The mother's emotional experiences during pregnancy can affect the development of the baby's brain (O'Donnell et al., 2009). Stress causes increased levels of the hormone cortisol which can pass through the placenta. Neurologists have identified that the presence of this 'stress hormone' during gestation disrupts brain development and functioning, and it has been suggested it may result in a range of behavioural problems, especially attention problems (Clavarino et al., 2009).

ADHD is the most commonly diagnosed childhood psychiatric disorder, with an estimated prevalence of at least 4 per cent (Brown et al., 2001). Rodriguez and Bohlin (2005) concluded from their research, undertaken in Sweden, that pre-natal exposure to both stress and smoking (nicotine) were independently associated with later symptoms of ADHD in children, especially boys. As young children by nature are highly active, ADHD is difficult to diagnose. What actually causes this condition is a complex combination of genetic and environmental factors (Rodriguez and Bohlin, 2005). What has been identified through magnetic resonance imaging (MRI) is that the frontal lobes of the brain in children exhibiting ADHD are damaged, and this area of the brain is linked to the way in which we are able to control our behaviour (Kelly et al., 2007).

Stress continues to be an important factor after birth as babies cannot manage their own cortisol. Infants who are in a distressed state will produce higher levels of this hormone, rather than the relaxed hormone oxytocin, and in a stressed state an infant has a reduced capacity to engage with the world around them. The influence of this stress hormone can also have long-term effects on the overall development of the brain (see Figure 1.1). As adults, we have developed strategies which alleviate stress but babies have not developed the required skills to deal with stressful situations.

Habits or automatic responses are being formed and physically embedded by the production of certain chemicals in infancy and it takes until about 4 years old to establish a normal adult pattern of high levels of cortisol in the morning, lowering later in the day (Gerhardt, 2004). Detailed research shows how love and attention, particularly from the key carer (usually mother), critically from six months to a year, reduce stress and stimulate the development of the 'social brain' (2004). Research shows that infants of depressed mothers appear less responsive to faces and voices as early as the neonatal period (Field et al., 2009).

Whilst it may not be possible for ECEC professionals to impact on this early period of life, knowledge and understanding of the antecedents of a child's behaviour can inform practice to better support the needs of individuals. It can also support practice in more general ways in terms of ensuring consistency of care, establishing key workers for each child, and highlighting the importance of being responsive and creating a calm environment.

Figure 1.1 demonstrates the effect of *global neglect* (this means severe neglect, including sensory deprivation) on the developing brain. A vast amount of stimulus and support is required to try to reconnect some of the neural pathways before they are permanently pruned out.

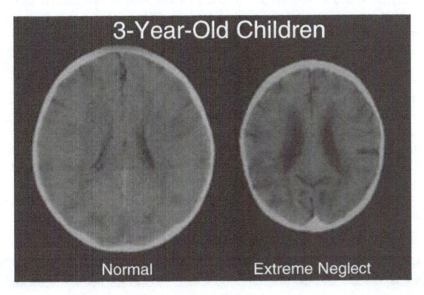

Figure 1.1   These images illustrate the negative impact of neglect on the developing brain. In the CT scan on the left is an image from a healthy 3-year-old with an average head size. The image on the right is from a 3-year-old child suffering from severe sensory-deprivation neglect. This child's brain is significantly smaller than the average and has abnormal development of the cortex (Perry and Pollard, 1997). These images are from studies conducted by a team of researchers from the Child Trauma Academy (www. ChildTrauma.org) led by Bruce D. Perry, M.D., PhD.

Source: The Margaret McCain lectures series, Inaugural lecture by Bruce D. Perry, *Maltreatment and the Developing Child*, 2004

It is not suggested that ECEC professionals engage in diagnosis of any medical condition but they are often best placed to identify possible signs and symptoms and alert parents and other professionals who support the child and suggest that timely intervention may be needed. Whilst it is not possible at present to treat a damaged brain medically and repair it, it is possible through early intervention in terms of additional and specific support to mitigate the problems and achieve better outcomes. It is essential that all those caring for young children understand the importance of the child's previous experience. As soon as a child starts their formal education, record keeping and a teacher's awareness of their prior learning is, rightly, seen as vital. The importance of learning and experience from pre-birth to 3 has been ignored for too long.

The breastfeeding debate

Breast-fed children are still 30 per cent less likely to have behaviour problems than bottle-fed infants, when compared with other factors such as deprivation and parental age (Heikkila et al., 2011; University of Oxford, 2011). Breast milk contains large amounts of essential long-chain polyunsaturated fatty acids, growth factors which support the development of the brain and the central nervous system. Through a randomised study, causal inference has been made between breastfeeding and intelligence (Kramer, 2008).

Another factor is the importance of the interaction between mother and child when breastfeeding; unless milk is expressed, this role falls solely to the mother so a strong bond can be established. In addition, breastfeeding tends to take longer (in terms of the mother/child interaction) than bottle feeding and the baby will pause, allowing for all-important mother/child 'conversations' (Trevarthen and Aitken, 2001). This closeness and communication, that mirror a conversation, support the mother in talking or singing to the child and help to develop auditory pathways which allow the infant to identify speech patterns and syntax.

REFLECTIVE ACTIVITY

Consider these questions:

- If breastfeeding provides ideal opportunities to assist bonding and support language acquisition, what could you do with babies and young children in your care to emulate this?
- Would it be helpful to find out whether children in your setting have been breast-fed? If so, how could you gather this information sensitively?
- Would it be helpful to compare your results from such an investigation with those of another setting? If so, why?

Conclusion

As seen from the research discussed, there is a range of prenatal factors that a foetus may have to contend with prior to the actual birth. After entering into the world, the child may still be disadvantaged by the care and experience received. The ECEC practitioner can endeavour to mitigate the impact of negative early experiences on a child's learning and development by offering a range of experiences and opportunities within a secure, stimulating environment and also by offering support to parents. Early intervention can result in long-term gains including better educational and employment outcomes. This intervention needs to be at a point where children are still able to form new neurological pathways and it has been shown that at this early stage, the impact is greater. The longitudinal HighScope study in the USA recognised the cost-effectiveness to society of spending more on supporting children and families earlier, leading to long-term social and financial gains for society (Heckman, 2008). We know now that the first 1000 days of life constitute the most sensitive period for determining lifelong health. We are just beginning to learn more about how these early days affect brain development. It is certainly a sensitive period but it is not yet clear if it is critical in the sense that damage cannot be remedied by later interventions. What is clear is that whether we wish to intervene to prevent physical health problems such as coronary heart disease or delayed development leading to learning difficulties, then the earlier the intervention occurs, the better. Also, a better understanding of how children develop from conception up to the point where they first come into contact with an ECEC professional can and should inform practice and provision.

A response to the case study considering normative development

Discussion

You would possibly suggest that Edward sees either the health visitor or the doctor to ascertain whether a physical problem exists. You might endeavour to meet with both parents to discuss this as there may be language barriers.

Actual outcomes

No physical problem was diagnosed, which came as a relief to both parties involved. The nursery team were still perplexed as to why Edward continued walking in this manner. After conversations with the parents, it became clear that Edward was rarely outside and when he was, he was still in the buggy; even on trips to the supermarket he always went in the trolley. He had not been walking enough to actually move his physical development on since beginning to walk. The team working alongside the parents planned a range of activities to allow Edward to progress his development.

Further reading

Barr, R. and Hayne, H. (2003) 'It's not what you know, it's who you know: older siblings facilitate imitation during infancy', *International Journal of Early Years Education*, 11 (1): 7–21.

Bruce, T. (ed.) (2010) *Early Childhood: A Guide for Students*, 2nd edition. London: Sage. See pp. 91–2.

Bruce, T. and Meggitt, C. (2006) *Child Care and Education*, 4th edition. London: Hodder Arnold. See pp. 222–30, which outline normative development patterns.

Goswami, U. (2008) *Cognitive Development: The Learning Brain*. Hove: Psychology Press. See pp. 61–73 in the chapter 'Infancy: the physical world'.

Keenan, T. and Subhadra, E. (2010) *An Introduction to Child Development*, 2nd edition. London: Sage. See Chapter 1, 'The principles of developmental psychology'.

 ## Useful websites

The UNICEF website has a wealth of valuable information at: http://www.unicef.org.uk

You will find a report on levels and trends in child mortality from 2010 at: http://www.unglobalpulse.org/sites/default/files/reports/UNICEF_Child_mortality_for_web_0831.pdf

You will find information from Children in Scotland, the national agency for voluntary, statutory and professional organisations and individuals working with children and their families in Scotland, at: http://www.childreninscotland.org.uk

You can read the article 'Prolonged breastfeeding may be linked to fewer behaviour problems' at: http://www.sciencedaily.com/releases/2011/05/110510154618.htm

Read 'Investigating how the normal brain develops to improve treatment for patients with brain injury', an article from Cambridge Neuroscience, at: http://www.neuroscience.cam.ac.uk/research/cameos/DevelopingBrain.php

Read 'Pre-birth to 3 – the importance of relationships' by Suzanne Zeedyk, an article for Education Scotland, at: http://www.ltscotland.org.uk/video/p/genericcontent_tcm4639129.asp?strReferringChannel=earlyyearsandstrReferringPageID=tcm:4-633862-64

References

Barr, R. and Hayne, H. (2003) 'It's not what you know, it's who you know: older siblings facilitate imitation during infancy', *International Journal of Early Years Education*, 11(1): 7–21.

Bing-Chen Han, Hang-Fei Xia, Jing Sun, Ying Yang and Jing-Pian-Peng (2010) 'Retinoic acid-metabolising enzyme cytochrome P450 26a1 (cyp25a1) is essential for implantation: functional study of its role in early pregnancy', *Journal of Cellular Physiology*, 223(2): 471–9.

Brown, R.T., Freeman, W.S., Perrin, J.M., Stein, M.T., Amler, R.W., Feldman, H.M. et al. (2001) 'Prevalence and assessment of attention deficit/hyperactivity disorder in primary care settings', *Paediatrics*, 107: e43.

Bruce, T. (2004) *Developing Learning in Early Childhood 0–8*. London: Sage.

Bruce, T. and Meggitt, C. (2006) *Child Care and Education*, 4th edition. London: Hodder Arnold.

Casey, B.J., Galvan, A. and Hare, T.A. (2005) 'Changes in cerebral functional organization during cognitive development', *Current Opinion in Neurobiology*, 15: 239–44.

Children in Scotland (2011) Briefing on foetal alcohol harm. Available at: http://www.childreninscotland. org.uk/ (accessed 17.06.11).

Clavarino, A., Mamun, A., O'Callaghan, M., Aird, R., Bor, W., O'Callaghan, F., et al. (2009) 'Maternal anxiety and attention problems in children at 5 and 14 years', *Journal of Attention Disorders*, 13(6): 658–67.

Dehaene-Lambertz, G. and Baillet, S. (1998) 'A phonological representation in the infant brain', *NeuroReport*, 9: 1885–8.

DiPietro, J.A. (2004) 'The role of prenatal maternal stress in child development', *Current Directions in Psychological Science*, 13: 71–4.

Doherty, J. and Hughes, M. (2009) *Child Development: Theory and Practice 0–11*. London: Pearson Education.

Field, T., Diego, M. and Hernandez-Reif, M. (2009) 'Depressed mothers' infants are less responsive to faces and voices', *Infant Behaviour and Development*, 32: 239–44.

Gerhardt, S. (2004) *Why Love Matters*. London: Routledge.

Goswami, U. (2008) *Cognitive Development: The Learning Brain*. Hove: Psychology Press.

Hanson, J.W., Jones, K.L. and Smith D.W. (1976) 'Foetal alcohol syndrome – Experiences with 41 patients', *JAMA*, 235 (14): 1458–60.

Heckman, J. (2008) *Schools, Skills, Synapses*. Available at: http://www.heckmanequation.org/content/resource/schools-skills-synapses

Heikkila, K., Sacjer, A., Kelly, Y., Renfrew, M.J. and Quigley, M.A. (2011) 'Breast feeding and child behaviour in the Millennium Cohort Study', *Arch Dis Child.*, 9 May.

Huotilainen, M. (2010) 'Building blocks of foetal cognition: emotion and language', *Infant and Child Development*, 19: 94–98.

Johnson, M.H., Dziurawiec, S., Ellis, H.D. and Morton, J. (1991) 'Newborns' preferential tracking of face-like stimuli and its subsequent decline', *Cognition*, 40: 1–19.

Kelly, C.A.M., Margulies, B.A. and Castellano, F.X. (2007) 'Recent advances in structural and functional brain imaging studies of attention-deficit/hyperactivity disorder', *Current Psychiatry Reports*, 9(5): 401–7.

Kotulak, R. (1997) *Inside the Brain: Revolutionary Discoveries of How the Mind Works*, 2nd edition. Kansas City, MO: Andrews McMeel Publishing.

Kramer, M.S. (2008) 'Effects of prolonged and exclusive breastfeeding on child behaviour and maternal adjustment: evidence from a large, randomized trial', *Pediatrics*, 121: e435.

Lemoine, P., Harrousseau, H., Borteyru, J.P. et al. (1968) 'Les enfants de parents alcooliques: A nomalies observes: A propos de 127 cas', *Ouest Med.*, 25: 477–82.

Meltzoff, A.N. and Moore, M.K. (1983) 'Newborn infants imitate adult facial gesture', *Child Development,* 54: 702–9.

NOFAS (2011) National Organisation on Foetal Alcohol Syndrome – UK at: http://www.nofas-uk.org/index.php (accessed 17.06.11).

O'Donnell, K., O'Connor, T.G. and Glover, V. (2009) 'Prenatal stress and neurodevelopment of the child: focus on the HPA axis and role of the placenta', *Developmental Neuroscience*, 31: 285–92.

Ostera, E.M., Ostera, A.R. and Simpson, P.M. (1997) 'Mortality within the first two years in infants exposed to cocaine, opiate or cannabinoid during gestation', *Paediatrics*, 100: 79–85.

Perris, E.E., Myers, N.A. and Clifton, R.K. (1990) 'Long-term memory for a single infant experience', *Child Development*, 61: 1796–807.

Perry, B. and Pollard, D. (1997) Altered Brain Development Following Global Neglect in Early Childhood, *Society for Neuroscience: Proceedings from Annual Meeting*, New Orleans.

Rakic, P. (1995) 'Corticogenesis in human and nonhuman primates', in M.S. Gazzaniga (ed.), *The Cognitive Neurosciences* (pp. 127–45). Cambridge, MA: MIT.

Rodriguez, A. and Bohlin, G. (2005) 'Are maternal smoking and stress during pregnancy related to ADHD symptoms in children?', *Journal of Child Psychology and Psychiatry*, 46(3): 246–54.

Scottish Government (2008) *The Early Years Framework*. Edinburgh: Scottish Government. Available at: http://www.scotland.gov.uk/Resource/Doc/257007/0076309.pdf

Szalavitz, M. and Perry, B.D. (2011) *Born for Love*. New York: Harper.

Tickell Review (2011) *The Early Years: Foundations for Life, Health and Learning – An Independent Report on the Early Years Foundations Stage to Her Majesty's Government*, 30 March.

Trevarthen, C. and Aitken, J. (2001) 'Infant intersubjectivity: research, theory and clinical applications', *Journal of Child Psychology*, 42(1): 3–48.

University of Oxford (2011) 'Prolonged breastfeeding may be linked to fewer behaviour problems', *ScienceDaily*, 11 May. Available at: http://www.sciencedaily.com/releases/2011/05/110510154618.htm (accessed 21.06.11).

Zeedyk, S.M. (2006) 'From intersubjectivity to subjectivity: the transformative roles of emotional intimacy and imitation', *Infant and Child Development*, 15: 321–44.

CHAPTER 2

PLAY AS ACTIVE LEARNING

Key ideas explored in this chapter

- what play is and how we can define play for ourselves and to others
- the importance of play in terms of learning and how to justify a play-based approach
- the role of the ECEC professional in promoting and facilitating play activities as active learning.

What is play?

Play is surprisingly complex and abstract to define. It is something taken for granted as part of childhood and it is easy to assume our own understanding of what constitutes play and our experience of it is consistent with that of everyone else – certainly amongst our peers. In the context of early childhood education and care, play is so important that it is vital to be able to define it for ourselves and others; to understand and acknowledge that our own experience shapes our understanding and to use our own experiences as a starting point to enable us to facilitate play and extend children's learning.

Sandberg and Samuelson (2010) conducted a research study looking at how pre-school teachers remember their own childhood play experiences, and how they perceive children's play today. The purpose of the study was to 'investigate, identify, and describe different ways that pre-school teachers view play'. The researchers made four assumptions, summarised as:

- play is important
- all participants (Swedish pre-school teachers) have played as children and studied theories of play
- play is not well developed in pre-school, despite heavy emphasis
- pre-school teachers might understand the significance of play through an examination of their own childhood experiences.

The study identified two characteristic perspectives: the idealised and the pragmatic, the former being more common. The idealists viewed their own childhood as the norm and better than today. They perceived such changes in society as watching TV and using computers as dangerous, and they described play from a biological perspective so that 'there is something, given by nature, for each age that is general and stable and that transcends both culture and time' (Piaget, 1962, cited in Sandberg and Samuelson, 2010: 5). They identified the pragmatist view as being that of those teachers who felt children's play today is no different from their own experience. These teachers saw play as 'an expression of culture, something that is constructed and created … and therefore appears differently in different periods of time and in different societies' (p. 13). Two themes emerged from this study comparing adult experiences and recollections and perceptions of childhood and play today: namely time for play and the effect of media on play. The key point made in conclusion by the writers was that the idealised perspective was more common.

REFLECTIVE ACTIVITY

Consider your own childhood and play experiences. Start by taking just a minute to identify your favourite, most significant recollection of play from your childhood. Jot it down on a piece of paper. Ask other adults for their recollection in the same way. Are there similarities?

Tim Gill uses this as a starting point for his lecture 'Risk and Childhood' (available at: www.teachersmedia.co.uk/videos/tim-gill-risk-and-childhood or Google RSA lectures/Tim Gill).

Does your response and that of other adults tell you anything about your view of play today? Do you have an idealised view or a pragmatic view?

It is important to consider the socio-cultural factors that impact on children's play experiences to help us understand how these might differ from our own. These would include:

- gender – are boys given more freedom?
- class – middle-class children are over organised, whilst lower-class children have more freedom but a less stimulating environment and are restricted by hazards
- disability – the disabled are more ordered and controlled by adults
- formal education – which is ordered by adults
- the 'built' environment children live in, e.g. high rise
- parents' work commitments – (both) longer hours
- single parenting – 22 per cent of UK children are brought up by a lone mother
- pollution
- the impact of the media – parent paranoia and the blame culture.

Tina Bruce (1991) has usefully identified 12 'characteristics' of play and these are referenced in many texts (for example, Bruce and Meggitt, 2002; O'Hagan and Smith, 2004), drawn on by students and adapted and revised. She also identified and explored the difference between what she has called 'free-flow' play and 'structured' play, and in 1991 provided a very useful shorthand summary of the characteristics of free-flow play as:

Free-flow play = wallowing in ideas, feelings and relationships + application of developed competence, mastery and control.

When students are asked to define play, the most commonly occurring words are 'fun', 'chosen', 'spontaneous' and 'freedom'. Many also include the fact that it is a 'way to learn' but this is maybe because of the context in which they are asked the question! (When I have asked this question outside of a classroom setting, nobody has ever mentioned learning.)

It can be helpful simply to consider what play might look like and a suggestion from Australia is:

- Children may play on their own in solitary play, alongside someone else but independently in parallel play or with other children in co-operative play.
- Play may be structured, where someone else makes the rules and decisions.
- Play may be unstructured, where the child is self-directed or takes all the initiative (Northern Territory Government, 2012).

REFLECTIVE ACTIVITY

Consider your own definition of play and discuss it with colleagues and/or other students.

(Continued)

(Continued)

Find the list of 12 characteristics of play (Bruce, 1991 and in many other texts). Consider whether you agree with them, whether the above is a good summary and try to write a similar summary for structured play.

Ask those who are not tussling with this as part of their professional development, also ask children and consider the range of responses against your own and textbook definitions.

Almost always when asked to define play, or provide words they associate with play, adults will first say it is 'fun'. Sadly, however, it is not always fun. Some children are excluded and we hear the heart-rending cry 'nobody will play with me'. Adults' pleas to let the excluded child join in are rarely more than temporarily effective. Paley (2004, cited in McIntyre, 2012) coined the phrase 'You can't say you can't play!' in an attempt to establish this as a mantra, rather than calling attention to the left-out child. It would be an interesting piece of action research in any setting to see if this had an impact. Being left out of play has a huge impact on a child's self-esteem, especially when it happens a lot. Adults in ECEC settings will spend much time and thought on how and when to intervene in children's play and this is one reason why they will wish to. It is interesting to consider that despite the pain caused by this kind of experience, children still want to join in and keep trying. This is testimony to the power and importance of play.

There are three characteristics of play, identified by theorists and often identified by students, that really help our understanding of the importance of play to children's learning and development. These might be summarised as:

1   Play is a chosen activity that may be freely chosen or chosen from what has been offered within a structured environment. The choice may be initiated by an adult but taken up and taken forward by the child.
2   The child sets the pace, determines rules and boundaries and so cannot fail.
3   Play is not a 'means to an end' but a central activity done between adult-directed activities. It is a process and has no other purpose or product.

Play and learning

It can be difficult to identify the role of the ECEC professional or any adult in facilitating learning through play, or for them to identify the learning that is taking place when children are playing. In order to do this, it is helpful to start by exploring the theory and research. Each ECEC professional needs to be able to justify a play-based approach for themselves and to others and this can be done by determining how play relates to learning theory.

Development and learning

Before we can examine what we mean by 'active' learning, it is important to establish a view of learning and before doing that to establish the difference between development and learning.

- **Development** is about the general way a child functions, e.g. running, jumping. It is spontaneous.
- **Learning** is provoked. It occurs in specific situations when a problem needs to be solved.

Each will impact upon the other; they are inseparable. The ability to reach, for example, provides opportunities for learning. The ability to bring the thumb and forefinger together in a 'pincer' grip enables the child to start manipulating tools such as cutlery, a toothbrush and a pencil. As the child grows, the proportions of the body change, i.e. the head gradually becomes a smaller proportion of the overall body size and weight, enabling the child to balance. There are many examples and it is worthwhile exploring these by examining tables of normative development, such as in Bruce and Meggitt (2006), as suggested in Chapter 1 (see Further reading).

Nature versus nurture

The inescapable link between development and learning reflects the link between nature and nurture:

- **Nature** is the extent to which the child's development is to do with the natural process of maturation.
- **Nurture** is the extent to which development progresses as a result of experience.

The debate over which most influences outcomes for children continues, but it is now clear that each plays a part. Research, such as that mentioned in Chapter 1, continues to give us a much better understanding, and it is clear that nurture plays a significant role.

Psychologists refer to how the environment can influence 'gene expression' – in other words, genes produce a range of potential outcomes. Our genes, the genetic code we are born with, can be seen as 'nature' whilst the environment (all the many facets including relationships, diet, education) can be seen as 'nurture'. A useful framework for understanding the interactions between genes and the environment is referred to as the 'reaction range'. Simply explained, this is the upper and lower limits or range of possibilities that a genetic code allows. An example would be to consider how intelligence, whilst it is genetically influenced, is not fixed at birth.

Instead, it means that an individual inherits a **range** for potential intelligence that has upper and lower limits. Environmental effects will then determine where the person falls within these genetically determined boundaries. (Passer et al., 2009: 99)

There is no way at present to measure these genetic reaction ranges and the concept has most often been applied in the study of intelligence. These studies indicate that the influence of environmental factors is significant. To fully understand how development works, it is necessary to explore both nature or the biological factors and nurture or the environmental factors, as it is the interaction between these that explains both consistency and change (Bee, 1995).

Learning theories

Theories of how we learn can be broadly categorised as:

- psychological 'behaviourist' theories – including Skinner (1938) and Thorndike (1898)
- cognitive development theories – including Piaget
- social theories – including Vygotsky (1896–1934), Bruner et al. (1958) and Bandura (1977).

All these theories overlap and 'build' on the ideas of each other. It is possible to find applications for each when studying how people learn and so it is unhelpful to try to determine 'best' theory.

Behaviourist theory

The behaviourist theories of Thorndike (1898) and Skinner (1938) currently receive a 'bad press' – they are unfashionable. This may be partly or largely because their experiments involved rats and the famous example of Pavlov's dog.

Very much simplified, Thorndike's classical conditioning theory can be stated as: responses or behaviour followed by a pleasurable or satisfying consequence will be repeated and strengthened whereas those followed by a negative consequence will be avoided and weakened (Thorndike, 1898). Considering the date of his experiments and publication, it seems surprising that educators, certainly in the first half or more of the last century, chose to pin children down in soulless classrooms and beat them to make them learn! Classical conditioning is where the elicited behaviour is a reflex-like response, for example salivation. The response is elicited by a stimulus, such as the sound of a bell.

Similarly simplified, Skinner's (1938) operant conditioning theory can be stated as responses or behaviour emitted by the learner (pressing a lever) followed by negative or positive consequences (food drops down). Again, the suggestion is that where a learner's action is followed by a positive consequence, the behaviour is reinforced and something is 'learned'. Unfortunately, approaches based on this theory have become associated with tortuous methods whereby pain is inflicted following an action, providing forceful negative reinforcement. However, behaviourist theory is evidenced strongly in learning experiences provided through computers where the learner presses the right buttons, gets the desired response or inputs the correct answer and gets the right response. Where you see the learner responding to a stimulus or taking an action and getting immediate feedback and this can be repeated and repeated, you are seeing behaviourist learning theory in action.

REFLECTIVE ACTIVITY

Observe a young child or adult (or ideally a range of children and adults at different times) 'playing' computer games or using an online learning package to learn, e.g. children's computer maths or an adult learning a foreign language online.

Record your observations and analyse them, trying to determine where behaviourist learning theory is applied and where this is classical conditioning or operant conditioning.

Finally, reflect on these observations and consider where the activities, particularly of children observed, sit in terms of playfulness. Ask yourself:

Are they playing?

Which characteristics of play (Bruce, 1991) can you identify?

Does this experience fit your own definition of play?

Cognitive development theory – Piaget

Piaget provided a very structured view of the stages a child progressed through, just as they progress through the developmental milestones. It has been argued that his theory was genetic, maturational and hierarchical (Child, 1973). Piaget considered that conceptual growth occurred as the child actively attempts to adapt to the environment whilst organising actions into schemata. The child does this through a process of assimilation and accommodation. The first schemata involve grasping or sucking anything that comes near the hand or mouth. It is much easier to see how the very young baby assimilates and accommodates new information building on the reflex actions he is born with but much harder as the child begins to walk and talk. It is often unclear how the learning is connected.

REFLECTIVE ACTIVITY

Observe a very young baby – ideally for a few short periods – and focus on how they are building on reflex actions to explore their environment. These questions may help:

What are they touching – blankets, clothes, food, toys, Mum?

Are they touching hand to hand?

Are they grasping and pulling objects towards their mouth?

Can they focus on the object and do they?

Note the exact age of the baby and the context of each observation. If possible, leave a gap of at least a week and observe again. Try to analyse progression.

When a baby is exploring the environment and learning from experience in this way, it might be fair to say they are 'playing'. It is worth considering how else a baby might learn. It would be laughable to suggest we 'teach' a baby from birth and yet there is an almost constant drive, in our society, to bring formal education forward earlier and earlier. It is in these first months of life that the child learns more and more quickly than at any other time.

Piaget postulates a theory of cognitive development from birth to adolescence that follows a definite and, in his view, inevitable sequence of maturational steps. This starts with the biological mechanisms of the newborn, such as reflexes, latching on to the breast, sucking. The child then progresses from this 'sensori-motor stage' through the 'pre-operational stage', where muscle development enables control of the head and focus of the eyes. This is followed by the concrete operational stage where concepts are formed through interaction with concrete objects and experiences, for example counting using cubes. Finally, each individual may reach the formal operations stage characterised by highly developed systems of abstract operations. At this point, an individual can assimilate and accommodate new information, new ideas and new concepts in abstract form. A graphic example of this might be understanding the laws of physics to build a rocket to go to the moon (not exactly something one can practise). Piaget postulated that many people never fully achieve this final stage in their learning, in other words many people always need concrete examples to aid understanding. Again, as with Thorndike's theory, reflection on this aspect of this learning theory leads me to question why we still rush to move our children towards a formal education that usually requires the ability to understand concepts in the abstract and learn without involving more than one or two senses (usually sight through reading and hearing through listening to a teacher), and provides learning opportunities that are neither concrete nor operational. A play-based approach can provide concrete operational and sensory learning experiences that meet each child's individual needs.

Social learning theory

Social or socio-cultural learning theorists such as Vygotsky, Bruner and Bandura provide different structures or frameworks for our thinking but no one theory of learning provides the ultimate definition that will suffice for all individuals in all situations. The theorists all see learning as a process of constructing knowledge and understanding through interaction with others and the environment; a process of developing skills through activities that use and build on skills already established; a continuing process that takes place within a community through interaction.

Vygotsky has been called a social-constructivist theorist and emphasised the importance of play in young children's learning (Mulholland, 2002). He postulated the theory of the zone of proximal development (ZPD) where a learner can engage with new concepts that are, as it were, only just beyond their reach and can do this successfully with the support of a 'more able other' (not necessarily an adult or teacher). As a psychologist, his research had already, like Piaget, led him to theorise that each child went through specific stages of cognitive development. He identified the importance of what he termed the 'potential concept stage', when a child begins to identify and manipulate attributes of a concept but cannot cope with complexity. He suggested that 'drill methods' of learning lead to the child developing 'pseudo-concepts' which give a false impression of their understanding. A clear example of this can be seen in maths where many of us were taught to add and subtract and multiply using 'tricks' such as 'borrow and pay back', or rote learning of tables without any real understanding of the concept of place value or multiplication.

Bruner et al. (1958) developed theories of how learners expand on, modify and adapt existing concepts to meet new demands. He went on to elaborate on ZPD, suggesting the process of 'scaffolding' for the learner struggling to assimilate new ideas, new concepts or indeed new skills. The 'scaffolding' may come from an adult or, again, a more able peer and might include resources or, in other words, concrete materials.

Bruner (GTCE, 2006) also gave us the theory of the 'spiral curriculum'. Very simply explained, he identified the importance of the learner re-visiting the learning, whether a concept or a skill, and building on the previous learning. He suggests that by encountering an idea, for example addition, frequently in many different situations and initially in simple concrete form and then gradually in more abstract complex forms, the learner can assimilate information and build a secure understanding. It is easy to see how these theories have built on each other and, in themselves, provide an example of the spiral curriculum.

REFLECTIVE ACTIVITY

Observe a group of children (ideally of mixed ages) playing together in a complex collaborative play situation, such as role play. (In this day and age, this may prove surprisingly hard to do as children are so often rigidly separated into age-related groups in all care and education settings, and it is quite rare to find a mixed-age group of children playing in a park, garden or street! If so, observe any group of children.)

(Continued)

(Continued)

Use a narrative approach and you could also use the schedule in Chapter 4 (Figure 4.1).

Focus your observation on how they engage with each other, trying to write down what they actually say to each other. Try to write down exactly what they do for a short period of 10–15 minutes.

Analyse your observation and try to identify the roles they take on, for example:

- Are the children leading the play?
- Are they taking on specific roles, such as doctor or nurse?
- How are they negotiating their roles?

Try to identify what they might be learning through their play. It might be that some or all of the children are:

- developing or consolidating concepts, basic skills, ideas, feelings, moral values, spiritual ideals and values
- supporting physical development, such as fine or gross motor skills
- learning to interact socially
- integrating experiences, such as pretending to read to another child in the role of 'teacher'
- practising skills.

The play might be helping children to develop emotionally by:

- developing confidence and self-esteem
- practising social skills
- providing an emotional outlet
- providing an opportunity to test reality
- providing an opportunity to explore feelings (and possibly strong emotions)
- allowing them to experience success
- giving them time to relax, particularly their minds
- allowing them time to explore relationships.

A series of short observations, carefully analysed, will provide a rich resource for your own learning and can be discussed and shared with colleagues and fellow students – remember the importance of confidentiality and use initials, etc. According to Hutchin (2010), an observation needs to describe as accurately as possible what was seen and/or heard. Knowledge of child development is important: what are you likely to see?

The social learning theory proposed by Bandura (1977) has become perhaps the most influential theory of learning and development. He believed that direct reinforcement could not account for all types of learning and argued that learning can occur through observation, by seeing a behaviour modelled. Indeed, he asserts that *most* human behaviour is learned observationally through modelling and that it is from observing others we form an idea of how new behaviours are performed.

He saw this process of modelling as a four-step process requiring:

1   Attention — the learner must be paying attention to the behaviour being modelled.
2   Retention — the learner must remember what has been modelled and retain this memory.
3   Reproduction — the learner must be physically able to reproduce the modelled behaviour (or something close to it).
4   Motivation — the learner must have a good reason to imitate; they must be motivated to copy and display the modelled behaviour.

He identified self-efficacy as a key attribute of the successful learner. In layman's terms, self-efficacy could be looked at as self-confidence towards learning – an 'I can do it!' approach. He postulated that high self-efficacy affected the learner's behaviour and effectively increased their ability to learn – success breeds success. An important characteristic of play identified earlier in this chapter was, 'The child sets the pace, determines rules and boundaries and so cannot fail'. This means that the child engaged in play-based learning will always experience success, developing confidence or 'self-efficacy' and increasing their ability to learn.

Example

A mother may butter the bread at the table when a baby is at the table in the high chair. The baby can observe and this may happen every day but the baby does not start to butter the bread or even attempt to because the baby is not *attending* (perhaps distracted by toys or even too young to focus at that distance); the baby cannot physically *reproduce* the modelled behaviour (fine motor skills not yet developed); the baby is not *motivated* to display this behaviour (sees no need to butter own bread when Mum can do it!). However, it is impossible to know how much is *retained* at this point.

REFLECTIVE ACTIVITY

Think about how you learned to do 'ordinary' things, such as butter the bread, put clothes on, wash, wash up, etc. Did anyone 'teach' you?

(Continued)

(Continued)

It is unlikely that you were taught to do all the myriad tasks you perform. Many adults cannot recall being 'taught' to read because they learned without much difficulty at a very young age. We know that seeing adults reading, modelling that behaviour, plays a significant part in the success or failure of learning to read (Browne, 2009). There may be other complex tasks that you appear to have 'picked up'. You have learned by observing.

It is important to remember that 'We also learn fears, prejudices, likes and dislikes and social behaviours by watching others' (Olsson and Phelps, 2004: 824). This is only too clear to see when we look at areas of conflict in the world where fears and prejudices are passed from generation to generation – for example, when parents are called in to discuss a child's aggressive behaviour and are soon raising their voice and shaking their fist at the teacher. It is clear that 'human capacity to learn by observation, which is also called modelling, far outstrips that of other creatures' (Passer et al., 2009: 320). It is also clear how children at play, when that play is of high quality, supported by adults who know when to intervene and how to interact, will be attending and motivated, and have opportunities to reproduce behaviour they have observed in a situation where they can only be successful. They are more likely to have high self-efficacy, be relaxed and happy, and therefore repeat the behaviour and retain the learning.

Social learning theory and play

The correlation between social-constructivist theories of learning and the promotion of a play-based approach to learning in the early years are clear to see and can perhaps be summarised as:

- the child learns by engaging with others, particularly more able peers who can 'scaffold' learning
- the child learns by building on what *they* already know and can do, and this will be different for each child all the time
- the child learns through experiencing success and through positive reinforcement as this is a stimulus to further learning
- the child learns by re-visiting the same learning in different situations and applying learning from one situation to another

REFLECTIVE ACTIVITY

Refer back to the three types of learning identified by Goswami (2008) in Chapter 1. These were:

- learning by imitation
- the ability to connect cause and effect – explanation
- associative learning – analogy.

Can you identify how these correlate with the learning theories discussed?

Can you identify occasions where children are learning in these three ways from your observations of them at play?

There are many other theories both of learning and of play and 'you need to have an open mind and to look at various theories, bringing together those ideas that are useful from each so that you can use them in your work' (Bruce and Meggitt, 2002: 127). It is sensible to ensure you have a sound understanding of some important theories rather than a superficial knowledge of all of them. A summary of learning theory might be: 'a process of personal adaptation to the circumstances of our lives. Learning allows us to use our biological heredity to profit from experience and adapt to our environment' (Passer et al., 2009: 281).

'Active' learning

Learning must surely always involve a degree of activity whichever theory we decide is applicable. This term, 'active learning', can confuse (I have seen a number of student teachers making reference to it in their documentation simply because children are physically moving about). The term implies a high level of involvement in, engagement in and ownership of the learning. The learner needs to be operating in their environment, engaging with others, using their senses and actively participating, though they may not be moving much to do this. The learner needs to be:

- making choices
- negotiating
- using their own ideas and imagination
- being physically and intellectually active
- experimenting, exploring and investigating.

In fact, these are all the things they will be doing when they are playing!

Planning for play

It is not an easy task to plan for play if the activities in the setting or classroom are going to be child-led and meet the individual needs and interests of a number of children by enabling them to:

- make choices
- negotiate
- use their own ideas and imagination
- be physically and intellectually active
- experiment, explore and investigate.

It can be difficult to see how and what the ECEC professional *can* plan. It is challenging. It is more challenging than planning a formal maths lesson for a class of 10-year-olds. Some of the considerations include:

- knowledge of normative development, to determine the stage that the child/ren are at
- knowledge of how children learn
- knowledge of the 'lived lives' of the children.

Tassoni and Hucker (2000) identify key points of good practice when planning play that include considering the individual needs of children, hence the need for knowledge of normative child development and where each child fits into this. They also include planning as a team and involving both children and parents, on the basis that all 'stakeholders' need to take some ownership of the plan, the play and therefore the learning. Parents will be key to understanding the 'lived lives' of children and can extend and integrate learning experiences. Listening to children and involving them in decisions and their own learning is powerful – it enhances learning (Kinney, 2005).

Another aspect of good practice raised in many texts is that of routine. There can be a danger that this is just a hangover from Victorian times that haunts and hampers our society. At the same time as the establishment of a routine is promoted, there is also a demand for flexibility and spontaneity in planning and in the opportunities provided.

There are certainly some 'must-haves' in terms of regularising a setting for young children, and it is true that establishing a sense of security will help young children develop and learn. Entry to a childcare setting should not mean that the child 'fits in' to the setting, to the curriculum, to the routines already established, but rather that those providing the care and education follow the needs and interests of the child. There is evidence to suggest that stable relationships and consistency of care develop a sense of security, reduce anxiety and aid learning (Sylva et al., 2004), but I am unable to find research evidence to support the fact that simply giving children meals at the same time every day and adhering to a rigid timetable is beneficial. In the famous story of 'Pollyanna', she responds to her aunt's description of the 'routine' she expects her to follow with the exclamation, 'But when will I *live*!'

There will be a number of fixtures in any setting, such as start and finish times, and children can benefit from a structured, stable environment that can enable them to operate independently because they know the boundaries and expectations. However, it may be more helpful to start from the child, asking yourself what their needs and interests are and how you can best accommodate their different needs and interests rather than *starting* with 'establishing a routine'.

The first step in planning for play needs to be finding out (through observing, talking and listening to children and their parents, and exploring the community and environment in which they live their day-to-day lives) three key things:

- what it is they are interested in and what can they relate to – motivation, making choices
- what they need to learn – relevance to their lived lives
- what stage they are at in terms of their development – what is their 'zone of proximal development'?

(Continued)

centre about two miles from the school. She put a great deal of effort into the creation of it with seed packets, an attractive green watering can, gardening gloves and a piece of fake grass on the floor. When I visited the class, the garden centre had been in the class for over a week. None of the children were playing in the area for the first half an hour or so and I asked the student about it. She was very disappointed that after a short flurry of interest on the first morning it was set up when she had drawn their attention to it, they had then ignored it. She said she knew why they were not interested – it was because few of them lived in homes with gardens and they had never been to a garden centre. She was very honest and admitted that she had just rushed in with a 'good idea' and demonstrated that she had learned a great deal from this and the whole five-week placement.

Later on in my visit, three girls suddenly opted to play in the 'garden centre' context. They were very animated, talking to each other; one sat in a chair they pulled over, one was sweeping and one was re-arranging things on the shelf. They had turned it into a hair salon!

The next step in planning for play will be to decide on the context/s you will set up or the activities you will organise and how you will introduce things. Sometimes this may be part of an ongoing theme or topic; it could be linked to a story or something the children have spoken about; or it may be that you simply introduce the resource and see where the children take it. For example, bringing three large cardboard boxes into a nursery and simply leaving them on the carpet led to a range of imaginative and very creative play by one group of children, finally culminating two weeks later in the creation of a very good 'den' (a supply of new cardboard boxes was required over the period!).

Whilst having a plan and considering your own involvement is important to enable you to resource play, it is vital that changes are expected. It is in the changes, the fluidity, the flexibility where the children's voices will be heard and where creativity and learning will flourish. Smidt (2011: 74) writes: 'you may want to think very carefully about the effect of telling children what the learning outcomes are for the activities they are involved in. You are, in effect, determining the outcomes for them and nothing could be less creative than this.'

Supporting play

There are three things an adult can do to affect the outcome when children are playing; they can interrupt, intervene or interact. You may need to do all three at some point and it is all about getting the balance right. There should be as few occasions as possible when you interrupt but it is sometimes inevitable, particularly in more formal settings, for example the dreaded routine imposed by the timetable and sometimes for safety.

When should an adult intervene?

- to help individual children 'join in'
- to extend learning
- when asked to by children
- when children are aggressive (often an opportunity for sustained shared thinking)
- to re-direct for safety reasons, particularly to reiterate rules for safety
- when children are distressed.

How should adults intervene?

- gently and sensitively
- after observation and thought
- swiftly and decisively if there is danger – and then by reflecting together
- with as little disruption as possible – for example, introduce another resource such as more or different containers at the water trolley, or by joining in as a character, asking a question, asking permission, making a suggestion. (Adapted from McIntyre, 2012)

Interacting effectively with children at play is the most important aspect of the adult role. This is very difficult to explain and very hard (if not impossible) to teach. The best way to develop your skills in interacting effectively is to do it! However, just doing something over and over does not necessarily enhance skill; you must also be able to reflect on and learn from experience. Reflection on your own interactions should be part of your evaluation in the planning cycle. Similarly, you can learn a great deal about what works and what doesn't by observing others interacting with children at play, but again it is the reflection that is important (Dewey, 1933, cited in Pollard and Tann, 1992).

There are a number of other important ways to support children and enhance learning through play. The Northern Territory Government (2012), in Australia, suggests we can support children's play by:

- allowing for extended periods of time for children to remain in 'the flow' of their play
- providing resources such as safe household items and materials
- making enough space to focus on the play activity
- catering for choices of activity, materials and equipment

- role-modelling to encourage and extend ideas
- challenging children with more complex thinking, novel ideas or experience.

This provides a useful, practical summary and encompasses the key elements of the adult role in providing a play-based approach to active learning.

Current policy

All four themes of the English Early Years Foundation Stage (EYFS) emphasise the importance of meeting the individual needs of children (Hutchin, 2010). The standard demands that learning and development take place through play and active learning stating on its 'Play practice cards' that 'play underpins all development and learning for young children'. Another card states: 'In their play children learn at their highest level' (DCFS, 2008: 7, cards 3.3 and 4.1).

In Scotland, the new curriculum guidelines currently being implemented in schools promote a play-based approach as previously adopted in nursery settings (3–5-year-olds) extended into Primary 1 (5–6-year-olds) and beyond. A statement in one of the early Curriculum for Excellence documents, *Building the Curriculum 2* (Scottish Government, 2007: 5) states: 'all areas of the curriculum can be enriched and developed through play'.

The Welsh Assembly Government's (2002: unpaginated) Play Policy seeks to reflect the importance of children and a desire to meet their needs. It states their belief that 'play is the elemental learning process by which humankind has developed'.

The Department of Education, Northern Ireland (DENI, 2012) currently states on its website that children should be provided with a rich variety of play activities and other experiences in a stimulating and challenging environment and allowed to learn without experiencing a sense of failure.

These policy statements are important in establishing the central importance of play in learning so that it will it be given greater value as a key part of the learning curriculum (O'Hagan and Smith, 2004). Children will not have more opportunities for high-quality play just because it is stated in policy documents. It is about what ECEC professionals do with the opportunities these new policies and documents provide.

Further reading

Hutchin, V. (2010) 'Meeting individual needs', in T. Bruce (ed.) *Early Childhood – A Guide for Students*, 2nd edition. London: Sage. This is Chapter 4 in the book.

McIntyre, C. (2012) *Enhancing Learning Through Play: A Developmental Perspective for Early Years Settings*. London: Routledge. This is an excellent, in-depth, dissertation on play and Chapters 1 and 7 are especially relevant.

O'Hagan, M. and Smith, M. (2004) *Early Years Child Care and Education: Key Issues*, 2nd edition. Edinburgh: Bailliere Tindall. See Chapter 2, 'Promoting children's learning through play'.

Useful websites

A photo album from the University of Sydney showing creative use of outdoor play space can be found at: http://sydney.edu.au/health_sciences/sydney_playground_project/photo_album.shtml (accessed 26.07.12).

An initiative from the Scottish Government to engage parents and carers of very young children with the process of developing literacy can be found at: http://www.playtalkread.org/play (accessed 26.07.12).

Dr Tessa Livingstone reports on how Britain's young are overworked and underplayed in *The Telegraph* at: http://www.telegraph.co.uk/news/uknews/2059471/Child-Of-Our-Time-Whatever-happened-to-our-childrens-playtime.html (accessed 26.07.12).

References

Bandura, A. (1977) *Social Learning Theory*. New York: General Learning Press.

Bee, H. (1995) *The Developing Child*. New York: HarperCollins.

Browne, A. (2009) *Developing Language and Literacy 3–8*, 3rd edition. London: Sage.

Bruce, T. (1991) *Time to Play in Early Childhood Education*. London: Hodder and Stoughton.

Bruce, T. and Meggitt, C. (2002) *Child Care and Education,* 3rd edition. London: Hodder and Stoughton.

Bruce, T. and Meggitt, C. (2006) *Child Care and Education*, 4th edition. London: Hodder Arnold.

Bruner, J.S., Goodnow, J.J. and Austin, G.A. (1958) *A Study of Thinking*. New York: Wiley.

Child, D. (1973) *Psychology and the Teacher,* 2nd edition. New York: Holt, Rinehart and Winston.

Department for Children, Schools and Families (DCFS) (2008) *Practice Guidance for the Early Years Foundation Stage*. Available at: https://www.education.gov.uk/publications/eOrderingDownload/eyfs_practiceguid_0026608.pdf (accessed 27.07.12).

Department of Education, Northern Ireland (DENI) (2012) *Statement on Early Years Education*. Available at: http://www.deni.gov.uk/index/support-and-development-2/early-years-education.htm (accessed 26.07.12).

GTCE (2006) *Research for Teachers: Jerome Bruner's Constructivist Model and the Spiral Curriculum for Teaching and Learning*. Available at: http://www.gtce.org.uk/pdf/tla/rft/bruner0506 (accessed 24.10.11).

Goswami, U. (2008) *Cognitive Development: The Learning Brain*. Hove: Psychology Press.

Hutchin, V. (2010) 'Meeting individual needs', in T. Bruce (ed.) *Early Childhood: A Guide for Students*, 2nd edition. London: Sage.

Kinney, L. (2005) 'Small voices ... powerful messages', in A. Clark, A.T. Kjorholt and P. Moss (eds) *Beyond Listening – Children's Perspectives on Early Childhood Services*. Bristol: Policy Press.

McIntyre, C. (2012) *Enhancing Learning Through Play: A Developmental Perspective for Early Years Settings*. London: Routledge.

Mulholland, C. (trans.) (2002) *Play and its Role in the Mental Development of the Child*. (First published 1933.) Psychology and Marxism Internet Archive. Available at: http://www.marxists.org/archive/vygotsky/works/1933/play.htm

Northern Territory Government (2012) *Play-based Learning*. Available at: http://www.det.nt.gov.au/__data/assets/pdf_file/0015/960/play-based_learning.pdf (accessed 24.07.12).

O'Hagan, M. and Smith, M. (2004) *Early Years Child Care and Education: Key Issues*, 2nd edition. Edinburgh: Bailliere Tindall.

Olsson, A. and Phelps, E.A. (2004) 'Learned fear of 'unseen' faces after Pavlovian, observational, and instructed fear', *Psychological Science*, 15: 822–828.

Passer, M., Smith, R., Holt, N., Bremner, A., Sutherland, E. and Vliek, M. (2009) *Psychology: The Science of Mind and Behaviour*. New York: McGraw-Hill.

Pollard, A. and Tann, S. (1992) *Reflective Teaching in the Primary School: A Handbook for the Classroom*. London: Cassell.

Sandberg, A. and Samuelson, I.P. (2010) 'Preschool teachers play experiences then and now', *ECRP*, 5(1): 1–16. Available at: http://ecrp.uiuc.edu/v5n1/sandberg.html

Scottish Government (2007) *Curriculum for Excellence: Building the Curriculum 2 – Active learning in the early years*. Edinburgh: Scottish Government. Available at: http://www.scotland.gov.uk/Resource/Doc/325191/0104856.pdf (accessed 27.07.12).

Skinner, B.F. (1938) *The Behaviour of Organisms: An Experimental Analysis*. New York: Appleton-Century-Crofts.

Smidt, S. (2011) *Playing to Learn: The Role of Play in the Early Years*. London: Routledge.

Sylva, K., Melhuish, E., Sammons, P., Siraj-Blatchford, I. and Taggart, B. (2004) *Effective Pre-School Education: A Longitudinal Study funded by the DfES 1997–2004 (EPPE Project)*. London: University of London, Institute of Education. Available at: www.ioe.ac.uk/projects/eppe

Tassoni, P. and Hucker, K. (2000) *Planning Play and the Early Years*. London: Heinemann.

Thorndike, E.L. (1898) *Animal Intelligence: An Experimental Study of the Associative Processes in Animals*. New York: Macmillan.

Vygotsky (1896–1934) in R.W. Rieber and A.S. Carton (eds) (1987) *The Collected Works of L.S. Vygotsky* (translated and with an introduction by N. Minick). New York: Plenum Press.

Welsh Assembly Government (2002) *Play Policy*. Available at: http://wales.gov.uk/docrepos/40382/40382313/childrenyoungpeople/403821/623995/play-policy.pdf (accessed 26.07.12).

CHAPTER 3

PLAY AND RISK

Keys ideas explored in this chapter

- the importance of the opportunity to take risks as part of learning and development
- how increased 'risk aversion' translated into legislation, policy guidelines, attitudes and behaviour is impacting upon children's learning and development
- some of the ways in which an ECEC professional can mitigate the negative impact of a risk-averse society.

Defining 'risk'

The word 'risk' immediately leads us to think of hazard and danger, particularly in the physical sense. When we discuss the issue of risk in terms of young children, inevitably we focus on climbing trees and crossing roads but, in fact, risk taking is much broader than that and permeates every aspect of our lives no matter how hard we try to avoid it. Boholm (2003: 166, cited in Christensen and Mikkelsen, 2008: 113) defines risk as: 'a situation or event where something of human value (including humans themselves) has been put at stake and where the outcome is uncertain.' This definition is helpful in broadening our understanding of risk and moving the discussion beyond health and safety issues.

It is helpful to focus on the last words in this definition – 'where the outcome is uncertain'. We live with uncertainty every day though we try hard to pretend otherwise for our own sanity. These uncertainties range from more minor physical accidents to death and from losing your job to winning the Lottery. There are constant physical, social and emotional uncertainties in our daily lives. Malaby (2002: 285) in an interesting medical study states, that 'the fundamentally unpredictable quality of experience, its contingency, is a key universal of human experience'. If we accept this finding, it becomes clear that it is important for young children to have the opportunity to experience uncertainty and engage with risk. Risk, uncertainty, chance and challenge permeate our lives and it could be argued that those adults who are open to risk taking are more successful, not just materially but in terms of reaching their full potential and leading full and happy lives.

REFLECTIVE ACTIVITY

Think about people you know personally and people you know of, such as sports personalities, politicians, business people or celebrities, in terms of whether you would consider them risk-takers. Ask yourself these questions:

- Are they disposed to take risks?
- What kind of risks do they take?
- Are they successful in their field because they are risk-takers?
- How do you define risk for yourself?

There is an increasingly lively debate about how 'risk averse' we are becoming as a society and how this impacts on all our lives, but most importantly on the development and learning of our children. This centres around physical risks and particularly the outdoor environment, play and supervision of children in their daily lives. It is a difficult area. An example of this occurred during a discussion about the issue of providing opportunities for risk taking in order to develop children's self-esteem, independence and confidence. One participant who was also a parent stated very forcefully that 'it's not a teacher's role to allow children to take *any* kind of risk. As a parent I want to know when I send them to school they will be *perfectly* safe and come home in one piece at the end of the day'. Once this statement had been made, it was difficult to develop the discussion. Such statements are not uncommon. It was difficult to argue against such a firmly held viewpoint of a parent about their own child. However, it is vital to engage with this issue, to engage with other professionals and parents and to open up and move the debate forward.

Opportunities for children to take risks, by which we mean children making decisions for themselves, are diminishing, particularly in the outdoor environment. There is concern about what children now do instead of playing outside in the playground, garden, street, park or wasteland. It appears the majority of our children from an early age spend increasing amounts of time watching TV or playing computer games and less time playing outside. It appears they spend more time engaged in passive, supervised activities.

It seems clear from discussions, from media reports and from some research evidence (Hillman et al., 1991; Thomas and Thompson, 2004) that this is happening and that parents and professionals are concerned but feel powerless to stop the progress towards an increasingly risk-averse society in which children become more passive and less independent. Newman and Blackburn (2002) found that children today appear to have become less able to cope with and overcome stressors and obstacles, and this in turn appears to be partly because they are sheltered from challenging opportunities.

Indeed, they go on to say that having a preoccupation with sheltering children from risk has contributed to children's health problems, including suicides and eating disorders (Gill, 2004). ECEC professionals can play an important role in helping to reverse this trend.

There is significant data to show the state of children's overall well-being. UNICEF (2007) produced a table showing overall levels of child well-being across countries. This was used in the OECD report *Doing Better for Children* (2009). It is interesting to note the two countries at the top and bottom of the table (Netherlands and Sweden are at the top, and the USA and the UK are at the bottom), and consider the attitudes within these societies to outdoor play, risk and challenge, and provision for early childhood education and care and then look at column 5 which shows 'Behaviours and risk'. The 'risky' behaviours referred to here are teenage pregnancy, smoking and drinking. The figures suggest that where children engage with more risky, adventurous outdoor play from an early age and are given greater independence, they engage in less risky anti-social behaviour in their teenage years and beyond.

The main findings of this report include: 'All countries have weaknesses that need to be addressed and no country features in the top third of the rankings for all six dimensions of child well-being (though the Netherlands and Sweden come close to doing so); the United Kingdom and the United States find themselves in the bottom third of the rankings for five of the six dimensions reviewed' (UNICEF, 2007: 3).

REFLECTIVE ACTIVITY

Examine the table online at: http://www.unicef-irc.org/publications/pdf/rc7_eng.pdf (Innocenti Report card 7, page 2).

Consider and discuss the information with colleagues/fellow students/parents.

Use the internet to find out more about practice and provision in other countries and see Part 3.

Of course, the interpretation of such complex, wide-ranging data cannot give us any definitive answers. It would be easy, for example, to misinterpret the statistics in column 2, 'Health and Safety', where again Sweden is at the top of the table, and assume that this position identifies a country where children are very protected, perhaps even 'wrapped in cotton wool'. In fact, this data refers to factors such as low birth-weight, immunisation programmes, breastfeeding, infant mortality and amount of physical activity. These are the real risks to children's health and well-being, not the opportunity to climb trees, experiment, explore and make their own mistakes.

REFLECTIVE ACTIVITY

On a visit to Sweden, we found ourselves sitting in a primary school staffroom talking to the head teacher just after school had finished for the day. After about 10 minutes, we heard a noise above our heads and then saw a football bounce down from a flat roof outside the window. This was quickly followed by two boys of about 10 dropping down onto the path from the flat roof. They collected the ball and ran off happily. The head teacher did not falter in her conversation and just glanced up following our gaze, saying, 'Oh! They have their ball'. We, all experienced teachers now working in higher education, had all just about gasped and tensed ourselves for the expected rush to reprimand the boys and check them for broken limbs.

This, we felt, was a fine example of the difference in perspective between our two cultures. From reflection and discussion, we all felt the Swedish attitude was right and that our own response was determined by the culture of risk aversion we live and work in.

How do you think you would respond to the same incident, and why?

The evidence that tells us this is having a negative impact on children's learning and development

There is some evidence to support the assertion that there are tangible benefits to play activities that involve elements of risk. Peter Moss and Pat Petrie of the Thomas Coram

Research Unit at London's Institute of Education strongly assert that risk is inherent in human endeavour. Their research supports the fact that for children not to engage with risk leaves them vulnerable as we learn to assess and manage risk by encountering it (Moss and Petrie, 2002).

It is asserted that children allowed to take risks in play will:

- be better able to assess risk and therefore deal with any situation as an adult
- be better equipped to cope in an unpredictable world .
- be less likely to seek out inappropriate high-risk activities as they get older
- develop better social skills
- be more creative, pro-active and problem-solving
- develop a positive disposition that will develop their capacities, allowing them to progress more quickly and reach their full potential
- develop resilience and mental well-being.

Conversely, it is frequently asserted that children 'wrapped in cotton wool' will:

- be unable to assess risk and be more likely to put themselves at risk throughout life due to poor judgements
- be unable to cope with the variety of situations they will inevitably encounter and suffer from stress-related illnesses as a result
- be less successful learners and therefore not reach their full potential
- lack resilience and persistence, affecting their learning abilities
- be more likely to take risks, such as taking drugs, driving fast or getting involved in extreme sports, with long-term adverse outcomes or even death.

Across the UK, the high rate of teenage pregnancy, substance misuse, binge drinking and engagement in more extreme sporting pursuits suggest something is missing from the process of learning and development. Many parents, ECEC professionals and media pundits feel the lack of opportunity to take risks in play and to operate more independently from an early age, is resulting in these longer-term negative outcomes – but is it?

There is data to evidence the changes to children's early lives (Hillman et al., 1991; Thomas and Thompson, 2004) and the state of their well-being (UNICEF, 2007). There is also evidence that where practice and provision are different so are the outcomes – particularly when we examine what happens in Scandinavian countries. However, it is not possible to see some form of practice or provision in another country and simply adopt it wholesale. There are a multitude of inter-connected socio-cultural factors that result in current practice and provision in any one country, area or setting. We can, however, learn from looking at how things can be done differently, adapt approaches using some and not others and can be stimulated to look at our own with a fresh perspective.

Christensen and Mikkelsen (2008) carried out a study of 35 10–12-year-olds across 14 families in Copenhagen exploring their risk management strategies. They found that 'when a child takes risks then s/he simultaneously engages with managing them' and that accidents present important learning opportunities in terms of social relationships rather than simply causing physical harm. They found, as have other studies, that the number of accidents involving boys was greater and that 'risk-taking behaviour is especially valued among boys'. However, their study goes beyond others in identifying that although girls engaged less with physical risk taking, they 'took risks in the emotional and social domains of their relationships and interactions'. The study highlights how both sexes avoided serious conflict or causing harm to themselves or others by rushing into risky activities. By 'navigating the social terrain', balancing their 'risk-willingness and self-care' and making assessments, they actually managed risk in their everyday lives. The study provides an example of the learning provided when children are allowed to engage in managing risk themselves. Of course, the authors do not suggest children are expected to manage all situations for themselves, and emphasise that 'it is important for adults to engage with children about risk in ways that are meaningful to the children themselves'.

REFLECTIVE ACTIVITY

Carry out some formal observations of children in your own setting. You could adapt and use the observation schedule in Chapter 4 or design your own. Observe children playing outside and focus on risk-taking behaviour. Observe one child for a short time (for a maximum of 10–15 minutes) and try to observe a number of children in similar play environments, perhaps some during the same session or over a week. Observe boys and girls. Analyse your observations, discuss with colleagues and consider if there are noticeable gender differences, individual differences or any patterns in behaviour. It would be very valuable to share observations with others in different settings and discuss.

Use the information to inform your planning.

The authors of another study, Backett-Milburn and Harden (2004), found that each family 'developed its own configuration of risk' and drew on their own experiences to do so. The evidence from these and other studies supports the assertion that risk is a social construct. If this is the case, then it can be re-constructed. A social construct can change and evolve if we understand what impacts upon its construction.

REFLECTIVE QUESTIONS

What is your own 'construct' of risk?
What is the 'construct' of risk in your setting?
Are they the same?
Can you identify what impacts upon your own 'construct' of risk?

Exploring the debate

It might be very helpful to the debate on this issue to change the language! As soon as the word 'risk' is introduced into any conversation, images associated with the A&E department and courtrooms start flashing into everyone's mind and it is difficult to get beyond that. It might help to use terms such as 'challenging environments', 'opportunities for decision making or self-regulation', 'independence', 'choice' and 'self-discipline'.

Another barrier to healthy debate are the 'myths' surrounding Health and Safety legislation. The Health and Safety Executive has a section on its website devoted to the myths they feel are often used as an excuse, for example, in not providing exciting opportunities for children (HSE, 2011). One pertinent 'myth' can be found in No. 24 (March 2009): 'Health and safety rules take the adventure out of playgrounds.' The reality, say the HSE, is that they are 'all for playgrounds being exciting and challenging places' but 'what's important is to strike the right balance – protecting children from harm whilst allowing them the freedom to develop independence and risk awareness'. This sounds absolutely right and sensible and straightforward but in fact this is what lies at the very heart of the problem.

First, we need to examine our shared understanding of what constitutes an 'exciting and challenging place'. On this web page, the HSE go on to say that 'poorly maintained and badly designed' play spaces do not strike the right balance. This implies their understanding of the ideal play space is one designed, built, maintained and supervised by adults. The image that springs to mind is of the small play parks built by developers in the middle of new housing estates with soft surfaces and brightly coloured slides and swings, surrounded by carefully landscaped garden areas with clearly marked paths and a bench for the supervising adult. This is what the Free Play Network and PLAYLINK on their website would designate a 'place of woe' (see Useful websites). On this website, they explore through many examples what they call 'places of woe: places of possibility' in terms of play space. They rightly note that 'this is contested territory' and that their examples of woe may be seen by many as ideal. I suspect the majority would pass the HSE standards for maintenance and design but they leave little or no room for imagination, problem solving or indeed risk taking. The spaces they have identified as places of possibility are much more natural and less enclosed but with places to hide and involving wood, rocks and water.

The evidence from Forest Schools (http://www.forestschools.com/) of the benefits to children of playing and learning in a natural outdoor environment also supports the argument for places of possibility as defined by the Free Play Network and PLAYLINK as play spaces that provide the necessary challenge and stimulation. The Danish *Skovbornehave* (wood or nature kindergartens) (Jensen, 2010) also evidence the benefits of the natural environment.

REFLECTIVE ACTIVITY

Go onto the website http://www.freeplaynetwork.org.uk/playlink/exhibition/woepossibility/ index.html and explore the images for both 'woe' and 'possibility'. Focus on one example from each and identify the opportunities the space would provide for children to use their imagination, make decisions and choices, impact on and change the environment, challenge themselves, explore using their senses and take risks. When you have identified an opportunity for risk taking, consider:

- the possible benefits
- the level of risk
- whether the risk is acceptable, particularly when set against the benefits.

If you are unable to access the website, you could take two or more photos of very different play areas and explore them in the same way.

In a live talk 'Learning to love risk', broadcast on BBC Radio 4 in a programme produced by David Stenhouse, the travel writer Nick Thorpe (2010) identified key issues with regard to risk taking and learning. He talks about a trip to Easter Island in a reed boat with a group – *none* of whom could sail at the outset. You can read the transcript or listen to the talk at http://www.nickthorpe.co.uk/journalism/broadcasting/love-risk-bbc-transcript. These key issues can be summarised as:

- the impact of media and commerce on our thinking and responses as professionals or as parents
- the escalation in anxiety about risk
- the fact that we live in a risk-averse culture of blame
- the idea that risk taking is innate and necessary
- the notion that worrying is pointless
- the need for balance
- the difficulty in striking that balance
- children needing a foundation of safety
- exposure to risk being connected to learning.

Notably, he highlights the importance of strong foundations to enable children to 'fully embrace the risk they need to take to grow' and rather beautifully refers to the 'ultimate insurance of love' that provides this foundation. This is confirmed by the work of Anna Freud in the Second World War that showed that children were less emotionally damaged by bombing and its consequences, such as losing their homes, if they remained with their mothers, rather than being physically safe through evacuation to the country (Burlington and Freud, 1942, cited in Bruce, 2004).

This, in turn, brings us to the question of attachment. The psychiatrist John Bowlby also studied evacuees after the Second World War and developed his theory of the importance of attachment to the mother. Libby Brooks (2006: 47), in her interesting text exploring modern childhood in Britain, wonders 'if annexing children's territory and fencing its borders with fear will result in an extended failure to attach: to other adults, to the environment, to the capacity to be alone'. This last point is particularly interesting as an often overlooked aspect of development.

REFLECTIVE ACTIVITY

At one point, Nick Thorpe (2010) says: 'All babies are risk-takers, of course. Only later does fear take over. A child cannot learn to walk without taking the risk of falling.'
Do you agree? Discuss with colleagues and other students.

Reflecting on his trip to Easter Island, Thorpe (2010) realises that the risks were not all physical. An important part of the experience involved emotional risks from living in a confined space with seven other people. At one point, he states that when he returned to his comfortable life, he 'found the courage to go freelance and write a book'. This is not the learning one would have expected someone to take from a physically adventurous trip and it suggests we may be limiting a wide range of learning when we 'wrap our children in cotton wool'.

How professionals might provide opportunities

This is certainly a challenging area for ECEC professionals. There is an emphasis on risk assessment and the aim can appear to be to eliminate all risk. It is hard to strike a balance between the risks and the benefits of challenge when only one side of the equation is being considered (Ball, 2002, cited in Gleave, 2008). It might be more helpful to first make an assessment of the purposes and benefits of an activity, then carry out a risk assessment and set one against the other in order to make a balanced judgement.

In her recent book on learning from Forest Schools about risk and adventure in outdoor play, Sara Knight (2011: 4) suggests that 'early years practitioners are uniquely placed to mediate the pressures from family, culture and community and to give every child the opportunity to stretch themselves and maximise their potential'. This is a heavy responsibility and whilst they are indeed uniquely placed, it does not mean this is a simple or easy task! However, Knight does go on to give some very useful practical suggestions and guidelines as to how this might be managed. She explores the four elements, of earth, fire, water and air to show how, by going into the outdoors and allowing children to engage fully with their natural environment, learning can be extended. An important aspect of learning here is how to manage risk.

Perhaps the most interesting of these four elements in this context is the chapter on 'fire'. As Knight (2011: 44) says, we seem to have 'ceased to think about the safety of fire and tend only to think of the danger of fire', and she uses the fact that she is the lady who 'lights fires with 3-year-olds' to grab the attention of groups when giving talks. She points out how unused our children are to even seeing an open fire, let alone building one themselves or cooking on one. The Forest Schools approach shows how it is possible, with sensitive adult intervention, to *safely* involve children as young as 3, in building and cooking on an open fire. There is no suggestion that children are left to their own devices or 'play with fire'. Her suggestions of how children can be introduced to the activity through role play first and then gradually develop the necessary skills and knowledge, such as the need to think about the position and a means of dousing the fire before you even start, show how this essentially risky activity can still be engaged in, along with the raft of learning opportunities across the curriculum that it provides. There is learning related to science and particular skills.

Bruce (2004) writes about the importance of children learning about 'transformations' and how some are reversible and some irreversible, noting that, 'this is why cooking with children, or having bonfires and barbecues, helps them to see how materials transform, either reversibly or irreversibly, like burning wood or charcoal into ash' (p. 113).

However, perhaps the most important aspect of learning and development in such an activity is about dispositions. Knight writes in her concluding chapter: 'When the brain is at its most plastic and malleable, and developing at its fastest rate, is the time to establish the dispositions to support children through the whole of their lives' (Knight, 2011: 117).

The findings from a research report by Forest Schools (Forest Research, 2012) included:

- Children developed confidence through having the freedom, time and space to learn and demonstrate independence.
- Children developed their social skills through team activities, sharing tools, participating in play and seeing the consequences of their actions on peers.
- Language development was promoted through engagement with sensory experiences.
- Children were motivated as they were fascinated and became able to concentrate for longer periods.
- Children developed greater physical stamina as well as their gross and fine motor skills.
- Children developed their knowledge and understanding of the natural environment and a greater respect for the environment.

All of the above are key to successful learning and development, and it would be hard to imagine a classroom situation where a research study would find the same list of positives.

REFLECTIVE ACTIVITY

Consider:

- the possibility of lighting an open fire with children from your own setting
- making your own list of safety considerations and the process you would go through before actually lighting a fire
- exploring guidelines by doing an internet search for 'campfire building safety' as a starting point
- discussing the idea with colleagues, other students or parents in terms of the benefits as well as the risks.

It is not suggested that you immediately rush outside and start lighting fires with 3-year-olds but it will provide a starting point for discussion – you will get attention!

Risk assessment

A risk assessment is simply a careful examination of what ... could cause harm to people, so that you can weigh up whether you have taken enough precautions or should do more to prevent harm. (HSE, 2006: 1)

It is vital to risk-assess activities but this should be looked on as an enabling process, not as a barrier or an excuse for not providing opportunities. It provides the means to balance the risks against the benefits and ensure the activity is 'safe enough'.

It is useful first to be clear about the difference between risk and hazard:

- A **hazard** is anything that may cause harm.
- A **risk** is the chance, high or low, that someone could be harmed by the hazard.

In carrying out a risk assessment, first ask:

- Who might be harmed and how?

And secondly:

- How serious could the harm be?

Control measures are what you use to eliminate or control the risk of the hazard causing harm, and the law requires you to do everything 'reasonably practicable' to protect people from harm. It does not expect you to eliminate *all* risk.

It is important to remember when carrying out a risk assessment that:

- ignorance is not an excuse – you have responsibilities!
- the information MUST be shared with all parties concerned (and you might be asked to prove you have done this).

This could be deemed 'invisible' (it's a mental process) but we must document our findings (proof). You should keep it simple but your risk assessment procedures must be deemed 'suitable and sufficient'. All local authorities will have their own prescribed style and content and you must adhere to this.

- REMEMBER – risk assessment is NOT a form or a folder on a shelf!
- Risk assessments must be reviewed on a routine basis and in the light of any incidents or situational changes.
- When carrying out your risk assessment, in line with guidelines from your local authority and setting, try *starting with the benefits* of the activity in terms of children's learning and development – this may help restore balance and perspective.

The recent Tickell Review (2011: 6) recommends that whilst 'keeping children safe is of course a non-negotiable element of any early years framework … practitioners should not have to undertake written risk assessments when they take children out, but instead be able to demonstrate, if asked, the ways that they are managing outings to minimise risk'. It will be interesting to see how this impacts on practice as it may be seen as leaving the practitioner *without protection*. It could be suggested that if there is an accident, that clearly demonstrates any risk has not been adequately minimised. This may be something to discuss with colleagues.

Looking for opportunities

Much of the debate centres on policy and attitudes within society. Gill (2007) provides evidence from research and statistics to support the fact that changes in attitudes, policy and legislation, as well as media coverage that often appears to be the driver of all of these, are impacting on the lives of children and that more reach adolescence with emotional and behavioural problems. It is important that individuals, particularly childcare professionals, not only engage in the discourse around this issue but look for ways to strike the right balance between protection and freedom. Tim Gill (2004: unpaginated) also notes that where threats to children clash with what is deemed essential, for example car travel, there is less 'obsessive control' but 'where spaces can be regulated excessive controls are deemed necessary'. Childcare settings do seem to come under the latter, for example a nursery not being allowed to take children out-side through a door and down a step until a white border is painted on the step. The following activity is a suggestion as a starting point to engage with colleagues and parents and gain a sense of perspective.

REFLECTIVE ACTIVITY

Carry out an audit of outdoor provision in your setting.
Examine under headings (you could use photographs):
Space – including:

- looking at access to any outdoor spaces
- whether you can access these regularly or occasionally (include places you could visit such as parks or a piece of woodland).

Resources – including:

- fixed resources or free natural resources such as sticks, earth and water
- cheap consumables such as chalk and compost
- expensive resources such as bikes and climbing frames
- clothing, identifying whether this is provided by the setting or parents or both.

Staffing – including:

- numbers and legislation re ratios
- strengths and weaknesses
- likes and dislikes
- training
- attitudes

Time – considering the following questions:

- Is there time for outdoor play every day?
- Is the outdoor environment available all the time? Or at certain times? Or just when staff feel it is appropriate?
- What are the constraints on time?
- If it is timetabled, does it actually happen?

An audit will help you identify the real opportunities and threats to the provision of risk, challenge and adventure in the outdoors within your setting. Use this audit as a starting

(Continued)

(Continued)

point to develop the outdoor play space in your setting. Draw up an aim or target for increasing the time children spend outdoors, increasing access to the outdoors and developing the space to provide challenge. *It would be useful to engage with parents on this issue.*

You could audit the indoor environment in the same way, by considering how much opportunity for risk taking of all kinds is provided.

The following is a case study where a student on the BA Childhood Practice degree at the University of Aberdeen implemented a plan to introduce a woodwork bench with real tools to her setting. This is an example of dissemination of good practice from the Cameron House Nursery School explored in detail by Bruce (2004).

I had been to training at a nearby school where I had heard about the introduction of a work bench with real tools in order to encourage autonomous play by giving the opportunity to use real tools safely. I discussed the idea with staff in the nursery. The staff and I visited another setting that had done this and saw that the experience was working well and no child had been hurt. One colleague was anxious about the idea but agreed when assured that we introduce it when more staff are on hand and we can ensure close supervision. I sent out a letter to parents inviting involvement and two asked to see the risk assessment beforehand.

I told the children they were going to have the opportunity to explore real tools and discussed this with them. Some parents said their child had 'been talking non-stop about it ever since'. The children sat in front of the work bench and I introduced the tools one by one. I explained the use of each tool and emphasised safety. I wrote down the conversations we were having as the start of a woodwork floor book, to which we later added photos of models and of correct use of tools. I then asked the children to come up with rules to help them keep safe. We identified a comprehensive list together that included:

- Wear goggles to protect our eyes.
- Use two hands when using the hammer.
- Only two people at the work bench at one time.

The staff and I are happy that we introduced this activity. The children were thrilled and spent hours creating models. It definitely encouraged their imagination. The girls needed more reassurance and encouragement but were keen to try. They sometimes take models home, sometimes paint them and we feel their confidence has grown. This is clear from observing one child in particular who now moves freely around the room making decisions about what to make and whether to paint it.

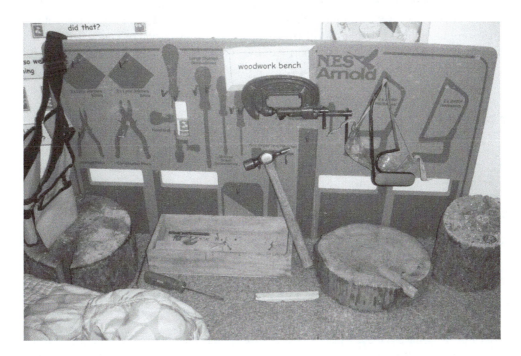

Figure 3.1   The workbench with 'real' tools at Cowgate Underfives Centre, Edinburgh

Conclusion

There is evidence that children have less risk and challenge throughout their childhood than in the past and there is evidence that this is impacting upon their learning and development, as well as their physical and mental health and well-being. It appears we have become increasingly risk averse as a society and many people, particularly ECEC professionals, are aware of the need to redress this trend. There are a number of projects and approaches which can help us in looking for ways to do this and we can learn much from looking at approaches and most importantly attitudes in other countries, notably those in Scandinavia. Playing and learning outdoors is a key element in redressing the balance. Striking the right balance between keeping children safe enough to allow them to learn to risk assess for themselves, develop resilience and self-reliance, keep physically fit and learn from experience, or 'wrapping them in cotton wool' is difficult but extremely worthwhile. Getting the balance right can provide the early learning and develop the right disposition towards learning that will last a lifetime and ensure positive outcomes. There is evidence that this kind of early and ongoing intervention can prevent the risky behaviours we see increasingly in the teenage and post-teenage years, such as drug taking, drinking and unwanted pregnancy. Striking the balance is about professionals in every setting prioritising the provision of greater challenge, greater independence in all activities and exploring the outdoor environment against a background of sensible and transparent risk assessment. It is important to engage with parents, particularly, as well as the wider community on this issue, bearing in mind the statement from the parent earlier in this chapter.

 ## Further reading

Beck, U. (1992) *Risk Society: Towards a New Modernity*. London: Sage.

Gill, T. (2007) *No Fear: Growing up in a Risk Averse Society*. London: Calouste Gulbenkian Foundation. Available at: http://www.gulbenkian.org.uk/pdffiles/--item-1266-223-No-fear-text-only-19-12-07.pdf (accessed 20.10.11).

Gleave, J. (2008) *Risk and Play: A Literature Review*. Available at: www.playday.org.uk – see particularly parts 2, 6 and 7.

Knight, S. (2011) *Risk and Adventure in Early Years Outdoor Play: Learning from Forest Schools*. London: Sage – see particularly the introduction, conclusion and Chapter 4.

 ## Useful websites

Images of play spaces labelled places of woe or of possibility from the freeplay network can be found at: http://www.freeplaynetwork.org.uk/playlink/exhibition/woepossibility/index.html

Details of the nature/nurture early intervention project at Camphill Schools Aberdeen can be found at: http://www.camphillschool.org.uk/page/nature-nurture-project

Forest Schools is an innovative educational approach to outdoor play and learning – see their website at: http://www.forestschools.com/

Mindstretchers is a company of people dedicated to providing children with multi-sensory and real-world educational environments through training and consultancy, educational products, nature kindergartens and charitable endeavours, at: http://www.mindstretchers.co.uk/

References

Backett-Millburn, K. and Harden, J. (2004) 'How children and their families construct and negotiate risk, safety and danger', *Childhood*, 11: 429.

Brooks, L. (2006) *The Story of Childhood: Growing Up in Modern Britain*. London: Bloomsbury.

Bruce, T. (2004) *Developing Learning in Early Childhood: 0–8 years*. London: Sage.

Christensen, P. and Mikkelsen, M.R. (2008) 'Jumping off and being careful: children's strategies of risk management in everyday life', *Sociology of Health and Illness*, 30(1): 112–30.

Forest Research (2012) Summary of Report, Social and Economic Research Group. Available at: http://www.forestresearch.gov.uk/pdf/SERG_Forest_School_research_summary.pdf/$FILE/SERG_Forest_School_research_summary.pdf

Gill, T. (2004) 'Bred in captivity', *The Guardian*, 20 September. Available at: http://www.guardian.co.uk/society/2004/sep/20/childprotection (accessed 29.0711).

Gill, T. (2007) *No Fear: Growing up in a Risk Averse Society*. London: Calouste Gulbenkian Foundation.

Gleave, J. (2008) *Risk and Play: A Literature Review*. Available at: www.playday.org.uk

Hillman, M., Adams, J. and Whitelegg, J. (1991) *One False Move...: A Study of Children's Independent Mobility*. London: Policy Studies Institute.

HSE (2006) *Five Steps to Risk Assessment*. Available at: http://www.hse.gov.uk/pubns/indg163.pdf (accessed 29.03.11).

HSE (2011) *Health and Safety Myths*. Available at: http://www.hse.gov.uk/myth/index.htm (accessed 29.03.11).

Jensen, C. (2010) 'Introducing children to outdoor living', *Children in Europe*, 19/2010. Available at: www.childrenineurope.org

Knight, S. (2011) *Risk and Adventure in Early Years Outdoor Play: Learning from Forest Schools*. London: Sage.

Malaby, T. (2002) 'Odds and ends: risk, mortality and the politics of contingency', *Culture, Medicine and Psychiatry*, 26(3): 283–312.

Moss, P. and Petrie, P. (2002) *From Children's Services to Children's Spaces*. London: Routledge.

Newman, T. and Blackburn, S. (2002) *Interchange 78: Transitions in the Lives of Children and Young People: Resilience Factors*. Available at: http://www.scotland.gov.uk/Publications/2002/10/15591/11950

OECD (2009) *Doing Better for Children*. Paris: OECD.

Tickell Review (2011) *The Early Years: Foundations for Life, Health and Learning – An Independent Report on the Early Years Foundations Stage to Her Majesty's Government*, 30 March.

Thomas, G. and Thompson, G. (2004) *A Child's Place: Why Environment Matters to Children*. Green Alliance and Demos. Available at: http://www.green-alliance.org.uk/uploadedFiles/Publications/A%20Childs%20Place%20Final%20Version.pdf

Thorpe, N. (2010) *Learning to Love Risk*. Live talk on BBC Radio 4, 24 October. Available at: www.nickthorpe.co.uk/journalism/broadcasting/love-risk-bbc-transcript

UNICEF (2007) *Child Poverty in Perspective: An Overview of Child Well-being in Rich Countries*. Innocenti Report card 7. Available at: http://www.unicef-irc.org/publications/pdf/rc7_eng.pdf page 2

CHAPTER 4

CREATIVE APPROACHES TO TEACHING AND LEARNING – KODÁLY

> **Key ideas explored in this chapter**
>
> - the importance of the promotion of creativity
> - the background of the Kodály philosophy of teaching music
> - how such a methodology can aid language acquisition, promote cross-curricular learning and support the development of creativity.

Creativity within the curriculum

The Cambridge Primary Review acknowledges that years of prescription and micro-management should be replaced by the encouragement of independent judgement grounded in professional collaboration and the best available evidence. Furthermore, it has been consistently argued that a broad and rich curriculum in the primary phase should be a statutory entitlement, as inspection evidence shows that curriculum breadth and high standards in the 'basics' are interdependent (Alexander, 2009). This both provides an essential foundation for future learning and choice and is vital to the pursuit of standards. Unfortunately and increasingly, the gap between 'entitlement' and 'reality' often amounts to the creation of a 'two-tier' system of education with a strong focus on the perceived basics of literacy and numeracy and the ensuing marginalisation of other subjects. No one would deny that these are extremely important areas of any curriculum, but the concern is very much with 'how' these are taught.

In Scotland, the new Curriculum for Excellence (Scottish Government, 2007) aims to restore teacher autonomy, in an attempt to make the curriculum fit the child and not the other way around. The first step in the implementation of the Curriculum for Excellence has been to smooth the transition from Nursery into P1 with the intention of continuing the child-centred, play-based approach. However, many teachers appear very unsure of what this actually means, which is understandable since creative approaches to education have been discouraged over the past two decades. Rather, evidence from regular visits to schools over the past 10 years, would support what Alexander (2010) outlines as a culture of compliance and dependency which has steadily subsumed the majority of school staff teams.

Many authors today, including Robinson (2001) and Goleman (1998), stress the importance of transferable or 'soft' skills and particularly the importance of developing problem-solving and creative thinking skills throughout a child's education. There is an increasing awareness that employers value people who can think intuitively, are imaginative, innovative, good communicators, team players, flexible, adaptable and self-confident. This is now being given greater attention within Higher Education, so that in addition to subject and knowledge content, courses will help students to demonstrate:

- a breadth of knowledge, understanding and skills beyond their chosen discipline
- a capacity for independent conceptual and creative thinking
- an ability to communicate effectively for different purposes and in different contexts
- an ability to work independently and as part of a team. (UoA, 2012)

Goleman (1998) states that these are the necessary skills for social and economic development, and that these so-called 'soft skills' have been for too long ignored or badly dealt with by education. In other words, these are the skills which we definitely need for the future and which we should be promoting in schools. I would suggest here that if we look at quality early years education, these are in fact the skills which we do promote in children, and particularly within a pre-school context: 'All I really need to know ... I learned in kindergarten' (Fulghum, 2003: unpaginated).

The skills outlined above do not appear by chance. Optimal environments and opportunities for teaching and practice must be created in order to promote them in children. Gardner (1993) identifies a number of interesting aspects of the behaviour or typical responses of creative people that he suggests they may have in common:

- very fast growth in the chosen domain once they have committed themselves to it
- a high level of self-absorption and self-promotion
- a mix of childlike and adult in their behaviours
- a feeling of being under siege when being most creative
- being 'productive' each day.

Similar observations are also made by Laevers (2005) in his discussion of raising the child's level of well-being and involvement, through observations of such characteristics as concentration, energy, complexity and creativity, facial expression and posture, persistence, precision, reaction time, language used and satisfaction at the end of the process.

REFLECTIVE ACTIVITY

Observe a child involved in a free play situation for a period of 10–20 minutes. Use the observation schedule to record your findings.

Context ....

Observe how the child interacts with the learning context or activity for one ten-minute period. Full transcripts of conversations should be supplied. If space does not permit, these should be appended.

Start time ....   Finish time ....

Aim of observation: *to observe level of involvement and engagement of child in self-directed activity*

Resources within context:

Identify children e.g. AB, CH or Girl A, Boys X & Y	What they are doing	What they are saying

Analysis – *What have I learned about the child's level of involvement and engagement in self-directed activity?*

Figure 4.1   Observation Schedule

Then, observe the same child for a similar period of time in an adult-directed task. Record your findings.

Now, compare the findings from the two observations with Gardner's list of desirable attributes. Which situations are more conducive in promoting these skills and qualities?

REFLECTIVE ACTIVITY

Case study

My own teaching experience in secondary school in Sweden provides evidence to substantiate how creativity can be promoted. Having come across an aspect of subject content in which pupils appeared to be interested, there was the autonomy to decide, collaboratively with pupils, on how to develop this interest in ways that would engage them and allow them to facilitate experimentation with teaching and learning across other areas of the curriculum.

The Diary of Anne Frank

This took place when working with two different groups of pupils in secondary school in Sweden. One class involved teaching a group of 15-year-olds who had English as their native language and who were reading through a dramatisation of *The Diary of Anne Frank*. At the same time, they were studying the Second World War in Social Sciences as part of the Swedish curriculum. The dramatisation of the play contextualised the historical aspect because they could then relate this to someone of their own age. At the same time, Swedish TV broadcast a documentary about Auschwitz, underscored by Gorecki's 3rd symphony. The students then asked if they could use some of our English classes within the wider school context – together with the students learning English as a foreign language – to perform the play. The students took control of this, divided up the larger class into smaller groups and each set took on a scene from the play and performed this – underscored by the music – for other classes. The pupils took control of their learning and many of these desirable skills and qualities were in evidence. Bearing in mind that this was taking place in English, a foreign language for the majority of the class, the evidence of learning was very clearly demonstrated through pupils being able to deviate from the 'script' and improvise their lines if necessary. Interestingly enough, the Swedish Social Sciences teacher did not wish to be involved (because it was too uncomfortable to deviate from his 'script'?), but did organise a visit from an Auschwitz survivor to talk to the pupils. Altogether, these cross-curricular experiences had a very powerful effect on the students, particularly the effect of the music.

Within such a project, as in the case study above, it is possible to observe in pupils the greatest satisfaction in learning and also the dispositions to be involved and creative. In other words, the teacher has to 'let go' in terms of always being in control, although still having end goals in mind. The example from a secondary school may be easier for adult readers to 'tune in to'. The key factors, such as motivation, involvement, the desire and ability to concentrate, and confidence, that engage learners in learning and support creative thinking and problem solving remain the same at any age. This is the type of active learning which can be promoted at any stage. Students on our EYPGCE programme, engaged in exploring the use of this and other creative approaches, noted how they felt able to give greater control and 'ownership' over to the children. One student expressed this during a conversation saying: 'I am more aware of the environment, definitely and making it "theirs". It's their classroom – not my classroom ... and about giving the children a say. I think that has had the biggest impact. I've noticed a big change in the way that I approach things ... I've been going with what the children have chosen, rather than what has been established.'

Robinson (2001) suggests that creativity is basically an attitude that comes easily to young children but is one that must be sustained and strengthened through education. Picasso apparently said: 'All children are artists. The problem is how to remain an artist once [they] grow up.' Bruce (2006) develops this point further by stating that the links between creativity and childhood play are of central importance in the development and learning of young children. In order to promote this, children need to experience a balance of child- and adult-led activities, as children cannot be expected to find out absolutely everything for themselves, and above all, children need to be given opportunities to make choices and decisions, some of which may involve taking risks.

REFLECTIVE ACTIVITY

Why is the concept of creativity important?

Teaching in Sweden, within state education, I was involved initially in English language teaching but, later, also asked to teach Music to 7–16-year-olds (in Swedish). This allowed the opportunity to experiment with a combination of music and language teaching and revealed clearly how one complements the other. I became aware of 'low achievers' academically who found working with music inspirational but who then were able to combine the two curriculum areas and begin to be creative in ways that enhanced their confidence, self-esteem and subsequent motivation towards greater academic achievement. Returning to Scotland in 1997, I found an imposed curriculum increasingly compartmentalised and focused above all on the importance of literacy and numeracy, with perceived 'softer' subjects, such as music, increasingly marginalised.

How would you describe the curriculum guidelines you are presently working with? Is it a prescriptive curriculum? Is creativity prescribed within it? Is there room for you to adopt different approaches within the guidelines?

Developments in brain research

Gardner (1993) discusses the fact that some modes of thinking dominate in different types of activity, for example the aural in music and the kinaesthetic in dance or the mathematical in physics. The important point here is that these draw on different areas of intellect simultaneously. Current brain research through use of MRI scanning techniques can highlight which parts of the brain are being used in any action and this research has immense significance for our understanding of creativity and intelligence (see Chapter 1).

Balbernie and Zeedyk (2010) discuss the high degree of plasticity and adaptability of the newborn brain, which is ready to be shaped by relationships and experiences. Forming and reinforcing connections between the brain cells or *neurons* are the key tasks of early brain development. Balbernie and Zeedyk compare the revisiting of previous connections to laying down pathways and use the analogy of developing a motorway system in the brain from the beginnings of a little used track. Neurons make connections with others across the gap between them called the *synapse* in a process called *synaptogenesis*. Neurons that make successful connections remain whilst the brain rids itself of those that are unsuccessful in another process called *synaptic pruning* (Doherty and Hughes, 2009). Connections made most often trigger a robust response and these are developed through interactions with others, being active and involved, and learning through exploration and discovery. Every time the pathway is revisited, it is strengthened and the link speeds up. The process is known as 'hard-wiring' and 90 per cent of hard-wired connections will be complete by the age of 3. Conversely, the connections which are not reinforced will wither and die, which Balbernie and Zeedyk refer to as the 'use it or lose it' syndrome.

Therefore, in terms of supporting creativity, there are enormous implications for professionals working with children to ensure that children's development promotes activity across all areas of the brain. Perry and Pollard (1997) present a slide (see Figure 1.1 in Chapter 1), which shows the brain scans of two children aged 3: one normal and one suffering from extreme neglect. This comparison clearly demonstrates which child has been exposed to a wealth of experiences and which child has not. This reinforces the necessity for a broad and balanced curriculum for children.

Robinson (2001) is clear that creative development in individuals is a sophisticated process that must balance learning skills with stimulating the imagination to explore new ideas, and that creative insights often occur by making unusual connections or seeing analogies between ideas that have not previously been related. Creativity works like our multi-faceted brain and thrives on contact between different areas of specific expertise. We need to promote development in all areas of the brain to enhance and stimulate creativity.

Kodály methodology uses active approaches to learning which, whilst based on promoting musicianship, if fully understood by the teacher, will also promote skill development across other areas of the curriculum, in line with current curriculum principles.

Zoltan Kodály (pronounced Koh-dah-ee)

Kodály (1882–1967), a Hungarian composer and music educator, developed a clear structure for music education, in an approach which he claimed should begin nine months before the baby is born. This, as we now know from current brain research, is an extremely important concept, yet Kodály was writing about this in the 1930s and 1940s. He recognised the importance of the voice as the most important musical instrument and therefore the most direct way of making a musical response, as well as learning musical concepts and skills. Research into his life and work (Hein, 1992) demonstrates that he, in relation to his time, also had a clear understanding of the psychology of child development and hence his methodology is accessible to very young children. The Kodály music method is child developmental and highly sequential. However, it is not just confined to a method of teaching music for young children, as Kodály methodology can also be studied at an adult level (see The British Kodály Academy in Useful websites).

Kodály Music Education

Kodály Music Education provides evidence of promoting multi-faceted development in children and in ways which children perceive as fun. Kodály developed his music education throughout the 1940s and 1950s. This was achieved through an amalgamation of different existing musical components and pedagogy observed in his travels throughout Europe and the USA. However, the goals, philosophy and principles are all attributed to Kodály, and together form a viable philosophy of music education (Choksy, 1986).

The stimulus for Kodály came initially through work for his PhD thesis on the structure of Hungarian folk songs. He had observed that the level of music on offer to children in schools was very poor (Bonis, 1964). I would assert that this is very much the case today in parts of the UK, partly at least through a lack of regular access to specialist provision in primary schools. He concluded that this was not the result of a lack of interest on the part of children, but a lack of suitable music composed for the purpose. In an attempt to 'wage war on musical illiteracy', he set about collecting examples of Hungarian folk songs, possibly closer to the musical rhymes we remember from childhood, which he intended should be presented to young children as quality music. This also caught the attention at the time of literary scholars.

Kodály discovered that the typical characteristics of Hungarian folk songs contained an accented opening, falling melodic line and use of a pentatonic scale (think of using only the black notes on a piano) (Eosze, 1962). However, as he travelled more widely collecting songs from other countries, he noticed that these characteristics were common to all songs from all languages he encountered.

More recently, Trevarthen (2004) in his study of communication between babies and their parents or carers, also noted that these first songs and rhymes have the same prosodic or musical features in different languages. Malloch (1999) calls this a theory of communicative musicality – in other words, early musicality is a powerful tool in building memories and furthermore musicality may be at the source of the ability to be socialised in the human way (Cross, 1999). This is further corroborated by Bruce (Bruce and Meggitt, 2005) who uses evidence from studies in neuroscience to emphasise the importance of music in helping language and memory to develop. She describes how mothers, for example, without prompting, will use a kind of high gliding speech and falling pitch to 'Up we go!' whilst lifting a baby, for example, out of a pushchair or pram.

The theory of communicative musicality is defined as a sharing of:

- pulse (with which the baby is familiar from the mother's heartbeat pre-birth)
- quality of sound (regular gentle phrases)
- narrative form.

Kodály's research had presented the same data in his analysis of songs for young children. The stanzas generally had four lines with rhyming vowels at the end of lines 2 and 4, use of a dancing rhythm (iambic) and a duration of 15–20 seconds:

Here is my finger

Here is my thumb

Here is my nose

And here is my TUM!

Wiggle baby's finger, thumb, nose and finally give a tummy tickle. (Geoghegan, 2002: 22)

As the baby's communication skills develop, they learn to anticipate the 'punch line' and can predict timing and rhyming. Through this type of singing game and rhyme, young children learn about pulse, rhythm, simple pitch shifts and rhyming syllables at specific points and variations in the beat to regulate excitement, and these skills are well developed in children who are exposed to this type of loving interaction with adults, long before actual speech develops. Trevarthen (2004) describes this adult/baby interaction as promoting 'dispositions to learn' and 'dispositions to teach'. In terms of language development, the baby is learning about the rules of communication but, at a metacognitive level, communication about communication. A further comparison with language development here is that the baby is being exposed, through the use of these songs and rhymes, to patterning in language structure, particularly onset (the initial sound in a word) and rime (the end sound or phoneme in a word).

Kodály insisted, in working with young children, that all music making should involve active learning, a concept only now being acknowledged as important for young children in school. Participation in Kodály singing games and rhymes allows young children to develop musical skills through constant repetition, and these are practised, initially, all from memory. The 'theory' of music is implicit as the teacher knows exactly what the theory is, but this is not made explicit until much later on, when the song or rhyme is very familiar and internalised. Singer and Singer (1977), Pulaski (1981) and Riess (1981) in Moyles (1989) all concur that internal thinkers concentrate better, show less aggression and more inclination to enjoy what they do.

If we take the verse in Figure 4.2 as an example, a mother could be calmly rocking her baby whilst repeating the words, or singing the tune. It contains lots of repetition and follows the stanzaic pattern above. It also fits into Kodály's requirements for the musical skills involved, for example use of the pentatonic scale and a very limited pitch range appropriate to tiny vocal chords. Initially, the young baby

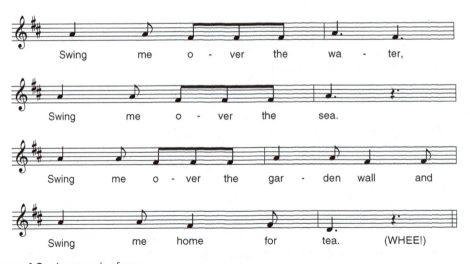

Figure 4.2 An example of verse

would be feeling the pulse, familiar from pre-birth, from the mother's heartbeat. For toddlers, the rhyme can be further developed on a one-to-one basis with an adult, for example each holding an end of a scarf, swinging this to the pulse. Add additional interest by putting a small toy animal on to the scarf and emphasise the 'punchline' by tossing the small toy gently in the air on the 'swing' of the last line. The child is still feeling the pulse of the music and language, but in a different and more exciting way. With older children, for example at the pre-school stage, this can be further developed with a large class of children, grouped into threes, where one child is in the middle and the other two join hands around them. The song can be sung in the same way, with the pulse being kept by the children with joined hands swinging backwards and forwards. On the punchline, the children lift their hands into an arch and the child in the middle progresses clockwise to the next pair, walking the beat as they go. The musical skills here, of pulse, rhythm, pitch and length of note, are being reinforced and developed through constant repetition but are not being made explicit to the child at this stage.

Geoghegan (1999: iv) discusses other advantages of Kodály methodology which are important to child development: 'singing songs will aid the child's language development: when we sing or say a rhyme, the pronunciation of the words is much clearer and slower and therefore more easily understood and imitated.' This type of activity is also extremely helpful for children who are learning English as an additional language (E2L learners). Second language acquisition follows exactly the same pattern as the first language, but where singing and rhymes can be of significance is in the clear enunciation of words. When we speak normally, we elide words and often drop in pitch at the end of phrases, yet when we sing, each word is articulated clearly, in a way that would sound very strange if spoken. If you learned a foreign language at school, you may well have forgotten the grammar rules, but can probably still remember some of the songs you learned.

Geoghegan also points out that the child is developing other things too, besides musical skills, such as social and emotional relationships, taking turns, self-esteem and confidence, listening and reasoning skills, spatial awareness, memory and co-ordination, as well as fluency of speech and a better understanding and use of language – in other words, the 'soft skills' that we know are essential in order to promote creativity.

Kodály, in Bonis (1964), realised that singing, connected with movement and action, is a much more ancient, and at the same time, more complex phenomenon than is a simple song. This was clearly demonstrated when taking part in a Kodály workshop which included some eminent professors of music, who experienced some difficulty with the co-ordination required, whilst young children with their malleable brains could pick up words, tunes and actions very quickly. Perhaps this was an example of some neural pathways in adults not having been used for a very long time!

The use of a simple rhyme also exemplifies Bruner's spiral curriculum theory of learning (Bruce and Meggitt, 2005) being constructed, co-constructed, revisited and built upon in a way that meets the developmental age and stage of the child. However, with Kodály methodology, none of the theory would at this stage be made explicit to the children, and this was the stimulation for an analysis and reflection on the parallels between language teaching and the Kodály approach.

Music teaching for ages 0–8

Music is perceived by the average primary class teacher as the most difficult subject to teach well, perhaps because it involves use of the voice in a different, exposed manner, which is intensely personal. Hennessy (2007) discusses the fact that very often the generalist class-room teacher is extremely anxious about their ability to teach music yet *confidence develops through sustained engagement with both musical thinking and musical activity.*

However, if we look at Kodály's philosophy, he clearly understood the importance of music teaching beginning with quality experiences for the very youngest children. This emphasises what Craft (2002) describes as the distinction between 'outcomes' and 'processes'. Kodály understood the value of the processes, yet current educational policy has clearly shifted towards the outcomes. If we deny children the opportunity to take part in quality music experiences (processes), are we not also denying the child the opportunity to develop one of their potential strengths? Recent classroom observations have shown only one student who carried out a music lesson during school experience, nor can I recall many examples of any meaningful planning for music activities.

REFLECTIVE ACTIVITY

Carry out an audit of music or music-related activities in your setting over a normal week. Analyse the results.

What percentage of time is spent on such activities?

Who leads these?

Why?

Relevance to the professional context

Kodály, in his travels to the UK during the first half of the 20th century, came across the teaching of sol-fa in schools:

Tonic sol-fa is a pedagogical technique for teaching sight-singing, invented by John Curwen who adapted it from a number of earlier musical systems. It uses a system of musical notation based on movable 'do', whereby every tone is given a name according to its relationship with other tones in the key: the usual staff notation is replaced with anglicised solfège syllables (e.g. do, reh, me, fa, so, la, te, do) or their abbreviations (d,r,m,f,s,l,t,d). (wikipedia.org/wiki/Tonic_sol-fa)

The system is familiar to most people from Maria's song in *The Sound of Music*.

What Kodály observed in practice was that this sight-singing technique was being taught in UK schools on a purely theoretical basis. He asserted that the whole psychological process of music making was faulty and needed to be inverted. With his understanding of how children develop and learn, he developed his own pedagogical process through which concepts and skills are developed. This always begins with the total musical experience and moves gradually to the abstractions for that experience, that is, from the known to the unknown, from sound to symbol (Choksy, 1986).

It appears that this is exactly the opposite of what we are doing today in the teaching of language and literacy through an increasing preoccupation with abstract terminology, in ways that confuse rather than help children. Yet, just as Kodály was waging war on musical illiteracy in Hungary in the 1920s, so is the UK experiencing alarmingly high levels of adult illiteracy.

Kodály writes:

> What is to be done? Teach music and singing at school in such a way that it is not a torture but a joy for the pupil; instil a thirst for finer music in him, a thirst which will last a lifetime. Music must not be approached from its intellectual, rational side, nor should it be conveyed to the child as a system of algebraic symbols, or as the secret writing of a language with which he has no connection. (Bonis, 1964: 120)

I would suggest that although the 'algebraic symbols' here related to the UK in the 1950s in terms of music teaching, the parallel is very clear in terms of teaching reading today and in particular the UK government preoccupation with the teaching of synthetic phonics. Phonics represents one way of promoting literacy in children, but not '*the* way to teach reading'.

Although professionals are well aware of the necessity of the preparation stage in terms of the development of language and literacy, this important stage is not always being given sufficient attention as ECEC professionals are often being pressurised into using formal approaches too soon.

REFLECTIVE ACTIVITY

Case study

A student visit to a school in an area of socio-economic deprivation revealed a language lesson under way with Primary 1, during the summer term. The children were being asked to analyse and break words down into constituent parts, digraphs and phonemes. These

(Continued)

(Continued)

terms, along with consonants and vowels, were actually being used and 'parroted' by the children. Following discussion with the class teacher, the only explanation or justification was that this was school policy for the Literacy Hour.

For reflection:

- How did you learn to read?
- Were you familiar with this type of terminology?
- Are you secure in your understanding of it now?
- Can you identify any benefits to the child in this setting from deconstructing language in this way?
- What possible disadvantages could this cause to the child?
- What possible problems might this create for parents or for working in partnership with parents?
- Might this create more significant problems with some parents? Why?

Kodály, in Eosze (1962: 86), saw the parallels to this in music making where 'mechanical training in instrumental playing, making music with the fingers instead of the soul, the omission of any thorough musical grounding ... are the direct causes of the increasing numbers of second rate professional musicians and amateurs who overrate their own capabilities'. Robinson (2001) agrees with this statement and notes that many highly trained people, such as musicians, are not necessarily musical.

Kodály's analysis was expressed in terms of a top-down approach without paying attention to the laying down of the foundations. Fifty years ago, he spoke eloquently and somewhat ahead of his time about the importance of the period from 3 to 7 years old in terms of the education of children being greater than in the succeeding years. He was quite sure then that anything that is left out, or badly taught, during those years could not be remedied later on. He felt that the entire future development of a human being was decided in those years. His thinking, over 50 years ago, though modified by recent research on the one hand, is also closely aligned with current research and knowledge.

Fabian (2002: 123) writes: 'When children are introduced to formal instruction or abstract thinking too soon, they may learn knowledge and skills at the expense of the disposition to use it.' Consider current UK government proposals to test children aged 6 in their ability to decode phonetic sounds, including the use of nonsense words. This is what we are at great risk of doing today with literacy teaching, whilst, on the other hand, in terms of music teaching, there is a great upsurge of interest in Kodály methodology, with justification for this approach in terms of supporting creativity and also from recent studies into brain research.

I am not advocating that all teachers should take part in Kodály teaching with their classes, as in order to carry this out successfully, it is important for the leader to be able to sing in tune and be confident enough to use their voice in singing with children and want to take part. However, it is well within the scope of most ECEC professionals to build up a repertoire of these simple songs and rhymes which can be used and developed on a regular and repetitive basis, with the understanding that these types of activities can have such an important positive effect on the all-round development of young children.

Ideally, it would be desirable to have one or two members of staff in a setting able to take the lead in involvement of children in this way, particularly with children aged 0–8, working with a bottom-up approach. In later stages, the music theory does become more specialised and perhaps some teachers would feel in need of more support from suitably qualified specialists.

REFLECTIVE ACTIVITY

Case study

Students on the Post Graduate Certificate (PGC) in Early Years at Aberdeen University experienced a morning session on Kodály methodology as a tool to use prior to carrying out field experience working with the 0–3 age group. Most students appreciated the workshops but there were some who said that they could not see how this method could possibly be viewed as creative as it was very much adult-led.

In an attempt to justify this approach, I explained that the promotion of both language and literacy and the promotion of musicality in children require an emphasis on high-quality materials and an understanding of the child's cultural heritage. Both areas develop simultaneously in the same way – listening, speaking, (singing), reading and writing. But through the whole-child approach of active involvement in singing games and rhymes, the child is using many more neural pathways than in just singing or reading or counting alone. The important aspect of this is that these processes are happening simultaneously and that it is the promotion of this ability that fosters creativity, which is the desirable life skill.

Many of the students who had tried out the Kodály approach in working with the 0–3s went on to experiment with this in their own classroom settings of Nursery to P3 and commented very favourably on the processes involved. One commented:

'It always stuck in my mind that Lucinda (Geoghegan) said that children who had this singing in tune and pitch and rhythm seemed to do better with reading and literacy and I

(Continued)

(Continued)

do find that this year we have some really able articulate children going into P1 who can really hear rhyming words and things and whereas last year I would have said I had some children who were just as able, but if you were doing matching rhyming words during storytime, then I don't think they could really hear it.'

Conclusion

Choksy (1986) discusses research from Hungary which shows that studies undertaken with children under the age of 2 show marked differences in the acquisition of speech and music between children who are sung to every day and children who have no music in their environment. Hungary today also has Kodály music primary schools and research carried out with those pupils ·has demonstrated associated improved results in maths and reading.

Changes to curriculum guidelines, such as the Curriculum for Excellence in Scotland, provide an opportunity for all ECEC professionals to explore ways to broaden and enrich the range of experiences offered to children.

Kodály methodology provides one tried-and-tested example of active learning, in an often neglected area of the curriculum, that could simultaneously raise standards in core skills, transferable 'soft' skills, music education and creativity. Early, sustained and repeated exercise of the brain through engagement in appropriate musical activities can enable more to 'use it' and not 'lose it'!

Further reading

Geoghegan, L. (1999) *Singing Games and Rhymes for Early Years*. Glasgow: National Youth Choir of Scotland. Contains lots of ideas and comes with a recorded CD of all songs.

Geoghegan, L. (2002) *Singing Games and Rhymes for Tiny Tots*. Glasgow: National Youth Choir of Scotland. As above.

Littley, M. (1992) 'Current theories about language learning and their relevance to Kodály pedagogy', *Bulletin of the International Kodály Society*, 17(1): 50–4.

Robinson, K. (2001) *Out of Our Minds: Learning to be Creative*. Oxford: Capstone. See pp. 1–16.

Useful websites

The British Kodály Academy – http://www.britishkodalyacademy.org/public_downloads/BKA%20Courses%20brochure%202012-2013.pdf

Pre-birth to Three: New National Guidelines from Education Scotland can be found at: http://www.ltscotland.org.uk/earlyyears/prebirthtothree/index.asp

The education principles of The National Youth Choir of Scotland are based on Kodály, and their website is at: http://www.nycos.co.uk/Education/Kodly

Information about International Kodály Society publications, courses and events can be found at: http://www.iks.hu

You can watch and listen to soprano Isabel Bayrakdaraian and the Sinfonietta Cracovia, conducted by John Axelrod, performing Gorecki Symphony No. 3, 'Sorrowful Songs' – Lento e Largo. Taken from 'HOLOCAUST – A Music Memorial Film from Auschwitz' on YouTube at: http://www.youtube.com/watch?v=miLVOo4AhE4. For the first time since its liberation, permission was granted for music to be heard in Auschwitz and a number of leading musicians were brought there to perform music for the film.

References

Alexander, R. (2009) *Children, their World, their Education: Final Report and Recommendations of the Cambridge Primary Review*. London: Routledge.

Alexander, R. (2010) The perils of policy: success, amnesia and collateral damage in systemic educational reform. Miegunyah Distinguished Visiting Fellowship Program, public lecture, Melbourne.

Balbernie, R. and Zeedyk, S. (2010) *Pre-birth to Three: New National Guidelines* (filmed conversations). Available at: http://www.educationscotland.gov.uk/earlyyears/prebirthtothree/nationalguidance/index.asp (accessed 24.07.12).

Bonis, F. (ed.) (1964) *The Selected Writings of Zoltan Kodály* (trans. I. Halapy and F. Macnicol). London: Boosey and Hawkes.

Bruce, T. (2006) *Early Childhood: A Guide for Students*. London: Sage.

Bruce, T. and Meggitt, C. (2005) *Child Care and Education*, 3rd edition. London: Hodder and Stoughton.

Craft, A. (2002) *Creativity and Early Years Education*. London: Continuum.

Choksy, L. (1986) *Teaching Music in the Twentieth Century*. London: Prentice-Hall.

Cross, I. (1999) 'Is music the most important thing we ever did? Music, development and evolution', in Suk Won-Yi (ed.) *Music, Mind and Science* (pp. 10–29). Seoul: Seoul National University Press.

Doherty, J. and Hughes, M. (2009) *Child Development: Theory and Practice 0–11*. London: Pearson Education.

Eosze, L. (1962) *Zoltan Kodály: His Life and Work* (trans. I. Farkas and G. Gulyas). London: Collet's.

Fabian, H. (2002) *Contextualised Learning for 5–8 Year Olds*. Dundee: Learning and Teaching Scotland.

Fulghum, R. (2003) *All I Really Need to Know I Learned in Kindergarten*, 15th edition. New York: Ballantyne Books.

Gardner, H. (1993) *Frames of Mind: The Theory of Multiple Intelligences*. London: Fontana Press.

Geoghegan, L. (1999) *Singing Games and Rhymes for Early Years*. Glasgow: National Youth Choir of Scotland.

Geoghegan, L. (2002) *Singing Games and Rhymes for Tiny Tots*. Glasgow: National Youth Choir of Scotland.

Goleman, D. (1998) *Working with Emotional Intelligence*. New York: Bantam.

Hein, M.A. (ed.) (1992) *The Legacy of Zoltán Kodály: An Oral History Perspective*. Budapest: The International Kodály Society.

Hennessy, S. (2007) 'Creativity in the music curriculum', in A. Wilson (ed.) *Creativity in Primary Education*. Exeter: Learning Matters.

Laevers, F. (2005) *Deep Level Learning and the Experiential Approach in Early Childhood and Primary Education: Experiential Education*. Leuven: Katholieke Universiteit, Belgium.

Malloch, S. (1999) 'Mother and infants and communicative musicality', in *Rhythms, Musical Narrative, and the Origins of Human Communication*, Musicae Scientiae, Special Issue, 1999–2000, pp. 29–57. Liege: European Society for the Cognitive Sciences of Music.

Moyles, J.R. (1989) *Just Playing? The Role and Status of Play in Early Childhood Education*. Philadelphia, PA: Open University Press.

Perry, B.D. and Pollard, D. (1997) Altered Brain Development Following Global Neglect in Early Childhood. Society for Neuroscience: Proceedings from Annual Meeting, New Orleans.

Robinson, K. (2001) *Out of Our Minds: Learning to be Creative*. Oxford: Capstone.

Scottish Government (2007) *Curriculum for Excellence: Building the Curriculum 2 – Active learning in the early years*. Edinburgh: Scottish Government. Available at: http://www.scotland.gov.uk/Resource/Doc/325191/0104856.pdf (accessed 27.07.12).

Trevarthen, C. (2004) *Learning About Ourselves, from Children: Why a Growing Human Brain Needs Interesting Companions*. Edinburgh: University of Edinburgh.

University of Aberdeen (UoA) (2012) *Graduate Attributes*. Available at: http://www.abdn.ac.uk/thedifference/graduate-attributes.php

CHAPTER 5

CREATIVE APPROACHES TO TEACHING AND LEARNING – TRANSIENT ART

Key ideas explored in this chapter

- 'transient art'
- 'creativity'
- how you might use transient art to support and extend children's learning in an ECEC setting
- whether it is possible to teach creativity.

Transient art

The essential element of transient art is impermanence. A number of different styles and 'ways of creating' come under the umbrella of transient art but the connecting element is this impermanence. For very young children, this could include creating from play dough, with crazy foam, by finger painting or with 'gloop' and these will all be very familiar. The truth is we generally rush children on from this initial engagement with transient art towards producing pictures, paintings and models that can be displayed or taken home. Just as with their play, adults impose structure and formalise the child's experience. We begin very early to limit choice and create boundaries and rules and constraints around art and craft activity. The process becomes subsidiary to the product and children begin to 'fail'. Pablo Picasso famously said that all children were artists, but how do we help them stay artists into adulthood? Many people seeing Picasso's comment might wonder why it is important for there to be more artists – many may not be much taken with his abstract art. The important point here is not just about art but about creativity and particularly creative thinking.

Probably the most famous transient artist today is Andy Goldsworthy. His work is made in the open air using materials that are to hand in remote locations that he visits, including the Australian outback and the North Pole as well as Yorkshire where he grew up and Cumbria where he lives now. He uses twigs, leaves, stones, snow and ice, even the rain. His work is ephemeral and short-lived though many

Figure 5.1a   **Figure 5.1b**

An example from a workshop with children under 3 years old and the ECEC professionals caring for them. This was set up initially as in Figure 5.1a with multi-coloured strips and shapes of paper laid out on a long strip of white paper in front of a large mirror. The babies could sit surrounded by the colours and shapes; the crawlers went to the mirror, and were encouraged to explore by picking up and dropping. The toddlers were able to tip containers of paper strips and shapes onto the paper or sprinkle them or place them. Fabrics such as pieces of netting were introduced and paint on another strip of paper. It was very dynamic, stimulating, free-flowing and fun. [Pictures courtesy of Alan Paterson, University of Aberdeen.]

pieces are photographed and published, often showing the work in progress, and his books are a work of art in themselves. You can see examples of his work simply by Googling 'Andy Goldsworthy' and if you go to the URL below you will see him drawing on slate with slate on the Cumbrian hills and making a 'rain shadow' when the rain comes and washes his drawing away (http://www.bbc.co.uk/learning-zone/clips/andy-goldsworthy-art-in-a-natural-environment/8230.html [accessed 26.07.12]).

Goldsworthy's work explores and uses the landscape and the natural world to convey an experience of the real, natural world. He does work mostly in rural landscapes but his view of the natural world includes all environments. He says: 'Nature for me isn't the bit that stops in the national parks. It's in a city, in a gallery, in a building. It's everywhere we are' (Goldsworthy, 2012: unpaginated).

In an interview in *The Guardian* in 2007, he said that 'he used to hate it when people referred to his work as childlike, or worse childish, believing himself to be a heroic conceptualist. "I used to say, 'Hey, I'm a grown-up and this is grown-up art.' But since I have had my own children", he has four, "and seen how intensely a child looks at things, you really can't describe that looking as naive. My work is childlike in the sense that I am never satisfied to look at something and say that is just a pond or a tree or whatever. I want to touch it, get under the skin of it somehow, try and work out exactly what it is"'.

When you view any of the images on the web of Goldsworthy's work and the artist at work, in particular, perhaps the most striking feature is the time given to the creation against the often very short lifetime of the work. Watching the drawing with slate on slate being washed away by the rain, this is particularly striking. The artist is very much like a child wallowing in free-flow play (Bruce, 1991). His work is purposeful but this is determined entirely by him. The purpose is in the process not the product and just like the child at play he cannot fail, or at least only in his own eyes. Imagine, in contrast, an artist commissioned to paint a portrait of the Queen. The constraints will be numerous and the product is paramount.

REFLECTIVE ACTIVITY

Consider the art and craft activities you did yourself when at school. Did you model something created by an adult? What happened to your drawings, paintings or 'creations'? Do you draw, paint or create anything now?

Consider the art and craft activities you provide for children in your setting. Do they focus on the process or the product? Are they more like the work of Goldsworthy or the artist

(Continued)

(Continued)

commissioned to paint the portrait of the Queen? Do adults provide a model that the children follow (here's one I made earlier)? What happens to their creations – do they take them home or are they displayed, and is this always the same and for all children? The 'crunch' question to ask is:

What decisions/choices are children making when they are engaged in art and craft activities?

CASE STUDY

Here is a mother talking about children making transient landscape art: 'This morning on a chilly day we created transient environmental art in the garden and then attempted to record it through photography and sketching. Quite by chance we took a photograph that defined the learning experience in an instant. My 13-year-old son sat within his "woodland sculpture" and sketched. I took a photograph and it all came together. We suddenly understood the power of art in inspiring, looking, creating and being.

The three of them went on to create a piece of environmental art against the ticking clock. I watched their behaviour and was truly amazed at the sophisticated skills they brought to the task. In no time the "ship" was created and the recording through photograph began all over again.

If I have one wish for all forms of education, it is that our children are exposed to their environment and that they have the opportunities to explore and be creative within varied environments. In the summer we are going to repeat the process but on the beach. I told them that at the end of the session and they immediately began discussing the possibilities.

This is active learning. They owned the process and I merely guided gently, mainly through the raising of questions. I am not sure we can do better than this whether we are teachers or parents or both. I enjoyed the session enormously, but more importantly, they loved it. I'll close and let the photographs speak for themselves.'

The text and photographs were found at: http://livingsimply.hubpages.com/hub/transient-art (accessed 26.07.12).

Another stunning example of a highly skilled adult demonstrating this art form can be found at http://www.linda-matthews.com/transient-art-here-today-gone-tomorrow/ (accessed 26.07.12) where you can see a video of Kseniya Simonova, a Ukrainian artist who recently won Ukraine's version of *Britain's Got Talent*. She uses a giant light box, dramatic music, imagination and 'sand painting' skills to interpret Germany's invasion and occupation of the Ukraine during the Second World War.

Transient art in an ECEC setting

Transient art might begin with babies and toddlers using finger paints, gloop or crazy foam but the approach and freedom of expression it provides can be continued and explored inside and outside. Students on the Post Graduate Certificate in Early Years at Aberdeen University experienced a two-hour twilight face-to-face session on transient art as a tool to use prior to carrying out field experience working with children in an alternative setting to their own (for most this was the 5–8 age group). As part of their assessment, they explored the use of this approach in their own and the alternative setting. The results were interesting – particularly to the students themselves.

One student, an experienced nursery teacher in a school in an affluent part of the city, wrote: 'Children in my setting found transient art initially quite difficult. They wanted their efforts to be permanent and couldn't understand why it could change.' One child in a class of Primary 3 children (7–8-year-olds) found it very challenging. The teacher felt this was because she was seeking 'the right answer'. Initially, this child 'copied' the image created by another child and did not want her artwork photographed. She then changed it to a creation of her own (see Figure 5.2 below).

Figure 5.2 'At this point I ask Child N about her picture which she has changed from the original (she didn't want the first one recorded). She told me very quietly, "It's the grass". I asked her about the animal. She tells me "It's a tiger". She does not seem willing to tell me anything else but agrees to let me take a photograph.'

Figure 5.3   'Child F said "I've made a forest. You get out of the car there and walk down here to the river. These pieces look like the water if you turn them over, they're blue."'

Figure 5.4   '"Can I make another picture now?" Child F created another picture. He described it as a campsite.'

Figure 5.5   A 4–5-year-old boy: *'It was a house now it's a rocket.'*

The teacher used the Leuven Child Involvement Scale (Heylen and Laevers, 2003; see also Bertram and Pascal, undated) to assess levels of engagement with this task and Child N scored low in contrast to Child F – see Figures 5.3 and 5.4.

It is interesting to note that this group, even those who appeared highly engaged in the activity, did not create abstract images. They are all pictures of scenes associated with the children's lives or the class topic. In her evaluation, the teacher noted: 'During the activity their discussion was animated as they created images' and 'During the plenary they said they liked the idea of their pictures being transient, "if you don't like it you can change it". One boy said it was "ace".'

Another student was able to explore the approach with four age groups: two pre-school groups, one at 3–4 years and the other at 3–5 years; one Primary 1 and 2 composite class (at 5–7 years); and a Primary 7 class (at 11–12 years), which resulted in a fascinating study.

In her evaluations she wrote: 'Ante-pre-school (3–4 years) pupils were keen to play with materials available – used ribbons as scarves/hairbands; tried tickling each other with the feathers; at one point threw the box of buttons all over the floor; hula-hooping with the hoop'. In contrast the pre-school pupils (4–5 years old) 'spent longer at the activity, discussion was continual and involved all pupils in the group, others were eager to participate and kept coming to see when there would be space available (limit of 4 at a time)'. Perhaps most interestingly she wrote: 'Pupils who showed lower levels of involvement were those who wanted to glue things down and make a picture they could take away – these pupils quickly moved on' (see an example in Figure 5.5).

In the evaluations after working with all age groups, she noted that those children keen to create a picture of 'real' things and especially those keen to make it permanent were less involved and did not engage with the activity for as long as those pupils who 'simply explored the properties of the materials and produced abstract artwork'. Of the 5–7-year-old group she wrote: 'Having completed one "picture" many pupils chose to move on to other activities. 5/6 pupils spent a longer period of time creating a variety of pictures, using different materials and at times adapting previous pictures. These pupils could have happily spent all morning on this task.' Consider the examples below:

Figure 5.6 Female P7   **Figure 5.7** Male P7

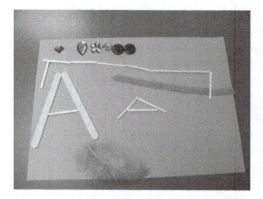

Figure 5.8   Female P2, 6–7 years old

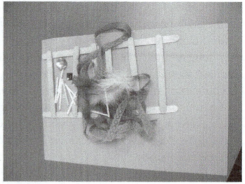

Figure 5.9   Male P1, 5–6 years old

Figure 5.10   Male, pre-school, 4–5 years old

Figure 5.11   Male, ante-pre-school , 3–4 years old

Figure 5.12

Figure 5.13

'Two girls, aged 4–5 years, one who speaks little English, work together outside on a larger artwork. Communication during this activity was minimal, and was conducted through gestures such as pointing and nodding/shaking heads.'

Other students provided interesting examples of materials to use for transient art such as fruits, vegetables, leaves and twigs and created images inside and outside.

 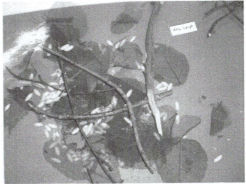

Figure 5.14   **Figure 5.15**

Examples of transient art using various materials

One excellent practical consideration in providing opportunities for transient art, such as the examples provided by our students and those you will have seen on the web, is the use and re-use of easily available, natural materials. The more expensive things can be used again and again. There are commercial sources such as the 'Mindstretchers' catalogue and website (at: http://www.mindstretchers.co.uk/cat/CW/EA62.html) where, in response to requests, they have expanded their range to include a 'transient art box'. However, you can build up a bank of resources as well as make use of naturally occurring materials such as leaves, stones, bark – even snow and rain.

Creativity

It was noted in the previous chapter that many authors today stress the importance of transferable skills and there is an increasing awareness that employers value people who can think intuitively, are imaginative, innovative, good communicators, team players, flexible, adaptable and self-confident. It was also argued that these skills do not come by chance; they are skills not qualities and they are best learned in the early years. In a recent conference presentation, Wiliam (2011: unpaginated) cited Papert (1998), quoting:

> So the model that says learn while you're at school the skills that you will apply during your lifetime is no longer tenable. The skills that you can learn when you're at school will not be applicable. They will be obsolete by the time you get into the workplace and need them, except for one skill. The one really competitive skill is the

skill of being able to learn. It is the skill of being able not to give the right answer to questions about what you were taught at school, but to make the right response to situations that are outside the scope of what you were taught in school. We need to produce people who know how to act when they're faced with situations for which they were not specifically prepared.

You will notice the reference there to the fact that it is *not* the skill of giving the *right answer* that really matters. It is interesting to reflect on the responses to the transient art projects described above and the pupils looking for the glue, the right response, the fixed response and the reality, and those exploring the materials, their imaginations and the possibilities!

It is also interesting to refer back to Gardner (1993) and the behaviour of creative people, again mentioned in the previous chapter, particularly the mix of the childlike and the adult in their behaviours. I wonder if those pupils less able or willing to engage in transient art have actually just been forced to 'grow up' more quickly. I suspect that in most formal education settings and activities, they would be seen as the 'good' children and would be successful at completing the tasks set, such as producing a good copy of Van Gogh's 'Sunflowers' or a pretty exact version of the 'Mother's Day' card the teacher modelled for them. Will they be able as adults to cope with the speed of change in the 21st century? Will they be divergent thinkers who can respond to new situations?

REFLECTIVE ACTIVITY

In her recent talk on TED.com in Edinburgh (2011), 'What do babies think?', Alison Gopnik said that when children play they are experimenting exactly like scientists posing a question, making a hypothesis and finding out what holds true. She says that children's 'playing around' is actually as close to 'rocket science' as we can get. They experiment and use scientific and mathematical processes of probability to problem solve quite naturally. She suggests they are the 'R&D division of the human race'.

Are children *naturally* divergent thinkers? Are they, as Picasso believed, *all* artists? Are they indeed *all* scientists, as Gopnik suggests? Are we *really* 'killing creativity', as Robinson (2001) believes?

Psychologists, educators and others have been attempting to pin down exactly what 'creativity' is for decades. I do not propose to attempt to give a definitive definition and would suggest it is unhelpful for any of us to try and do so. This would be rather like trying to catch hold of a piece of soap in the bath. It is worth exploring the ideas about creativity in order to identify what encourages it. It is important to consider creative ability in the widest sense to include creative thinking across the entire spectrum of ideas and problem solving in science, business, etc., not just the arts. Craft (2002) refers to 'little c creativity' that she describes as a kind of 'personal effectiveness' in terms of being able to cope with recognising and making choices. She sees this 'creativity for everyday life' as essential for children to thrive in tomorrow's world, as 'it is concerned with the skills involved in manoeuvring and operating with concepts, ideas, and the physical and social world' (p. 67).

Robinson (2001) acknowledges the many misconceptions about creativity but asserts it is not a separate faculty evidenced by some people or in only some activities. In other words, he suggests creativity can occur in any human activity. The last 30 years have seen a knowledge explosion and an unbelievably rapid development of technology, so that Kurzweil (1999: 57) can write: 'Before the next century is over, the law of accelerating returns tells us, earth's technology-creating species – us – will merge with our own technology … The intelligence that we are now creating in computers will soon exceed the intelligence of its creators.' There has been no shortage of creative thinking and innovation by a relatively small number of people in certain fields. The challenge is how to educate children born today for *their* future not our yesterdays.

REFLECTIVE ACTIVITY

How would you define creativity?

Think of famous people that you would consider to be creative. Are they all or mainly artists? Can you think of a scientist who you would consider to be creative?

Think of someone you know personally who you would consider to be creative. Why? Do you think this is a feature of their personality or that they are particularly intelligent or that they have been 'brought up' differently?

Write down any words you associate with creativity.

Do you think you have creative abilities? Can you identify an example of something you created or where you have demonstrated creative ability?

Ask at least two other people the same questions.

Do you think creativity can be taught?

Being creative is not always about creating 'something', for example a piece of art or music. It is, perhaps more often, about *creative thinking*. Psychologists divide thinking into divergent and convergent processes. Divergent thinkers would be adept at solving problems that require the generation of a number of different solutions, or in other words a variety of original responses. Today this might be called 'thinking out of the box'. The convergent thinker would be adept at taking given information and finding the one correct answer. Until quite recently, it was believed that the left and right hemispheres of the brain controlled and dominated different functions and different ways of thinking. People were categorised as 'left-brain' or 'right-brain' and women were predominantly seen as one and men the other. There is evidence now to refute this but nevertheless the brain is divided into two distinct halves that, whilst clearly and vitally working together, seem to determine intuitive and rational thinking.

REFLECTIVE ACTIVITY

Listen to the animated talk from Iain Gilchrist on 'The brain divided' at: http://www.ted.com/talks/iain_mcgilchrist_the_divided_brain.html?utm_source=newsletter_weekly_2011-10-25andutm_campaign=newsletter_weeklyandutm_medium=email (accessed 27.07.12)

Does this impact on your thinking about creativity or creative thinking?

Conclusion

It is important for children to have the opportunity to explore materials and develop confidence in their own creative abilities. Duffy (2006: 117) writes: 'Learning through the arts is beneficial in its own right and contributes to children's development in all areas of learning.' Using various approaches to transient art can provide opportunities for a range of sensory experiences and in-depth explorations.

Creative and imaginative experiences such as transient art can provide the opportunity to:

- develop the full range of human potential
- improve capacity for thought, action and communication
- nurture our feelings and sensibilities
- extend our physical and perceptual skills
- explore values
- understand our own and other cultures. (Calouste Gulbenkian, 1982 cited in Duffy, 2006)

The child can 'play' with materials, learn actively and take ownership of their learning experience. Children need to 'learn how to learn' more than they need to learn facts or skills – which may not be useful in their future, as it is pretty much an unknown. They need to develop a disposition that enables them to learn. They need to retain the artist that Picasso believed was already in them.

Further reading

Read about the Leuven Child Involvement Scale at: http://www.decs.sa.gov.au/farnorthandaboriginallands/files/links/link_104984.pdf and see Chapter 15.

Craft, A. (2002) *Creativity and Early Years Education: A Lifetime Foundation*. London: Continuum. See Chapter 10, 'Teaching and assessing creativity'.

Duffy, B. (2006) *Supporting Creativity in the Early Years*. Maidenhead: Open University Press. See Part 3, 'Theory into Practice', starting page 113.

Key, P. (2009) 'Creative and imaginative art and design', in A. Wilson (ed.) *Creativity in Primary Education*, 2nd edition. Exeter: Learning Matters. This is Chapter 10 in the book.

Useful websites

You can find a talk (18 minutes) by Alison Gopnik: What do babies think? On TED.com at: http://www.ted.com/talks/alison_gopnik_what_do_babies_think.html?utm_source=newsletter_weekly_2011-101andutm_campaign=newsletter_weeklyandutm_medium=email

You can also see Sir Ken Robinson on RSA Animate: Changing Education Paradigms at: http://www.youtube.com/watch?v=zDZFcDGpL4Uandfeature=related

References

Bertram, T. and Pascal, C. (undated) *Effective Early Learning Programme: Child Involvement Scale*. Centre for Research in Early Childhood, University College Worcester, St Thomas Centre, Birmingham. Available at: http://www.decs.sa.gov.au/farnorthandaboriginallands/files/links/link_104984.pdf

Bruce, T. (1991) *Time to Play in Early Childhood Education*. London: Hodder and Stoughton.

Craft, A. (2002) *Creativity and Early Years Education: A Lifetime Foundation*. London: Continuum.

Duffy, B. (2006) *Supporting Creativity in the Early Years*. Maidenhead: Open University Press.

Gardner, H. (1993) *Frames of Mind: The Theory of Multiple Intelligences*. London: Fontana Press.

Goldsworthy, A. (2012) *What is Art? ... What is an Artist?* Available at: http://www.arthistory.sbc.edu/artartists/photoandy.html (accessed 24.07.11).

Gopnik, A. (2011) What do babies think? A talk from TED.com in Edinburgh. Available: at http://www.ted.com/talks/alison_gopnik_what_do_babies_think.html?utm_source=newsletter_weekly_2011-101andutm_campaign=newsletter_weeklyandutm_medium=email (accessed 27.07.12)

Guardian, The (2007) Natural Talent: An Interview with Andy Goldsworthy. Available at: http://www.guardian.co.uk/artanddesign/2007/mar/11/art.features3 (accessed 26.07.12).

Heylen, L. and Laevers, F. (2003) *Involvement of Children and Teacher Style: Insights from an International Study on Experiential Education*. Leuven: Leuven University Press.

Kurzweil, R. (1999) 'The coming merging of mind and machine', *Scientific American*, 10(3): 56–61.

Robinson, K. (2001) *Out of Our Minds: Learning to be Creative*. Oxford: Capstone.

Wiliam, D. (2011) Conference presentation at the Hallam Conference Centre, London on 28 September for Cambridge Assessment Network, Embedding Formative Assessment with Teacher Learning Communities, www.dylanwiliam.net

PART 2
THE CHILD IN THE SOCIO-CULTURAL CONTEXT

Introduction

The five chapters in Part 2 focus on some of the changes in the 'lived lives' of children in the UK in the 21st century that impact on their health and well-being and ultimately on their learning and development. There is no attempt to provide answers to some of the factors identified that inevitably become problematised, particularly in the media, such as changes to family structure and changed attitudes and responses to the role of parents, but it is important to raise the awareness of all those involved in ECEC. There is increased understanding of the importance of family and community, as well as the physical environment, on children's ability to learn and reach their full potential. This is evident in the UK (highlighted in Part 1) and it is also true in other countries (highlighted in Chapter 9 and in Part 3).

In this second part, we will explore:

- change and inequality in family life, particularly the role of women, and how ECEC professionals might respond
- the role of parents and again the changes to values, attitudes and parenting style that impact on children's learning and development

- the influence and impact that the community has on children's learning and development and the agencies within it that can intervene
- the importance of early intervention and working in partnership with parents, families and the community
- the possibility that within a fast-changing society the 'school' is not keeping pace
- the nature, purpose and importance of technology in the lives and learning of very young children today.

Chapter 6, 'The impact of changes in family structure', explores how the concept and reality of family has changed from the traditional view held in the 1950s when the foundations of the structure of our educational provision were set. It will examine some of the relevant statistical information from recent studies and reflect on our changing conceptualisation of 'family'. Some key legislative changes are highlighted and discussed in this context with some comparison with Sweden. Inevitably, the role of women in society underpins this discussion which is pursued particularly in terms of ECEC practice and provision.

Chapter 7, 'The role of the parent in the 21st century', explores the changing role of the parent in the 21st century, developing the discussion from Chapter 6 to examine how changes to family structure impact on this role. The chapter continues by discussing the different demands on parents as a result of changes to work patterns, pressures from the media, and the explosion in information and legislation. In examining the role, it is important to discuss parenting styles and how these are affected by the increased demands of society and changes to values and attitudes. The purpose of this discussion is to raise the awareness of ECEC professionals and centres on the importance of the home environment and the values, attitudes and aspirations of parents or primary carers. Research and subsequent reports such as those from the Organisation for Economic Co-operation and Development (OECD) are drawn on to establish a correlation between poverty, an inability to access the support of professional services and failing within the context of formal education. It will explore the critical role of the ECEC professional in terms of working in partnership with parents.

Chapter 8, 'The role of the community in childcare and education', uses the 'ecological framework' identified by Uri Bronfenbrenner to examine the impact of the community on children's learning and development. It explores the support services available to very young children and families and examines the effectiveness of some of these in terms of early intervention. Suggestions are made that will help ECEC professionals develop their knowledge and understanding of their own community more fully and indeed why this is important. Again, it will explore how changes within communities (through case studies) can impact on outcomes for children.

Chapter 9, 'The place of the school in the 21st century', examines how little schools have changed in terms of, for example, structure, timetabling and curriculum compared to changes in society. Some recent initiatives and proposed changes are discussed.

There is a comparison with daycare in Sweden, linking with Chapter 11 in Part 3, and an examination of the evidence from Sweden on the efficacy of Free Schools. Some of the more radical perspectives are highlighted, such as those being explored by, for example, Sugata Mitra through his 'hole in the wall' research and other very current ideas from around the world, such as khanacademy.org. These examples both explore the use of IT and open up the debate about the place of IT in schools, as well as the impact the increasing use of IT is having on our children, which is looked at in the next chapter.

Chapter 10, 'The place of technology in early years care and education', explores the use of ICT and other technologies for children's learning across the curriculum. Through case studies and discussion, this chapter again highlights how swiftly the 'lived lives' of children today are changing and how this might impact on their learning and development, particularly in terms of language acquisition and dispositions towards learning. The discussion focuses on how to incorporate ICT in meaningful ways and in supporting quality interactions. One of the issues explored is about whether the introduction of computers and other technologies to very young children is appropriate, particularly the 'blanket' introduction of Smart boards that may simply be employed as a modern version of the blackboard. Some suggestions are made as to how professionals, systems and services can keep pace given the speed of change, drawing on valuable work elsewhere such as Developmentally Appropriate Technology in Early Childhood (DATEC). With reference to chapters earlier in this section, it considers the impact on family life as well as within care and education settings.

Throughout this part, the aim is to contribute to professional dialogue about changes to children's lives and therefore their changing needs and the nature of the curriculum. There are some suggestions for personal exploration, such as the community walk in Chapter 8, and many points highlighted for further discussion and reflection. There are some practical suggestions such as the guidance from DATEC in Chapter 10 but there is no suggestion that this section provides answers to these complex issues.

CHAPTER 6

THE IMPACT OF CHANGES IN FAMILY STRUCTURE

Key ideas explored in this chapter

- changes in family life, particularly the role of women in society
- inequalities in society and how these impact on children's long-term development
- how ECEC professionals might respond to these changes – implications for practice.

What is a family?

Society is constantly changing, with each generation believing 'things' are not changing for the better. The general public and politicians agree that families matter. Prior to any election, whether it be local or national, policy linked to supporting families is generally discussed. The 2010 Conservative/Liberal Democrat coalition government pledged to review the marriage penalty in the tax credit system as one of a range of measures to promote 'strong and stable families of all kinds as the bedrock of a strong and stable society'. Halsey (2000) analysed the family within the context of the 20th century and concluded that:

> few can doubt that the family as an institution is in trouble. Parliament and people are now casting around for solutions to what is seen as a problem of widespread disorder – rising divorce, lone parenting and child poverty … a collapsed community. (p. 20)

Over the past 30 years in the UK, one major change to children's lives relates to the composition and the stability of family life. High rates of divorce, or partnership dissolution, and higher proportions of children born to parents who are neither married nor cohabitating, means that an increasing number of children live apart from their natural fathers (Kiernan, 2004). This is a major change to the structure and dynamics of the family, leaving many children growing up without a consistent male role model. The Millennium Cohort study (2010) identified that one in four children by the age of 7 years was not living with their natural father; the impact of this on the family is frequently economic and psychological and was recently reported as having a biological effect on boys. There is evidence that an absent father can affect boys physically, by influencing male reproductive outcomes. If a father is absent before the age of 7 years, puberty is earlier; if the father leaves between the ages of 11 and 16, delayed voice breaking (a proxy for puberty) can be an outcome (Sheppard and Sear, 2011).

We perceive that the structure of families has changed recently, but families have always undergone a range of dynamic changes. A family is a group of people who are related by blood or marriage – this definition falls short of allowing for step-children and adopted children. The term 'household' is possibly more descriptive of the scenario we see in today's society, referring to a group of people who live together at the same address and share living arrangements. If you question people, the general view they offer is that of the nuclear family, the image that Edmund Leach (in the BBC Reith Lectures of 1967) calls the 'cereal packet' norm of the family fostered by advertisers who portray smiling families consuming their product. Advertising campaigns portray and promote the 'ideal family', but the reality is very different.

As their primary carers, children may have:

- a single-parent mother
- a single-parent father
- two parents: the biological mother and father living in a heterosexual relationship
- two parents: the biological mother and partner living in a homosexual relationship
- two parents: two 'fathers' living in a homosexual relationship with an adopted child (which could be born to a surrogate mother and be the natural child of one)
- two parents: one biological and a step-parent

- two working parents
- two parents, with only one working, i.e. mother at home
- a single parent who is working
- foster parents
- adoptive parents
- grandparents
- the State – looked after children.

You can probably add to this list!

It has been suggested that the word 'parent' is shorthand for all the important adults in a child's life (Whalley, 1997). Some changes to family structure may offer overall a wider family network compared to the traditional 'nuclear' family and indeed allow children the opportunity to form new relationships and develop negotiating skills. Some changes may leave children with a limited support network. Corsaro (2011) evidences throughout his study of childhood 'the importance of familiar, everyday routines for security in children's lives' (p. 229). It can be very difficult for a parent or parents to provide this security in the midst of divorce, separation or re-marriage to form a 're-constituted' family, perhaps involving numbers of children. Dramatic changes to family structure, which more and more children are experiencing, bring economic demands, changes in residence, school and friends, as well as emotional upheaval. Many children now experience the reorganisation of roles and relationships that means a re-distribution of family power, along with resources such as money, space, time and affection, sometimes more than once in their childhood (McClintic Pann and Crosbie-Burnett, 2005). ECEC practitioners need to fully support the needs of all family 'structures' and take time to consider their own beliefs and attitudes towards them.

REFLECTIVE ACTIVITY

When might a family not be a family? When might it be termed a household, and is there a difference between the two? For statistical purposes, the National Statistical Office (2012: 81) defines a household as: 'a person living alone or a group of people who have the same address as their only or main residence and who either share one meal a day or share the living accommodation.'

Could this be viewed by some people as a family?
  Is a family whatever we want it to be?
  Read the following five case studies. Decide which of these households constitutes a family and why you believe this to be so.

(Continued)

(Continued)

You may find the following criteria useful in determining family status:

- the degree of emotional commitment
- the degree of commitment to the future of the arrangements
- the degree of emotional interdependence
- the degree to which social and domestic life is interwoven
- the degree of financial interdependence
- the intimacy of the relationship(s)
- the duration of the relationship(s)
- the exclusivity of the relationship(s).

When you have considered these findings, share them with others. Look for similarities and differences. Some points to consider are listed after the case studies.

Case study 1

Betty and George have been married for eight years. They hardly speak to one another except to argue or to 'sort out' practical matters to do with the children, Jo (aged 4) and Chris (aged 6). Both pay their wages into separate accounts, although each pays half of the household bills. Betty does most of the necessary childcare during the week and George takes over at the weekend.

Case study 2

Surinder is a lone parent who cares for her daughter, Shama, aged 10. Shama's father does not support the family financially, as he is married with three other children of his own. He regularly brings the children to play with Shama and will sometimes child-mind to enable Surinder to go out by herself. Surinder spends a great deal of time with her mother, from whom she receives a lot of practical help. During the school holidays, Shama's grandmother moves into Surinder's house so that Surinder can continue to work.

Case study 3

Jason and Justin have lived together for nearly 12 years. Two years ago, they entered into a civil partnership. Last year, they had a child, a girl, using a surrogate mother. They have not carried out DNA testing to determine which one of them is the father. Jason is just about to finish paternity leave and return to work.

Case study 4

Jean and Eric, both divorced, have lived together for 5 months. Jean's children, Thomas, James and Edward (all aged under 5), live with them, as do Eric's son Paul (15) and daughter Sara (17) and Sara's baby, Amanda. Sara's boyfriend sleeps in the house most nights. The children, because of their ages, have little to do with one another. Jean 'will not get involved' with the care of Amanda, and Eric disapproves of Sara's boyfriend. The tenancy of the house is in Jean's name, but bills are paid by whoever has the means at the time, which is a cause of friction between Jean and Eric. The current arrangements were undertaken on a trial basis, the terms of which are not clear.

Case study 5

Glyn and Rita have been married for 18 years. They have no children. Rita has never worked outside of the home. Glyn has a good job which more than covers their regular outgoings. They own their own home, run a car and have regular holidays abroad. Glyn and Rita describe themselves as 'soul mates', although they do not spend as much time in each other's company as they used to.

Some points to consider:

1 Which criteria do you regard as most useful in determining whether these households could be called a family?
2 Are there any criteria that you would regard as critical in determining whether any particular household could be called a family?
3 How would you define the meaning of 'family'?
4 How much does your definition of family originate from your personal experience of family life?
5 Has your view of what constitutes a family changed after reading and studying these case studies?
6 What impact might a better understanding of 'family' have on your development as a practitioner?

Professionals and other caregivers of children need to learn about the structure of each individual family, rather than making assumptions about a particular family. Families need to play a key role in defining their own members and the significant relationships within them.

Having read the case studies, write up one for your own family. Consider your own case study against the same criteria.

Factors affecting family structure

Economic changes during the Industrial Revolution impacted on family life. Children contributed to the overall family income and the dynamics of family life altered, whilst what became known as the 'nuclear family unit' was retained. Towards the end of the

19th century, the employment of children was replaced by compulsory education. The dynamics of family life altered again in so much as children were dependent on their parents for support and were no longer contributing to the family income. The next dynamic change to family life was during the 20th century when the term 'teenager' was coined – these older children had formed an economic force influencing consumer markets whilst continuing in full-time education (Cunningham, 2005).

Feminisation of the workforce

Over the last 100 years, the impact of changes in legislation, technology and attitudes has resulted in the feminisation of the workforce. During the Second World War, women regularly took on the male role with childcare support to allow women to work. Many felt emancipated during this time; however when the war finished the nurseries closed practically overnight, the men returned to work and women went back to the home (Todd, 2005). The next significant impact, not just on women but on family life, was the availability of contraception, allowing deferred decisions about starting a family from 1961 onwards. Women now had the ability to plan their family and, generally, the number of times women became pregnant declined. The ability to control their fertility offered women the opportunity to return to the workplace, allowing families to be more secure in their overall income, but also women became a driving force in economic growth.

The increased participation of women in higher education and in the labour market outside the family home has impacted on family life in a number of ways. Today, work and education have become accepted points of social transition that take place alongside more traditional forms such as marriage and childbirth. The participation of women in the labour force has altered the dynamics between partners within the family unit. By having an increased level of economic independence, women have challenged the traditional, distinctive roles within the family unit.

Whilst gender is certainly still a key factor in the organisation of the family unit, the increasing economic independence of women raises a number of questions about gendered notions relating to family, childcare and domesticity in the home. This suggests that dual earning in households with dependent children places a strain on family resources, and that women, in particular, experience 'time squeeze' due to competing family and employment demands. Opportunities to work have enabled women to leave a marriage and seek a divorce. Divorce, remarriage and cohabitation are acceptable in today's society compared to that of our grandparents. Divorce rates are actually falling but this trend is due to fewer couples getting married.

Attitudes towards the role of women in the labour market have altered and these may be attributed to changes in society but also legislative change with regard to equal pay and sex discrimination laws. Between 1971 and 2008, the employment rate of women in the UK increased from 59 to 70 per cent, whilst male employment fell from 95 to 79 per cent (Office of National Statistics, 2008).

The introduction of civil partnerships has enabled same-sex parents to contract into legally binding relationships, and anti-discrimination laws linked to adoption have allowed same-sex couples to become families with children. It is possible due to the Human Fertilisation and Embryology Bill for same-sex couples to have the biological children of one partner. Within the population, these family structures are few. In 2007/8 just 80 gay couples adopted children compared to 2,840 heterosexual couples (Community Care, 2008) and in 2006 only 0.5 per cent of women receiving IVF cycles were registered as lesbian (Human Fertilisation and Embryology Authority, 2008).

Social theorists, including Beck (2002) and Giddens (1991), suggest that an increasing diversity in the nature of intimate relations and family structures is evidence of a shift away from traditional categories of social identity towards a more reflective, fragmented, individualised approach to organising our lives. An aspect which has not altered greatly since the 1950s is the fact that care for both children and the elderly generally falls upon women in our society, and this frequently creates a 'glass ceiling' with regard to their opportunities linked to career promotion and salary scales.

REFLECTIVE ACTIVITY

What are the family structures of the children in your setting?
  Who are the significant adults in each child's life?
  How do we build and maintain relationships with these significant adults?
  Consider a small group of families (4–6). (Select them randomly and identify them only by the first letter of their surname in alphabetical order.)
  Write down your responses to the following questions for each family:

1 Who are the significant members of the child's family?
2 How many of them have you met?
3 Whom do you meet regularly?

On the basis of these answers, prepare a brief response to the following questions. (You may want to think about each family separately or consider the whole group.)

1 What strategies exist in your setting to develop relationships with family members?
  Could you improve on this and meet more family members?
  Do you meet each child mainly in school/nursery/other setting/home?
  Could you alter your way of working to ensure that you meet other members of the family?
  What constraints prevent you from meeting other members of the family?
  In what circumstances might it be inappropriate to try to meet family members?

Maternity benefits

The introduction of a paid maternity leave scheme was established more than 30 years ago. The scheme may have been introduced but a distinct lack of childcare provision meant that most women left employment to raise their children, impacting on the employment market.

Statutory maternity leave and pay in the UK was extended in 2003 and 2007 and is amongst one of the longest in Europe (National Statistical Office, 2012).

The Social Justice Policy Group (2007: 8) reported that four in five people agreed it is 'better for pre-school children to be looked after by a parent at home rather than a childminder or day nursery' and only three in ten agree that 'we should be trying to encourage mothers to go back to work and contribute to the economy rather than making it easier to stay at home'. This response suggests that parents would support a cash benefit to allow them to stay at home. In some European countries such as Sweden, there is much stronger legislation supporting parents to stay at home in the first year of their child's life. However, in 2010 the Swedish government was critical of the new EU directive proposal, making it obligatory for women to be at home for the first six weeks after birth, believing that it should be the voluntary right of parents, not maternity leave by force. Given the increasingly diverse structure and needs of families, it would seem sensible to allow for flexibility. It does however appear that the desired outcome of one parent being able to stay at home with their child in the first 6–12 months is more and more seldom an option.

Childcare and support

> Parents in Scotland face some of the highest childcare costs in the UK, which are already the highest in the world. (Save the Children, 2011: 3)

In 2011, a typical childcare bill for youngsters under 2, before any state-funded nursery or school place is provided, was around £729 a month, frequently higher than a mortgage payment (Save the Children, 2011). This high cost of childcare can mean some parents have very little disposable income at the end of a month, again impacting on family life in so much as parents may undertake evening and weekend employment. Frequently women undertake part-time work, the outcome being that the family spends very little time together as a complete unit. Changes in family structure, separation and divorce, may lead to financial issues relating to childcare and support, with these issues requiring further mediation involving government departments or legal procedures.

Save the Children (2011) undertook research to consider a range of approaches that may address child poverty through childcare, and the following recommendations were made:

- provide for an entitlement to 15 hours a week of early education and care for 2-year-olds, starting with low-income families

- introduce an entitlement to publicly funded out-of-school care for 5–14-year-olds for children living on low incomes (covering school holidays)
- introduce entitlement to support towards the cost of childcare for student parents
- make representations to the UK government to increase support to parents to pay for childcare under Universal Credit.

At the same time, there are calls from other quarters asking for reductions in Child Benefit in order to engineer a lower birth rate; a reduction in support for second and subsequent children for the same reason (for example, free school meals only for the first child); only providing public housing for families up to two children and incentive measures such as tax breaks for childless couples. Childcare, the birth rate and almost everything to do with ECEC is at the heart of current debates and will inevitably impact on family structures, parenting and therefore children's learning and development.

The general trend in today's society is for women to start their family later. In 2009, the average age for women giving birth to their first child was 30 years old. As long as the woman is fit and following a healthy lifestyle, there should be no real concerns, although after the age of 35 years certain risk factors increase. Having children later on does impact differently on family life as, for example, other family members are also generally older. Grandparents often take on the role of childminder to allow mothers to return to work and, increasingly, children remain in the family home much longer than previous generations. In the 20th century, families had the opportunity to move into local authority housing. This opportunity is often no longer open and the advent of the 2008 credit crunch has meant young people find it increasingly difficult to get onto the property ladder. Also, the drive at the end of the 20th century to increase the number of university graduates has impacted on their ability to be considered for mortgages, often due to debt accrued whilst being a student.

The so-called 'baby boomers' are often carrying the burden of childcare and also offering financial support to their children to support another family unit.

The family into which a child is born often defines their outcomes as adults:

> Many of Scotland's children suffer significant disadvantages as a consequence of poverty and deprivation ... it is important to remind ourselves that an awful lot of things that really matter to babies and young children are not costly – either to families or the public purse – but they do take time and effort, and often education and guidance. Many of the things that matter to a child cannot be bought nor provided by the State. Much relies on what we do in our homes and families – and parents in particular have a key role to play.
> (Joining the Dots, 2011: 13)

Dysfunctional societies

Some rich countries are socially dysfunctional with poor health records, increased crime rates, high teenage pregnancies, low educational attainment, obesity and poor community values. Overall, the UK compared to other countries does not perform well (OECD, 2006). So where is it all going wrong? Social inequality seems to be at the root of many problems and generally health and social problems are worse in countries that are more unequal. The UK fits into this category. As this equality gap widens, trust declines and problems emerge within a society. In countries where inequality gaps are wide, mental health, drug use, obesity, teenage pregnancy and infant mortality are prevalent. These problems impact upon the family structure. Parents lack the ability to support their families and are at risk of psychological problems. Parents may have low self-esteem, and as discussed in Chapter 1, stress can have a huge impact on pre- and post-natal life.

In considering inequality, Feinstein and his colleagues (2007) reinforce the fact that socio-economic circumstances at birth have a considerable impact on outcomes later in life. Beyond income, family 'background' and the complex matrix of social and cultural factors, that make up the fabric of family life, play an important role in shaping the kinds of opportunities that are available to children. The overall cohesiveness of the family unit has a significant bearing on child development. A child's future health is influenced by pre-natal experiences; pregnant women having healthy food, not smoking, consuming limited amounts of alcohol and limiting stress can all impact on future life. Scotland's Chief Medical Officer, Sir Harry Burns (2011), sets out evidence suggesting the importance of positive early life experience for long-term health and well-being. For these reasons, socio-economic differences in health in the early years is not simply a matter of immediate concern, but has implications for decades to follow. Within the family, the child's ability to thrive is dependent on caring and nurturing parents.

A report by UNICEF (2011) jointly funded by the Department of Education identified that British parents spend insufficient time with their children because they are working too hard and attempt to compensate by offering a range of material consumables. The research was commissioned following an earlier UNICEF report which concluded that Britain was the worst country among 21 developed countries for children to grow up in; the 2007 report rated the UK as third from bottom for educational standards, second from bottom for teenage pregnancies and bottom for self-esteem. The report compared attitudes of children in Sweden and Spain where these children were significantly happier than their counterparts. What they rated most highly was the time spent with their family and friends and much outdoor activity. We cannot use the weather as an excuse as both Sweden and Spain also experience extremes of high and low temperatures. Dr Agnes Nairn, author of the UNICEF report, said:

> Parents in the UK almost seemed to be locked into a system of consumption which they knew was pointless but they found hard to resist … While children would prefer time with their parents to heaps of consumer goods, [their] parents seem to find themselves under tremendous pressure to purchase a surfeit of material goods for their children. This compulsive consumption was almost completely absent in both Spain and Sweden. (2011: 4)

The findings of the report took the whole spectrum of society into account, irrespective of class or race. So what are the differences? The report indicates that family time is given a much higher priority in Spain and Sweden. It revealed that the sharing of childcare tasks in Sweden, and mothers in Spain staying at home longer to look after children linked to the support of the extended family, were things that children valued, and wanted. Society seems to have shifted from when mothers could only spend time with their children to one whereby both parents work and therefore spend less time with the family, but compensate with material possessions. The media perpetuate this with heavy advertising campaigns, for example when a new children's film is opening and there is heavy-duty advertising pre-Christmas. Who is allowing this to happen? The children have no choice as it is the adults in society that allow this to occur.

The report offered the following recommendations:

- Ban all advertising directed at children under 12, as happens in Sweden.
- Foster a culture in which adults feel they can work fewer hours, arguing in favour of a living wage being set higher than the minimum wage.
- Councils should keep local amenities open longer for families to access.

Providing children with material possessions again reflects a change in family circumstances as during the 1980s and 1990s people experienced a higher level of disposable income and were in a position to offer their children more material possessions. The UK government commissioned a report, *Letting Children Be Children* (2011), looking at the commercialisation and sexualisation of children. The report concluded that there is a need for regulation to protect children from excessive commercial pressures and a need to be 'comprehensive and effective across all media' and to reflect more closely the views of parents and children. The UNICEF report (2011) suggests that the UK government should show strong leadership in order to support families and fight back against the ways in which the UK's materialistic culture embeds inequality in our society, affects family time and relationships, and has a negative impact on a child's well-being. Surely this is a sad reflection of the changes in family life, whereby we need government intervention in deciding what is best for our children.

REFLECTIVE ACTIVITY

What do you believe constitutes 'good parenting'?

Do you hold strong views on what constitutes a 'good parent'?

Have you heard of the phrase 'good enough parenting'? What do you think that means? (The term 'good enough parenting' was probably first coined by Bettelheim, 1987).

Is it right to promote your own views and how might you do this as an ECEC professional?

Can you identify some ways you could support parents to be 'good enough' that you would be comfortable with?

How can inequality be addressed?

In Scandinavian countries, social inequality is less prevalent. Society is on a more even keel with high taxes allowing for the redistribution of wealth. This suggests that reducing inequality impacts on attainment, education, health and living standards. The importance of intervening to remove some of these inequalities impacts not only on individuals, but also in supporting economic development, increased attainment and, according to the report, happier and healthier children within a family. Hallam (2008) reported that there is significant evidence of the positive effect of intervention in the early years. In order for these changes to occur, a shift in government policy is required, but also a shift in cultural attitudes. Perhaps in a parliamentary democracy such as the UK, this shift in cultural attitude needs to occur before government policy can be instigated.

The interactions that parents have with their children and the parenting styles adopted will inevitably shape a child's development. The Families in Britain report (2011) highlights that children growing up in a non-traditional family structure achieve poorer outcomes in relation to educational achievement, health and wealth, and participate in more anti-social behaviour.

If parents experience inequality, they will be less likely to help their children develop the skills needed to succeed in society, such as the ability to co-operate with others, develop empathy, develop self-confidence, and trust other adults that they come into contact with. If children have poor attachment, if the mother suffers from depression and there is poor parenting, this can influence the child's ability to thrive. In future years, certain conditions may occur such as mental health problems, learning difficulties, poor social skills and a range of physical health problems. The gap is wide; early on in life children with the most educated parents are 12 months ahead of those with the least educated parents. Children living in families below the poverty line are generally eight months behind those in an income bracket above (Millennium Cohort Study, 2010).

Families struggling in today's society tend to have lower incomes. They need to spend more time working which adversely impacts on family life and adds to stress within the family. To alleviate the stress, alcohol and drugs may provide a temporary escape mechanism, but take a heavy toll in the long term.

As we know, cognitive development in the early years influences later outcomes. When researchers reflect on cognitive assessments undertaken between the ages of 3 and 5 years, these correlate with later school achievement, academic attainment and occupational outcomes (Bradshaw, 2011). Living in disadvantaged circumstances frequently manifests itself in poor attainment (Schoon, 2007). Research supports the importance of early intervention which can improve the life chances of young children and the families they are part of in the long term (Melhuish et al., 2008). ECEC professionals have the opportunity to support parents, offering advice on the importance of establishing rules and boundaries, supporting healthy eating and good personal hygiene, stressing the importance of an environment which offers love, play, sleep, routine, talking, bedtime stories and outdoor play.

The Scottish government has initiated a new programme to encourage parents to play, talk and read with their children and this is being supported by an advertising campaign, available at: http://www.playtalkread.org. Some countries offer financial support for 'good parents' who adhere to particular conditions. In Mexico, for example, parents must ensure that their children attend school and have regular health checks, which seem to lead to increased school attendance and positive child health outcomes (OECD, 2006). In Australia, maternity payments are conditional on having children vaccinated and pilots are currently ongoing in Aboriginal communities whereby family payments have been tied to a wide range of behaviours including school attendance and housing tenancy conditions (Saunders, 2008).

REFLECTIVE ACTIVITY

Consider your own views on the issue of monetary recompense for being a 'good parent'?
How is a 'good parent' identified and by whom?
How much is good parenting worth?
You could discuss this with colleagues and fellow students.

Conclusion

We have no crystal ball to see how families will be organised in the future. What we do know and are fully aware of is the importance of 'family' in terms of outcomes for each child. Parents want their children to experience a good life and try to give them the best start possible. As an ECEC professional, that best start might be due to your early intervention to support the child and the family, so it may be that as ECEC professionals we need to rethink how we support children and families. It might be helpful to stress the importance of education and not simply the care of children from pre-birth to 3 as many children have already 'slipped through the net' before they enter any ECEC setting.

Further reading

Breakthrough Britain: Ending the costs of family breakdown, report for the Conservative Party, Volume 1: Family Breakdown at: http://www.centreforsocialjustice.org.uk/client/downloads/family%20breakdown.pdf. (accessed 15.09.11) (pages 22–30).

Pugh, G. and Duffy, B. (eds) (2010) *Contemporary Issues in the Early Years*. London: Sage. See Chapter 1, pp. 7–32.

Useful websites

Families in Britain report at: http://www.policyexchange.org.uk/images/publications/pdfs/Families_in_Britain.pdf (accessed 8.10.11).

Letting Children be Children: Report of an Independent Review of the Commercialisation and Sexualisation of Childhood at: https://www.education.gov.uk/publications/standard/publicationDetail/Page1/CM%208078 (accessed 21.08.11).

UNICEF (2011) *Child Wellbeing in UK, Spain and Sweden*. Available at: http://www.unicef.org.uk/Latest/Publications/Ipsos-MORI-child-well-being (accessed 18.10.11). The UK commissioned Ipos MORI to explore the links between inequality, materialism and well-being in children, and the policy implications of this for the UK government.

References

Beck, U. (2002) *Individualization*. London: Sage.

Bettelheim, B. (1987) *A Good Enough Parent: A Book on Child Rearing*. New York: Random House.

Bradshaw, P. (2011) *Growing up in Scotland: Changes in Child Cognitive Ability in the Pre-school Year*. Edinburgh: Scottish Government.

Burns, H. Sir and Department of Health, Physical Activity, Health Improvement and Protection (2011) *Start Active, Stay Active: A Report on Physical Activity from the Four Home Countries' Chief Medical Officers*. Available at: http://www.dh.gov.uk/prod_consum_dh/groups/dh_digitalassets/documents/digitalasset/dh_128210.pdf (accessed 17.05.12).

Community Care (2008) *Vulnerable Children Still Waiting Too Long for Placement*, 5 November. Children looked after in England (including adoption and care leavers) year ending 31 March 2008. Available at: http://www.commuitycare.co.uk/Articles/2008/11/05/109856/gay-couples-overlooked-in-adopters-shortage.html

Corsaro, W.A. (2011) *The Sociology of Childhood,* 3rd edition. London: Sage.

Cunningham, H. (2005) *Children and Childhood in Western Society Since 1500*. London: Pearson.

Families in Britain (2011) *The Impact of Changing Family Structures*. Available at: www.policyexchange.org.uk/images/.../pdfs/Families_in_Britain

Feinstein, L., Hearn, B., Penton, S., Abrams, C. and Macleod, M. (2007) *Reducing Inequalities: Recognising the Talents of All*. London: National Children's Bureau.

Giddens, A. (1991) *Modernity and Self Identity: Self and Society in the Late Modern Age*. Bristol: Policy Press.

Hallam, A. (2008) *The Effectiveness of Interventions to Address Health Inequalities in the Early Years: A Review of Relevant Literature*. Edinburgh: Scottish Government.

Halsey, A.H. (2000) 'Introduction', in A.H. Halsey and J. Webb (eds) *Twentieth-Century British Social Trends*. London: MacMillan.

Human Fertilisation and Embryology Authority (2008) *A Long Term Analysis of the HFEA Data*. London: HFEA.

Kiernan, K. (2004) 'Unmarried cohabitation and parenthood in Britain and Europe', *Journal of Law and Policy*, 26(1): 33–55.

Joining the Dots (2011) *A Better Start for Scotland's Children*. An independent report by Professor Susan Deacon. Available at: http://www.scotland.gov.uk/Resource/Doc/343337/0114216

Letting Children Be Children (2011) *Report of an Independent Review of the Commercialization and Sexualisation of Childhood*. Available at: https://www.education.gov.uk/publications/standard/publicationDetail/Page1/CM%208078

McClintic Pann, K. and Crosbie-Burnett, M. (2005) 'Remarriage and recoupling: a stress perspective', in P.C. McKenry and S.J. Price (eds) *Families and Change: Coping with Stressful Events and Transitions*. London: Sage.

Melhuish, E.C., Sylva, K., Sammons, P., Siraj-Blatchford, I., Taggart, B., Phan, M.B and Malin, A. (2008) 'Preschool influences on mathematics achievement', *Science,* 321(29): 1161–2.

Millennium Cohort Study (2010) available at: http://www.cls.ioe.ac.uk/page.aspx?andsitesection id=851andsitesectiontitle=Welcome+to+the+Millennium+Cohort+Study

National Statistical Office (2012) Statistical information available at: http://www.cso.gov.bw/

Office of National Statistics (2008) *Working Lives*. Available at: www.statistics.gov.uk/cci/nugget.asp?id=1654

Office for Economic Co-operation and Development (OECD) (2006) *Babies and Bosses: Recording Work and Family Life*, Vol. 4. Paris: OECD.

Saunders, P. (2008) 'From entitlement to employment', in L. Kay and O.M. Hartwich (eds) *When Hassle Means Help*. London: Policy Exchange.

Save the Children (2011) *The Childcare Trap*. Available at: http://www.savethechildren.org.uk/resources/online-library/making-work-pay-the-childcare-trap

Schoon, I. (2007) 'Adaptations to changing times: agency in context', *International Journal of Psychology*, 42: 94–101.

Sheppard, P. and Sear, R. (2011) *Father Absence Predicts the Age at Sexual Maturity and Reproductive Timing in British Men*. Available at: http://rsblsocietypublishing.org/content/early/2011/08/23/rsbl.2011.0747.full.html#ref-list-1 (accessed 18.10.11).

Social Justice Policy Group (2007) *Breakthrough Britain*. London Centre for Social Justice. Available at: http://today.yougov.co.uk/commentary/john-humphrys/british-children-unhappy-materialists; http://www.centreforsocialjustice.org.uk/client/downloads/family%20 breakdown.pdf.

Todd, S. (2005) *Young Women, Work and Family in England 1918–1950*. Oxford: Oxford University Press.

UNICEF (2011) *Child Well-being in the UK, Spain and Sweden: The Role of Inequality and Materialism*. Available at: http://www.unicef.org.uk/Latest/Publications/Ipsos-MORI-child-well-being.

Whalley, M. (1997) *Working with Parents*. London: Hodder and Stoughton.

CHAPTER 7

THE ROLE OF THE PARENT IN THE 21ST CENTURY

Key ideas explored in this chapter

- the role of parenting styles linked to changing values and attitudes within the 21st century
- some key external influences on family life
- the role of the ECEC professional team in working in partnership with parents.

Introduction

Childhood is a relatively modern phenomenon. During the medieval period, less than a quarter of children reached their first birthday and there was little concept of childhood (Cunningham, 2006). It was the writings of Rousseau during the Enlightenment period of the 18th century that advocated consideration of the child's interests, and it is just over 150 years since Joseph Chamberlain, Mayor of Birmingham, set up the National Education League to campaign for free secular and compulsory education. 'Childhood' began to be recognised early on in the 20th century; prior to this children were very much expected to contribute to the family economy as soon as they could secure employment. In 1944 the school leaving age was 15 years and this was raised to 16 years in 1973.

Recent governments have indicated that this could be raised to 18 years, which could lead to conflict as to where childhood ends.

Parenting remains a challenging role in the 21st century. Many might describe children as in this quotation:

> The children now love luxury; they have bad manners, contempt for authority; they show disrespect for elders; love chatter in place of exercise. Children are now tyrants, not the servants of their households. They no longer rise when elders enter the room. They contradict their parents, chatter before company, gobble up dainties at the table, cross their legs and tyrannize their teachers.

This complaint is widely attributed to Socrates, a Greek philosopher writing in Athens in the 4th century BC but, in essence, might be written today. Similar views are still held, particularly towards teenagers, supported by often negative media coverage.

The norm in society is to value children and becoming a parent is considered life-enhancing. Indeed globally, it appears that for women, having children is still the ultimate experience to offer fulfillment in their lives (Ulrich and Wetherall, 2000). Many women undergo invasive treatments to achieve motherhood, even when all other aspects of their lives are successful. The biological driving force still compels us to pass our genes on to the next generation.

As identified in Chapter 6, the traditional nuclear family is not the overall norm in today's society, having been replaced by a range of family structures. Whether there is only one parent living with the child, two or multiple step-parents involved, the vast majority of parents endeavour to provide the best care for their children. In generations past, this care was heavily focused around the basic requirements of warmth and food, which for some families is still the case.

Parents offer love, stability and support, but in an ever-changing, often more stressful world. In Chapter 6, we discussed how children in Britain have been found to be the least happy in Europe (OECD, 2006). Why is this? Have parenting styles and parents changed dramatically?

Attitudes to children and how childhood is changing

Our attitude to children and our view of childhood has not suddenly and dramatically altered with the advent of the 21st century but it continues to evolve. One aspect of change is legislation dealing with a range of issues linked to health, well-being and education where the 'best interests' of the child are the focus. Since the beginning of the 21st century, children have become increasingly prominent within policy and legislation. The protection and rights of children were initially documented in the United Nations Rights of the Child (United Nations, 1989). Governments either adopted this or developed policy specific for them, i.e. the Children Act (1989)/Children Act Scotland (2003). Policy continually develops (Scottish Government, 2004; EYPS, 2008) informed by research such as the Growing Up in Scotland reports (Scottish Government, 2011). Policy and legislation means parents have responsibilities rather than rights.

Legislation continues to reinforce the importance of listening to children's voices. The Children's Commissioner of Scotland holds annual 'blethers' (a Scottish word for a good chat) at: www.sccyp.org.uk/ – these are open to all children to gauge their views. Adults often assume that children can and cannot do certain things at certain ages and this is increasingly influenced by legislation that identifies the age at which a child can be left alone, drink alcohol, etc. In our society, adults are required to attend to and meet the basic needs of children. Children are seen to have the right to a 'childhood', physical care, love and an education. This is not the case in every part of the world. Our construct of childhood and how we parent is built from our own childhood experiences and from our own parents' values and beliefs.

The UNICEF (2007) overview of child well-being in rich countries rated UK children the lowest of all in 21 countries for both relationships and happiness. British children were fourth from bottom and only one point above for educational well-being. In this survey, the Netherlands and Sweden came out on top with the UK and the USA sitting in the bottom third. These results may or may not surprise us but they are certainly disappointing. They may reflect a change in attitude or a change to the experience of childhood – indeed this may be an improvement on 10 or 20 years ago – but they are only presented in comparison to other countries at present. They may be linked to cultural attitudes. In Sweden, children are very much seen as the future and the responsibility of all, with the state taking a more involved role in all aspects of childhood. A striking difference is the low level of bullying of all types in Sweden (15 per cent), compared to other countries where the rate can be 40 per cent (UNICEF, 2007). Could it be that where the level of bullying is low that the 'voice of the child' is being listened to?

REFLECTIVE ACTIVITY

Consider the following scenario:

A child is in hospital and needs to be given medication; the child refuses and is generally quite distressed. The parents support the medical team in holding the child firmly and forcing the medication into the child. The child is so upset that the medication is immediately vomited back out of the child's system.

Consider:
If this was an adult, would this intervention be allowed?
Would it be considered assault?
How does this example reflect the balance of rights and responsibilities of parents?

It would appear that in all democratic countries legislation highlights 'listening to children', but the reality is that, apart from a few countries, the needs of children continue to be met entirely by their immediate family as best they can and many children remain unheard.

How changes in legislation impact upon parenting styles

The United Nations Convention on the Rights of the Child (UN, 1989) was ratified by all nations except Somalia and the USA. Many governments fully support this legislation by making it an offence to subject children to any form of corporal punishment.

Changes are frequently the result of a trigger event, as seen in Sweden in 1975, where a 3-year-old girl was badly beaten by her father and taken to hospital with bruises over her entire body. The court acquitted the father, stating he had not exceeded his right to chastise his daughter (Svern, 1984, cited in Durrant, 1996). In 1979 the proposal to ban corporal punishment was passed unopposed.

> Children are entitled to care, security and a good upbringing; children are to be treated with respect for their person and individuality and may not be subjected to physical punishment or other injurious or humiliating treatment. (Parents Code, 2004: 3)

A key factor in this change was the way the law forbade mentally humiliating treatments such as ridiculing, frightening, threatening or locking up a child. This addressed the issue of the possibility of an increase in mental abuse if physical chastisement was removed. As with all legislation, these changes were fully supported by a public education campaign. This change in the law set a precedent whereby 99 per cent of Swedes became familiar with the law, a level of knowledge unmatched in any other study on knowledge about law in any other industrialised society (Ziegert, 1983). To support the legislation, secondary-age pupils are offered classes in parenting. Other countries that have passed similar laws include Finland, Denmark, Norway, Austria, Cyprus and Italy. The banning of corporal punishment, including that of mental mistreatment, has in most circumstances led to a reduction in child abuse. A government awareness campaign running in Scotland, 'Children are Unbeatable', is gathering momentum to outlaw smacking (http://www.childrenareunbeatable.org.uk/pages/scotland.html).

REFLECTIVE ACTIVITY

This debate continues in the UK. What is your view regarding corporal punishment of children by parents?

What might be the impact of introducing legislation preventing parents from punishing their own child as they see fit?

Try to consider as many 'pros' and 'cons' as you can. It might be helpful and enlightening to engage in a discussion of the issue with others.

Ways in which this legislation could affect parenting in the UK

Baumrind (1967), in her research during the 1960s, studied more than 100 pre-school children using a range of research techniques and identified four dimensions of parenting:

- disciplinary strategies
- warmth and nurturance
- communication styles
- expectations of maturity and control.

Baumrind identified that parents display one of the three key parenting styles (now accepted as four since Maccoby and Martin [1983] identified the 'uninvolved parent').

The styles we refer to are:

- **Authoritarian** – Children are expected to follow the strict rules set by parents, with failure to follow resulting in punishment. When children challenge this, the response can be, 'Because I said so.' Typically such parents place high demands on their children whilst not being responsive.
- **Authoritative** – Similar to authoritarian parents, authoritative parenting establishes rules and guidelines they expect their children to follow. These parents do display a more democratic and responsive parenting style by listening to their children. The element of punishment is replaced by forgiveness. These parents want their children to be assertive and socially responsible whilst developing self-regulation.
- **Permissive** – Sometimes referred to as 'indulgent parents', frequently taking the role of being a friend, being lenient and not expecting the child to demonstrate maturity and self-control. They communicate with their children very openly as they adopt the role and status of a friend.

- **Uninvolved –** These parents fulfil their children's basic needs but tend to communicate or interact little with their children. In extreme cases, this may result in rejection or neglect.

REFLECTIVE ACTIVITY

If you are a parent, consider what you believe is your parenting style.

In your setting or amongst your peers, what do you perceive to be the main parenting style? Which style do you believe is most effective? Why?

When you reflect upon this activity, you will identify that parenting is frequently a combination of styles. Only when we see these forms in their extreme should we begin to have concerns.

The parenting style adopted has an influence on the development of the child. Authoritative parenting generally leads to children who are happy, capable and successful (Maccoby, 1992). The parenting style we adopt is heavily influenced by each parent's prior experiences as a child and the influence from the fellow parent or carer. Parenting styles cross all social boundaries but some potential differences can be linked to culture, personality, family size, parental background, socio-economic status, educational level and religion.

Stress and its effect on today's society

The Oxford English Dictionary states that the term stress can be traced back to the early 14th century when stress had several distinct meanings, including hardship, adversity and affliction (Rutter, 1983). Stress is a stimulus, an observable response to a situation and we need *some* stress in our lives. It is the degree of stress and the absence of factors that help us cope with it that make the difference between stimulation and distress. Stress in families tends to be associated with particular conditions rather than the everyday stresses of daily life. This was shown in one of the first studies considering family stress carried out by the University of Michigan and the University of Chicago during the 1930s, looking at the impact of the Great Depression on families (Boss, 2002). Parenting can often seem to be a series of stressful situations and decisions. Many parents, perhaps increasingly today when both are likely to be working and working hours are longer, will 'take the line of least resistance', giving in to demands from children on the one hand and saying 'no' too often on the other. Consider the activity below.

REFLECTIVE ACTIVITY

Consider the following scenario:

Today your 6-year-old son is walking to school by himself for the first time. Consider how this makes you feel; what thoughts flood through your head and how much information have you imparted to him prior to the walk? Would you be a confident parent and see this as another rite of passage and let him get on with it, or would you be following closely behind and watching from a distance?

What would be your view of a parent allowing a 6-year-old to walk to school alone? Do the judgements of others create more stress for parents today than in the past?

Everyone experiences 'normal' stressful events that last for a short period of time; predictable events such as a birth or the death of an older relative are transition processes for both adults and children. Boss (1988) identified non-normative stressor events that affect us that are generally not predictable, and not repeatable. These could include a natural disaster, loss of employment, a car accident, winning the lottery – so stress is not always inherently bad!

What is important is the way in which the 'family', in whichever form it takes, deals with the event and the supportive network around them. McCubbin et al. (1980) concluded that it is frequently an accumulation of several stress factors over a length of time that affects the family.

How families cope and what tactics they employ to cope with stress will vary. For some families, stress will draw them closer, which may reflect a strong family bond, resilience in some or all family members or the presence of an extended supportive network. For others, cracks may begin to appear and the family unit slowly disintegrates. Stress is only problematic when it leads to a disruption in the family system. For most parents, normative stresses (McKenry and Price, 2000) such as lack of personal time, fretful babies and being with children all day will come and go and they will cope. For others, the stress builds up, they do not cope and the disrupted, dysfunctional family unit results in more stress.

Just over a quarter (26 per cent) of households with dependent children are single-parent families and there are 2 million single parents in Britain today. This figure has remained consistent since the mid-1990s (www.gingerbread.org.uk [accessed 05.03.12]). This is a distinct change to family structure and consequently a change to the experience of being a parent and of being parented, for many. For single parents, normative stress factors can compound into huge concerns as they have to cope with all eventualities on their own.

If the support of an extended family is not available, then the importance of having a strong social network becomes imperative, supporting the well-being of mothers and fathers. Many new mothers will relate to the scenario of rushing and finding it an effort to get to the mother and toddler group on time, but once there the support of and interaction with other adults make the effort worthwhile. Consider the factors in the case study below.

CASE STUDY

Two boys, Connor and Callum, of the same age (3 years and 8 months) attend a nursery class in a local primary school in Aberdeen. They live in very similar affluent homes, one street apart, in the West End of the city and they both have a younger baby sister. Their dads both work offshore in the oil industry and although they work for different companies on different platforms, their work schedules are the same – being offshore for two weeks and onshore for three weeks. Sometimes due to weather conditions, they cannot get back straight away and their return can be delayed for some days.

It seems the two boys' life experiences are almost identical. However, there is one key difference that has a dramatic effect. Connor's mother is happy with this lifestyle, perhaps because her own parents and her sister and family live nearby. They are very supportive and she has a large group of friends. She socialises when her husband is away, leaving the children with her parents from time to time to have a break. When he is home, she happily adjusts her schedule and they can still leave the children with family and have nights out together. Callum's mother is unhappy. She does not have any extended family living in Aberdeen as she grew up in Manchester. She has a few friends but has found it difficult to establish any really close relationships as she came to Aberdeen only a year before Callum was born. She is lonely and finds life stressful when her husband is away, and when he is home they often argue as she feels he does not understand how hard it is for her.

The two boys are quite different in nursery. Connor is relaxed and sociable, meeting all developmental milestones as expected. Callum is anxious, often crying in the morning when his mum leaves, often choosing solitary activities or struggling to interact with other children by being too boisterous and aggressive. Sometimes he is disruptive at story time at the end of the session, and twice he has fallen asleep in the home corner.

REFLECTIVE ACTIVITY

How much importance is placed in ECEC settings on providing support for parents?

How much importance is placed in ECEC settings on providing opportunities for social interaction between parents and between staff and parents?

How much importance is placed in ECEC settings on obtaining the kind of information in the case study above?

Attachment

In past generations, women tended to spend most of their time within the home and were the main carer for their children. As women have moved into full-time employment, this has changed and many children are now cared for within a range of settings. This may have an impact on attachment. It would be easy to assume that parents, particularly mothers, spend less time with their children today but in fact today's parents spend more time with their children than previous generations – 99 minutes per day compared to 25 minutes in 1975 (Future Foundation, 2000). However, there could be other reasons for this, such as both parents now sharing the childcare more equally, children going to bed later, or the whole family staying indoors and engaging in sedentary pursuits together such as watching television. This last thought gives rise to the question of the quality of time spent with children, which may have altered.

Bowlby (1969) identified the importance of a close bond forming between parents and their children. The concept of attachment integrates social, emotional and cognitive aspects of the child's mind. Cassidy (1999) observes, within this framework, that attachment is considered a normal and healthy characteristic of humans throughout the lifespan, rather than a sign of immaturity that needs to be outgrown.

Ainsworth et al. (1978) assessed levels of attachment between the mother and child by means of a stranger entering the room, extending the work of John Bowlby in what has become known as 'The Strange Situation Experiment'. If children feel securely attached to their main carer, they will use this as a secure base in order to explore; they will feel confident to try new things. If this attachment is poor or non-existent, the child may not feel confident to explore and some areas of development will be delayed.

The four types of attachment identified from the Strange Situation Experiment (adapted from Ainsworth et al., 1978) are:

Insecurely attached: detached/avoidant (Type A): The child focuses on the environment when in a room, does not cry on separation from the parent and shows no preference for the mother over the stranger. The child is not distressed by the separation.

Securely attached (Type B): The child explores happily and looks for the parent for comfort when needed. Securely attached children actively seek and maintain close proximity with the primary caregiver.

Insecurely attached: resistant/ambivalent (Type C): The child seems to need the parent at all times and can demonstrate passive and anger emotions. The child does not explore the environment. The child is upset on separation from the carer and is not easily comforted on reunion.

Insecurely attached: disorganised/disorientated (Type D): The child in the carer's presence demonstrates disorientated behaviours. At times, the child may freeze and not move. The child seeks comfort after separation but avoids eye contact and is generally ambivalent.

REFLECTIVE ACTIVITY

Consider some of the behaviours that you have observed in your setting and try to explain them to a colleague in the light of the above classification.

Infants are capable of forming more than one attachment with siblings, extended family members and with educators, but will express a strong preference for one person when they require comforting. The importance of a main or key worker for each young child in an early years setting is highly significant in supporting long-term emotional and social development. Children struggling with separation from their primary carer, for example when starting at any childcare setting, produce an increased amount of the stress hormone Cortisol, which has an impact on other hormones that produce pleasurable feelings and on the function of the brain. This physical effect of separation anxiety occurs, not just when the child is physically separated but also when the primary carer is emotionally detached. In other words, it is not just about the physical presence of 'Mum'. One study of nursery school children suggests that this emotional attachment can be replaced by another adult. If a member of staff takes on this role of being responsive to the state of the child moment to moment, the child can cope with separation (Dettling et al., 2000, cited in Gerhardt, 2004).

Type C (resistant/ambivalent) tend to be troubled by unresolved issues with parents whilst still unable to break away from the family. Type D (disorganised/disorientated) are the most at risk. As teenagers and adults, with the absence of alternative attachment figures, they may resort to bullying, aggression and excessive control. However, there is the opportunity during adolescence and adulthood, with the support of extended family and/or a loving partner, to reconcile past experiences (Werner and Smith, 1982).

When working with young children, we need to fully consider the importance of all interpersonal relationships within families. When observing any form of negative behaviour such as anger and withdrawal, we should consider if origins are linked to early attachment issues. The Nurture Group Network has currently around 1,500 nurture groups (NGs) active in the UK. They are grounded in attachment theory, and support the need for any person to be able to form secure and happy relationships with others in the formative years of their lives.

REFLECTIVE ACTIVITY

Investigate the availability of nurture groups in your area and consider their long-term role in supporting emotional and social development.

Each individual needs to develop strategies to reduce stress. For both adults and children, outdoor play and activities can reduce stress. 'Getting back to nature' may have been a key factor in why previous generations may not have felt so stressed during everyday activities (see Chapter 3 for further discussion).

Technology, media and its influence on family life

The pace of technology continues to be one of the key features that impact on family life and the access children have with the outside world. Parents today may know less about what their children are doing and learning, even though they are in the house with them, than previous generations. A very young child begins to use a mobile telephone when his mother holds it to his head and he asks to speak to someone. Children, 35 years ago, might have had to walk to the end of the street to use a call box, since there was no telephone in the house. Having access to a range of computer games and the internet is now the norm. If carers have no particular interest in these games, they are frequently played in isolation and older children may play online with a range of participants worldwide. Children spend time in front of screens before, during and after school. Narin et al. (2007) identified that one third of families accompany their mealtimes with the television being watched or a computer being used.

REFLECTIVE ACTIVITY

One setting featured in a case study report (Stephen and Plowman, 2003) used digital cameras not only as a way to share children's experiences with parents but also to reassure. When a mother was concerned that her child was not eating enough, a play leader photographed snack time. Another mother, upset at leaving her child in tears, could be shown a picture of her child playing happily on her return. This seems a very positive and practical use of technology to help build relationships with parents (see Chapter 10 for further discussion on technology).

Consider and discuss with others how you use technology as an educational tool. Can you use it in ways to strengthen and support home–setting links? Do you need to support aspects of the curriculum that are being limited or overtaken by technology?

Childhood and the role of the parent is imagined and depicted in moving colour images every minute of every day. It is packaged and sold to us as an ideal. Prior to the birth of the child, it is common for prospective parents to buy a range of parenting magazines to ascertain the best cot, pram and educational toys to support their child's development. In January 2009, the insurance group Liverpool and Victoria estimated that the cost of having a baby was £194,000 with advertising messages persuading parents how best to spend their money. Parents may be the first to be influenced by the media but this influence soon extends to the child. In an increasingly materialistic society, children are an important part of the economy. The child as a consumer is very lucrative and children's 'pester power' is well recognised. They increasingly have an influence on family expenditure on high-end purchases such as holidays and cars, as well as eating out. Children are exposed to thousands of advertisements per year and retailers use particular television channels for this niche market. Children who have no perception of the persuasive powers of advertising are drawn in by a set of images, and parents (perhaps on low incomes) may buy products even if this means incurring debt.

REFLECTIVE ACTIVITY

Reflect on the resources provided in your setting. Do they reflect this picture of a materialistic society? How natural are your resources? Do you rely on commercially produced toys? Do you make use of recycled, reusable resources that are cheap or free? If you use more expensive equipment and resources, do you feel pressured to do so? What are these pressures and are they the same for parents?

Ali et al. (2009) identify that by the age of 5 or 6, minors realise that advertisements offer advice as to which toys should be bought but do not realise they are being persuaded to purchase them; by 7 or 8 the persuasive nature of advertising is understood. In its quest to support healthy lifestyles, prevent disease and fight rising obesity, the UK government banned the advertising of unhealthy snacks and drinks that were high in sugar, fat and salt.

REFLECTIVE ACTIVITY

Watch television at a peak viewing time for children. What are the advertisements featured and how are they targeted at children? Do you believe that all advertising for food is covered by the government legislation of 2008?

When we log on to the internet, advertisers have already built up our consumer profile through 'cookies'. The average age children go online is between 7 and 9 years.

In the UK, 49 per cent of children and young people between the ages of 9 and 16 years use the internet in their own bedrooms at home; 47 per cent use it at home but not in their own bedroom (Cowie, 2012). When the television is moved from the main sitting room to a bedroom, parents have less control over what children view; the internet however allows children the opportunity to gain access to far more information, and to enter social networking sites. Most parents are aware of the need to be vigilant as to how their children are using the internet and are aware of the possibility of cyber bullying via the internet or by mobile phone, but find it increasingly challenging to prevent.

Conclusion

The role of a parent and the relationship between parent and child are fundamentally unchanged but the 'lived lives' of both parents and children have certainly changed and this is impacting on roles and relationships. Legislation has had an impact on shifting the emphasis and the balance from parental rights to parental responsibilities. Living in a single parent or reconstituted family has an impact, not least financially. The majority of mothers with a child in their first year of school are now working, which inevitably affects the amount of time parent and child spend together and how they spend that time. Technology has changed the way people live and how they spend their time. In many ways, the ease of communication through mobile phones and social networks can actually be isolating and can cause stress as well as connection and ease. The media, providing literally 'too much information', can cause distress and a distortion of reality for parents, leading them to overact and over-protect their child which impacts on the child's learning and development. Parenting today, despite people having fewer children and having children later in life, is arguably more challenging than ever.

ECEC professionals need to develop an understanding of what it is to be a parent today and to understand the needs and expectations of the parents of children in their care, as both the child and the parent (or primary carer) are their 'clients'. The relationship with the client is a key attribute of professional status – see Chapters 16 and 20. It is also vital to remember that parents and family are always the child's prime educators. This does not just mean in the sense of their first educator before they come to school but their first and foremost educator through to adulthood. They wield the greatest influence over the child and determine outcomes. In terms of effective early intervention, the ability of professionals to reach out to and engage with parents and families is often the key to success (DfES, 2004; Gasper, 2010). It is vital to acknowledge that there are barriers to dialogue and partnership between home and setting and to work to overcome these. It may be more challenging working with parents from minority, socially disadvantaged and non-English speaking groups but the importance of a meaningful ongoing dialogue cannot be too highly stressed. This should be a dialogue and not professionals imparting information and dictating what is 'right'

(Brooker, 2005). Good conversations develop when people listen (see Chapter 19). ECEC professionals need to develop an understanding of the role of the parent today and listen to the parents of children in their care. It is important to remember that, as Pugh and De'Ath (1984: 184) stated: 'The great majority of parents are concerned to do their best for their children, even if they are not always sure what this might be.'

Further reading

Bruce, T. (2005) 'People who matter to children', in T. Bruce (ed.) *Early Childhood Education*, 2nd edition. London: Hodder Arnold. This is Chapter 9 in the book.

Layard, R. and Dunn, J. with the panel of The Good Childhood Inquiry (2009) 'Conclusions', in The Landmark Report for The Children's Society: *A Good Childhood: Searching for Values in a Competitive Age*. London: Penguin. This is Chapter 9 in the book.

Lumsden, E. and Doyle, C. (2009) 'Working with families', in T. Waller (ed.) *An Introduction to Early Childhood*, 2nd edition. London: Sage. This is Chapter 12 in the book.

Thomas, N. (2004) 'Sociology of childhood' and 'Law relating to children', in T. Maynard and N. Thomas (eds) *An Introduction to Early Childhood Studies*. London: Sage. These are Chapters 7 and 9 in the book.

Useful websites

Children's Commissioner for Scotland – www.sccyp.org.uk/ (accessed 08.05.12).

Children are Unbeatable – http://www.childrenareunbeatable.org.uk/pages/scotland.html (accessed 23.03.12).

Getting it Right for Every Child – www.scotland.gov.uk/gettingitright (accessed 08.05.12).

References

Ainsworth, M.D.S., Blehar, M., Waters, E. and Wall, S. (1978). *Patterns of Attachment: Psychological Study of the Strange Situation*. Hillsdale, NJ: Lawrence Erlbaum.

Ali, M., Blades, M., Oates, C. and Blumberg, F. (2009) 'Children's ability to recognise advertisements on web pages', *British Journal of Developmental Psychology*, 27: 71–84.

Baumrind, D. (1967) 'Child-care practices anteceding three patterns of pre-school behaviour', *Genetic Psychology Monographs*, 75: 43–88.

Bowlby, J. (1969) *Attachment and Loss*, Vol. 1. London: Hogarth Press.

Boss, P.G. (1988) *Family Stress Management*. Newbury Park, CA: Sage.

Boss, P.G. (2002) *Family Stress Management: A Contextual Approach*, 2nd edition. Thousand Oaks, CA: Sage.

Brooker, L. (2005) 'Learning to be a child: cultural diversity and early years ideology', in N. Yelland (ed.) *Critical Issues in Early Childhood Education*. Maidenhead: Open University Press.

Cowie, H. (2012) *From Birth to Sixteen*. Oxon: Taylor and Francis.

Cassidy, J. (1999) 'The nature of a child's ties', in J. Cassidy and P.R. Shaver (eds) *Handbook of Attachment*. New York: Guilford Press, pp. 3–20.

Children Act (1989) www.legislation.gov.uk/ukpga/1989/41/contents (accessed 08.05.12)

Children Act Scotland (2003) www.scotland.gov.uk/Topics/People/Young.../children.../10258 (accessed 08.05.12).

Cunningham, H. (2006) *The Invention of Childhood*. London: BBC Books.

Department for Education and Science (DfES) (2004) *Every Child Matters: Change for Children*. London: HMSO.

Durrant, J.E. (1996) *The Swedish Ban on Corporal Punishment: Its History and Effects*. Family Violence Against Children for Society. Berlin: Walter de Gruyter, pp. 19–25.

EYPS (2008) http://www.eyps.info/ (accessed 08.05.12).

Future Foundation (2000) http://www.futurefoundation.net (accessed 08.05.12).

Gasper, M. (2010) *Multi-agency Working in the Early Years: Challenges and Opportunities*. London: Sage.

Gerhardt, S. (2004) *Why Love Matters*. London: Routledge.

McCubbin, H.I., Joy, C.B., Cauble, A.E., Comeau, J.K., Patterson, J.M. and Needle, R.H. (1980) 'Family stress and coping: a decade review', *Journal of Marriage and the Family*, 42: 125–41.

Maccoby, E.E. (1992) 'The role of parents in the socialization of children: an historical overview', *Development Psychology*, 28: 1006–17.

Maccoby, E.E. and Martin, J.A. (1983) 'Socialization in the context of the family: parent–child interaction', in P.H. Mussen and E.M. Hetherington (eds) *Handbook of Child Psychology, Vol. 4: Socialization, Personality and Social Development*, 4th edition. New York: Wiley.

McKenry, P.C. and Price, S.J. (2000) 'Families coping with problems and change: a conceptual overview', in P.C. McKenry and S.J. Price (eds) *Families Coping with Stressful Events and Transitions*, 2nd edition. Thousand Oaks, CA: Sage.

Narin, A., Ormrod, J. and Bottomley, P. (2007) *Watching, Wanting and Wellbeing: Exploring the Links*. London: National Consumer Council.

Office for Economic Co-operation and Development (OECD) (2006) *Babies and Bosses: Recording Work and Family Life*, Vol. 4. Paris: OECD.

Parents Code (2004) http://www.sweden.gov.se/sb/d/3926/a/27655

Pugh, G. and De'Ath, E. (1984) *The Needs of Parents*. London: Macmillan.

Rutter, M. (1983) 'Stress, coping, and development: some issues and questions', in N. Garmezy and M. Rutter (eds) *Stress, Coping, and Development* (pp. 1–41). New York: McGraw-Hill.

Scottish Government (2004) *Curriculum for Excellence*. Edinburgh: Scottish Executive. Available at: http://www.scotland.gov.uk/Topics/Education/Schools/curriculum/ACE/ (accessed 08.07.12).

Scottish Government (2011) *Growing Up in Scotland – 2011: Research Findings No.4/2011: Change in Early Childhood and the Impact of Significant Events*. Available at: http://www.scotland.gov.uk/Publications/2011/05/11160035/0

Stephen, C. and Plowman, L. (2003) *'Come Back in Two Years!' A Study of the Use of ICT in Pre-school Settings during Spring and Summer 2002*. Dundee: Learning and Teaching Scotland.

Ulrich, M. and Weatherall, A. (2000) 'Motherhood and infertility: viewing motherhood through the lens of infertility', *Feminism and Psychology*, 10: 323–36.

United Nations (UN) (1989) *United Nations Convention on the Rights of the Child (UNCRC)*. Available at: http://www.unicef.org/crc/ (accessed 04.01.12).

UNICEF (2007) *Child Poverty in Perspective: An Overview of Child Well-being in Rich Countries*. Florence: UNICEF Innocenti Research Centre.

Werner, E.E. and Smith, R.S. (1982) *Vulnerable but Invincible: A Study of Resilient Children*. London: McGraw-Hill.

Ziegert, K.A. (1983) 'The Swedish prohibition of corporal punishment: a preliminary report', *Journal of Marriage and the Family*, 45: 917–26.

CHAPTER 8

THE ROLE OF THE COMMUNITY IN CHILDCARE AND EDUCATION

Key ideas explored in this chapter

- the influence and impact that the community has on children's learning and development
- the 'ecological framework' identified by Bronfenbrenner
- the importance of early intervention in supporting particular communities by considering the role of supporting agencies.

Introduction

Children's lives are influenced by a complex range of factors, including the community they grow up in and the influences of wider society. Children experience the community through the eyes and ears of the 'key' adults in their lives, but their perspective is still bound to be very different as they do not have a lifetime of experience to draw on. We assimilate our knowledge and understanding of what goes on about us against our prior learning, just as Piaget (1962) suggested a young child assimilates new knowledge or any new skill against the schema they have already established. Sometimes young children are trying to assimilate knowledge and work towards an understanding of events in their community that are beyond their years. A student's report exemplified this when walking near the nursery and a 3-year-old commented, 'That is where the murders happen.' The child had obviously heard about this and may have understood what it meant but a 3-year-old is unlikely to fully understand the concept of murder. It can be challenging, as it was for this student to know how to respond.

What is a community?

A community includes the physical environment and the local neighbourhood and relates to our social networks and our sense of belonging. Governments and local councils constantly talk about 'building a community' (often related to some idealistic nostalgic past) and may be referring to the physical or social environment. In today's society, the virtual community impacts hugely on our lives, breaking down international boundaries (see Chapter 10). In the past, particularly in rural settings, a school building may have provided accommodation for a teacher so that the teacher lived within the community, often held in high regard. In today's society, staff for schools or any ECEC setting can travel some distance to the school and thus know little about the community around the setting. Even when staff are working in the same area that they live, particularly in larger towns and cities, they may not be aware of the very local community around the setting. Also, if staff return to an area that they grew up in after a period away (perhaps studying), it is easy to make assumptions and not realise how much things have changed.

In order to gain an insight into the community around your setting, it is a good idea to carry out a community walk, either alone or with the children to gain a better understanding of the community and how they view it. The Community Walk was developed by Liz Curtis at the University of Aberdeen:

> as part of a series of activities designed to support first and second year Primary Education students' exploration of the locale of the school in which they were to carry out their placement in order to further their understanding of a broader community context … The methodology for the walk was drawn from Margaret Roberts' work on personal geographies and, in particular, affective mapping (Roberts, 2003). (Curtis, 2010: 172)

This activity, slightly adapted for distance learning students, has been a valuable starting point for BA Childhood Practice and Early Years Postgraduate students over the last few years. Even if you live and work nearby or work in an area in which you grew up, it is still valuable to do this as much will have changed (Valentine, 2004).

REFLECTIVE ACTIVITY

A walk around the community

The purpose of the exercise is to give you the opportunity to explore at first hand the areas which surround your setting, roughly within a mile radius. Approaching geographical enquiry from a personal point of view offers you the opportunity to build up your own mental map based on your own experience of walking a particular route (Roberts, 2003). You should record your thoughts and feelings as you walk. This process will hopefully give you a richer framework to reflect on the socio-economic profiles of people living in the area.

Pre-walk tasks

Before you go on the walk, you should make notes on the following:

Which are the places in ... you have not visited and would like to?
Why?
Which are the places in ... you would not like to visit?
Why?
What has informed or influenced your thinking on these places?
Create a short table showing a maximum of five places which you would like to visit in your area and the reasons why.
Create a short table showing a maximum of five places which you might not like to visit in your area and the reasons why.
For example:

Places I would not like to visit	Reasons why
Westerhouse Lane	Level of dereliction, chipboard glazing, broken bottles, discarded needles and general littering, graffiti. Makes me feel threatened, scared and depressed.

Places I would like to visit	Reasons why
The Botanic Gardens	Well-kept, aesthetically pleasing, attractive café, comfortable seating, inspirational. Makes me feel happy.

You should make sure that you have a relevant map of the area, particularly if it is unfamiliar.

What you will need:

You might find a photocopy of your map a useful aid for jotting down thoughts or marking particular features which you observe.

(Continued)

(Continued)

Notebook: for the purposes of this exercise, you will find that a small notebook which can easily be fitted into a pocket is the most useful. You may find that a pencil is more useful than a pen, especially if it starts to rain!

Digital camera or camera or mobile phone.

Observational etiquette:

- Keep in mind during your walk that you might be walking through residential areas. Think about how you would feel if you were chatting to a neighbour and you saw someone with a notebook and camera taking notes about your street.
- Use of cameras: the idea behind using digital cameras is to help you build up an *aide memoire* of places and feelings encountered on your walk. Avoid taking photographs of people. Likewise, if you happen to walk by a school and it is playtime, avoid the temptation to take photographs of children playing.
- Personal safety: if at any point during your walk you find yourself approaching a situation which makes you feel uncomfortable, do not continue. Being familiar with the layout of streets on the map will increase your safety and it is a good idea to fold it to fit inside your notebook. This means that you are not attracting unnecessary attention to yourself on your walk.

Collecting observations:

- As you walk, you should be creating a profile of how the geography/design affects your feelings in terms of safety, comfort, interest, like, dislike of particular streets and places.
- You should also consider what triggers these particular feelings and record both your feelings and the evidence for them. You may take a photograph of an inviting green space or, on the other hand, a juxtaposition of buildings/signs which make you feel unwelcome.
- It is important that you make a written record, no matter how brief, of what you have photographed, as these notes provide a commentary and reminder of your first impressions.

Key questions for you to think about on the walk:

- How do I use public places?
- How is my use of public spaces controlled by me?
- How is my use of public space controlled by others and why?
- If I were to move into this area, which streets would I choose to live on and why?
- If I were to live in this area, which places might I avoid/make me feel unwelcome and why?

Post-walk tasks

Create your own map of your community walk, illustrating your feelings towards particular places. To do this, you can use a copy of the street map and annotate it using a key of your own design which indicates the range of your feelings. You might also choose to create your map using photographs which you have taken:

The key might include, for example:

attractive	clean	unpleasant	quiet	dull
dangerous	go on my own	interesting	frightening	exciting

Reflect on your community walk and your own thoughts and feelings. Consider the community from the perspective of a child. Think about how their thoughts and feelings might resemble or differ from that of your own.

Use photographs which you have taken on your walk as a basis for a discussion with children in the setting. Note down instances where the child's response is the same or different from your own. Make a note of children's responses which surprise you. It is a good idea to document this using photos annotated with what children say and create a 'Big Book' or panel for a wall display so that you, other members of staff and children can re-visit and develop the conversation about their community. This can prove a valuable starting point for learning experiences as well as helping to develop your own understanding of the community, children's perspectives on it and its impact on their learning and development. It is, of course, important to ensure any display provides a balanced but fairly positive view of the community.

Children and families in their communities

Family structures can be very different (see Chapter 6) and some may have strong networks and links with their community and have forged a sense of belonging which binds them not only to the physical area but also to many other people. Other families may be very isolated from the rest of their community and this is seldom because of simple physical isolation; it is just as likely to affect those living in densely populated cities. Children can develop their sense of belonging through going to playgroup, nursery or school. Children growing up in the same area but within a range of different families are all influenced by the community within which the family lives and works, but this can be different for each child. Communities are influenced in turn by government policy, media and many other external factors.

An 'ecological framework'

Urie Bronfenbrenner's book *The Two Worlds of Childhood* (1972) compared and contrasted the experiences of childhood in the USA and the USSR (now Russia and its border countries). This research led to the principles of the ecological model of child-hood. Bronfenbrenner (1979) likened his theory to a set of Russian dolls, in that each aspect of the affective environment layers upon another, and his model of such a structured or 'nested' environment is reproduced in the Te Whāriki approach in New Zealand to represent the significance of the environment and community in which children live, grow and learn (see Chapter 13).

Each child is influenced by a series of systems. Imagine the child at the centre and first around the child are the influences of the home. These will include the physical environment and people. This begins to extend to other places and people they see regularly which might be grandparents in their home, neighbours, childminder, playgroup, nursery and then school. This is identified as the **microsystem** – home, school, etc. Then beyond this there is an **exosystem** which has an indirect influence on the child. This would include the education and political systems where they grow up, as well as such things as parental contacts and work conditions. The **macrosystem** is the wider political climate and cultural context determined by legislation, history, beliefs and attitudes of the wider community and the social conditions.

The conceptual framework itself shows the main influencing factors that surround every child, though they will be different for each child. The interaction between these systems will always create differences for children growing up in the same community – even living next door to each other or in the same home as siblings.

How each layer influences the child

- **The microsystem** refers to the immediate surroundings of the individual. This includes the child's family, peers, school and neighbourhood. It is in the microsystem that the most direct interactions with social agents take place; with parents, peers and teachers, for example. For the very young child, these are the most important influences.
- **The exosystem** is concerned with the connection between a social setting in which the individual does not have an active role and the individual's immediate context. For example, a child's experience at home may be influenced by a parent's, perhaps Dad's, experiences at work. The father might receive a promotion that requires more travel, which might increase conflict with the wife and affect patterns of interaction with the child.
- **The macrosystem** describes the culture, meaning 'the ways of people', in which individuals live. Cultural contexts would include socio-economic status, poverty and ethnicity. Kirk (1999) elaborates on the importance of social support as an influence on the child's macrosystem in respect of parental functioning. This in turn critically influences the well-being and health development of young children.

Bronfenbrenner (1979) also refers to the mesosystem and the chronosystem. The mesosystem concerns the relations between the different systems or connections between contexts. Some common examples are the connection between family experiences and school experiences, school experiences and church experiences or family experiences and peer experiences. For example, children whose parents have rejected them may have difficulty developing positive relations with their friends or peers. Shelvin (2010) suggests that by responding positively to the relationships children form with those closest to them, they extend early bonds to those perceived to be at a greater distance. In other words, a child who has experienced reciprocal affection and respect and established strong relationships is likely to be more willing and able to engage in activities and establish relationships with others.

The chronosystem refers to the patterning of environmental events and transitions over the life of an individual, as well as socio-historical circumstances. For example, divorce is one transition. Research has identified that the negative effects of divorce on children often peak in the first year after the divorce. Two years after the divorce, family interaction is less chaotic and more stable. An example of socio-historical circumstance is the increasing opportunities for women to pursue a career.

This framework has been used by different disciplines in numerous different studies to clarify understanding of the impact of factors on development and learning. These include studies on chronic disease (e.g. asthma), access to services or opportunities such as play, change or trauma such as divorce, and perhaps most importantly in extending the understanding of mental health beyond what is known as the 'medical model'. Bronfenbrenner (2012) proposed a bioecological model of mental health which he likened to 'looking at the whole forest, not just one tree' (p. 1). The diagram produced to show this model certainly highlights the complexity of factors impacting on mental health. Many other diagrams have been produced using his Ecological Framework and these are freely available on the internet – try a search on Google for 'images for Urie Bronfenbrenner's ecological framework'.

An ecological perspective is an approach based on the interaction between human beings and their environment. It is useful as we need to see children in the context of their family, wider society and their cultural environment, and understand how all three interact to create a complex web of influences. It is therefore not possible to assume that every child will be negatively affected by certain factors or, if they are, that they will be affected in the same way, through growing up in the same community. It is helpful to build our knowledge and understanding of the communities children are growing up in, the experiences they are likely to have and the possible influences on their learning and development. If we know about their 'lived lives', we can make learning experiences relevant and meaningful, build on their interests and endeavour to intervene early to prevent or pre-empt problems arising from negative influences.

Using an ecological approach helps:

- **clarify the complexities** we face in understanding the interplay of psychosocial, social and cultural factors which may combine to result in a child and/or their family requiring support
- **ensure the best possible future** for the child by encouraging us to consider a whole range of options within the frame simultaneously.

An ecological approach can help us make connections from the perspective of the child, family members and/or workers which might not otherwise have been visible.

In summary, the main advantage of the ecological approach is in the attempt to grapple with social structures, the many influences on children's development and the complex interactions between these. It suggests that just as family members interact with each other, so the family, both collectively and individually, relates to the world outside. This occurs within a number of dimensions, which are:

- immediate family – within which individuals interact
- wider/extended family
- local community – formal (local agencies) and informal (friends, neighbours, clubs, shops, other facilities)
- wider society – providing the overarching structures of policy making, legal systems, media, etc.

As can be seen from the work of Bronfenbrenner (1979) and Fawcett (2009), some children enjoy strong informal supports characterised by loving families, protective neighbours and friends, which Bronfenbrenner terms the 'Wealth Model'. Although taken for granted by many, the experience of many other children is one of inadequate or even abusive parenting, no loving extended family and isolation from the community. There are children where immediate support systems are weak; where children are purposefully or inadvertently neglected, feel frightened and unprotected and some unloved.

It must be said that most children are loved by their parents and most parents want to do the best for their children. Unfortunately, the skills and emotions required to achieve this aim are not always readily available to the adults concerned. Equally, external factors such as poverty, unemployment and poor health militate against families achieving their aims for their children. Where informal support systems are weakest for children for whatever reason, it is more likely that their main supports will come from professional sources outside the family unit. The Millennium Cohort Study (2010) offers an insight into how the home environment and the community affect children. The survey concluded that language and literacy skills were more sensitive to the home environment than non-verbal and numeracy skills, with the relative gap in composite cognitive scores between children in advantaged and disadvantaged homes not widening between the ages of 5 and 7. Language skills develop though a range of personal interactions; if a child does not experience these, language development can be delayed. The report confirms that children from disadvantaged backgrounds are more likely to exhibit health problems. However, children from advantaged families suffer more from hayfever and eczema (Millennium Cohort Study, 2010). It has been suggested that these children may not be exposed to enough external environmental factors to strengthen their immune system. As far as child poverty is concerned, the survey identified that Scotland had the lowest rate of child poverty in the UK, and Wales the highest.

Within ECEC, there is a variety of 'professional support settings' available to children and families. In England, the Early Support Programme (DfES, 2004) introduced the concept of working alongside parents whereby the child's home becomes the early years setting with a range of services working in partnership with parents. The importance of inter-professional collaboration is a key feature of early intervention, but at times for families this may manifest itself in a disjointed experience.

When working alongside parents, we need to fully understand how children are perceived within their community. We should take into account the significant impact of the social and cultural context. Early intervention needs to be family centred and professionals need to work in partnership with children and parents (Carpenter et al., 2004).

Parents have an in-depth knowledge and understanding of their child's development. We also need to recognise the importance of cultural beliefs and practices. Woodhead (2005) discusses how the way parents care for their children is shaped in part by their cultural beliefs (or ethno-theories) about what is appropriate and desirable in terms of the goals for child development, and the means of achieving these goals. These goals may be set within a cycle of deprivation, leading parents to set low attainment levels for these children. Russell (2003) suggests that partnership between parents and professionals requires them to regulate different and new ways of thinking about situations and future events in order to reconsider expectations and plan accordingly.

An ecological framework in practice

The work of Bronfenbrenner and others has recognised and highlighted for us that children are not isolated beings. The ecological framework cannot be isolated from demographic data, as we need to fully consider specific population characteristics such as age, sex, income, health, ethnicity and education. Through understanding the importance of demographics, we can gain a clear insight into how the child's life is affected by the community.

Working with each individual child and their family highlights a complex set of variables changing over time. Children live within their varied family structures, within a range of changing communities, and are continually influenced by the wider social and political environment. No two children are the same. Their experiences, although sharing some similarities if they live within the same street, block of flats or village, can be vastly different, due to the range of other potential influences on their lives (see the case study of Connor and Callum in Chapter 7).

A study in Australia drew on Bronfenbrenner's work when researching childhood resilience to overcome adversity. This effectively illustrates the concepts of applying an ecological framework when working with children. Howard and Johnson (2000) discuss resilience and the outcomes for children 'at risk'. The study concluded: 'Clearly things that happen within the family, the school and the community – all Macrosystem environments in which the child is physically located – can have a major impact on the development of resilience' (p. 329)

CASE STUDY

A recent television documentary (*Panorama: Poor America* [accessed 16/02/2012] at: http://www.bbc.co.uk/iplayer/episode/b01c2y2b/ Panoramapo0ramerica/) demonstrated the need to consider Bronfenbrenner's framework. The programme revealed how high levels of adult unemployment have led to homelessness which has created 'tent cities' and children living in cheap motels – the mesosystem. This isolation has impacted upon their microsystem in so much as the children are becoming reclusive and not willing to mix in the wider community – possibly due to financial restraints not allowing money for travel and feeling that the accommodation in which they are living is not acceptable to entertain visits from friends. The documentary suggested that most children affected by the economic downturn could be as much as one to two years educationally behind their peers, having moved into a survival mode whereby their main concerns are linked to their family, lack of food and where they will have to spend the night. This gradual downward spiral has the cumulative effect of a cycle of poverty, a poor child being more likely to develop into an adult living in poverty, as suggested by UNICEF (2005).

The programme in the case study highlights the important role of inter-professional practice, where all agencies work together to support families. Anning et al. (2010) when discussing intervention, draw our attention to the way in which relations between settings can affect what happens within them, and argue the importance of recognising that environmental events and conditions outside the immediate setting can have a profound influence on behaviour and development. All ECEC practitioners need to understand their community and the way in which families and children are integrated within it. They need to consider the support they may require and how the community has a particular influence on the personal and social development of each child (Wenger, 2005). Social support significantly influences the child's macrosystem in respect of parental functioning and well-being and the healthy development of young children (Kirk, 1999).

Conclusion

The message for all ECEC professionals is that children are heavily influenced by variables within their environment and can be helped to develop internal support mechanisms and know how or when to access external ones. Early years educators are well placed to help children and families identify and access support. They play a key role in offering direct support and empowering others to develop support networks for themselves. An understanding of the concept of 'community' and the ability to apply an ecological perspective are frameworks from within which the skill base of early years educators can be developed. Children are educated, not only within the confines of the nursery, school or playgroup, but within their own families, social grouping and communities. Having an understanding of the interplay between these can help workers better understand each individual child.

Longitudinal research by Growing Up in Scotland (Scottish Government, 2011) found that those who would benefit most from access to a range of services from antenatal care to early childhood education and care are the ones currently least likely to access it.

Sir Harry Burns (2011: 6) states:

> Research is now clearly indicating that children born and brought up in difficult and deprived circumstances are more likely to experience physical and mental health problems later in life. By supporting their parents and by providing a range of services which increase stability in their lives, children are more likely to perform better at school, become more resilient in their response to challenge and develop into healthy adults. The real question is how to use available funds wisely. The best evidence supports this policy prescription: *invest in the very young and improve basic learning and socialisation skills.*

The need to support particular communities led to the introduction of the Sure Start Local Programmes (SSLPs) towards the end of the 1990s in England. These programmes gave full consideration to the communities they supported. Initially, Sure Start was targeted at 20 per cent of families considered the most disadvantaged. The Joseph Rowntree Foundation (2008) identifies that there are more than 4 million children living in poverty in the UK (cited in Roberts-Holmes, 2009). The correlation between poverty and a poor start to life is well documented from the time of conception, leading to low birth weight, bad housing, health issues and poor nutrition, in turn leading to an inability to thrive, unstable family life and ultimately a lower expectation of educational achievement. Roberts-Holmes (2009) identified that a 3-year-old living in poverty was educationally a year behind counterparts coming from a wealthier background. Poverty is a feature of most societies but Roberts-Holmes (2009) points out that some, notably Scandinavian countries, have successfully tackled child poverty by investment in their public services. The long-term benefits of early intervention are discussed in Chapter 12 in the context of HighScope. All ECEC professionals play a vital role in early intervention, particularly for specific communities and individuals. They can also help to ensure that children from different communities and backgrounds play and learn alongside each other to break down social barriers from an early age.

Further reading

Morgan, S. (2005) *Don't Eat This Book*. London: Penguin. See Chapters 10 and 11.
Selbie, P. and Wickett, K. (2010) 'Providing an enabling environment', in R. Parker-Rees, C. Leeson, J. Willan and J. Savage (eds) *Early Childhood Studies*, 3rd edition. Exeter: Learning Matters. This is Chapter 6 in the book.

Useful websites

You can access 'Valuing Places: Think Maps' to help with affective mapping on your community walk from the Geographical Association web pages at: http://www.geography.org.uk/projects/valuingplaces/cpdunits/thinkmaps/#top (accessed 28.07.12).
Getting it Right for Children and Families (2011) *Young People are the Future of Scotland*. Available at: http://www.scotland.gov.uk/Publications/2012/03/7790/1 (accessed 28.07.12).
Research on child poverty from the Child Poverty Action Group can be found at: www.cpag.org.uk/ (accessed 28.07.12).
UNICEF Innocenti Research Centre provides information about child-friendly cities and communities, including information on good practice, at: www.childfriendlycities.org (accessed 28.07.12).

References

Anning, A., Cottrell, D. and Frost, N. (2010) *Developing Multiprofessional Teamworks for Integrated Children's Services*, 2nd edition. Maidenhead: Open University Press.
Bronfenbrenner, U. (1972) *The Two Worlds of Childhood: US and USSR*. New York: Simon & Schuster.
Bronfenbrenner, U. (1979) *The Ecology of Human Development: Experiments by Nature and Design*. London: Harvard University Press.
Bronfenbrenner, U. (2012) The Association of Natural Psychology: Bioecological Model of Mental Health. Available at: http://www.winmentalhealth.com/urie_bronfenbrenner_bioecological_model_medical_model.php (accessed 31.07.12).
Burns, H. Sir and Department of Health, Physical Activity, Health Improvement and Protection (2011) *Start Active, Stay Active: A Report on Physical Activity from the Four Home Countries'*

Chief Medical Officers. Available at: http://www.dh.gov.uk/prod_consum_dh/groups/dh_digitalassets/documents/digitalasset/dh_128210.pdf (accessed 17.05.12).

Carpenter, B., Addenbrooke, M., Attfield, E. and Conway, S. (2004) 'Celebrating families: an inclusive model of family centred training', *British Journal of Special Education*, 31(2): 75–80.

Curtis, E. (2010) 'Engaging student teachers with the local community: a mapping approach', in T.K. Wisely, I.M. Barr, A. Britton and B. King (eds) *Education in a Global Space: Research and Practice in Initial Teacher Education*. Edinburgh: IDEAS, pp. 189–94.

Department of Education and Skills (DfES) (2004) *Early Support Programme* (family pack). Nottingham: DfES.

Fawcett, M. (2009) *Learning Through Child Observation*. London: Jessica Kingsley.

Howard, S. and Johnson, B. (2000) 'What makes the difference? Children and teachers talk about resilient outcomes for children "at risk"', *Educational Studies*, 26(3): 321.

Kirk, S. (1999) 'Caring for children with specialised health care needs in the community: the challenges for primary care', *Health and Social Care in the Community*, 7(5): 350–7.

Millennium Cohort Study (2010) Available at: http://www.cls.ioe.ac.uk/page.aspx?andsitesectionid=851andsitesectiontitle=Welcome+to+the+Millennium+Cohort+Study

Piaget, J. (1962) *Play, Dreams and Imitation in Childhood*. New York: Norton. (First published 1945; English translation 1951.)

Roberts, M. (2003) *Personal Geographies: Learning through Enquiry – Making sense of geography in the key stage 3 classroom*. Sheffield: Geographical Association.

Roberts-Holmes, G. (2009) 'Inclusive policy and practice', in T. Maynard and N. Thomas (eds) *An Introduction to Early Childhood Studies*, 2nd edition. London: Sage.

Russell, F. (2003) 'The expectations of parents of disabled children', *British Journal of Special Education*, 30(3): 144–8.

Scottish Government (2011) *Growing Up in Scotland – 2011: Research Findings No.4/2011: Change in Early Childhood and the Impact of Significant Events*. Available at: http://www.scotland.gov.uk/Publications/2011/05/11160035/0

Shelvin, M. (2010) *Count Me In! Ideas for Actively Engaging Students in Inclusive Classrooms*. London: Jessica Kingsley.

UNICEF (2005) *Children and Poverty: Global Context, Local Solutions*. Available at http://www.unicef.org/policyanalysis/files.child_poverty_final_draft_4_05.pdf (accessed 17.04.12).

Valentine, G. (2004) *Public Space and Culture of Childhood*. Aldershot: Ashgate.

Wenger, E. (2005) *Communities of Practice: Learning, Meaning and Identity*. New York: Cambridge University Press.

Woodhead, M. (2005) 'Early childhood development: a question of rights', *International Journal of Early Childhood*, 37(3): 97–8.

CHAPTER 9

THE PLACE OF THE SCHOOL IN THE 21ST CENTURY

Keys ideas explored in this chapter

- the real purposes of education
- how formal education might change to make it fit for purpose in the 21st century
- some alternative approaches.

Introduction

Although society has changed enormously since the UK commitment to national provision of education in 1870, in general the pace of change in schools has not mirrored these developments. It is odd to think that a 'visitor' from a school of the 1880s would be most amazed and probably overwhelmed by advances in transport and certainly by technology, yet the schools of today could possibly provide one of the more easily recognisable contexts. Some of the actual buildings are still in use, but also the way in which education is organised leads one to ask what we are teaching in schools today. What is the end goal of education, or what should it be?

- Do we view education as a preparation for the jobs market?
- Do we view education as a lifelong process without a finite goal?
- Is there something in between? Another way?

Goleman (1996, cited in Robinson, 2001) discusses the fact that although people are spending more time on desk study and computers, those entering the workforce appear to be less suited than ever before. It would certainly appear that although society has progressed, the ideologies of education have not. We cannot meet the challenges of the 21st century with the education ideologies of the 19th.

Robinson (2001) discusses this further by stating that we need to learn from the past without being dictated to by it and cannot approach the future by constantly looking backwards, teaching the same things in the same way, just because this is what we have always done.

The media is constantly informing us that employers are not finding the necessary basic skills for success in new employees, either from school leavers or university graduates. This would suggest that 'something is not right' about what we are teaching and how we are teaching it. Yet education, in many countries, is politically at the top of the agenda. We do not have to look back very far to remember the Blair government mantra in the UK of 'Education, Education, Education!' But did this actually produce anything that was better? There was increased financial investment, but also an increased desire to 'raise standards' through testing and accountability. This gives rise to the situation we currently find ourselves in, as stated by Robinson (2001: 5): 'Business expects education systems to give people qualities and skills required for the new world. The political response is to raise standards. Of what?'

History could demonstrate that employers have always had these aims in mind and quite probably around the time of the Industrial Revolution, the very first schools would be concerned with training children to be able to read and write sufficiently well in order to be able to operate machinery. At that time, it was also fairly easy to predict the likely outcomes in terms of knowledge and skills which children might require in order to be successful in the workplace. Broadfoot (2000) describes the traditional western model with its emphasis on academic, book-based learning; dividing children into year groups or classes by age; defined curricula, often agreed nationally and subject to external assessment.

In today's society, there is no guarantee that children will remain in one area of employment, or one geographical area, or even one continent. At this point in time, we cannot predict which jobs will exist in 10 years' time, mostly as a result of very recent advances in information technology (IT) – an area that will be addressed in more depth in Chapter 10. Can we really expect necessary and beneficial changes in education to come as a result of political decrees? Do we need new models of learning?

The 21st Century Learning Initiative (2011) discusses some interesting qualities of traditional education and also suggests some desirable qualities of the future.

Conventional academic success has traditionally involved:

- mastery of basic skills
- largely solitary study
- generally uninterrupted work
- concentration on a single subject
- much written work
- high analytical ability.

The 21st-century workplace now involves:

- mastery of basic skills
- working with others
- constant distractions
- working at different levels across different disciplines
- mainly verbal skills
- problem solving and decision making.

It has been suggested, most amusingly by Fulghum (2003), in his book *All I Really Need to Know I Learned in Kindergarten*, that the list of desirable qualities for the workplace can easily be observed in quality pre-school provision. If we are capable of developing and supporting these skills in very young children, what is it that we are failing to continue with in primary and secondary education to prevent further development? Laevers (2005) describes this as a challenge for education systems which are content based, to be able to 'nourish an exploratory drive' in children which keeps the spontaneity and delight in learning alive, as it is this intrinsic motivation that is required to set the foundations of lifelong learning.

Guy Claxton, Professor of the Learning Sciences at the University of Winchester, in an interview with Yvonne Roberts for *The Guardian* (September 2011), was posed the question: *What is education for in the 21st century?* His reply was very enlightening:

> Education means learning to think for yourself, learning to make and repair friendships, learning to see other people's point of view, learning not to be afraid of uncertainty or difficulty. Unfortunately the system, whether it be in a free school, an academy or a comprehensive school, seems to comprehensively neglect the development of those qualities in the obsession with exam results.

Schools are unlikely to succeed in this on their own. According to the OECD (2007), the majority of Europeans spend at least nine or ten years of their lives in school, but it is only through the complementary roles of home and community that schools will be able to help individuals fulfil their potential in an all-round capacity. Children are also products of a family and a culture, yet we live in an increasingly globalised world. Although many family values are based on our own experiences and traditions, with a clear link to the past (which can have both positive and negative effects), it is the globalising aspect, mainly because of developments in IT, which has underpinned the fast changes in society and therefore justifies the need to look more closely at the place of school and consider some alternative approaches.

Alternative methods

Do children actually need a defined and prescribed curriculum to learn? As teachers, we have found curriculum *guidelines* helpful, but more as a reference point to support teaching, to ensure that the content has been as relevant and broad as it can be. However, the following two sections describe other ways in which children have learned effectively, without a prescribed curriculum, but with the aid of IT.

The hole in the wall

Sugata Mitra, Professor of Educational Technology at Newcastle University, UK, began an experiment, the Hole in the Wall (HIW), in India, in 1999. He hoped to prove that children could be taught to use computers very easily and without any formal training, which he described as Minimally Invasive Education (MIE). He describes the situation where a computer was placed in an actual 'hole' in the wall in a series of remote areas of India. Initially, a hole was cut in the wall of an office slum of a New Delhi office and a computer placed, facing outwards, connected to the internet. The children in the area were not English speaking, yet within hours, it was clear that an 8-year-old child was teaching a 6-year-old to browse the web.

The experiment was repeated in another area of socio-economic deprivation in the centre of India and, within minutes, a 13-year-old school drop-out was observed investigating the machine, like a TV but which could 'do something'. A few hours later, he had organised a large group of friends to continue the browsing.

The results of these experiments produced very interesting data. For example, in one area where the computer was left for several months, there were requests for a faster processor and a better mouse. Girls were equally as interested as boys and although none of these children could speak English initially, after three months the children had learned to use around 200 English words, all associated with computer use.

Mitra continued with these experiments over a period of about five years and found that:

1   The children were self-motivated to learn the English alphabet – as the website Mitra left the computer connected to was in English.
2   Very often the younger children – aged about 6 years – were teaching the older children.
3   Children aged 6–13 were very capable of self-instruction – if they were in groups and if there was no adult intervention.
4   The children were able to use basic Windows, email, browse and play computer games. (Mitra, 1999)

Mitra's point is that the range of experiments, carried out in different climates within the Indian continent, could actually be replicated if carried out on a worldwide basis. The following case study provides some reflection on the first point above.

CASE STUDY

 1. The children were self-motivated to learn the English alphabet

I am always amused at the reaction of other adults to the fact that I am fluent in Swedish. It is not a language that is taught in UK schools and I did not have any knowledge of the language before I moved to live there as an adult. However, in the same way as the children experimented with the computer, I began to listen to others around me and pick up the language, using a variety of clues, verbal and non-verbal and visual signals. I can speak the language, read the language and write it too, but I never had a teacher to help me with this.

How does this work? *Intrinsic motivation*: for me, it was the desire to be able to live, work and shop in this foreign country; for these Indian children, it was the desire to find out, explore and experiment with something new.

My experience of learning a foreign language, through listening and watching, was very different from the way in which I learned French or German at school. Learning Swedish was important because I could see the benefit to me in being able to use the new skills. Likewise, the Indian children were able to use the computer skills that they acquired.

No one formally assessed my knowledge of the language and I was not required to perform any external test of my competence and be graded or labelled as a result. The Indian children were tested at intervals, but with the end aim of collecting and analysing data.

The second point above, 'Very often the younger children – aged about 6 years – were teaching the older children', is also interesting as we have an in-built assumption that younger children learn from older children, yet Mitra discovered that very often it was the younger children who were teaching the older ones. This raises an issue about our western tradition of grouping children chronologically. If we look at quality nursery provision, which can quite happily involve a mixed age group of 3–5-year-olds working together, why do we insist on changing this situation as soon as children are eligible to start school? We do have vertically grouped classes in some UK schools, but this is never really presented as a desirable feature by parents, teachers or school management.

Regarding the third point, 'Children aged 6–13 were very capable of self-instruction – if they were in groups and if there was no adult intervention', there were no time limits imposed on the children and Mitra discovered that the children formed themselves naturally into collaborative working groups. This often involved one child manipulating the keyboard whilst another group of three or four would be giving advice. Yet, when the whole group was tested, all scores were very much the same. Mitra also describes the situation where around 16 other children were present, giving wrong advice to the small group, yet, when tested, they too had a similar score. This, Mitra suggests, was from learning by watching and demonstrates evidence of learning being essentially a self-organising system. Laevers (2005) would support this view as he advocates a system where testing should target complex competences where many skills and dimensions are brought together.

Collaborative learning is a current term within education, but it can have different meanings in different settings. Recent primary classroom observations in Scotland would suggest that teachers are very likely to instruct children to collaborate and that in order to achieve an end product, children are carefully grouped and roles, such as *manager, timekeeper, recorder, reporter, resource manager, interpreter*, are assigned to individual children within these groups. There is very little room for choice for pupils and the situation is very much under the control of the adult. This may work for some classes, and no doubt can be justified by ensuring that roles are changed regularly for children, but for those observed, it is generally too structured and limiting in its scope to allow children to be particularly active or creative.

In contrast, in a maths lesson observed in a Swedish upper-primary classroom recently, the whole lesson had been carried out in English, and was concerned with learning about parts of the body. To follow on from the language/biology aspect of the lesson, the class teacher had made up some maths problems (in English) where the children used prior experience from the lesson in order to be able to solve these. Different problems were allocated and the children were asked to organise themselves into groups of 4–5 and to find somewhere to work quietly in order to come up with a solution to the problems. They were not restricted to being inside the classroom. The class teacher moved around the groups, to offer help and support if required, but did not intervene unnecessarily. The children were very much in control of the tasks and the choice of groupings, and the format was an excellent example of collaborative learning. This example is much closer to Mitra's findings.

An analysis of the two types of teacher roles observed would favour the Swedish teacher who was facilitating children's learning but not directing it. The Scottish primary teacher role, from recent observations, continues to be very adult-controlled and directive. A novel by Henning Mankell (2002), a contemporary Swedish author, describes a visit of Scottish primary schoolchildren to the Culloden Battlefield outside Inverness, together with their 'bestämda lärare' – determined/controlling/firm/ teachers. Is this perhaps how we are viewed from outside the UK?

However, it is not only primary-age children who can work collaboratively. Trevarthen (1982, cited in Laevers, 2005), a key author regarding the 0–3 age range, urges us to 'take into account the perspective of the young child' and provides evidence to support children as young as 16 months being able to organise themselves into a working group.

CASE STUDY

I recently observed an example of two young boys organising themselves into a working group. One was aged 20 months and the other 16 months. Both children have parents who are professional dancers; both boys spend a lot of time in dance studios on a regular basis and are very comfortable in this type of environment. On this particular evening, there was an end-of-term performance organised by students on the professional programme. The two children were up late, but seated at the front of the audience, in their respective pushchairs. When the quality of the performance was good (by anybody's standards), the two boys sat still and were totally engrossed in the dance. However, when the performance did not hold their attention, they began to squirm, make noises to attract each other, without using actual language, and generally indicate that they were both bored. Their behaviour was discussed later and likened to two old men, such as the two 'critics' who made regular appearances on the Muppet Show. However, we all had to agree that their judgement of the performance, even at that age, was very discerning.

The Khan Academy

Another good example of how IT can be used to harness and develop children's interest in learning is through the Khan Academy (http://www.khanacademy.org). This is a not-for-profit organisation with the mission of providing a free world-class education to anyone, anywhere.

Salman Khan is a young entrepreneur, who, whilst working as a hedge fund manager in the USA, was offering online tutoring to younger relatives to help with their maths. Eventually, the cousins made him aware that they preferred the online video tutoring to the face-to-face events. The reasons for this became clear as:

- the children could pause and repeat the video at will
- they did not experience being made to feel stupid either by asking questions or by having to respond to an adult asking if they understood
- they could discuss amongst themselves and learn from each other
- they could still review the teaching material a year later.

Having reflected on the feedback, Khan decided to make some of his tutorials available to the public through YouTube, and as a result of the very positive comments received, has expanded this initial idea into a major website which is regularly used by over 1 million students (including Bill Gates for his own children and he now contributes financially to sustain and extend the 'academy'). Everything on the site has been developed by Khan himself and ranges from basic arithmetic to tutorials in advanced maths and sciences.

Some schools have adopted Khan's approach and, as a result, have turned the classroom experience upside down. The teachers no longer stand at the board and 'teach' but instead give a Khan video link as homework, for the children to work through at their own pace, and then the traditional 'homework' part is done in class, on a collaborative basis. One of the clear elements of good practice is the fact that children are encouraged to work through the materials at their own pace – and move forward when they feel that they have mastered that particular aspect. Compare this with normal practice where an aspect is taught, tested and then everyone in that 'set' moves on to the next aspect. The traditional model, according to Khan, means that a student who scores 70 per cent still moves on at the same rate as the student who has scored the full 100 per cent. Khan's method allows the pupil to work through the remaining 30 per cent.

In a TED talk, Khan (2011) explains his philosophy whereby the teacher role moves from the didactic to the facilitator, in itself much more complex. Instead of looking at a teacher/child ratio, he talks about a student/valuable 'human' time with a teacher ratio. Feedback from teachers has shown that some children, whom they had previously assessed as 'slow', in fact just needed more time to assimilate the information from the materials and once they had understood the problem, were also able to progress enthusiastically. This was also well supported by peer-to-peer tutoring, not necessarily only by an adult.

Again, as ECEC professionals, we should not be surprised by Khan's findings, which support what we know to be good practice in early years education. The above are excellent examples of a possible way forward, but we should also consider where we are now.

Successful curriculum models

This is a familiar term associated with schools of today but not new in terms of education theory. However, the term has only dominated education policy during the last 40 years, where within the UK we have moved from no published curriculum documentation to a very tightly defined and prescribed curriculum and now, at least in Scotland, a move away from prescription towards a freer interpretation, as promoted by the *Curriculum for Excellence* (Scottish Government, 2004).

Starting Strong (OECD, 2004) identifies and presents five curriculum outlines which support good practice in working with young children. These comprise:

- experiential education – effective learning through well-being and involvement (see Chapter 15 of this book)
- the HighScope curriculum – active learning through key experiences (see Chapter 14 of this book)
- the Reggio Emilia approach – truly listening to young children (see Chapter 12 of this book)
- *Te Whāriki* – a woven mat for all to stand on (see Chapter 13 of this book)
- the Swedish curriculum – goals for a modern pre-school system (see Chapter 11 of this book). (OECD, 2004)

It is interesting to note that the above relates to Belgium, the USA, Italy, New Zealand and Sweden, but it is sad to note that none of the practice in the UK is included in this at present. It would be a good idea to look at the commonalities of practice in these diverse countries.

First, all have a central focus on the individual child, in accordance with human rights principles and supported by socio-cultural theories in learning, for example those of Bronfenbrenner (1979), who sees the child as being influenced by the family, community and wider society, but where the child is also capable of exerting an equal influence in the opposite direction. This is extremely important in terms of the ways in which we view children: as beings to whom things are 'done' or beings who are capable of exerting their own influence on others and the environment?

All of the above curriculum outlines have been promoted by individuals with a genuine concern for the welfare and development of young children and for whom it is extremely important that children should be encouraged to have the greatest amount of freedom possible, within these guidelines.

Our understanding of how young children learn has developed vastly over recent years and we are much more aware of the importance of babies being active promoters of their own development (Laevers, 2007). In order to be able to support this, Laevers sees the need for any curriculum for young children to be based on an open framework. In relation to the Swedish curriculum, Sylva et al. (1999, cited in OECD, 2004) describe this as:

- key values, skills and understanding formulated by the state for children from the early stages right through the school system
- a few general goals decided at national level, following discussion with the main stakeholders
- goals worked towards in practice together with children, adapting these to meet the needs, understanding and interests of individual children and their lived lives.

Adopting this type of curriculum allows for a great deal of freedom for teachers to develop content to match the needs and interests of children and allows for the same content to be covered and revisited with increasing levels of complexity, always ensuring that the shared and stated goals are being used to underpin learning. However, this is not necessarily what we see in schools at the moment, where students have informed us that they have not been able to pick up on the interests of an individual, as told by the class teacher: 'The children will be covering that next year, so we cannot do it now.' Such statements serve only to reinforce the 'recipe' approach to education which is prevalent in primary schools today and which would appear to go against good practice as promoted by Bruner (1996) in the *spiral curriculum,* which encourages children to revisit and assimilate new knowledge and experiences in the light of what is already known.

Free Schools

It is interesting to note that although the OECD (2004) report praises the Swedish education system, a recent report from Skolverket (2012), paints a less positive picture. This report is concerned with the effects of increased numbers of Free Schools within a market-driven economy for education, since the early 1990s. A previous report by Skolverket (2006) outlined the main aims:

- a wider range of schools and freedom of choice for parents and children together with increased influence
- more specialisation and flexibility
- better quality – competition amongst schools would encourage children to achieve more and teaching would be revitalised
- more cost-effectiveness.

The 2012 report states that many of the objectives have been met, but also admits to a chaotic system subject to constant change. There is a wider choice of schools available for children and more children are opting against going to the neighbourhood school. It is interesting to note that this is presented as the child's choice, not the choice of parents. A variety of schools with a particular profile have emerged; this could be, for example, a music school or a football school, or increasingly, a general profile. A number of problems have emerged from this:

- The school 'market' is driven by local authorities, private owners, schools, parents and children all exerting influence but market forces do not always provide equity and better quality.
- Across the whole country, there is a diversity of provision, resulting in inequality and this is reflected at local and regional levels.
- Local authorities are still responsible for education but are also competing with other 'actors' in the market. They must guarantee the right to education of all children resident within their area but must also provide the funding for this, no matter where the child chooses to attend school.

Problems have arisen where, as a result of changing schools, numbers left in the original school can become unsustainable, leading to a drop in the quality of provision and, in some cases, school closure. Rather than being more cost-effective, Free Schools have incurred increased costs for local authorities as the situation is unstable and unpredictable. For example, a child may choose to attend a school with a particular profile in another local authority from the one in which they live, but the home authority still has to pay the costs of this. This particular finding is the exact opposite of one of the intended aims.

The report also highlights the fact that 'choice' for children and parents tends to be asserted by articulate and well-educated families, thus causing further divisions within society and most definitely less choice for some, which goes against the democratic principles upon which the Swedish education system is based.

The information in this report certainly gives justification to anecdotal evidence that we were given by university staff in Sweden during a visit in 2010, who voiced the concern that divisions being caused within the education system were making it very difficult for many schools to be able to deliver the broad curriculum expected, particularly in the post-16 sector (*gymnasieskolan*) and thus also impacting on university entrance.

Conclusion

No education system is ever going to be perfect, nor can it ever be transported whole-sale from its surrounding culture. This does not mean, however, that it is not relevant to examine other school systems and analyse the similarities and differences between them and the one with which we are familiar. Our central thought must always be concerned with promoting development and learning in children in the best way possible.

What we have ascertained is that work in many countries in pre-5 settings, respects the intuitive abilities of children and that the education practices which promote this are those which are most likely to help prepare children for success in later life. The Curriculum for Excellence (Scottish Government, 2004) states that the new curriculum will:

- build on real strengths: the existing guidance for the 3–5 curriculum is working well
- provide better continuity between children's pre-school experiences and Primary 1, especially in learning and teaching approaches
- provide more emphasis on active learning through Primary 1 and beyond.

This does, however, require the use of imagination and creativity on the part of those adults responsible for delivery.

Further reading

Laevers, F. (2005) 'The curriculum as a means to raise the quality of early childhood education: implications for policy', *European Early Childhood Education Research Journal*, 13(1): 17–29.
Organisation for Economic Co-operation and Development (OECD) (2004) *Starting Strong: Curricula and Pedagogies in Early Childhood Education and Care – Five Curriculum Outlines*. Paris: OECD.
Organisation for Economic Co-operation and Development (OECD) (2007) *Schools for the 21st Century*. Commission staff working paper. Paris: OECD.
Pound, L. and Miller, L. (2011) 'Critical issues', in L. Miller and L. Pound (eds) *Theories and Approaches to Learning in the Early Years*. London: Sage. This is Chapter 11 in the book.

Useful websites

Khanacademy.org – http://www.ted.com/talks/salman_khan_let_s_use_video_to_reinvent_education.html
Mitra, S. 'The Beginnings' – http://www.hole-in-the-wall.com/Beginnings.html

References

Broadfoot, P. (2000) 'Comparative education for the 21st century: retrospect and prospect', *Comparative Education*, 36(3): 357–71.
Bronfenbrenner, U. (1979) *The Ecology of Human Development: Experiments by Nature and Design*. London: Harvard University Press.
Bruner, J. (1996) *The Culture of Education*. Cambridge, MA: Harvard University Press.
Fulghum, R. (2003) *All I Really Need to Know I Learned in Kindergarten*, 15th edition. New York: Ballantyne Books.
Khan, S. (2011) *Salman Khan says 'Let's use video to reinvent education'*. Available at: http://www.ted.com/talks/salman_khan_let_s_use_video_to_reinvent_education.html
Laevers, F. (2005) 'The curriculum as a means to raise the quality of early childhood education: implications for policy', *European Early Childhood Education Research Journal*, 13(1): 17–29.

Laevers, F. (2007) *Deep Level Learning and the Experiential Approach in Early Childhood and Primary Education: Experiential Education*. Leuven: Katholieke Universiteit, Belgium.

Mankell, H. (2002) *Danslärarens återkomst*. Stockholm: Ordfront förlag.

Mitra, S. (1999) *The Beginnings*. Available at: http://www.hole-in-the-wall.com/beginnings.html

Organisation for Economic Co-operation and Development (OECD) (2004) *Starting Strong: Curricula and Pedagogies in Early Childhood Education and Care – Five Curriculum Outlines*. Paris: OECD.

Organisation for Economic Co-operation and Development (OECD) (2007) *Schools for the 21st Century*. Commission staff working paper. Paris: OECD.

Robinson, K. (2001) *Out of Our Minds: Learning to be Creative*. Oxford: Capstone.

Scottish Government (2004) *Curriculum for Excellence*. Edinburgh: Scottish Executive. Available at: http://www.educationscotland.gov.uk/thecurriculum/whatiscurriculumforexcellence/index.asp

Skolverket (2006) *Schools Like Any Other? Independent Schools as Part of the System 1991–2004*. Stockholm: Swedish National Agency for Education.

Skolverket (2012) *En bild av skolmarknaden*. Stockholm: Swedish National Agency for Education.

The Guardian (2011) How do we make our schools fit to face the 21st century? 4 September. Available at: http://www.guardian.co.uk/education/2011/sep/04/how-do-we-make-schools-fit-for-children

The 21st Century Learning Initiative (2011) The strategic and resource implications of a new model of learning. A Headmasters' and Headmistresses' Conference presentation. Available at: http://www.21learn.org/site/wp-content/uploads/PP.pdf

CHAPTER 10

THE PLACE OF TECHNOLOGY IN EARLY YEARS CARE AND EDUCATION

Key ideas explored in this chapter

- the place of technology in the lives of young children today
- what educational technology actually is
- the use and place of technology in ECEC
- key issues such as appropriateness, speed of change and impact on children's overall learning
- how practitioners can use technology appropriately.

Introduction

The title of this chapter is perhaps misleading as it suggests that there is a question about *whether* there is a place for technology in early years care and education. In fact, trying to deny that there *is* a place for technology would be rather like trying to put the genie back in the bottle. All our lives are affected by technology. We all use technology every day. It is part of the world that a child is born into and it is vital that they can and do engage with it. Prensky (2001) refers to those born in the last decades of the 20th century as 'digital natives', by which he means they have grown up in a digital world and are 'native speakers' of the language of technology. He asserts that because they have grown up in such a different environment, they 'think and process information fundamentally differently from their predecessors' (p. 1). Prensky cites Dr Bruce D. Perry (see Figure 1.1 in Chapter 1) in stating that 'different kinds of experiences lead to different brain structures' (p. 1). Those of us who have not grown up with technology, either because of age or our experience, are, in comparison, 'digital immigrants'. We have to learn the new language and will always retain an 'accent'. Again, he relates this to neuroscience, saying that 'a language learned later in life, scientists tell us, goes into a different part of the brain'.

It is clear that the question is not whether children should engage with technology but *how* they should engage with it, in other words what is 'appropriate'? Just as a child needs to develop literacy skills, they now need to develop 'technological literacy' or 'computer literacy' or perhaps 'digital literacy'. I will use the term techno-literacy in this chapter. We need to determine what constitutes techno-literacy and then how we can teach it or at least help children develop it. It is not easy for the 'immigrants' to teach the 'natives', and it may be helpful to explore our own starting points to identify the way forward.

I came across the most wonderful book when researching this chapter, by Jean Rice and published in 1976. It is called *My Friend the Computer* and it was in the old library of the Aberdeen College of Education. I was 20 in 1976 and remember very well that long hot summer. The company I worked for selling 'airtime' to advertisers on Yorkshire and Tyne-Tees Television in central London introduced a computer system at enormous expense to operate the timing of advertisements and the invoicing. The system failed. Enormous amounts of paper were generated, adverts went out at the wrong time and companies were not being invoiced. A year later, they introduced another more successful system. Here was my first example of how computers became irresistible. Despite the failure, extra work and expense, the company, like all similar companies around that time, ploughed on until they got a system that worked. This delightful book (Rice, 1976) is full of pictures that *I* recognise, such as a telex machine, Pascal's adding machine and ENIAC. The latter is described as:

> the first all-electronic computer. It was built by Eckert and Mauchly at the University of Pennsylvania in 1946. The ENIAC weighed 30 tons and occupied a whole room. It could do a problem in 2 hours that would have taken 100 engineers a year to do. (1976: 26)

The book provides very simple explanations of how things work, including:

> The computer seems to be very smart. Actually, the computer is not smart at all. It has an IQ of zero. It cannot think by itself. It has to be told what to do. It is an extension of

man's mind. Since man has to tell the computer what to do, man has complete control over it. (1976: 7)

This would still be true of computers we are using in our homes and schools – but for how much longer? It seems that technology has moved so fast and become so complex that we do not even try to give an explanation of how it actually works. Even back in 1976, some computer operations were done in 'nanoseconds' and some stores were already using codes for groceries. These were explained as 'a billionth of a second' and 'a scanner at the checkout detects the marks and sends a signal to the computer so that your purchase is recorded' (p. 19). Perhaps this could be a starting point for young children? A back-to-basics approach first exploring how technology is used in everyday life.

A 'digital divide'

There does seem to be a tendency to encourage young children to simply use a computer, a hand-held computer game console, a mobile phone etc. without any suggestion that they might want to understand more about how it actually works. So much is hidden from view such as barcodes and paying by credit card (or now using 'Ping' on your smartphone) and there is so much that so many adults do not begin to understand, that perhaps this is impossible. Is this the 'digital divide'?

Siraj-Blatchford and Whitebread (2003) suggested that techno-literacy or access to and the ability to use digital technology such as the internet, email, mobile phones and social networking sites is a 'citizenship issue'. In 2003 they suggested it was already impossible to participate fully with political life and in society without access to and understanding of digital technology and this is surely increasingly the case. Is this the 'digital divide'?

Research has shown a difference in the kind and degree of engagement with technology between boys and girls. Boys are more keen from an early age to play computer games that are competitive, require problem-solving skills and rapid reactions, whilst girls use social networking sites or 'games' that are less interactive. Is *this* the 'digital divide'?

Stephen et al. (2012), reporting on a survey of 346 3–4-year-olds in 2005, acknowledged concern about the development of a digital divide created through economic background. Their data suggested that there is no simple divide between the experiences of economically advantaged and disadvantaged children. Instead, they found 'a complex relationship between family circumstances and ICT experiences, one that is the result of family practices, parental attitudes and children's own preferences' (p. 187). There is no clear evidence of a digital divide or, if one *is* developing, then how and why? We should not therefore make assumptions but should remain alert and concerned about the issue.

REFLECTIVE ACTIVITY

You could carry out your own research to explore:

- what experiences children have of technology – that is, how they engage with it and from what age
- how aware they are of the uses of technology in day-to-day life – for example, in shops, at traffic lights or when controlling things in the home
- whether boys and girls engage with technology more or less the same or differently.

This information can inform your planning and your practice.

The technology children are growing up with today

It is fascinating and somewhat unnerving to consider the dramatic changes technology has brought to all of our lives. It is important for us to consider this in some detail in order to gain a proper perspective of the importance of technology in the education of young children. Whatever age you, the reader, are, I can guarantee that the experiences of a child aged 0–8 today are radically different, largely because of technological changes, to your own early experiences. Obviously, for older readers the difference is even more radical. To emphasise the contrast, I have provided a case study based on myself (case study 1) and another for my great-nephew born last June, 55 years later (case study 2). Case study 3 provides an example from the generation in between.

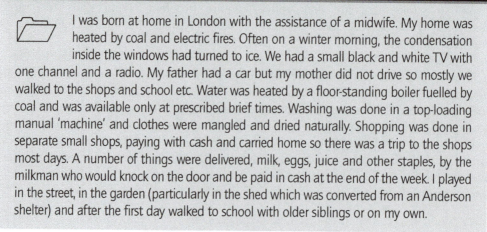

CASE STUDY 1 (1956–64)

I was born at home in London with the assistance of a midwife. My home was heated by coal and electric fires. Often on a winter morning, the condensation inside the windows had turned to ice. We had a small black and white TV with one channel and a radio. My father had a car but my mother did not drive so mostly we walked to the shops and school etc. Water was heated by a floor-standing boiler fuelled by coal and was available only at prescribed brief times. Washing was done in a top-loading manual 'machine' and clothes were mangled and dried naturally. Shopping was done in separate small shops, paying with cash and carried home so there was a trip to the shops most days. A number of things were delivered, milk, eggs, juice and other staples, by the milkman who would knock on the door and be paid in cash at the end of the week. I played in the street, in the garden (particularly in the shed which was converted from an Anderson shelter) and after the first day walked to school with older siblings or on my own.

CASE STUDY 2 (2011–)

Roscoe was born in a London teaching hospital. I heard about it within hours with pictures via mobile phone technology and email. He arrived home to colour television (high definition) with about 1000 channels and internet access. His home is always warm courtesy of gas central heating, with hot water on demand from a combination boiler. Both parents have laptops and smartphones and drive. The car has a SatNav system so that there is no need to use a road map. Roscoe's clothes disappear into the automatic washer-drier and come out dry, usually with no need for ironing because of the high-tech fabrics. His food is heated in a microwave in seconds, including sterilising equipment. Shopping can be done without leaving home via the internet and is paid for electronically using smart cards (either credit or debit). Even in small shops, his mother will generally pay with a card and when getting on buses or the Underground will use an Oyster card. There is absolutely no chance that he will play 'in the street'; hopefully he will play in a garden but I think it unlikely he will be walking to school on his own for many years. It is very likely that he will be operating the TV, DVD player, computer, iPod, iPad, certainly the phone and mobile phone, possibly taking photographs and using other technology that we are not yet aware of before he can read and write. His parents' generation was similarly affected by technology and is already becoming au fait with new terminology – see the next case study.

CASE STUDY 3 (1981)

Back in the early 1980s, I was having lunch at my sister's house with her 2-year-old daughter and my parents, her grandparents. My sister had a nice new modern kitchen with a microwave oven which was relatively new on the scene in those days. She heated baked beans for my father (granddad) in the microwave and as she put them on the toast in front of him, my niece piped up saying, 'Granddad you mustn't eat them yet because the molecules are still agitating'. As you can imagine, Granddad nearly fell off his chair! He was not a very old granddad and was an engineer and academic who did actually know about 'agitating molecules' but did not expect to be told this by a 2-year-old. It went further because as he chuckled he proceeded to blow on the beans saying, 'Yes, you're right. I had better cool them down', only to be told rather impatiently, 'It's no good blowing on them – you have to move them about!'

There is little chance of a child born today growing up without interacting with, using and being affected by technology, particularly digital technology, and much of what they will use as adults most of us are quite unaware of now. Tapscott (1998: 128) and others refer to the 'Net Generation' and point out that 'the N-Gen is destined for a world of knowledge work'. Stephen et al. (2008), exploring how 3–4-year-olds used technology at home, found that they are active and discriminating users of technology with decided preferences and a view of their own competencies. Most of us are only aware of a small amount of the impact and use of digital technology today – rather like the tip of an iceberg! Few of us can begin to imagine what may change over the next 20–30 years. This is particularly challenging for anyone engaged in the education of children and this includes all ECEC professionals and parents. There are some burning questions to be answered, including:

- What do children, particularly very young children, need to know about technology?
- Do they need to use computers, mobile phones, cameras, etc. at a very early age? Are they disadvantaged if they do not have access and opportunities to engage with technology?
- Is there really a 'digital divide' between those who have access and can use computers, etc. and those who haven't and can't?
- Is this a 'citizenship issue' in the sense that those who are not technologically or computer 'literate' are unable to fully participate in a democratic society? (Siraj-Blatchford and Whitebread, 2003)
- Does using computers etc. help children's learning in general, such as their literacy skills, or is it damaging to other, perhaps more important, areas of learning?

These are not questions to which I have the answer and I do not believe anyone else has the answer either. I do believe they are questions that anyone involved in the care and education of children of any age needs to engage with. As with almost every aspect of care and education, there are no easy answers, no definitive answers – just an ongoing debate and exploration trying to use research and theory and apply these to each individual situation. Given the speed of change in technology, we will need to keep re-examining and re-visiting this issue. It might be important to allow children in care and education settings to make 'active and discriminating use' of technology and continue to decide their preferences and develop their own competencies, as they are already doing at home (Stephen et al., 2008). Metcalfe and Simpson (2011: 129) emphasise 'integrating the use of new technologies across the curriculum in ways that meet the needs and interests of children' as essential to their full, safe and effective participation in an increasingly technology-based society.

What is educational technology?

Educational technology might include computers, television, i-pads, i-pods, mobile phones, cameras, interactive whiteboards, robotic or remote-controlled toys, interactive toys such as the V-Tech range, and doubtless other things that are not yet widely available but already invented as I write. However, talk about educational technology mostly centres on digital technology and within that largely the use of computers. The use of computers in ECEC settings then largely centres on 'games' designed to facilitate learning to read, write and do number work – the 3Rs? Certainly in classrooms these activities are now extended to the Interactive White Board (IWB), one of which is now in every classroom I go into. I visited about 30 different primary classrooms over the last academic session, mostly early years, and have done for the last seven years. I would seriously question how 'interactive' these tools are in the way they are being used. They appear to be used more as a modern blackboard and frequently pale in comparison when they fail to work at all, go to 'sleep' unexpectedly, require blinds drawn and even then cannot be seen clearly, or when the teacher (in this case student teachers) cannot produce a good model of writing on them.

REFLECTIVE ACTIVITY

Within the setting where you work or are placed, examine the use of the IWB:

- How often is it used?
- Is it available for children to use as and when they wish?
- Is it used by individuals/groups or by an adult for a group?
- Could the things done on the IWB just as easily be done on a whiteboard/blackboard?

Are you confident in using the IWB? Can you model good writing on the IWB? If not, what can you do about it? Are there opportunities to develop your skills in this area?

Great claims are made for the efficacy of technology used to support learning, particularly computer technology. Many of these claims are made by those who produce and sell the hard- and software. Educational technology is often seen as the 'answer' to solving the problem of individual difficulties, particularly with literacy and maths that are seen to require individualised 'programmes'. There are now many online tutoring facilities available, as well as educational 'games', either online or available to buy. The quality of all of these is difficult to assess and largely goes unmonitored. Siraj-Blatchford and Whitebread (2003: 8) stated: 'ICT has potential to enhance educational opportunities in early years … it can encourage discussion, creativity, problem solving, risk taking and flexible thinking.'

This is certainly true. The potential is there and we cannot ignore the possibilities or the desire and need for young children to use and engage with ICT in ECEC settings, whether playgroup, nursery or school, as they do at home and in every aspect of their everyday lives. Already quite young children are engaging with serious problem solving through online games. *Fortune Magazine* reported that:

> The Defense Advanced Research Projects Agency (DARPA) in the US is already using social media to harness new talent by running a public computer game called Foldit, in which competitors try to fold proteins, one of the most difficult biochemistry impediments to curing disease. Mis-folded proteins lead to diseases such as Alzheimer's and cystic fibrosis. Since 2008 more than 236,000 gamers have registered and contributed to helping to decipher the structure of an enzyme responsible for causing AIDS in rhesus monkeys. (Easton, 2012: 25)

There is no age restriction on participation so a 12- or 13-year-old may contribute to a cure for cancer (Easton, 2012). It is 'creativity, problem solving, risk taking and flexible thinking' that needs to be the focus.

CASE STUDY 4

In a Primary 1 classroom, a student teacher delivered a very well-planned lesson involving small groups of children engaging with games to support the learning of phonic skills. They were grouped into threes or fours and moved on to each 'station' to experience each game over the session. One game was on the Interactive White Board. It involved a word appearing and four pictures. The children had to identify the correct picture to match the word. The medial or initial sound in each word was the same. The words came up in sets in rising degrees of difficulty and a score accumulated in the top corner as one was touched correctly matching word and picture. One boy in the first group almost immediately realised that if he kept touching the correct picture, the score kept going up. The others quickly caught on and so they would each bang the screen as many times as possible raising the score before moving on to another word. There was little focus on learning the sounds. A number of other children in the class were quite distracted by this lively game on the IWB and so did not fully focus on their 'game'. The student teacher became aware of the problem quickly and tried to discourage children from just banging on the board to get the score up but did not have much luck as they reverted as soon as she moved away.

REFLECTIVE ACTIVITY

In the case study above:

- What might the children have been learning – about phonics, IT skills or learning?
- What do you think the student teacher should do differently next time?

CASE STUDY 5

A male student teacher with a Primary 1 class (5–6-year-olds) was operating what had begun to be called a 'soft-start' in line with the class teacher's usual practice. This involved a number of activities set up first thing in the morning that the children could choose from. These might be described as structured play activities. One was a game on two computers that happened to be beside me. It involved clicking on and dragging words into boxes around an image. Two girls sat down and one quickly completed the activity with very little difficulty and was rewarded with a flashing cartoon character saying, 'Yes, you are right!' She was uncertain what to do next and then decided to drag them back to the bottom and start again. The other girl seemed unsure what to do and clicked and dragged a few words before noticing what the other girl was doing. She watched the second time, seemed disenchanted and drifted off. The first girl waited until she caught the attention of the teacher who came over and re-set the screen with a new 'game'. She completed this quickly and then went off to another activity.

REFLECTIVE ACTIVITY

In the case study above:

- What were the two girls learning?
- Is it possible to tell whether the second child was unable to operate the computer or unable to meet the challenge of the language activity?
- Is it interesting that this activity attracted two girls?

What is best practice in terms of using technology?

It would seem obvious that best practice in terms of using technology should not be any different to best practice in general. It might therefore help to think about what we are really trying to do with or for young children. Previous chapters have highlighted the importance of play, the importance and impact of the environment and key people in the child's life. We have focused on ways to encourage creativity and the importance of understanding the 'lived lives' of children so that we can build on prior experiences and learning. We have emphasised the importance of social learning and play-based approaches in line with social-constructivist theories of learning espoused by Lev Vygotsky, Jerome Bruner and Tina Bruce.

Vygotsky identified what he referred to as the zone of proximal development, which is the space between what a child already knows or has mastered and the knowledge that is still beyond their capabilities (Krogh and Slentz, 2011). In this space, learning is challenging but not frustrating and with help from a teacher, parent or more able peer, the child can understand and learn. It is quite easy to relate this part of Vygotsky's theory to learning with technology such as on the computer. I have seen so often with my own children and their friends how they cluster round the computer pointing and gesticulating, puzzling together over how to go forward in the latest game. I have often been assisted by my children or (much younger) colleagues when learning how to use new software or functions.

Bruner developed this concept further in terms of 'scaffolding' children's learning. He suggests this supports children in moving from where they are now to where adults want to take them. Bruce (2005: 36) points out that 'this is different from a situation where the adult goes with the child and helps them learn more about what interests and fascinates them'. As she rightly asserts, the differences are 'subtle and sophisticated' and the ECEC professional needs to develop the ability of knowing which to use, perhaps not least when using technology to support children's learning. This is surely a key aspect of our professional knowledge and skill, to know when to lead and when to follow, when to lead the child towards the learning intention we have determined or simply when to intervene and when to stand back. Bruner ([1960/1977]2006) also introduced the idea of the spiral curriculum where he suggested the child needs to be introduced to essential elements of learning on any subject at their own level and revisit and build on their understanding. He famously stated that 'any subject can be taught to any child at any age in some form that is honest' (Bruner, [1960/1977]2006: 56). This suggests that we can teach children about technology at an early age. However, he also puts forward the view that 'as a criterion for any subject taught in primary school, whether, when fully developed, it is worth an adult's knowing, and whether having known it as a child makes a person a better adult' (Bruner, [1960/1977]2006: 55). This seems more problematic with regard to teaching about and with technology as we know that this will be radically different by the time the child reaches adulthood. It may be more important for the child to know about technology, what it can and might do for us and how to make good use of whatever is available but not necessarily practise the use of what will soon become redundant. Achieving high levels of literacy and numeracy accompanied by a positive disposition towards learning will be more valuable to an adult in 2020–30 who will need to be able to adapt to and use technology not yet invented. These high levels of literacy and numeracy might be achieved using digital technology, making the learning relevant to children today, but this should not be at the expense of developing a positive disposition towards learning.

Developing positive dispositions towards learning

It is vital that children have a positive disposition towards learning, meaning that they are motivated to learn, curious, determined and willing and able to concentrate. A 'disposition' simply means 'what you are disposed to do' and in terms of ECEC really focuses on maintaining a positive disposition towards learning. The word 'maintaining' is used because all babies start with a positive disposition towards learning (Gopnik et al., 1999). Sadly, some have already lost or begun to lose this by the time they enter formal education. Perhaps the most important aspect of the role of all adults in a young child's life, particularly ECEC professionals, is to maintain and nurture these positive dispositions towards learning. Dowling (2010) suggests this may be achieved through:

- secure attachments – with a key person in the setting
- models of positive dispositions – particularly from a key person
- opportunities to repeat and practise patterns of behaviour that reinforce these dispositions
- adults encouraging and extending children's interest – developing autonomy
- adults explicitly valuing the child's efforts, for example through descriptive praise.

Dispositions are different to attitudes (Katz, 1995). The latter are concerned with a set of beliefs whereas a disposition demonstrates the attitude in behaviour. The EYFS (2012) identifies excitement, motivation and interest as dispositions for learning. These are three things we need to consider when planning activities around ICT or other technologies, just as we should when planning any activity. If children are excited, motivated and interested, there is more chance they will engage in discussion, be creative, problem solve, take risks and develop flexible thinking. These three dispositions towards learning correlate with the three domains.

Carr (2001) suggests a child needs to be:

- ready – see themselves as a learner
- willing – because they recognise the environment offers scope for learning, and
- able – because they have sufficient knowledge, skills and understanding to be ready and willing.

Many criticise users, not only children but any user, of email and online chat in terms of the detrimental effect on literacy skills because spelling, punctuation and grammar are not used properly. Armstrong and Casement (2000) have written a book about how computers put our children's education at risk with quite a lot of emphasis on children learning to write. They feel quantity and speed are promoted over quality and reflection. However others, such as Tapscott (1998), suggest these tools can improve communication skills, saying, 'Time spent using these services is time spent reading. Time spent thinking about your response is time spent analysing. And time spent composing a response is time spent writing' (p. 134). I would agree with this but cannot help point out that he has used a conjunction 'and' quite improperly to start a sentence! The essential point here seems to be about the communication skills required for the 21st century and Tapscott may be right when he says, 'Writing is like a muscle; it requires exercise. These kids are developing a powerful muscle that will serve them well in future work environments' (p. 135). We are, after all, very unsure what these work environments will be.

REFLECTIVE ACTIVITY

Explore some ideas for using technologies with young children using the internet. You could start with http://www.futurelab.org.uk/resources. This is the resources site for Futurelab which is an independent not-for-profit organisation committed to developing creative and innovative approaches to education, teaching and learning. You can download and read 'Neuroscience and technology enhanced learning' at: http://www.futurelab.org.uk/sites/default/files/NTEL_online_AW.pdf. This document focuses on the potential for the sciences of mind and brain that are providing new insights (see Chapter 1) and fresh perspectives on education to inform the design and use of technology-enhanced learning.

Use a search engine and search, for example, for 'digital literacy' or 'technology in learning' and explore new ideas and information. The only way to keep up to date with technology is to use it and particularly to use the internet. It is quite true that if you can buy something in the shops, such as the newest smartphone, it is already effectively out of date. It is also true that nobody else is able to keep completely up to date so – don't panic! Begin with what you are comfortable with and what you have access to. Remember, all those children a century ago who learned to read and write with a slate, a piece of chalk and the Bible. Also, consider the many children in parts of India who study computing in schools that do not have any computers, only a blackboard, and then go on to study computer science at university successfully.

Think about what you use and are most comfortable with – this might be using a digital camera, sending email, working with 'Word' or 'PowerPoint' or playing particular games on a computer. You may have 'old-fashioned' technology such as overhead projectors. These have been used in Reggio Emilia (see Chapter 12), for example, to explore light and shadow and expand images to great effect. Think about how you might encourage children to use it in your setting.

Plan one activity that involves children (this could be one or two or a large group) in using technology. Implement your plan and then reflect on and evaluate the learning using these questions:

- Were the children able to be creative, solve problems, take any risks or think flexibly?
- How autonomous were the children?
- Did the activity encourage positive dispositions for learning?

You will notice you are not asked to consider whether children reached a learning intention such as 'We are learning to count to 10'.

What are children learning?

Stephen and Plowman (2008) identified three kinds of learning with technology:

- operational learning which refers to the use of technology
- learning about areas of the curriculum which could be finding information, identifying sounds or rhymes (literacy skills) or identifying shapes, sorting and categorising (maths)
- acquiring positive learning dispositions such as confidence and persistence.

It may be that too much time is spent on the first two whilst the emphasis should in fact be on the last point. Children do not present with major problems in learning how to operate, for example, a hand-held computer game or a mobile phone. Often, adults are left behind when new technology arrives, whether in the home or a classroom. Much of the learning about other areas of the curriculum can be done in other, more traditional ways.

REFLECTIVE ACTIVITY

With regards to 'finding information', interestingly I have not yet seen children in nursery or early years' classes using computers for this. I have seen them looking at non-fiction books to find out information about, for example, animals. This is merely anecdotal evidence from observing student teachers but it is worth considering:

- Would it be better to encourage very young children to search for information on the internet or in rather out-of-date books?
- When you are looking for information about, for example, how to grow roses, do you go to the library or the bookshop or do you switch on your laptop at home and type 'how to grow roses' into the 'search' box?
- You most likely search the internet as I do, but is it important for children to develop skills using this or books? This would be a good point to discuss with colleagues, other students and perhaps parents.

Developmentally Appropriate Technology in Early Childhood (DATEC) refers to a project with the central aim of contributing towards the development of common agreements regarding appropriate ICT curriculum content for young children across Europe. The partners in the project included the Institute of Education, London, the School of Education, Cambridge, Goteburg University and Chalmers Tekniska Hogskola (both Sweden), the University of Evora, Spain and the Association of Professionals in Education of North Alentejo, Portugal. DATEC conducted a systematic and comprehensive survey of current (and planned) developments in ICT for young children's education.

Outcomes of this project included case studies (that can be viewed at: http://www.datec.org.uk/datecfrm1.htm), curriculum guideline materials and a policy statement giving authoritative guidance on developmentally appropriate practice in ICT education for 0–8-year-olds.

DATEC produced a final report identifying seven principles for good practice and these can be read in full in an extract at: http://www.327matters.org/Docs/DATEC7.pdf

These seven principles are:

1   **Applications should always be educational** rather than simply 'fun' and have broad aims beyond 'drill-and-practice' programmes. These, they feel, 'risk reducing children's intrinsic motivation to learn' because they rely on an external reward (such as a smiley face).

2   **Applications should always encourage collaboration** and they cite Light and Butterworth (1992: 2), saying: 'Activities requiring joint attention and which involve children learning to share provide a better cognitive challenge for young children than activities where they work alone.'

3   **Applications should always be integrated with other aspects of the curriculum** which means integrating the use of technology into play and projects to make them relevant to children. They highlight the problem of many schools in particular creating computer suites that isolate the activity from the rest of the curriculum. They also suggest that computers should not be used on a rota basis or as a 'reward' as this again isolates the activity, reducing relevance. Children need to see computers, etc. as a 'tool' for learning – something they can use whenever appropriate and chosen, just like they would go and pick up a crayon or pencil to draw.

4   **Applications should always ensure that the child is in control** rather than the child being subjected to a programme of learning. Activities for which there is only one correct answer and children are rewarded for speedily finding it follow a behaviourist theory of learning. The DATEC report says: 'There is consensus among informed early childhood educators across Europe about the importance of developing children's early awareness and positive disposition towards literacy and numeracy' (p. 3). Computers are excellent at routine tasks, finding the one correct answer by quickly eliminating wrong answers. Many programmes designed to help young children learn literacy and numeracy skills use this approach. The report states: 'Computers should be used as a means to fulfil a function which cannot be achieved better through other means' (p. 4).

5   **Applications should always be chosen because they are transparent**, which means the functions should be clearly defined and intuitive. One example they give of this is the 'drag and drop' facility where the child would 'pick up an item with a click, drag it to somewhere else and then drop it in that place with another

click' (p. 5), as this simulates real life where you pick something up and put it down in another place.

6 **Applications containing violence or stereotyping should be avoided** and the report goes on to discuss issues of equality. We must always be able to justify our choice of programmes, functions and access when providing ICT opportunities for very young children.

7 **Applications should always consider and show an awareness of health and safety issues**, including the amount of time children spend sitting at a computer (at any one time and as a proportion of their day), ergonomics (appropriate position when using the computer to avoid repetitive strain, for example) and balance: 'use of the computer should not be at the expense of outdoor opportunities and experiences'.

These principles provide an excellent guide for planning and providing ICT learning opportunities for young children and underpin curriculum guidelines across Europe. The report also emphasises the importance of involving parents and, like Stephen et al. (2012), highlights that research shows settings often have little knowledge about children's ICT experience at home. As with all learning, it is vital that we build on what children already know and make learning experiences relevant and enjoyable. To do this effectively, home–school communication is essential.

Conclusion

We have explored some of the issues but given the speed of change, I would suggest it is incumbent upon us all to continue exploring and learning for ourselves – alongside our children. I hope I have highlighted the need to focus on the fact that we have to keep trying to teach children for their tomorrow and not our yesterday – in fact, not even for our today. The seven principles from DATEC (above), plus ensuring the involvement of parents, are a valuable guide to planning and providing learning experiences for children. Reflection on learning theories, such as those of Vygotsky and Bruner, is still wholly relevant in this context and all the understanding of what constitutes best practice to support children's development and learning should be applied. We should embrace technology, particularly digital technology, starting with what we know and building from there, as we would with any learning journey, but be mindful of the impact on what we are trying to achieve. Children may not need to use a computer to learn to read, and they do not need to practise skills specific to today's technology such as using a mouse or keyboard as these become obsolete and can easily be learned when needed. They do need to learn about technology, understand its uses and power and be positively disposed to learn about each new thing that will surely come along in the next few decades.

Further reading

Bruce, T. (2005) 'Ten principles in a modern context', *Early Childhood Education*, 3rd edition. London: Hodder Arnold. This is Chapter 3 in the book.

Dowling, M. (2010) 'Dispositions for learning', in *Young Children's Personal, Social and Emotional Development*, 3rd edition. London: Sage. This is Chapter 5 in the book.

Stephen, C., McPake, J. and Plowman, L. (2012) 'Digital technologies at home: the experiences of 3- and 4-year-olds in Scotland', in L. Miller, R. Drury and C. Cable (eds) *Extending Professional Practice in the Early Years*. London: Sage. This is Chapter 15 in the book.

Tapscott, D. (1998) 'N-Gen learning', in *Growing Up Digital: The Rise of the Net Generation*. New York: McGraw-Hill. This is Chapter 7 in the book.

 Useful websites

Developmentally Appropriate Technology for Early Childhood – curriculum guidance at: http://www.datec.org.uk/datecfrm1.htm

FutureLab – Innovation in Education research and resources at: http://www.futurelab.org.uk/resources

For suggested activities for using ICT in the early years from West Dumbartonshire, go to: http://www.educationscotland.gov.uk/resources/s/genericresource_tcm4378872.asp?strReferringChannel=earlyyearsandstrReferringPageID=tcm:4-623087-64

References

Armstrong, A. and Casement, C. (2000) *The Child and the Machine: How Computers Put Our Children's Education at Risk*. Beltsville, MD: Robins Lane Press.

Bruce, T. (2005) *Early Childhood Education*, 3rd edition. London: Hodder Arnold.

Bruner, J. (1960/1977/2006) *The Process of Education*. Cambridge, MA: Harvard University Press.

Carr, M. (2001) *Assessment in Early Childhood Settings: Learning Stories*. London: Paul Chapman.

Dowling, M. (2010) *Young Children's Personal, Social and Emotional Development*, 3rd edition. London: Sage.

Easton, N. (2012) 'Fortune's guide to the future', *Fortune Magazine*, 16 January, pp. 20–33.

EYFS (2012) *Statutory Framework for the Early Years Foundation Stage 2012*. London: Department of Education.

Gopnik, A., Melsoff, A. and Kuhl, P. (1999) *How Babies Think: The Science of Childhood*. London: Wiedenfeld and Nicholson.

Katz, L. (1995) *Talks with Teachers of Young Children*. Norwood, NJ: Ablex.

Krogh, S.L. and Slentz, K.L. (2011) *Early Childhood Education: Yesterday, Today and Tomorrow*, 2nd edition. London: Routledge.

Metcalfe, J. and Simpson, D. (2011) 'Learning online: the internet, social networking and e-safety', in D. Simpson and M. Toyn (eds) *Primary ICT Across the Curriculum* (in the series Transforming Primary QTS). Exeter: Learning Matters.

Prensky, M. (2001) 'Digital natives, digital immigrants', from *On the Horizon*, MCB University Press, 9(5), October. Available at: http://www.marcprensky.com/writing/prensky%20-%20digital%20natives,%20digital%20immigrants%20-%20part1.pdf

Rice, J. (1976) *My Friend the Computer*. Minneapolis, MN: T.S. Denison and Co.

Siraj-Blatchford, J. and Whitebread, D. (2003) *Supporting Information Communications Technology in the Early Years*. Maidenhead: Open University Press.

Stephen, C. and Plowman, L. (2008) 'Enhancing learning with information and communication technologies in pre-school', *Early Child Development and Care*, 178(6): 637–54.

Stephen, C., McPake, J. and Plowman, L. (2012) 'Digital technologies at home: the experiences of 3- and 4-year-olds in Scotland', in L. Miller, R. Drury and C. Cable (eds) *Extending Professional Practice in the Early Years*. London: Sage.

Stephen, C., McPake, J., Plowman, L. and Berch-Heyman, S. (2008) 'Learning from the children: exploring preschool children's encounters with ICT at home', *Journal of Early Childhood Research*, 6(2): 99–117.

Tapscott, D. (1998) *Growing Up Digital: The Rise of the Net Generation*. New York: McGraw-Hill.

PART 3
INTERNATIONAL EDUCATIONAL APPROACHES

Introduction

This part takes a closer look at five approaches that readers may be quite familiar with. These are the approach taken in Sweden in recent years, in Reggio Emilia in Italy, in New Zealand with the introduction of Te Whāriki, in the USA through the HighScope project, and experiential education (EXE) arising from research by the University of Leuven and Ferre Laevers. These were chosen initially as aspects within our courses for BA Childhood Practice students, and more recently for our Early Years Postgraduate Certificate students. These five approaches also form the focus of the paper 'Starting Strong: Curricula and Pedagogies in Early Childhood Education and Care – Five Curriculum Outlines' from the OECD (2004) as part of their project 'Thematic Review of Early Childhood Education and Care Policy', launched in 1998. The report stems from a workshop hosted in Sweden in 2003. It underpins and justifies our own understanding of the importance of these approaches and the value in studying alternative approaches. It is our belief that it is imperative for all those involved in the care and education of children, to remain vigilant and critical of the political forces constantly seeking to effect change in the sector. One way to help in this process is to widen our perspectives and look at approaches taken elsewhere. This is not with a view to adopting such approaches wholesale, as each is very much a part of its own socio-cultural context, but to help us examine our own practice more closely by comparison and adopt new ideas where appropriate.

In this third part, we will explore:

- the background to the provision of ECEC in Sweden, the principles of the Swedish pre-school curriculum and the rights and expectations of children aged 0–8 growing up in Sweden
- the provision and practice in Reggio Emilia, identifying and examining some key elements that have been adapted and adopted elsewhere and identifying key learning from this approach that might enhance provision and practice
- the provision and practice of Te Whāriki, examining some key elements and identifying key learning from this approach that might enhance provision and practice
- the research project known as HighScope, identifying and examining some of the key messages and implications of the research and identifying key learning from this approach that might enhance provision and practice
- quality enhancement of practice through the use of Ferre Laevers' approach to supporting emotional well-being in children and supporting involvement
- whether we can learn/take from other places and practices to help us look more closely and analytically at our own provision and whether we learn more from the commonalities or differences.

Chapter 11, 'Practice and provision for children aged 0–8 in Sweden', looks closely at provision and practice in Sweden, examining what can be learned, adopted or adapted to enhance provision and practice. It examines and compares childcare and education between Sweden and the UK considering aspects such as costs, qualifications of staff, curriculum goals and school timetables. It also explores issues such as the provision and quality of school meals, access to outdoor play and risk taking/ management of risk. The approach to preparation for reading through language acquisition, as opposed to acquisition of literacy skills, is also considered. This is drawn together through analysis and reflection on the impact of family life and outcomes for children.

Chapter 12, 'Practice and provision in Reggio Emilia', looks closely at provision and practice in Reggio Emilia, examining what can be learned, adopted or adapted to enhance provision and practice. Some key literature is reviewed to examine how the 'Reggio Approach' has been reified and adopted in other countries, notably the USA. Again, some elements from the approach are selected to examine against the background of an approach that is deeply rooted in the politics and culture of a particular part of the world. Just as in Sweden and indeed New Zealand, it has arisen and been developed against this background and at a particular historical time. In exploring any of these approaches and encouraging readers to do the same, we are cognisant of the fact that it would be a mistake to try and transplant any approach wholesale from one place to another. There is, however, such a wealth of theory, practice and literature that it is vital to consider what aspects we can take and adopt and what we may need to change in our own practice to make them work for us (Gardner, 1993).

This chapter explores parental involvement and what is referred to as a 'pedagogy of relationships', the image of the child as 'competent', documentation for recalling and reflecting and the environment seen as the 'third teacher'. The purpose of identifying these key features is to reflect on our own practice to determine what 'kind of soil' we need and whether we can provide it.

Chapter 13, 'Practice and provision in New Zealand – Te Whāriki', looks closely at Te Whāriki, the early childhood curriculum introduced in New Zealand in the late 1990s, examining what can be learned, adopted or adapted to enhance provision and practice. This innovative curriculum was designed to incorporate equitable educational opportunities in a bicultural society. The philosophy and theory underpinning the development of this early childhood curriculum must be viewed against the historical and political context in New Zealand, just as in the preceding chapters regarding Sweden and Italy. This curriculum document was developed and then implemented against a background of integration of all services responsible for the care and education of children (the first country in the world to do this); also against two decades of activism and persuasion by women and in partnership with Maori and Pakeha, reflecting the Treaty of Waitangi to ensure it was genuinely bicultural. It examines how the image of the competent and confident learner through the strands of well-being, belonging, contribution, communication and exploration, at the heart of this approach, can provide answers for others working in culturally diverse settings.

Chapter 14, 'HighScope', looks at the theory behind HighScope, The Perry Pre-school HighScope Project that originated in Ypsilante, Michigan, USA in 1962, and ran until 1967. At this time, the city was the centre for the Ford and GM car industry and schooling in the USA was racially segregated; this also applied to housing. The approach has provided a wealth of evidence from a longitudinal study showing the effects on children of a play-based approach to early education as well as long-term educational attainment, employment and stable relationships in adulthood. How it has been implemented and adapted since the start and evidence for effectiveness can be quite clearly tracked and considered, as this approach is the result of a research project. From research evidence, it is possible to consider the effects of this approach, and also from the associated research consider early intervention initiatives. It identifies some specific practices that readers might wish to explore and adopt in their setting.

Chapter 15, 'An approach to experiential education – Ferre Laevers', looks at the theory and work of Ferre Laevers. There is a particular focus on the emotional well-being of children and their levels of involvement and engagement through use of 'The Leuven Involvement Scale' (LIS). This educational model, which has been influential throughout Europe and beyond, emerged from an action research project involving 12 Belgian pre-school teachers reflecting critically on their practice. They examined the reality of the life and educational experience of pre-school children. The data was analysed and discussed by a team of researchers and their key finding, that *too many opportunities to sustain children's development remain unused*, resulted in the development of the LIS. Laevers' analysis of the child and its absorption in learning, where children are able to gain a deep, motivated, intense and long-term learning experience, at the very limit of their capabilities, is acknowledged worldwide. We have found that students who are already ECEC professionals, introduced to this 'tool' find it useful, valuable and informative on a number of levels. The chapter guides the reader through some simple stages towards exploring the use of the scale in practice.

Although each of these five chapters looks at a separate and seemingly quite different approach, it is hoped readers will begin to see the important similarities. It is significant to note that none of these approaches, identified around the world as models worthy of study, emanate from the UK. This is not to suggest that there is no good practice in and around the UK, but set against the background of recent OECD reports that identify UK children as some of the unhappiest in the developed world, it does suggest there may be a good deal to learn from others. One key similarity between these approaches is the integration of care and education and an emphasis on the emotional well-being of young children. For example, the Swedish Ministry of Education and Science was quoted in OECD (2004: 23) stating: 'The Swedish Pre-school should be characterised by a pedagogical approach where care, nurturing and learning together form a coherent whole'. There is also a common awareness that curriculum goals should provide direction based on agreed values, attitudes and norms rather than focus on content. The content, as can be seen very clearly in the Reggio Approach, emerges from children's individual interests, ways of thinking and ways of expressing themselves.

We are educating our children for an unknown future. We are doing so in an increasingly globalised world where international collaboration and communication become easier and more important by the day. Even though we are developing curriculum, pedagogy and practice within our own cultural context and cannot copy directly from elsewhere, we can and should learn from whatever models we can access and then take our own position.

References

Gardner, H. (1993) *Frames of Mind: The Theory of Multiple Intelligences*. London: Fontana Press.
Organisation for Economic Co-operation and Development (OECD) (2004) *Starting Strong: Curricula and Pedagogies in Early Childhood Education and Care – Five Curriculum Outlines*. Paris: OECD.

CHAPTER 11

PRACTICE AND PROVISION FOR CHILDREN AGED 0–8 IN SWEDEN

Key ideas explored in this chapter

- the background to the provision of ECEC in Sweden
- the principles of the Swedish pre-school curriculum
- the rights and expectations of children aged 0–8 growing up in Sweden.

This chapter will look at practice and provision of education and care in Sweden and compare this with the current situation in the UK. In terms of the health and well-being of children, Sweden scores consistently high (according to rankings as published in the OECD *Starting Strong* reports, 2001, 2006, 2009). Although it is never possible to adopt policy wholesale from one country to another, because of inherent cultural differences and traditions, it is possible to highlight some aspects of provision which do have a particularly significant and positive impact on children.

Sweden, Norway and Denmark comprise the group of Northern European countries known as Scandinavia. Sweden is the third largest country in Europe, with a landmass 2.5 times the size of the UK, half of which is covered by forest. However, the population is only around 9 million which equals about 16 per cent of the UK. From this, it can be clearly appreciated that although there are some large cities, the most well-known being Stockholm and Gothenburg, the country comprises a relatively small population spread over a very large area.

Politically, throughout the greater part of the 20th century and up to now, Sweden has championed a welfare regime that promotes principles of universalism administered by an all-powerful state. This is in stark contrast to the UK which operates a targeted and interventionist approach. The Swedish model has involved a redistribution of wealth acquired through high levels of national and local taxation which in turn has promoted a fairly high level of income equality (Ekström and Hjort, 2010). The state has traditionally been the main provider of social services such as education, childcare, care of the elderly and healthcare (Esping Andersen, 1990). However, although Sweden has not been immune to the effects of globalisation, privatisation, consumerism, EU regulations and changes to immigration legislation over recent decades, the state continues to be the main provider of universal services for its citizens: 'Sweden, in comparison to most other countries, can still be characterised as a country with limited income differences in which the state is the main welfare provider' (Ekström and Hjort, 2010: 366).

In order to provide this high service level through redistribution by taxation, there has, since the 1960s in Sweden, been an expectation that all adults, able and willing, should have the opportunity to be in paid employment and contribute to the 'overall good of society'. Within families, it is taken for granted that both parents should work (or study) and there are very favourable universal benefits for parents to support family life with young children. During 2010, approximately 80 per cent of Swedish children had a working mother and 90 per cent a working father (http://www.sweden.se).

Provision for children in Sweden within the education system is divided into four categories:

- the pre-school which covers childcare and education from 1 to 6 years – parents pay towards this cost
- the pre-school class which is for 6-year-olds (voluntary) – free
- compulsory school which covers ages 7–16 – free
- post-16 education which is voluntary but attended by most students – free.

It follows that a high level of parental employment also necessitates a high level of childcare provision. Education and childcare in Sweden are two areas which have been affected by market deregulation in recent times and the compulsory school system, which covers ages 7–16, has been particularly influenced by market forces. However, the Swedish model for provision of care and education for children has been praised within the OECD (2006) and promoted as a role model. The reasons for this include:

- respect for the child – that childhood has a value in itself and not only as a preparation for adult life
- that pre-school is well developed and has stable financing from government
- that fees are low
- that personnel are well-educated compared with the majority of other OECD countries.

These points merit closer examination.

Costs of daycare for children

All pre-school activities are heavily subsidised through taxation, but for children aged 1–6, parents are also expected to contribute towards the cost of this. However, compared with the UK, where childcare costs can very easily represent a higher financial commitment than a mortgage, the costs are very manageable. Costs are means-tested against the family's total taxable income. (Although Sweden is a member of the European Union, it has, like the UK, retained its own currency, the Swedish Krona – SEK. A simple conversion rate would be to think that around 10SEK = £1.)

A current (2012) example of this, translated from Uppsala Local Authority but which would apply to the whole of Sweden, would involve on a monthly basis:

Monthly fees for child 1: 3 per cent of monthly income, but at a maximum of 1260 SEK (£125);

Monthly fees for child 2: 2 per cent of monthly income – but at a maximum of 840 SEK (£85);

Monthly fees for child 3: 1 per cent of monthly income – but at a maximum of 420 SEK (£40);

No charge for any children beyond the third child.

The total maximum cost per month for any family with three or more children would currently be around £250 for full daycare.

(Figures correct for 2011 with reference to http://www.uppsala.se.)

Parental allowances

It is unusual for a child under 1 year to be in full pre-school provision, as allowances paid to parents are also very generous in order to enable them to be at home with their young child. This allowance covers a period of 480 days per child and can be paid out at any time up until the child's eighth birthday. Of this amount, 60 days are reserved for the 'other parent' to encourage the father to make use of this time together with the child. In the case of multiple births, an additional 180 days per additional child is added on to the total. The amount payable is roughly equivalent to 80 per cent of the parent's normal salary. Fathers are also given an additional 10 days in connection with the child's birth, in order to be present at the birth, get to know the new baby and take care of other children in the family.

In addition to this, *either* parent also has the right to stay at home to look after sick children. This is paid as a 'temporary allowance' and can be paid for a maximum of 60 days per year per child under the age of 12; it is paid at the same rate as described above, although special rules apply to periods longer than 60 days (see http://www.forsakringskassan.se).

REFLECTIVE ACTIVITY

Investigate the current situation in your area with respect to similar allowances. Reflect on this.

- Compare, for example, the average costs of full-time childcare for one, two or three children in a family in your area.
- In particular, consider the situation for fathers who stay at home with children. What benefits are they entitled to in relation to the child's birth or other paternity leave?
- What conclusions can you draw?

Respect for the child

In Sweden, there is a highly developed view of the child based on democratic values which gives respect for the child as a person in their own right and a belief in the child's inherent skills and potential. As childhood is regarded as having a value in itself, and the child is viewed as being competent, the pre-school years are of great importance in the child's growing understanding of itself, the opportunities it has and its everyday reality (Skolverket, 2008).

Awareness and understanding of the child's competence encourages children to take part in decision making concerning their own interests from a very early age. This is based on a highly developed level of respect for children's views, supported by the fact that parents are encouraged to negotiate with rather than dominate children's thinking. From a very early age, children are encouraged to use their influence in decision making and participation in more formal situations too, such as separation and divorce.

Another area in relation to the rights of the child, in which Sweden led the way, was in demonstrating that 'society can no longer accept that physical violence is used against children as a means of education or punishment' (Skolverket, 2008: 85) and which resulted in 1979 legislation outlawing any form of corporal punishment in the home. This in turn became a criminal offence in 1982 (Ahlberg et al., 2008). Explicit core values which all staff working with children must subscribe to and promote, include tolerance, equality of rights and respect for truth, justice and human dignity, and it is also the duty of staff to make parents aware of these (Torney-Purta and Schwille, 1986; Skolverket, 2010a).

Childhood has a value in itself and not only as a preparation for adult life

This statement should not come as a surprise to us as it will be very familiar to ECEC students within the UK as a tenet held by early pioneers such as Froebel, Montessori and Steiner (Bruce, 2005). The educational culture of the pre-school has developed over a lengthy period so that there is a general consensus over how children of pre-school age best develop and learn. The revised curriculum (Skolverket, 2010a) documentation stresses the importance of promoting development in children, together with a lifelong love of learning which should be fun.

> The early childhood centre should become a community of learners, where children are encouraged to participate and share with others, and where learning is seen as primarily interactive, experiential and social. Learning to be, learning to learn and learning to live together are each important goals for young children. (OECD, 2006: 221)

Qualifications of staff

There are two distinct groups of qualifications for working with children aged 1–12. (It is a reasonable assumption to make that the vast majority of children are at home with a parent until at least 1 year old, and possibly longer.) These two types are divided between teacher (*lärare*) qualifications and Early Years Practitioner (EYP) or assistant (*fritidspedagog*) qualifications. Yet even within teaching qualifications, there is a further division between those for pre-school and those for compulsory school. The pre-school teacher (*förskollärare*) degree qualification is valid for working with children aged 0–6, but the new compulsory school teaching qualification (*grundlärare*) also allows the teacher to work with children in the pre-school class (voluntary but attended by almost all 6-year-olds) and to teach grades 1–6, which is the equivalent of our primary education.

As of 2011, there have been further changes made to these qualifications. It is now possible for EYPs who have a post-16 qualification (*barnskötare*) within pre-school to upgrade their qualifications to that of pre-school teacher, through part-time study over three years, with a minimum entry requirement of five years' experience in a relevant setting. An incentive here might well be the pay differentials.

The out-of-school care worker (*fritidspedagog*) also takes a similar degree route with some commonalities with teacher education, but the actual role involves working as a classroom assistant during school hours and then as an out-of-school care worker either before or after school. However, compared with the myriad of qualifications and part-time job roles that exist within care and education settings in the UK, the Swedish model does provide some coherence for these professionals within the working day. There are similarly significant pay differentials between the two roles.

From a recent discussion with a head teacher of a primary school in Sweden, it became clear that the out-of-school care worker could also be involved in teaching within the classroom. This was more likely to be around supporting the principles upon which the curriculum is built, and also possibly within expressive arts subjects if the staff member had a particular interest. In other words, the core subjects are likely to be left to the 'qualified teachers' (*grundlärare*).

It is also worth noting at this point that out-of-school care, whether before or after school, is situated in the actual classrooms which are used for teaching children during the day – as opposed to school halls. Halls and other facilities can be used too, appropriate to the needs of the activities on offer. When the expansion to out-of-school care began, during the 1990s, teachers were somewhat bemused at classrooms for 7–10-year-olds (grades 1–3) being refurbished as areas that were more recognisable as kitchens and living rooms, with lots of soft areas for children to relax in. This was in response to the requirement from government that the premises used had to be suitable for the purpose. However, this has contributed significantly to promoting the seamless service which is appreciated by children and parents alike, with few transitions during the day and a continuity of staff between formal school and leisure-time activities. However, well-educated personnel with a high degree of educational competence contribute towards a guarantee of quality, a factor which has been extremely important, particularly during periods of economic cutbacks.

Entitlement to well developed pre-school provision

Apart from making it possible for parents to combine parenthood with work or study, the goal of Swedish ECEC has been, through the provision of educational activities of high quality, to support and stimulate the child's development and learning and contribute to good conditions for growth. In 1996, the responsibility for ECEC shifted from Social Services to Education. The aim in transferring ECEC to the educational sector was to reinforce the close educational links between ECEC, school and school-age childcare. As part of this transition, it was decided that the pre-school class for 6-year-olds should be integrated into school. This was one response to the public debate during the 1990s on reducing the school starting age from 7 to 6 years. Since then, further legislation has produced the introduction of the pre-school class for 6-year-olds as a separate, voluntary school form to encourage co-operation between 1–6 provision and the compulsory school (aged 7–16) with all forms of staffing described above being able to teach there. It is interesting to note, however, that the 'focus' of this class has also changed, as previously it was known as *'lekskolan'* which translates as *'play-school'* and is now *'förskolan'* which translates as *'pre-school'*, a fact which does appear to underpin the shift in emphasis from Social Services to Education.

The dual focus on education and care has been consistently promoted through overarching goals which foster democracy, equality, solidarity and responsibility as stated in the pre-school curriculum. Daycare settings generally operate a family structure which can place children of different age groups together and not, as is often the case in the UK, in 'baby rooms' or other groupings according to age. The thinking here is quite clear: to support children in learning from each other and from older children as they would do at home.

Follow the link below to view the video 'Sweden – Early Years':
http://www.teachersmedia.co.uk/videos/sweden-early-years

Pre-school curriculum (Lpf 98, revised 2010)

The transfer of responsibility for ECEC to Education in 1998 also introduced the first curriculum for pre-school. This is closely linked to the curriculum for compulsory school as both are based on a mutual view of knowledge, development and learning. An underlying motive was also to strengthen the bonds between pre-school and school, through allowing a greater emphasis on the education of very young children in daycare but also in allowing the influence of the successful ways of working with young children in pre-school to permeate the school system.

This thinking is also reflected in the current Curriculum for Excellence 3–18 guidelines in Scotland, which state:

> The aim is to bring the 3–5 and 5–14 curriculum guidelines together to ensure a smooth transition in what children have learned and also in how they learn. This will mean extending the approaches which are used in pre-school into the early years of primary, emphasising the importance of opportunities for children to learn through purposeful, well-planned play. (Scottish Executive, 2007: 1)

The principles upon which the Swedish pre-school curriculum is built and which are shared by the compulsory school system are:

- the importance of democracy as a basis for the national school system
- the development of knowledge and skills
- the promotion of development in all children and a lifelong love of learning
- the encouragement of respect for the intrinsic value of each person as well as for the environment we all share.

The use of the word 'democracy' is quite striking in its impact, but perhaps we should not be surprised, given the Swedish view of the young child as discussed earlier. The document then spells out further principles and values:

- the importance of the pre-school years in setting foundations for the love of lifelong learning, which should be fun, and promoting positive attitudes towards others
- the importance of partnership with the home, developing respect for society and preparation for future active participation in civic life
- the importance of promoting internationalism in a multicultural context
- the importance of adults as role models – adult actions influence children's understanding and respect for rights and obligations that underpin a democratic society
- the role of the adult in looking for development possibilities in children, through involvement with individuals and groups.

What is not stated is how teachers and other staff should promote these values, either through learning experiences or outcomes. There is a large degree of autonomy for staff in how this should be achieved. As a result, the 2011 Swedish pre-school curriculum document is a mere 16 pages long.

How do the above statements compare with the aims of the new Curriculum for Excellence (CfE) 3–18 being introduced in Scotland? This document promotes desirable qualities, known as the 'Four Capacities', stated as:

- successful learners
- confident individuals
- responsible citizens
- effective contributors.

CfE 3–18 justifies the adoption of more active learning approaches in primary school in an effort to counteract more formal approaches that have become prevalent in recent years, and it states:

> Research indicates that developmentally appropriate practice is most conducive to effective learning. For example, it suggests that there is no long-term advantage to children when there is an over-emphasis on systematic teaching before 6 or 7. (Scottish Executive, 2007: 6)

However, the 3–18 Curriculum goes on to *specify* learning experiences and outcomes, even for very young children. The Swedish pre-school curriculum, on the other hand, describes *goals* for children to strive towards. Every child should be given the opportunity to develop:

- openness, respect, solidarity and responsibility
- the disposition to be aware of and understand the situation of others and develop willingness to help others

- the disposition to discover, reflect on and take a stance on a range of ethical standpoints and day-to-day problems
- an understanding that all people are of equal value regardless of social background and regardless of sex, ethnic grouping, religion or other held belief, sexual orientation or disability
- respect for all life and the desire to take care of the immediate environment.

Roles and responsibilities for the pre-school teacher, the staff team and, where appropriate, the child, are also clearly stated. The goals lean heavily towards promoting the social and emotional development of children but do not include specific goals that children should be expected to achieve at different points in time.

The original curriculum document was produced in 1998 and has now been subject to a 10-year review (Skolverket, 2008) which discusses some interesting findings. It states clearly that the original aim had been to move towards a stronger emphasis on children's learning as well as an increased focus on children's development. The context has also to be taken into account as results are likely to take a long time – 10–15 years, to impact on practice – but at this stage some trends have been identified.

The justification for integration of care and education has been supported through the OECD *Starting Strong* (2001) publication, which values the role of the pre-school as the first link in the chain of lifelong learning and suggests that continuation of this integration should then be promoted by government between pre-schools and the compulsory school. The OECD emphasises the importance of a more unified view on learning in pre-school and school and that operations for younger children should be included in a strong and equal partnership with the rest of the educational system.

The OECD (2006) describes two distinct pathways that have developed. French- and English-speaking countries advocate 'preparation for school' and focus on the development of cognitive abilities. In these countries, pedagogical methods and content have grown closer in pre-schools and schools, but at the expense of child-centred, activity-based approaches. In contrast to this, the Nordic countries, in particular, have developed another type of methodology which primarily promotes the development of social and emotional well-being. It reinforces the view of the child as curious, competent and eager to learn, and development of children is followed through carefully assembled documentation which is used by staff as a starting point in joint reflection with regard to the child's learning. The Swedish pre-school has a long tradition of influence from the work of Reggio Emilia (see Chapter 12).

The first type of curriculum model described above, also brings with it an increased value on assessment of children and this was recognised by the Scottish Executive in its approach to the new curriculum guidelines. Where the previous 3–5 documentation had provided examples of learning processes that children should experience, in contrast, the 5–14 curriculum specified particular goals to be attained. Unfortunately, experience has shown that the assessment-driven agenda on the part of school management teams was more likely to permeate downwards to the 3–5 areas rather than the other way around.

However, the Swedish report (Skolverket, 2008) points out that there is increasing evidence of assessment of children taking place now within pre-school as this has taken on importance as preparation for school. The report makes it very clear that this is highly undesirable, quite contrary to the curriculum tradition and in particular is the exact opposite of the 'Swedish good example' as highlighted by the OECD. The trend appears to be that the curriculum is narrowing and is what Jensen, Brostrom and Hansen (2010) refer to as 'the schoolification of daycare'.

This is also supported by the OECD (2006) with regard to a review of the pre-school curriculum in the Nordic countries:

> In the early childhood field, an instrumental and narrow discourse about readiness for school is increasingly heard. Faced by this challenge, it seems particularly important that the early childhood centre should become a community of learners, where children are encouraged to participate and share with others, and where learning is seen as primarily interactive, experiential and social. Learning to be, learning to learn and learning to live together are each important goals for young children. (OECD, 2006: 221)

Play-based methods do not really feature in the early years of the Swedish compulsory school and may initially look very formal when compared with our expectations for primary 5–8-year-olds in Scotland. However, first we have to remember that there is a significant age difference. The Swedish child in 'Early Level' starts school in the August of the calendar year in which he is 7. The debate on an earlier start during the 1990s resulted in children having the right to start school at age 6 if their parents chose to (Skolverket, 2010b). However, the percentage of 6-year-olds in First Grade (åk 1) has steadily decreased over time, perhaps in conjunction with the steady increase in pre-school provision.

At this point, it would be a good idea to look at an average weekly timetable for a pupil in Second Grade in a small country town, who would be 8 years old, the equivalent of Primary 4 in Scotland. The example below would be very typical.

CASE STUDY

Look at the example timetable and use the bullet points to help you understand it.

Some helpful information for interpretation:

- this class is divided into two groups – Red and Green – as noted by R and G
- the total number of pupils could be around 25, although this is likely to be higher from Fourth Grade
- the division for this particular class would be geographical in terms of where the children lived and how this would relate to school transport (buses)

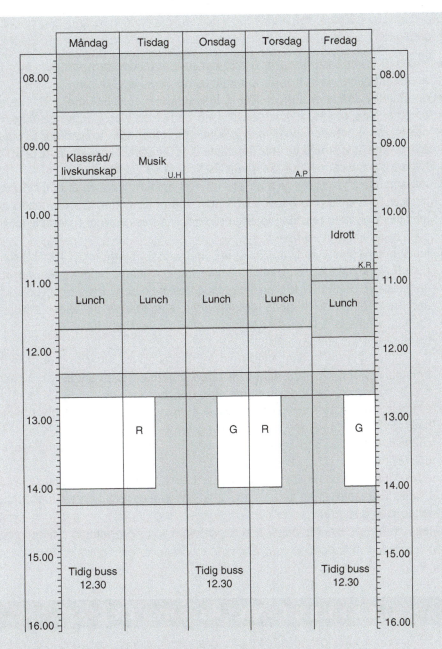

Figure 11.1   An example of a Swedish Year 2 class timetable (8-year-olds)

(Continued)

(Continued)

- this class starts each day at 8.30 am, because of school transport from outlying areas, although many schools in larger towns begin at 8.00am
- on Monday afternoons, the whole class is together until 2.00pm
- on other days, the teacher works with only half of the class (either the red or the green group) between 12.40 and 2.00pm; the other half go home or to out-of-school care. It is stated on this timetable that the early buses leave at 12.30
- two days per week, the children finish school at 12.20pm
- the amount of contact teaching at this level amounts to a total of 17½ hours per week per child. Teachers may do more than this as they work in teams and may be involved in teaching in other classes. The class teacher timetable for this class could look very different
- lunch is served very early at 10.50; in some schools it is from 10.30. This stems from the original Swedish tradition where young children, before there was public transport, often had to walk long distances in country areas to get to school and the break was, until quite recently, often referred to as the 'Breakfast Break'
- the lunch hour is extended on a Friday after PE, so that changing time is not taken out of the child's free time
- it is quite unusual to hear bells rung as classes follow individual patterns for timetabling. Some breaks might be taken together, for example the morning break, but others can be at the discretion of the class teacher who could, for example, ask the children to come back in 20 minutes. Maths in action? Children have to be able to tell the time to know when to return!
- children are outdoors for breaks in all weathers. The notion of 'indoor playtimes' does not exist
- school lunchtimes are staggered across the whole school – as there may be Grades 1–9 represented in the same area. The younger children eat first as their school day is shorter
- teachers always eat with pupils and conversation around mealtimes is encouraged.

REFLECTIVE ACTIVITY

- Find out about the school day and week of an average 8-year-old in your community.
- Compare the similarities and differences.
- Are there aspects of the Swedish curriculum that you like? Why?
- Are there aspects that could possibly be introduced in your setting?
- What aspects would be very difficult to introduce in your setting? Why?

From my experience as a parent of three children who grew up within Swedish state education and also from working there as a teacher over a period of about 20 years, there are other significant differences which are worth discussion. First, each school publishes an annual booklet (*telefonkatalog*) which contains class lists of all pupils, class by class, with their home addresses and telephone numbers. Over a 20-year period, I was never aware of anyone withholding their private details and interestingly some of the parent occupations represented included high court judges and national government ministers. I think that this is a good example of the rights of the child being foremost in facilitating contact amongst classmates.

Contact details of all school staff are also included in this booklet, although from a recent conversation with a head teacher, this year, for the first time, staff home addresses have not been printed. However, personal telephone contact details of staff must still be included as staff must be contactable by parents, or pupils, for at least an hour per week outside of the teaching schedule. The majority of school staff tend to suggest contact time as 'evenings – at home'. Interestingly enough, although this possibility existed, I am certain that I never made use of this facility as a parent and certainly received very few calls from parents either, but everyone is aware that the right exists. One reason for this might be the ease of access to schools and school staff that does exist as a right for parents. It is quite common for parents to turn up in order to spend a whole day in the class with their child, although interest in this does seem to lessen as the child gets older. I found this in stark contrast to locked schools and secure entry systems on my return to Scotland, which presumably came into force after the tragic events of Dunblane in 1996.

Pupils eagerly await the annual issue of the school directory, together with an annual collection of class photographs (*skolkatalog*), where each pupil is named. These two publications comprise the most read 'textbooks' for pupils within the compulsory school and form the basis of many a dinner-table conversation within Swedish families.

The importance of promoting internationalisation within a multi-cultural context

Another area where Sweden has promoted the rights of individual children concerns the promotion of mother-tongue (home language) tuition. At present, almost 20 per cent of children in Grades 1–9 were either born abroad or else have a parent whose first language is not Swedish (Skolverket, 2009). The entitlement to taking part in this tuition is that the child must already be able to use the language in communication with a parent. Local authorities are then obliged to provide teaching in that other language, for around 40–60 minutes per week. Where possible, as was the case where I worked, if there were sufficient numbers of pupils with that language, in this case, English, then it is possible to group the children together and hold vertically grouped sessions. Initially, teaching took place during the child's timetabled hours in school but increasingly this has moved to outside the working timetable and thus become marginalised in practice.

However, the 2009 report states that around 50 per cent of eligible children take part in this tuition, and, surprisingly, the findings of the report have shown that this appears to be highly significant for the children's performance across all areas of the curriculum. Those students who take part in mother-tongue tuition score a higher than average grade rating at age 16, the end of compulsory school, compared with the Swedish population as a whole. The report has not been able to draw any conclusions as to why this is the case and is likely to be the subject of further study.

One possible reason, suggested by the study and supported by language research, is that 'participation in mother tongue tuition generates good knowledge of the mother tongue, which is positive for students' general academic performance, which in turn results in higher grade ratings' (Skolverket, 2009: 49). This may be the case, but I wonder if it is also linked to being able to utilise different areas of the brain (see Chapters 1 and 4) which is likely to produce more flexibility in thinking. It is not so long ago that language researchers viewed bilingual children as being disadvantaged and with a handicap to overcome. The Swedish report also comments on the fact that it does appear to be 'ironic that participation in non-compulsory tuition emerges as having a possible effect that could be of benefit for the school's teaching in general' (Skolverket, 2009: 19).

As parents in Sweden, we valued this provision for our children as although we only ever spoke English at home, we were also aware that as parents, we could never insist that our children undertook any formal language development in English. Home language tuition provides children with the tools and skills to learn about and in the language of their family and can also promote a sense of identity and self-esteem within that culture. By comparison, I feel that provision for immigrant children in the UK could be vastly improved, particularly since language research shows that children can cope with a school language on a superficial level within about two years, though it takes around five years of learning a new language to be able to use it efficiently in an academic manner (Skolverket, 2009).

Conclusion

This chapter has given a background to the universality of ECEC provision in Sweden and stresses the standardised approach, entitlement and affordability of this. In contrast, we have a situation in Scotland, replicated throughout the rest of the UK, where provision is very diverse. We have a wide variety of pre-school provision in the public, private and voluntary sectors. In addition, costs vary enormously between types of provision and there is no standardisation of qualifications for staff working with our youngest children. Although some regulation of the workforce which is encouraging EYPs to study at a higher level, is now taking place, in Scotland at least, this is through the medium of top-down control through the lens of management. In contrast to Sweden, we do not have a uniformity of staff educated in child education and development to support our youngest and most vulnerable members of society.

Perhaps the most striking contrast between the two systems is concerned with the view of the child as a competent individual, capable of decision making in ways which will have a direct impact on his environment. This is well supported by an OECD (2006) report which places Sweden close to the top of the table and the UK very near the bottom in terms of well-being.

It is not possible to adopt a different system wholesale but we can use experience from other countries as a basis for discussion and in ways to influence thinking and motivate change. A fair comment might be that the UK finds itself today in a similar position to the situation that Sweden was in before any reforms of pre-school provision took place. Even within Sweden, these changes did not take place overnight.

Further reading

Swedish children's literature presents a very good view of the child, and, in particular, the well-loved author Astrid Lindgren portrays some very independent Swedish children, both boys and girls. See, for example:

The Best of Pippi Longstocking
Emil in Lönneberga
The Bullerby Children

Or, for information about the social and cultural debates brought about by Astrid Lindgren's writing, see: http://www.astridlindgren.se/en/more-facts/her-role-literary-world/books-which-gave-rise-debate

Useful websites

General information at the official gateway to Sweden – www.sweden.se

'Early Childhood Education and Care Policy in Sweden' – paper produced for a workshop presentation at the international OECD conference 'Lifelong Learning as an Affordable Investment', 6–8 December 2000, Ottawa, Canada. Available at: http://www.oecd.org/dataoecd/2/22/1917636.pdf (accessed 26.07.12).

Skolverket's Child and Recreation Programme – http://www.utbildningsinfo.se/content/1/c4/03/74/The%20Child%20and%20Recreation%20programme.pdf (accessed 26.07.12).

The Swedish Social Insurance Agency – http://www.forsakringskassan.se/irj/go/km/docs/fk_publishing/Dokument/Publikationer/Faktablad/ff_tfp_4089a_tillfallig_foraldrapenning_vid_vard_av_barn.pdf (accessed 23.10.11).

Uppsala (information) – http://www.uppsala.se/

References

Ahlberg, J., Roman, C. and Duncan, S. (2008) 'Actualizing the "democratic family?" Swedish policy rhetoric versus family practices', *Social Policy*, 15(1): 79–100.

Bruce, T. (2005) *Early Childhood Education*, 3rd edition. London: Hodder Arnold.

Ekström, K.M. and Hjort, T. (2010) 'Families navigating the landscape of consumption in the Swedish welfare society', *Journal of Macromarketing*, 30(4): 366.

Esping Andersen, G. (1990) *Three Worlds of Capitalism*. Princeton, NJ: Princeton University Press.

Jensen, A., Brostrom, S. and Hansen, O. (2010) 'Critical perspectives on Danish early education and care: between the technical and the political', *Early Years*, 30(3): 243–54.

Organisation for Economic Co-operation and Development (OECD) (2001) *Starting Strong: Early Childhood Education and Care*. OECD: Paris.

Organisation for Economic Co-operation and Development (OECD) (2006) *Starting Strong II: Early Childhood Education and Care*. OECD: Paris.

Organisation for Economic Co-operation and Development (OECD) (2009) *Starting Strong III: Early Childhood Education and Care*. OECD: Paris.

Scottish Executive (2007) *A Curriculum for Excellence: Building the Curriculum 3–8*. Edinburgh: Scottish Executive.

Skolverket (2008) *Ten Years after the Pre-school Reform: A National Evaluation of the Swedish Pre-school*. Västerås: Edita Västra Aros.

Skolverket (2009) *With Another Mother Tongue: Students in Compulsory School and the Organisation of Teaching and Learning*. Västerås: Edita Västra Aros.

Skolverket (2010a) Läroplan förförskolan Lpfö 98 Reviderad 2010. Available at: http://www.skolverket.se/2.3894/publicerat/2.5006?_xurl_=http%3A%2F%2Fwww4.skolverket.se%3A8080%2Fwtpub%2Fws%2Fskolbok%2Fwpubext%2Ftrycksak%2FRecord%3Fk%3D2442

Skolverket (2010b) *Facts and Figures 2010*. Stockholm: Swedish National Agency for Education.

Torney-Purta, J. and Schwille, J. (1986) 'Civic values learned in school: policy and practice in industrialised nations', *Comparative Education Review*, 30(1): 30–49.

CHAPTER 12

PRACTICE AND PROVISION IN REGGIO EMILIA

Key ideas explored in this chapter

- the provision and practice in Reggio Emilia
- some key elements that have been adapted and adopted elsewhere
- key learning from this approach that might enhance provision and practice.

In many education circles, certainly within Schools of Education across the world, Reggio Emilia has come to be synonymous with 'early years' and is now referred to as 'the Reggio Approach'. It is in fact an area in Northern Italy that most people, if they have heard of it at all, will know for its cheese and wine. However, after the Second World War, parents in this part of Italy, dynamically led by Loris Malaguzzi, started an innovative pre-school system that survives today. This was certainly a response to the ravages of war and the rigid systems that had been imposed by Mussolini. The political context cannot be ignored, as Dahlberg et al. (2007: 12) write (quoting the Mayor of Reggio Emilia in 1960): experience of fascism 'taught them that people who conformed and obeyed were dangerous, and that in building a new society it was imperative to safeguard and communicate that lesson and maintain a vision of children who can think and act for themselves'. The political context can never be ignored and perhaps this is something we can learn or be reminded of through study of the Reggio Emilia pre-schools. We sometimes ignore it and perhaps out of choice as it is challenging. It is hard for those of us who study and practise within the ECEC sector and who are acutely aware of the importance of early learning, for its own sake and for later outcomes, to acknowledge that the main 'driver' for provision is women's role in society, particularly in the labour market (Osgood, 2012). Economic factors certainly drive the expansion of provision. It is interesting and valuable to examine situations, such as those in Reggio Emilia and in Sweden, where this has also impacted on the type and quality of provision.

Loris Malaguzzi, already disenchanted with the public school system, had left his post as a primary school teacher to study psychology in Rome. He was inspired by Vygotsky, Dewey, Piaget and Bruner and built on their thinking about how children learn together in a social context, how capable and competent children are, how important culture and expressive arts are to developing the mind and particularly Dewey's belief in democratic principles that evidently matched his own. The development of these pre-schools arose and has been sustained, as perhaps with all such educational initiatives, by a political movement or 'will'. Initially, this was a reaction to fascism and war, and, as is often the case with matters concerning young children, changes to the lives of women after the war played an important part. Women moving to the city and leaving their homes to work in industry wanted good quality childcare and they came from a rural culture where family was important (Valentine, 1999). It was natural perhaps that the pre-schools set up reflected this. Parental involvement is a key feature.

Other key features of this approach must include:

- participation and collaboration – all parties involved in children's education participate equally and collaborate, including families, children and teachers. There is no hierarchical system for staff so no promoted staff structure but a teacher and an *atelierista* (professional artist also seen as a teacher) to a class of 24 children that stay together for the whole three years
- an image of the child as competent, strong, powerful, full of potential and 'connected' to adults and other children – part of society with 'rights' rather than 'needs'
- an 'emergent curriculum' – meaning that the curriculum is fluid, allowed to be uncertain, without prescribed outcomes, and arises from and follows children's interests
- documentation – children's activities are closely observed, extensively and continually documented and reviewed with the child, teacher and parents

- the environment – parents are considered to be the child's first teacher, then there is the 'teacher' in school, which here means all staff including the *atelierista*, and the environment is seen as the 'third teacher'
- importance placed on the expressive arts – the presence of the full-time *atelierista* attests to this.

What is perhaps most remarkable about the Reggio Approach is that a relatively small initiative has sustained and grown over many years. Some factors that have helped sustain it might include the fact that Jerome Bruner, Howard Gardner, Lillian Katz and others became interested and wrote about it, spreading the word. Loris Malaguzzi, who died unexpectedly in 1994, lived long enough to continue the momentum of the project he began in 1947. His vision of 'a pedagogy that sees learning as a shared relational experience involving child, parents, educators and the local community' (Allen and Whalley, 2010: 134) has been sustained. Carlina Rinaldi has been a remarkable advocate of the approach, writing, travelling and speaking still. However, despite these strong and influential characters, it is important to note that the approach has sustained and importantly continued to develop in Reggio Emilia itself, despite a complete dearth of research evidence to support it. It appears to have been a conscious decision not to engage in longitudinal research to 'prove' the worth of the approach. This is in contrast to the HighScope project which was fundamentally about research and evidencing the benefits of early intervention. Both are powerful and interesting examples within the world of education and particularly early education, but it is sometimes hard to see where either *seriously* influence provision. It is hoped that both have seriously influenced *practice* and it seems that in this respect the Reggio Approach has the 'edge'. It has certainly 'been the catalyst for significant reflection on provision and practice in Early Years settings in England' (Allen and Whalley, 2010: 134). However, beyond the world of ECEC, it is a battle to convince many protagonists (notably politicians) of the value of what they see as expensive childcare provision.

The many visitors are impressed by what they see. People writing and speaking about visits to the Reggio *scuole dell'infanzia* often express how impressed they are by the quality of the work the children produce, as well as by the beautiful environment they find and the sense of community. Attempts have been made to emulate the approach taken, particularly in the USA but also in Sweden where the Reggio Emilia Institute was established to support this, and in New Zealand. This global interest led to the establishment of a private organisation called 'Reggio Children' in 1995. The exhibition 'The Hundred Languages of Children' toured the world and the catalogue of this has been published and drawn on in other publications. However, it is important to reiterate that it is not possible or sensible to attempt to *copy* an approach to education and care such as this. The approach is deeply rooted in the politics and culture of a particular part of the world. It has arisen and been developed against this background and at a particular historical time. Gardner (1993: xvii) wrote: 'It is a mistake to take any approach and assume like a flower you can take it from one soil and put it in another one. That never works. We have to figure out what aspects of that are most important to us and what kind of soil we need to make those aspects grow.' We can explore each of the key features identified and reflect on our own practice to determine what 'kind of soil' we need and whether we can provide it.

Katz, speaking from a wealth of experience and study around the world, identifies the main points we can take from Reggio Emilia. She says (1994: 8) that

[if] we have been right all along:

- all young children have active and lively minds from the start

- the basic dispositions to make sense of experience, investigate it, care about others, relate to them, and adapt to their physical and cultural environment are dispositions within children from the start

- these inborn dispositions can flourish, deepen and strengthen under the right conditions

[then we can learn a lot from the Reggio Approach about what those conditions are].

Parental involvement

The Reggio Emilia pre-schools were started essentially by parents as a reaction to political events, as discussed above, but here the family and social context have remained central to the approach. Rinaldi (2006) writes at length about the changes to society, to the structure of the family and to the role of women and how this has impacted upon children and upon the approach to ECEC provision. She refers to 'our society' as 'fragmented', 'indistinct' and 'segmented' (p. 31). She writes: 'we have to talk about families and no longer the family, because of its increasingly varied and complex make-up' (p. 32), and goes on to list the relevant considerations in understanding the 'complex geography of the family'. Despite the massive changes to family life, for example the fact that women work outside the home and many families consist of one adult and one child, the parent or parents still remain the child's first educator. Rinaldi (2006) talks of parenthood and the role of the educator as a 'state of becoming', and in Reggio Emilia they continue to seek the 'active, direct and explicit participation of parents in the for-mulation of the educational project' (p. 27).

It is interesting to note, however, that in Reggio Emilia parents are *not* encour-aged to become involved in work in the classroom, as this is seen as disruptive to routines and children's learning. It would be a mistake to think that the approach is entirely flexible or non-prescriptive. Some aspects are quite rigid. The mere men-tion of 'disruption to routine' seems at odds with everything we see, read and hear about the Reggio Approach. However, there is certainly a very special relationship with parents and if it is not built around their involvement in the classroom, it is well worth examining how it is established and maintained. Key factors appear to be that:

- it is developed over time, particularly through the same two teachers working with children over three years
- parents receive lots of detailed information about what their child is doing and learning daily
- parents collaborate in documenting children's learning
- parents are involved in the administration, including being on the school council and establishing policy
- parents are involved in the upkeep of buildings, repairs and helping with outings and organising celebrations
- contact begins before the child starts and parents stay with their child for at least a week, gradually withdrawing for a smooth transition
- the school provides adult learning opportunities, such as talks on child health or practical guidance on diet with cookery sessions
- parents are involved in research
- there is plenty of personal contact and interaction.

It has been suggested that to talk of 'home–school links', as we might, just does not do justice to this special relationship, and the child/family/teachers are the school (Valentine, 1999).

REFLECTIVE ACTIVITY

What is parental involvement in your setting?
  Try to answer these questions:

- How do parents first hear about your setting?
- How is contact made with parents and families? How often is it made?
- How do parents/families/the community contribute to the day-to-day life and running of the setting?
- Do parents take the lead in any activities or are they just invited to attend? What is the expectation?
- How do you establish contact with parents/families that do not/cannot attend organised events?
- Do you feel there is a sense of partnership with parents? Is this important?

Participation and collaboration

The Reggio Approach has been described (by those who provide it) as 'a pedagogy of relationships'. Participation and interaction at every level by all parties, including families, children, teachers and the whole community, is seen as centrally important. They have created a 'Charter of Rights' for children and parents that confirms the right to participate and describes the child as 'entrusted to the public institution'. The politics and culture of this part of Italy play an important part. Co-operatives, for example, are a particular feature and these might be agricultural or industrial. There are many squares where people gather and interact, often engaging in lively discussions over conflicting views that are seen as normal and healthy and a means to learn. In other cultures, these might be seen as arguments, unhealthy and in need of repression. In other more chilly climates, people may have less opportunity to meet in this way! Importantly, the welfare of children is still seen as a collective responsibility. This is something that older people today may say we have 'lost' in the UK. It is difficult to say whether this was truly so firmly established across all social classes here as we might like to think.

The lack of hierarchical structure is interesting. There are no principals or head teachers or promoted members of staff. There is a teacher and an *atelierista* for every 24 children. The ratio of 2:12 is slightly higher than in the UK but this is between two members of staff deemed to be equally well qualified – they are, however, differently qualified. Rinaldi (1994: 47) describes staff development as a 'vital and daily aspect of our work', about 'interaction with children and among ourselves', as 'a right' and 'a new concept of didactic freedom … to discuss and challenge ideas, to have an interactive collegial relationship'.

REFLECTIVE ACTIVITY

Do you recognise this model of staff development?

It is unlikely that the hierarchical system of staffing in our education system will change in the near future. This is deeply ingrained in our culture, not just a system in our educational establishments.

If ECEC settings abandoned this hierarchical culture, what do you think would be the impact:

- on staff?
- on the sector?
- on children?

Is this something that could or should be emulated?

The image of the child as 'competent'

Children are imagined as competent, full of potential, curious and imaginative. They are seen as capable of expressing emotions, feelings and ideas, not as empty vessels. Children are seen to be searching for meaning with 'tenacity and effort' from birth (Rinaldi, 2005). This is a positive model not a deficit model. The period of early childhood is seen as valuable in its own right, not as a stepping stone to later childhood or adulthood, not as a preparation for education or working life. Children are not seen as the only learners in the school as teachers and parents are also learning. All are learning together, co-constructing knowledge and understanding and this 'ethos' underpins everything. Our education system and each setting everywhere has an underpinning ethos but it is rarely so explicitly expressed. It seems to me that the approaches we admire and study and write about most often have an explicit ethos that is clearly expressed, reviewed and openly discussed.

REFLECTIVE ACTIVITY

What is your image of the child?
   Take a moment to reflect on this and write down your thoughts. It may help to visualise particular children and particular situations that define and express your image of the child.
   What is the 'ethos' of your setting?
   Take a moment to reflect on this and write down your thoughts. It may help to visualise particular children and particular situations that define and express the ethos of your setting.
   Reflect on how closely your thinking correlates with the Reggio Approach.
   Is your model positive or deficit?
   Is the period of early childhood seen as valuable in itself or as preparation for education and adult working life?
   Who are the learners in your setting – only the children?
   Are your image of the child and your understanding of the ethos of your setting shared with colleagues, children and parents?
   Can you express the ethos of your setting explicitly?
   Is it expressed explicitly?

Bruce (2005) discusses the three 'most typical lenses' through which the child has been and still is viewed and outlines these as:

- **the empiricist lens** derived from the philosophy of John Locke (1632–1704) – where the child is viewed as an empty vessel to be filled up by adults
- **the nativist lens** influenced by the philosopher Jean Jacques Rousseau (1712–1778) – which is quite opposite to the empiricist lens, where the child is seen as pre-programmed to develop in certain ways

- **the interactionist lens** originating from the philosophy of Immanuel Kant (1724–1804) – which takes from each of the first two and where the child is seen to need some 'filling up' or instruction but is already partly pre-programmed. It is the interactions both within the child and with external stimuli that determine what, how and how well the child learns. Here, the adult role is 'a little like having conversations, dancing together or making music together' (Bruce, 2005: 10).

Documentation

Documenting children's learning is an important aspect of the Reggio Approach and entails a continual process of close observations which are then shared and interpreted. The process values multiple perspectives, so necessarily involves the child, parents and teachers. The purpose is to gather evidence every day to inform plans for the next steps in children's learning:

> Documentation offers the teacher a unique opportunity to re-listen, re-see and re-visit ('recognition'), both individually and with others, the events and processes in which she was the co-protagonist, whether directly or indirectly. (Rinaldi, 2006: 58)

Within the Reggio Approach, documentation is seen as a tool for recall and reflection. It is clearly an important part of the 'pedagogy of listening' (Rinaldi, 2006). It is essentially a collected and collated narrative that is then interpreted initially by the person recording it and then shared with others, including the 'subject' (the child), and is open to reinterpretation. It could be the end point of a learning experience but is often the starting point. This approach allows the teacher (or adult) to give value to the meaning the child has made and hence value it. It is a way of listening to children. It gives the child a voice. They are not anonymous. The child is seen and heard.

REFLECTIVE ACTIVITY

Consider 'work' displayed in your setting or in an 'average' classroom. Reflect on the following questions:

- How much of what is displayed is the children's own 'work'?
- What 'learning' does it evidence?
- How many displays show a number of versions of the same thing?
- What is the purpose of these displays?

- How else is children's learning documented and displayed or fed back to them?
- Do children or parents engage with the documentation of their learning?
- How is the child's learning assessed? Are they assessed against a norm? Are they assessed against each other?

It has been suggested by Rinaldi (2006: 57) that documentation 'does not mean a final report, a collection of documents, a portfolio that merely assists with memory, evaluation and archives: it is a procedure that sustains educational action (teaching) in the dialogue with the learning processes of the children'. Teachers need to document the process rather than archiving products. Documentation of the process of learning for individuals or groups of children, as appropriate, can become the focus and starting point for further learning; it can be part of the 'spiral' of learning that Jerome Bruner identified; it can become a 'scaffold' to future learning and be part of a process of 'reciprocal learning'.

The 'third teacher' – the environment

The environment in which children learn in a *scuole dell'infanzia* is designed (many but not all are purpose built) to encourage participation by having a series of linked spaces, rather than separate spaces for certain groups or classes or for particular activities. These spaces work around a central 'piazza' or atelier, just as the town environment centres around squares. The focus is on creating a light, multi-functional space that is open to change. The design allows and encourages children to operate independently, integrating inside and outside and allowing access to resources. They are intended to be multi-sensory and make much use of windows, mirrors, see-through storage containers and white walls. Valentine (1999: 18) writes:

> These schools are not, however, painted in the bright primary colours that many adults misconceive to be favoured by children. Instead there is a pervasive feeling of light and space brought about by the use of light or white walls ... it is the children themselves who contribute colour through their clothing and belongings, their artwork and their sculptures.

This is in stark contrast to the vast majority of pre-school settings that I visit where there is usually an eye-boggling mix of bright, often primary colours; windows plastered with pictures, posters etc. or covered by blinds; a lack of space emphasised and exacerbated by clutter, and children only standing out because they are contrastingly dressed in an often drab school uniform. The environment is something that ECEC practitioners, no matter what hierarchical level they are on, can change. You can see in the pictures (Figures 12.1 and 12.2) the outside environment at the Cowgate nursery in Edinburgh as it began and how it is now. A large outside environment takes time but can still be changed.

Figure 12.1   The Cowgate outdoor space at the start

Figure 12.2   The Cowgate outdoor space now

The Reggio Approach is founded on the belief that children are entitled to a 'rich, complex' environment with a 'wealth of sensory experiences', and this is written into their Charter of Rights. The intention is to create an environment in which children, teachers and parents – everyone – feels at ease. The spaces, both internal and external, are linked together and all are free for all to access and use. Each space has a purpose but is flexible and takes on the 'identity' of the children according to how they choose to use it. Colours are subtle and resources are natural and largely recycled. These are sourced through the ReMida Creative Recycling Centre, a joint project that collects and distributes surplus and recycled materials (Thornton and Brunton, 2009). Thirty years ago under the Inner London Education Authority (ILEA), there was a similar project serving all the schools in London. This was obviously a much larger undertaking, servicing a population of millions and many schools, but nevertheless made good use of recycled and reclaimed paper, polystyrene, fabric, etc. for creative use in schools. This is an approach that might be usefully revived in your area if it does not exist.

REFLECTIVE ACTIVITY

Look at the environment you provide for children in your setting. Look at it critically.

Does each space have a purpose?

Is it fit for purpose – or at least the purpose you and the children have for it?

Does the environment reflect the image of the child and the ethos of your setting as you defined and expressed these earlier?

What can you change?

Target one aspect or part of the environment. This could be the role-play corner or book corner or the area for snacks – any area. Observe how the children use it. Talk to the children about how they would like to change it. Talk to parents about how they would like to change it and how they might contribute – resources, time or ideas. Consider whether this area is multi-sensory and how it might be more so. Make changes and then observe closely again, talk to children again, talk to parents and other members of staff. Document how children use and learn in the area using photos, written observations and transcribed conversations/comments. Share the documentation with children and parents.

Finally, consider the outside environment. Is it easily accessible? Do you consider it as part of the learning environment? Could you make more and better use of the outdoors and perhaps bring the outside in?

CASE STUDY

The following case study shows how two settings within one authority explored the Reggio Approach more fully.

One chapter from Clark et al. (2005) entitled 'Small voices ... powerful messages' by Linda Kinney, tells how two settings within Stirling Council explored methods of consultation in small groups with the children to develop a 'pedagogy of listening'. Stirling Council began in 1996 and determined to have a focus on the people who used its services rather than the mechanics of service delivery. Having already established a Children's Committee, the Council decided, in 1999, to create a new children's service to bring together a wide range of provision for children and families. They recognised that a real change to children's services would require commitment to:

- making the most of people and their skills
- promoting decision making at the most practical level
- encouraging self-evaluation and reflection within a culture of working in partnership and achieving high quality.

Listening to children developed within this context.

Two centres took forward the exploration into consultation with children and two key questions emerged:

- What do we want to ask children?
- How can we ask in a way that is meaningful to children?

To seek answers to these questions, certain methods evolved and were employed, including:

- small group discussions – these operated within the key worker system to develop trust and confidence over time
- survey sheets and photograph boards – these adopted the Reggio Approach to documentation using photos of the community in which the setting was situated, other pictures and symbols that would help children express their views which were then documented (they would then be used to return to events and ideas for recall, review and reflection)
- concrete figures – these might be puppets or play figures used to help children describe events and people, and to project or predict what would happen next.

All of these tools together might be described as ways to support and build a 'narrative'.

This project had a significant impact on staff who had thought they knew children and their interests but were surprised to find that they did not and also how perceptive children were. They found it was important to record what was actually said by children rather than an adult interpretation. There was significant impact on practice as a result, including:

- working to improve observation skills and techniques and use them more
- increased 'intensity' of dialogue between staff and children and more opportunities for professional dialogue and group learning
- feeling compelled to take action as children's voices were being heard.

The impact on children included the following:

- They were more confident in sharing and expressing their views.
- They could listen for longer.
- On entry into P1, teachers complained these children were 'far too assertive' (this led to ongoing debate and a 'transition initiative').

The impact on parents was varied. Many were initially very cautious as they felt this approach did not reflect the 'real world' where children were 'seen and not heard' and need to conform to be successful. In time, many parents became 'proud' of the child's ability to express views and opinions and were amazed at their capabilities.

There was an impact on services and this was challenging as 'Taking action takes courage. Taking action as a result of listening to children means sometimes having to change decisions already made' (Clark et al., 2005: 122). One important area they felt compelled to respond to was the clear message for enhanced outdoor play opportunities. The Council reviewed this and felt they better understood:

- the importance of the environment and the need for this to be inspiring
- the value of children learning about their learning through documentation, making it visible to provide opportunities for debate, discussion and dialogue
- the importance of adult interactions so that adults and children research and learn together
- the notion that adult relationships with children must always be respectful, meaningful, trusting and reflective.

(Continued)

(Continued)

Stirling Council produced 'Children as Partners: A guide to consulting with very young children' in 2001. I think it is fair to say that the huge challenge for Stirling, unlike Reggio Emilia, was in attempting to impact on society through services rather than the wider society setting up services it wants and supports. Linda Kinney sums this up in conclusion saying: 'There are many challenges in working in this way, not least the gap between our professional view of children as rich in potential with rights to be heard, and the wider view of children in our society, which in the main continues to regard adults' rights as paramount' (Clark et al., 2005: 126).

Adopting approaches such as these would require a fundamental shift in the education and training of teachers and ECEC professionals. Rinaldi (2005) quotes Loris Malaguzzi as saying:

> we need a teacher who is sometimes the director, sometimes the set designer, sometimes the curtain and the backdrop, and sometimes the prompter. A teacher who is both sweet and stern, who is the electrician, who dispenses the paints, and who is even the audience – the audience who watches, sometimes claps, sometimes remains silent, full of emotion, who sometimes judges with scepticism, and at other times applauds with enthusiasm. (2005: 27)

All ECEC professionals interacting with young children will need to:

- see themselves as learners
- focus on the process not the product
- perhaps reconsider their image of the child
- listen.

Conclusion

Understanding the Reggio Approach requires and deserves broader and more in-depth study than one chapter allows. However, the critical issues, as with study of any alternative approaches, are around how the ideas, approaches, strategies or theories can be applied in another context or culture. There is clearly much to be learned and some elements that could be more easily adopted or adapted. A key feature of the Reggio Approach that I feel could impact quite easily and quite quickly on any culture or setting is the attitude to and influence of the environment. The physical environment can be changed, even if it is just small changes in your own classroom. Style and use of documentation might be influenced but more slowly. The amount and quality of communication with parents may be more problematic, given that it is so heavily influenced by cultural attitudes, but is important enough to merit further sustained attention.

Further reading

Dahlberg, G., Moss, P. and Pence, A. (2007) 'Constructing early childhood: what do we think it is?', in *Beyond Quality in Early Childhood Education and Care: Languages and Evaluation*, 2nd edition. London: Routledge, pp. 43–52. This is Chapter 3 in the book.

Kinney, L. (2005) 'Small voices … powerful messages', in A. Clark, A. Trine Kjorholt and P. Moss (eds) *Beyond Listening: Children's Perspectives on Early Childhood Services*. Bristol: Policy Press. This is Chapter 7 in the book.

Rinaldi, C. (2005) 'Documentation and assessment: what is the relationship?', in A. Clark, A. Trine Kjorholt and P. Moss (eds) *Beyond Listening: Children's Perspectives on Early Childhood Services*. Bristol: Policy Press. This is Chapter 2 in the book.

Thornton, L. and Brunton, P. (2009) 'The context', 'The environment and resources' and 'Documentation', in *Understanding the Reggio Approach*, 2nd edition. London: David Fulton. These are Chapters 1, 3 and 7 in the book.

Useful websites

To listen to and view a video of 'The Hundred Languages of Children' as 'an illuminated poem', see: http://www.angeliquefelix.com/articles/reggio-children-are-image-builders
An interesting short document entitled 'Documenting stories worth telling' by Emily Holznecht is available at: http://emh.kaiapit.net/DocumentingStoriesWorthTelling.pdf

References

Allen, S. and Whalley, M. (2010) *Supporting Pedagogy and Practice in Early Years Settings*. Exeter: Learning Matters.

Bruce, T. (2005) *Early Childhood Education*, 2nd edition. London: Hodder Arnold.

Clark, A., Trine Kjorholt, A. and Moss, P. (2005) *Beyond Listening: Children's Perspectives on Early Childhood Services*. Bristol: Policy Press.

Dahlberg, G., Moss, P. and Pence, A. (2007) *Beyond Quality in Early Childhood Education and Care: Languages and Evaluation*, 2nd edition. London: Routledge.

Gardner, H. (1993) 'Complementary perspectives on Reggio Emilia', in C. Edwards, L. Gandini and G. Forman (eds) *The Hundred Languages of Children*. Norwood, NJ: Ablex Publishing.

Katz, L. (1994) 'Images from the world', in L. Katz and B. Cesarone (eds) *Reflections on the Reggio Emilia Approach*. Urbana, IL: ERIC/EECE.

Osgood, J. (2012) *Narratives from the Nursery: Negotiating Professional Identities in Early Childhood*. London: Routledge.

Rinaldi, C. (1994) 'Staff development in Reggio Emilia', in L.L. Katz and B. Cesarone (eds) *Reflections on the Reggio Emilia Approach*. Urbana, IL: ERIC/EECE.

Rinaldi, C. (2005) 'Documentation and assessment: what is the relationship?', in A. Clark, A. Trine Kjorholt and P. Moss (eds) *Beyond Listening: Children's Perspectives on Early Childhood Services*. Bristol: Policy Press.

Rinaldi, C. (2006) *In Dialogue with Reggio Emilia: Listening, Researching and Learning*. London: Routledge.

Thornton, L. and Brunton, P. (2009) *Understanding the Reggio Approach*, 2nd edition. London: David Fulton.

Valentine, M. (1999) *The Reggio Emilia Approach to Early Years Education*. Dundee: Scottish Consultative Council on the Curriculum.

CHAPTER 13

PRACTICE AND PROVISION IN NEW ZEALAND – TE WHĀRIKI

Key ideas explored in this chapter

- the provision and practice of Te Whāriki
- some key elements
- key learning from this approach that might enhance provision and practice.

Te Whāriki – a socio-cultural curriculum

Te Whāriki is the Maori name given to the pre-school curriculum in New Zealand, and it means 'the woven mat'; this name embodies an understanding of the importance of family and community, and its influence on initial and long-term development. This metaphor of a Whāriki, a woven mat for all to stand on also describes a spider's web model of curriculum in contrast to a 'step' model (Penn, 2000). The metaphor describes the weaving together of the principles, strands and goals defined within this innovative bicultural early childhood curriculum. It should be understood as 'a tapestry worked in common by many hands that is inclusive of multiple perspectives, cultures, and approaches' (OECD, 2004: 17).

When the draft version of Te Whāriki was published in 1993 as curriculum guidelines, it was a ground-breaking document based on the theories of Vygotsky (1978), developing the idea that:

- children learn what aspects to value in their community through shared relationships
- children's learning and development are based on how they perceive the world around them and so are linked to the culture they grow up in
- children use their acquired knowledge to make sense of the world around them.

Reedy (1993: 17) has described the holistic approach of Te Whāriki and its bicultural paradigm as:

> encouraging the transmission of my cultural values, my language and tikanga, and your cultural values, languages and customs. It validates my belief systems and your belief systems also. (Te Whāriki is a whāriki woven by loving hands that can cross cultures with respect that can weave people and nations together. Te Whāriki is about providing a base that teaches one to respect oneself and ultimately others.)

The holistic ethos of this approach took time to develop, and, as discussed in other chapters in this book, there are constant conflicts between government policy and practice, when introducing new curricula.

Developing the ethos

Te Whāriki is founded on the following aspirations:

> to grow up competent and confident learners and communicators healthy in mind, body and spirit, secure in their sense of belonging and in the knowledge that they make a valued contribution to society. (Ministry of Education, 1996: 9)

The philosophy and theory underpinning the development of this early childhood curriculum must be viewed against the historical and political context in New Zealand. A key factor in determining the status and importance of early education in New Zealand was when in 1986, the administration of childcare was brought within the department of education. To support this change in 1988, an integrated diploma-level early childhood teaching qualification, comparable to a primary teaching qualification, was introduced. New Zealand became the first country in the world to integrate responsibility for all early childhood services within the education system (Moss, 2000), although it took more than 25 years to achieve this. This integration, though initiated by the belief that care and education are inseparable within quality early childhood services, was also in response to the evident inequalities in funding and resources for the early childhood sector (Smith, 2011). Integration or care and education then initiated changes to funding, resources and regulation in the sector and the introduction of a three-year training programme for early childhood teachers. These significant reforms were championed by women over many years and the change of government in 1990 slowed and shifted the focus of change (Smith and May, 2006, cited in Smith, 2011). Again, as in Italy in Reggio Emilia (see Chapter 12) and in Sweden (see Chapter 11), the political landscape of the early years sector is driven by women often conflicting with government agendas around economic growth.

REFLECTIVE ACTIVITY

How well are 'care' and 'education' integrated in your setting or in your authority? Where does the responsibility lie in terms of quality assurance, inspections and qualifications of staff – is it with Social Services or the Education department? Is there a difference in responsibility between age groups of children, for example 0–3 being the responsibility of Social Services and 3+ that of Education? Do you think changing responsibility would effect change for children, families and services, and if so how?

Helen May and Margaret Carr of the University of Waikato, with the Kohango Rea National Trust (for Maori immersion early childhood programmes) submitted a highly original curriculum project and acceptance followed (OECD, 2004) in 1991; both had early education backgrounds and had written various policy documents. In developing this curriculum, the authors consulted closely with all parties, giving full consideration to the Maori perspective and culture. The authors were opposed to a subject or stage-based approach to the curriculum and were conscious that the early childhood sector as a whole was against the imposition by the new government in 1990 of a curriculum focused on academic goals as preparation for school (Smith, 2011). The final curriculum document

> avoids the traditional domains of children's development – physical, intellectual, social and emotional – and instead focuses on a holistic approach of providing a safe and trustworthy environment, meaningful and interesting problems, avoidance of competition and risk of failure, opportunities for collaborative problem-solving and the availability of assistance from teachers. (Smith, 2011: 151)

An outline of the curriculum

Te Whāriki is built around four principles:

1   Empowerment (Whakamana)

The early childhood curriculum empowers the child to learn and grow.

2   Holistic development (Kotahitanga)

The early childhood curriculum reflects the holistic way children learn and grow.

3   Family and community (Whānau Tangata)

The wider world of family and community is an integral part of the early childhood curriculum.

4   Relationships (Ngā Hononga)

Children learn through responsive and reciprocal relationships with people, places and objects.

   These principles are then further developed into learning strands with general goals. The goals are more clearly defined through the identification of learning outcomes encompassing knowledge, skills and attitudes. Some questions for reflection are provided, along with some examples of experience which would help meet the outcomes. These examples are given for three age categories. The curriculum addresses the pre-school period of early childhood in New Zealand and Te Whāriki divides this into:

- infant – birth to 18 months
- toddler – 1–3 years
- young child – 2.5 years to school entry age (in New Zealand this is age 5).

There is acknowledgement of the considerable variation between individuals and settings, the overlap between these age categories and the need for flexibility and choice to ensure needs are met. The statement, 'Children from birth through to eight years of age have developmental needs and capacities that differ from those in any subsequent time of their lives', clearly underpins the entire document (Ministry of Education, 1996). The whole document is available at: http://www.northcotecreche.org.nz/pdf/whariki.pdf (accessed 22.05.12). It is very clear and easy to read.

Table 13.1   Te Whāriki learning strands and goals

Strand 1 Well-being (Mana Atua)	The health and well being of the child are protected.	Goals: Children experience an environment where: • their health is promoted • their emotional well-being is nurtured • they are kept safe from harm.
Strand 2 Belonging (Mana Whenua)	Children and their families feel a sense of belonging.	Goals: Children and their families experience an environment where: • connecting links with family and the wider world are affirmed and extended • they know that they have a place • they feel comfortable with routines, customs and regular events • they know the limits and boundaries of acceptable behaviour.
Strand 3 Contribution (Mana Tangata)	Opportunities for learning are equitable and each child's contribution is valued.	Goals: Children experience an environment where: • there are equitable opportunities for learning, irrespective of gender, ability, age, ethnicity or background • they are affirmed as individuals • they are encouraged to learn with and alongside others.
Stand 4 Communication (Mana Reo)	The language and symbols of their own and other cultures are promoted and protected.	Goals: Children experience an environment where: • they develop non-verbal communication skills for a range of purposes • they develop verbal communication skills for a range of purposes • they experience the stories and symbols of their own and other cultures • they discover and develop different ways to be creative and expressive.
Strand 5 Exploration (Mana Aotūroa)	The child learns through active exploration of the environment.	Goals: Children experience an environment where: • their play is valued as meaningful learning and the importance of spontaneous play is recognised • they gain confidence in and control of their bodies • they learn strategies for active exploration, thinking and reasoning • they develop working theories for making sense of the natural, social, physical and material world.

Source: The Te Whāriki Early Childhood Curriculum, Ministry of Education (1996)

May (2009) discusses how Te Whāriki promotes the idea that children must be supported in developmentally appropriate ways on a continuum of learning and growing, and acknowledges that individual children grow and learn in different ways and at a different pace. The idea of testing at set key points does not align with this approach.

Through Te Whāriki, the New Zealand government has tried to address the issue of social inequity. Unlike Australia, the indigenous population was consulted, allowing differences and diversity to be addressed and giving consideration to the importance of culture. Bronfenbrenner's (1979) model of Russian dolls fitting together can be reproduced in Te Whāriki to represent the significance of the environment and the community in which children live, grow and learn.

Te Whāriki was only one strand of the 10-year strategic plan for early education in New Zealand (Ministry of Education, 2002). There is ongoing research studying the overall effect of this plan, and whether the needs of diverse community and national groups have been fully met. Increased provision and uptake of places for very young children can provide opportunities for early intervention, but, as is so often the case, government focus remains on the economic agenda. During 2007, children were offered 20 hours per week of funded places, for children aged 3–4 years, with the proviso that the centres were teacher led. New Zealand has seen an increase in the number of children attending daycare, particularly for 1-, 2- and 3-year-olds. All-day provision has increased from 42 per cent in 2007 to 63 per cent in 2008, offering parents the ability to return to work and effectively supporting economic growth (Ministry of Education, 2008).

The nature of the curriculum

Te Whāriki has frequently been defined as a socio-culturally informed curriculum for children (Anning et al., 2008; Cowie and Carr, 2004; May, 2002; Rogoff, 1990; Wenger, 1998). It has drawn attention from other countries as it demonstrates the strength and flexibility of establishing curriculum aims and principles based on agreed values, rather than having a specific content which may not equip children for a future we cannot envisage. The guidelines are supported by its inspirational metaphor of the woven mat; the principles and aims of the curriculum are inter-woven with the culture (Ministry of Education, 1996). Unlike the system in the UK, it is not an academically driven policy discourse, taking a much more inclusive and holistic approach. However, the new Curriculum for Excellence in Scotland (Scottish Government, 2009) identifies similar key principles in the four capacities identified:

- confident individuals
- effective contributors
- responsible citizens
- successful learners.

The aim is to develop these four capacities in all children between the ages of 3 and 18 years.

REFLECTIVE ACTIVITY

Compare the *aims* of two curricula, either past or current, in the UK or from another country. Can you identify whether these aims are based on broad, holistic underpinning principles attuned to the culture, or are they narrow, prescriptive and politically defined?

As described above, the authors of Te Whāriki, Helen May and Margaret Carr, 'wove a broad framework of agreed principles and approaches rather than a traditional content or activities curriculum' (OECD, 2004: 17). This socio-cultural approach to curriculum – influenced by psychology and learning theory developed by Piaget, Erikson, Bronfenbrenner, Vygotsky and Bruner (May, 2001) – seeks to nurture learning dispositions, promote bi-culturalism and reflect the realities of young children's lives (OECD, 2004). The focus on nurturing dispositions towards learning distinguishes this curriculum from the traditional concept of a school curriculum that focuses on content. It is clearly acknowledged that each child is a unique individual who will develop and learn at its own rate, often with delays and spurts, whilst still proceeding through universal maturational stages. As children, at all ages, are seen as co-constructors of their own knowledge, and as development is seen as culturally determined, then the richness of their learning experiences will enhance their understanding and knowledge.

The adult role, in terms of management, organisation and practice is clearly defined as:

- the arrangement of the physical environment and equipment
- the scheduling of activities and events
- the setting down of organisational philosophies, policies and procedures
- the nurturing of the inclusion and support of parents and connections with the community
- awareness of the ages of the children, group size and groupings (Ministry of Education, 1996).

There are also directives regarding the management role in ensuring staffing meets requirements and training availability. Perhaps more interesting and pertinent to the development of positive dispositions towards learning or the positive 'mindset' referred to by Dweck (2006), which is the focus of this curriculum, are the roles and responsibilities of adults identified in the key requirements. These include:

- providing resources, challenges and support for the child's widening interests and problem-solving capacities, and particularly for creative expression, symbolism and representation

- providing opportunities for unfamiliar routines, new and self-directed challenges that keep pace with their physical co-ordination and development, co-operative ventures and sustained projects
- encouraging sustained conversations, queries and complex thinking, including concepts of fairness, difference and similarity
- interacting with children to provide opportunities to use language to explore and direct thinking and learning tasks
- recognising the child's developing sense of humour, which springs from new understandings about how things 'ought' to be (adapted from Ministry of Education, 1996).

The last bullet point is perhaps the only one that is a little surprising and unusual. It is however delightful and I suspect an indicator of the cultural context. It is something that we might take from this document to enable us to reflect on our own curriculum and practice. All the requirements that can be translated into adult roles and responsibilities focus on the motivational aspects of learning. They are about the learning dispositions or 'mindset' Te Whāriki seeks to establish. Dispositions are about habits of mind; they are about the behaviour that demonstrates an attitude and they are in turn shaped by and shape social interactions. If we believe that children learn best through social interaction including play, then inevitably encouraging an ongoing positive disposition towards learning will lead to better outcomes. The EYFS (2012) identifies excitement, motivation and interest as dispositions for learning. The Curriculum for Excellence (Scottish Government, 2009) identifies 'successful learners' as one of the four capacities which, whilst not explicitly stated, can be interpreted as a positive disposition towards learning. Te Whāriki is explicit and clear and this is surely one of its strengths. Smith (2011: 15) asserts: 'Te Whāriki seeks to support children's autonomy, exploration, commitment and aspirations.'

Family and community, as one of the four principles, are identified as integral to children's learning and development, and perhaps specifically to the development of learning dispositions. Bronfenbrenner (1979) identified the importance of community as a key determinant in children's development and learning (see Chapter 8). Both Te Whāriki and the Reggio Approach (see Chapter 12) consider the community, and draw upon this to plan and support learning, allowing children to develop at their own pace and allowing them more autonomy over their learning. Both models are admired and studied as good practice and, whilst it is not possible to copy an approach and transport it wholesale, we can learn by comparison and adapt approaches where relevant. In some ways, it might be easier to consider Te Whāriki as there are documented curriculum guidelines to draw on.

Adopting such a holistic approach has implications for practice. ECEC professionals must place more emphasis on the aspects of planning, observation and recording; need to develop close home links to get to know and understand the children's personal interests; work with children and parents to support learning as co-constructors.

The learning environment

In the UK, the influence of a 'traditional curriculum' still prevails, in that we segregate the curriculum into specific identified elements or subjects. This might be areas of development such as social, emotional, physical and cognitive, or subject areas, such as literacy, numeracy, health and well-being, science, etc. Nuttall and Edwards (2007) highlight in their discussion of curriculum frameworks that these 'represent highly localised, contextual responses to time and place, particularly to the dominant discourses of educational provision at the time the frameworks were written' (p. 14).

The OECD (1999) acknowledges the need for comparative studies between curricula documents to be considered and this should remain an aspect for future research. The work of Alvestad and Duncan (2006) compared teachers' perspectives on children's learning between Norway, Sweden and New Zealand in 2002. The study concluded that although their view of learning was articulated in various ways, all teachers in the three countries took a similar view of learning. They believed learning must be meaningful to children and build on prior learning and experiences in the home. They also felt that children's learning in the very early years would lead to a better life situation now and in the future (Alvestad, 2004). The study recognised that with all strategies teachers run the risk of simply repeating and reinforcing their traditional practice. What emerged was that through considering different curricula, a shift occurred in both their thinking and their practice, and they were continuing to search for new ways in their educational work with children. Alvestad, Duncan and Berge (2009) identified that we can often become entrenched in our curriculum and do not reconsider our practice to improve the learning environment.

REFLECTIVE ACTIVITY

If possible, visit another setting where different approaches to learning are evident. Write down your observations and reflections during and after a visit – you might like to begin a 'learning log', 'reflective journal' or 'portfolio' if you have not already done so.

Consider curricula from other countries. Compare and reflect on:

http://www.regjeringen.no/en/dep/kd/Selected-topics/compulsory-education/the-norwegian-education-system.html?id=445118 (the Norwegian curriculum) (accessed 09.05.12)

http://www.sweden.gov.se/sb/d/7172 (the Swedish curriculum) (accessed 09.05.12)

http://www.minedu.govt.nz/ (the New Zealand curriculum) (accessed 09.05.12).

Taking a holistic approach, as in Te Whāriki, may help create an environment where children feel safe to develop at their own pace. They are offered the opportunity to take risks and make mistakes and learn from experience. ECEC professionals become facilitators creating a stimulating environment and allowing child-initiated learning to develop, as opposed to a traditional adult-determined environment and adult-led learning.

Pairman and Terreni (2001) in New Zealand drew from the Reggio Emilia programme, accepting that the environment as the third teacher could be applied in their context. The environment, certainly within a setting, is something we can control and change. We can allow children more control and influence over their environment and use it to create and support learning experiences.

Learning Stories

The OECD (2004) identified two particular challenges for the implementation of Te Whāriki amongst others that the authors, May and Carr, have discussed. These are concerned with resources for early childhood and assessment. Both are common to many other countries. The former is concerned with funding, regulation, accountability and training. Discussion of these aspects may be of interest but not impact on practice. An understanding of assessment, on the other hand, is fundamental for all ECEC professionals. Te Whāriki is not assessed against milestones or standards and because of its emphasis on holistic goals, dispositions or attitudes rather than knowledge or skills, assessment is difficult. It is particularly problematic when aligned with primary school curricula and expectations, or in other words when it is to be used on entry to school and by those who wish to assess children in narrow, summative terms.

Learning Stories is a process of formative assessment designed to provide a 'running record' of children's learning and development. This method has been informed by the research of Black and Wiliam (1998) in studying assessment 'as' and 'for' learning. They found, in particular, that: 'In general, feedback given as rewards or grades increases ego – rather than task-involvement ... Feedback that focuses on what needs to be done can encourage all to believe that they can improve' (Black and colleagues, 2002, cited in Carr and Lee, 2012: 20). The Learning Story provides feedback that is not making a summative judgement. It should be a collaborative task to produce involving the ECEC professional and child, and has the primary aim of discovering 'what the learner knows, understands or can do' (Carr and Lee, 2012: 20). This approach also recognises the value of the teacher as researcher and research as narrative. Carr and Lee (2012) cite research that identifies how story-telling and story-sharing contribute to identity construction and also link storying and reading ability. The format for these Learning Stories has now been developed using digital technology, including photographs and video, and a number of examples can be seen in Carr and Lee (2012).

Assessment when used for learning should motivate and develop children's skills and dispositions. The use of Learning Stories was developed by Carr (2001) in response to the need to develop new tools for assessment 'as' or 'for' learning (Black and Wiliam, 1998). These learning stories capture the children's learning in a story format. The story gives the context of the learning, the contribution of participants and the learning they demonstrate. We gain a sense of how the children feel about themselves, others and their activities. The inclusion of children's voices in Learning Stories illustrates their full inclusion and continued ownership.

Carr (2001) and Carr et al. (2005) identified five steps in the Learning Stories framework:

1   deciding whether valued knowledge lies here or elsewhere, whether there's anything of interest going on
2   deciding whether to get involved or not
3   deciding whether to engage with challenge, and whether to persist when difficulties arise
4   deciding whether to express a point of view, and what form that will take
5   deciding whether to take responsibility in this social setting.

These five areas align to the strands and goals of the curriculum and also relate to dispositions for learning.

Documenting children's learning as Learning Stories could be thought of as recording 'critical incidents' (Tripp, 1993). Documenting these Learning Stories changes the role of the practitioner to action researcher and participant observer.

As Learning Stories are written, key themes can emerge, developing into a learning narrative. These stories allow the practitioner to summarise not only how things are, but how things could be (our sense of the possible), how things are expected to be and how things ought to be (Bruner, 1996).

The Learning Stories are constructed by the practitioners, but are shared with the children and their families. Through the sharing of these stories, connections are developed between the home and school environments. By the sharing of these stories, the identity of each child as a competent learner is valued and respected within the group. Pictures and appropriate language are carefully selected and used. Learning Stories allow us to review learning that has just happened and reflect upon previous learning. Documentation is a key aspect and can include photographs and video as well as hand-written or word-processed stories. This approach can be seen to be following the same direction as the documentation in Reggio Emilia, playing a key role in the learning process and not merely testing or categorising children, nor putting any 'ceiling' on their learning with pre-determined norms or standards. Smith (2011: 151) states: 'This assessment approach orients children and teachers to learning goals involving mastery, persistence and striving towards increased competence, rather than performance goals, which are oriented towards avoiding failure.'

REFLECTIVE ACTIVITY

Observe one context and construct a learning story. Support this story by recording using photographs, video, voice recordings and drawings from the child. The next stage is to ask a range of open questions and, from the response, gauge involvement.

Questions along these lines could be asked to ascertain learning and engagement:

- Why did you build it that way?
- What do you mean when you say ...?
- Can you think of any other ways to ...?

Learning stories allow us to review learning though our interactions with the child.

As one teacher, Karen Ramsey said: 'Everyone waits with bated breath as they hear stories they have heard so many times before, but never lose interest in hearing again' (Karen's story in Carr et al., 2005: 204).

> The first time we introduced the children to their stories being on tapes, it was an exciting time. Once the video was playing and children saw themselves they automatically went and got their files and began to look through them as they watched the footage. The videos sparked children's conversation as they revisited and talked through their learning experiences. I thought this was amazing: children had made very clear links with their files and videotapes. (2005: 204)

Conclusion

We need to reflect upon our practice, consider a range of approaches and draw from them to support the children in our care to meet their needs now. We should also reflect upon what their needs will be in 20 years' time when they are required to contribute to the economic development of their country, ensuring they are equipped with the skills they need to succeed. We do not know what specific knowledge or skills they may need when they reach adulthood, but we can be sure they will need to be able to learn and need to be motivated to learn. They will need what has been described as 'soft skills', which include the ability to socialise, collaborate, empathise, work in a team and remain open to new ideas – in other words, be lifelong learners. Te Whāriki seems to make this explicit and acknowledges that the development of positive dispositions towards learning that can have long-term benefits and produce lifelong learners, happens in the first years of life.

Further reading

Carr, M. and Lee, W. (2012) 'Why story?' and 'Recognising and re-cognising learning continuities', in *Learning Stories: Constructing Learner Identities in Early Education.* London: Sage. These are Chapters 2 and 5 in the book.

Smith, A.B. (2011) 'Relationships with people, places and things – Te Whāriki', in L. Miller and L. Pound (eds) *Theories and Approaches to Learning in the Early Years.* London: Sage. This is Chapter 10 in the book.

Useful websites

Te Whāriki – Early Childhood Curriculum, Ministry of Education. Available at: http://www.northcotecreche.org.nz/pdf/whariki.pdf (accessed 28.07.12).

The Herbison Lecture honours Dame Jean Herbison in recognition of her outstanding contribution to education. A leading New Zealand researcher is chosen each year to present the Herbison Lecture. Many can be downloaded from this site: http://www.nzare.org.nz/awards/herbison_lecture.html (accessed 10.05.12).

An article from Black and Wiliam, entitled 'Inside the black box', can be found at: http://blog.discoveryeducation.com/assessment/files/2009/02/blackbox_article.pdf (accessed 28.07.12).

A paper from Pakai for REACH at Victoria University is available at: http://reach.uvic.ca/PPT/Pakai_paper.pdf (accessed 28.07.12).

References

Alvestad, M. (2004) 'Preschool teachers' understandings of some aspects of educational planning and practice related to the national curricula in Norway', *International Journal of Early Years Education*, 12(2): 83–97.

Alvestad, M. and Duncan, J. (2006) '"The value is enormous – It's priceless I think!" Preschool teachers' understandings of the early childhood curriculum in New Zealand: a comparative perspective', *International Journal of Early Childhood*, 38(1): 31–45.

Alvestad, M., Duncan, J. and Berge, A. (2009) 'New Zealand and ECE teachers' talk about Te Whāriki', *New Zealand Journal of Teachers' Work*, 6(1): 3–19.

Anning, A., Cullen, J. and Fleer, M. (eds) (2008) *Early Education: Society and Culture*, 2nd edition. London: Sage.

Black, P. and Wiliam, D. (1998) 'Assessment and classroom learning', *Assessment in Education*, 5(1): 7–71.

Bronfenbrenner, U. (1979) *The Ecology of Human Development: Experiments by Nature and Design*. London: Harvard University Press.

Bruner, J. (1996) *The Culture of Education*. Cambridge, MA: Harvard University Press.

Carr, M. (2001) *Assessment in Early Childhood Settings: Learning Stories*. London: Paul Chapman Publishing.

Carr, M. and Lee, W. (2012) *Learning Stories: Constructing Learner Identities in Early Education*. London: Sage.

Carr, M., Hatherly, A., Lee, W. and Ramsey, K. (2005) 'Te Whāriki and assessment: a case study of teacher change', in J. Nuttall (ed.) *Weaving 'Te Whāriki': Aotearoa New Zealand's Early Childhood Curriculum Document in Theory and Practice*. Palmerston North: Dunmore Press, pp. 187–214.

Cowie, B. and Carr, M. (2004) 'The consequences of socio-cultural assessment', in A. Anning, J. Cullen and M. Fleer (eds) *Early Education: Society and Culture*, 2nd edition. London: Sage.

Dweck, C. (2006) *Mindset: The New Psychology of Success*. New York: Random House.

EYFS (2012) *Statutory Framework for the Early Years Foundation Stage 2012*. London: Department of Education.

May, H. (2001) *Politics in the Playground*. Wellington: Bridget Williams Books.

May, H. (2002) 'Early childhood care and education in Aotearoa – New Zealand: an overview of history, policy and curriculum', *McGill Journal of Education*, 37(2): 101–12.

May, H. (2009) *Politics in the Playground: The World of Early Childhood in New Zealand,* 2nd edition. Dunedin: Otago University Press.

Ministry of Education (1996) *Te Whāriki He Whaariki Matauranga: Early Education Curriculum*. Wellington: Learning Media.

Ministry of Education (2002) *Pathways to the Future: Nga Huarabi Aratiki – A Ten Year Strategic Plan for Early Childhood Education*. Wellington: Learning Media.

Ministry of Education (2008) *State of Education in New Zealand*. Available at: http://www.educationcounts.govt.nz/__data/assets/pdf_file/0020/41663/890829_MoE_State-of-Education.pdf (accessed 14.11.12).

Moss, P. (2000) *Training and Education of Early Education and Care Staff*. Report prepared for the OECD. London: Thomas Coram Research Unit, Institute of Education, University of London.

Nuttall, J. and Edwards, S. (2007) 'Theory, policy and practice: three contexts for the development of Australasia's early childhood curriculum documents', in L. Keesing-Style and H. Hedges (eds) *Theorising Early Childhood Practice: Emerging Dialogues* (pp. 3–22). Castle Hill, NSW: Pademelon Press.

Organisation for Economic Co-operation and Development (OECD) (1999) *Classifying Educational Programmes: Manual for ISCED-97 Implementation in OECD Countries*. Paris: OECD. Available at: http://www.oecd.org/dataoecd/41/42/1841854.pdf

Organisation for Economic Co-operation and Development (OECD) (2004) *Starting Strong: Curricula and Pedagogies in Early Childhood Education and Care – Five Curriculum Outlines*. Paris: OECD.

Pairman, A. and Terreni, L. (2001) *If the Environment is the Third Teacher What Language Does She Speak?* Early Childhood Education ECE Educate, New Zealand Ministry of Education.

Penn, H. (ed.) (2000) *Early Childhood Services: Theory, Policy and Practice*. Buckingham: OUP.

Reedy, T. (1993) 'I have a dream', Early Childhood Education: National Curriculum Conference, Christchurch.

Rogoff, B. (1990) *Apprenticeships in Thinking*. Oxford: Oxford University Press.

Scottish Government (2009) *Curriculum for Excellence*. Edinburgh: Scottish Executive.

Smith, A.B. (2011) 'Relationships with people, places and things: Te Whāriki', in L. Miller and L. Pound (eds) *Theories and Approaches to Learning in the Early Years*. London: Sage.

Tripp, D.H. (1993) *Critical Incidents in Teaching: Developing Professional Judgement*. New York: Routledge.

Vygotsky, L. (1978) *Mind in Society*. Cambridge, MA: Harvard University Press.

Wenger, E. (1998) *Communities of Practice*. Cambridge: Cambridge University Press.

CHAPTER 14

HIGHSCOPE

| Key ideas explored in this chapter |

- the research project known as HighScope
- some of the key messages and implications of the research
- key learning from this approach that might enhance provision and practice.

Introduction

The Perry Pre-school HighScope Project originated in Ypsilante, Michigan, USA in 1962, and ran until 1967, when the city was the centre for the Ford and GM car industry. At that time, schooling in the USA was racially segregated and this also applied to housing. There was, nationally, a continuing concern with the plight of disadvantaged children (Blackwell, 1994), which had begun in the 1950s. Questions had been raised as to whether the practice of adapting the curriculum for those children was providing the desired effect of 'inoculating children against failure and breaking the cycle of poverty' (p. 123). In the US 1960 census, the city had around 30,000 inhabitants, 30 per cent of whom were African Americans and 27 per cent of whom were living in poverty (Schweinhart et al., 2005).

David Weikart, then head of special education in Ypsilante, was concerned about the low achievement rates of African American students and their drop-out rates from High School. As part of his post-graduate study, he opted to carry out a research project to answer the question: 'Does participation by disadvantaged children in an early education programme improve their intellectual and academic abilities?'

The major influence on this particular research question was the fact that educational 'experts' at the time advised him strongly against this approach (Schweinhart et al., 2005).

The Perry Elementary School was chosen for the study because of its high rates of educational failure of African American children. The school's then principal, Eugene Beatty, was pro-active in educational reform and lent support to the project. The only African American teachers in Ypsilante were employed at this school and in special education services.

Results from the HighScope Perry Pre-school Study are most significant because they identify the short- and long-term socio-economic benefits to society from a high-quality pre-school education programme for young children living below the poverty line. The benefits, for the original group of children, have been shown to *increase* for the participants over a period of more than 40 years.

Project design

Families were selected from low socio-economic status as defined by parental occupations, low achievement in terms of parents' schooling and number of rooms per household. From these households, where children were deemed to be at high risk of school failure, a sample of 123 African American children, aged 3–4, was chosen. Of these, 58 were randomly assigned to a high-quality pre-school programme and 65 to no programme.

This may immediately ring alarm bells today for some as to the ethics of the approach. Were the 65 not assigned to the high-quality programme 'deprived' of the possibility of improving their life chances by not being included in the 'treatment'? However, the non-programme group was given access to the same quality of pre-school provision that was on offer city-wide at the time. It would be untrue to state that they were given no access to pre-school provision.

Value of the research

This was a longitudinal study, in that it was cyclical, regularly revisiting over a period of 40 years the same children and providing a continuous account of their life achievements. This has provided extensive quantitative data upon which to base sound judgements. Heckman (2005), however, offers the criticism that the data collection and reporting has relied too heavily on conventional statistical analysis and that some strong qualitative evidence in support of early intervention may well have been understated. *In other words, the research may be even more significant than the published data allows.*

The above comment relates to the fact that the educational aims of the programme, in line with current US policy at the time, were to raise the educational achievement of children, through inputs designed to improve cognition. This of course resonates with current UK policy in terms of 'raising standards' in education and which ignores development of the equally desirable 'softer' skills such as social skills, perseverance and motivation, which the accountability climate does not measure. (This aspect is discussed in more depth in Chapter 4.)

The collected data is of interest to a wide range of professional groups and the focus of this has shifted over time, as more data has emerged. Data was collected annually between the ages of 3 and 11, and then at ages 14, 15, 19, 27 and 40. Initially, the project data was concerned with cognitive testing and educational achievement, but widened in its scope as the children matured into adults and took their place in society.

Over a period of more than 40 years, the data has been extensively analysed for its impact on:

- intellectual achievement – using standardised IQ testing (the Standford Binet scale, which was the norm for the time)
- school experience – in terms of number of years completed and academic achievement
- lifetime earnings
- crime rates
- divorce – and an increased capacity to form and maintain long-term relationships
- return on investment.

As the participants grew older, the impact of the programme on all-round development and increased social responsibility became increasingly clear, as the programme group significantly out-performed the non-programme group. Repeated cost-benefit analyses have provided justification for investment in this type of pre-school programme in promoting lifetime benefits to children (Schweinhart et al., 2005).

As professionals engaged with young children, we are very often aware of working in an intuitive manner, as, implicitly, we are able to predict and facilitate situations and experiences that we can see will be of benefit to the individual child. However, the

HighScope data is able to present a solid theoretical grounding for this. There is now a growing understanding of how early cognitive development influences later life behaviours, opportunities and experiences (Schweinhart et al., 2005). This is also reinforced by Blackwell (1994) who discusses the unmeasured effects of the programme in terms of participants' overall well-being and satisfaction later in life, and further states that 'all who care for young children have at their hands formative possibilities if they provide high quality day care along the lines of the HighScope curriculum' (p. 24).

What did the programme involve?

Weikart's aim was to expose children in the programme group to a standard type of nursery provision which would foster social and emotional development but which would also have a clear focus on developing cognition in an attempt to prevent school failure. This was through a 'front-loaded' approach as opposed to waiting until problems had been identified at a later stage in school and then providing resources to try to right the problems.

The children attended part-time nursery provision of 2.5 hours per day on five weekday mornings, over a period of two years. The teaching year ran from mid-October until mid-May, so in no way did this model equate with full-time daycare provision. The HighScope curriculum was based on a sound theoretical approach using Piaget's view of the child which was a central focus for early years education during the 1960s. Piaget viewed child cognitive development as the emergence of logical forms of thought that become more effective in helping individuals adapt to the demands of the environment (Blackwell, 1994).

Other typical approaches to pre-school education of the time were based on an interpretation of Froebel or Montessori principles but could often be described as laissez-faire. These could be interpreted as 'child-led' in that activities and contexts were provided in response to the desires and interests of children but where the adult role was very much to stand back and observe what the children decided to do with them. The focus here would be more on children 'having a nice time and learning to socialise with others'. Bruner later challenged this approach by asking what adults could do to progress the learning of the child who repeated the same activity time after time, but did not actually appear to be learning anything from this (Bruner, 1983, cited in Smidt, 2011). However, this was the type of provision most favoured by the middle classes at the time.

The third typical approach of the time was adult-led and highly didactic where routines and activities were prescribed by adults and the children did as they were told. This was a behaviourist approach, with a focus on stimulus and response with rewards. It was an approach likely to have a strong literacy and numeracy focus and be based on a 'content' curriculum. From recent observations in UK pre-school provision, it might appear that the middle class of today would not find fault with this model and it certainly resonates with recent and current national policy.

The 123 children were assigned to one of these three types of pre-school provision, thus providing further data from a project within the main project.

Weikart and his team of teachers decided upon three main principles for the programme:

1   The pre-school curriculum had to be based on a coherent theory of learning and teaching. After a period of experimentation and trial and error, this emerged by the end of the project as Piagetian.
2   The provision had to support each child's capacity to develop individual talents and interests. A similar statement appears in the principles for curriculum design in Scotland (Scottish Executive, 2004: 14): 'The curriculum should respond to individual needs and support particular aptitudes and talents.'
3   Researchers and teachers had to work as partners with an equal balance of theory and practice.

Teachers worked with the children in the mornings and made weekly home visits of around 1.5 hours to each mother and child on weekday afternoons, with the exception of Fridays which were used for team meetings, training and paperwork. This is one of the significant factors contributing to the success of the project and has a very different focus from what we would describe as 'partnership with parents' today. Each teacher carried out one or two family visits per afternoon and would be able to help reinforce the programme principles in a less formal manner. Teachers received training to enable them to perform this task.

CASE STUDY

As a newly qualified teacher, my first teaching post was in an inner-city school in Scotland. I was given responsibility for running a 40/40 part-time nursery class in an area of the city populated by a majority of families living below the poverty line, with high unemployment, high crime rates, low educational attainment, yet most in possession of Alsatians or other large potentially aggressive dogs, as a form of personal security. If the children were playing outdoors towards the end of the nursery session, then the mothers would frequently reach over the railings and haul the child up and over by one arm, to avoid having to walk round to the front door and also to avoid having any verbal contact with school staff. It took me quite a long time to move from a 'critical' approach to these parents to an eventual understanding that the parents themselves viewed school as an alien world, where they had presumably 'failed' earlier in their own lives.

(Continued)

(Continued)

By enlisting support from a very understanding management team, the nursery staff started inviting the mothers into school one afternoon a week, initially to provide free coffee and tea and an opportunity to chat amongst themselves, then, once we had begun to build up a more trusting relationship, we were able to start having discussions with them about their children and education-related matters. For many of these parents, taking that first step across the threshold of the building was a frightening experience.

CASE STUDY

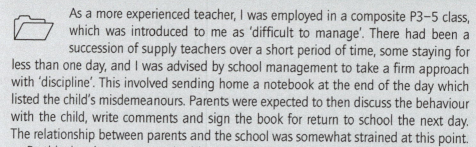 As a more experienced teacher, I was employed in a composite P3–5 class, which was introduced to me as 'difficult to manage'. There had been a succession of supply teachers over a short period of time, some staying for less than one day, and I was advised by school management to take a firm approach with 'discipline'. This involved sending home a notebook at the end of the day which listed the child's misdemeanours. Parents were expected to then discuss the behaviour with the child, write comments and sign the book for return to school the next day. The relationship between parents and the school was somewhat strained at this point.

By this time in my career, I had learned that in order for any meaningful learning and teaching to take place, good working relationships have to be formed between teachers and children and also between teachers and parents. I kept the 'book' but instead of listing the child's faults, I started to list what the child had done well that day. Again, this did not happen overnight, but over a short period of time, behaviour began to improve, support from home for the children began to improve and this in turn impacted in a positive way on the way the parents viewed the school.

REFLECTIVE ACTIVITY

How well are you really acquainted with the home backgrounds of the children in your care? Discuss this with colleagues

Carry out an audit of ways in which you communicate with parents. Consider the following:

How do you go about building up relationships with parents?
How often does this involve listening to what parents are telling you?
How often does this involve you imparting information to parents?

How much information is sent home to parents in printed form?

Can all of your parents read?

Can you think of other, more inclusive ways, of involving parents in their children's education?

Weikart's HighScope curriculum did not magically appear overnight, but evolved gradually through reflection on practice over a period of five years, always with the child's learning as the central focus (Schweinhart et al., 2005). This moved over time from a position of experimentation and not being guided by developmental theory or objectives to an eventual model of early childhood education with a strongly explicit Piagetian base. This views the child as an intentional learner – a view now promoted at an even earlier stage, in babies (Goswami, 2008), and has a clear focus on meeting the needs and interests of the individual.

The curriculum provided by HighScope has a strong emphasis on active learning on the part of the children and over time the focus shifted from measuring the child's attainment to being able to view the child's developmental status and provide a variety of materials from which active learning could arise (Blackwell, 1994). This was described as moving away from a 'deficit model' to an 'asset model' and teachers were aided in this by moving their thinking away from curriculum content to viewing the curriculum as a developmental tool which could provide children with opportunities to exploit their strengths.

This also changed the role of the teacher from leading to allowing the child to lead. This encouraged the child to do the talking and the adult role became very much to listen and respond appropriately. This provided an enhanced teacher–child dialogue. From the child's point of view, this meant that they had to discuss with an adult what they planned to do that day, followed by carrying out the planned activity and then further discussion supported by an adult about how the activity had progressed. This developed into the plan/do/review technique and is a fundamental principle of the HighScope curriculum.

For Weikart, it was also very important that there was consistency in the daily routine. This is easily justified by the fact that young children need predictability and stability in terms of provision. For some children, this might be the opposite of what they experience at home. This type of routine will help to promote the security that young children need. However, the consistency of the routine did also allow for flexibility, in order to support children's interests and to be able to adapt in a spontaneous way.

The layout of the classroom had to be well planned with thought given to the nature of the materials available – a balance of natural and commercial – and storage considered so as to be attractive and accessible to the young child. This helps to promote independence, use of initiative and, importantly, the making of choices. This type of approach is also favoured by Ferre Laevers (see Chapter 15), and is an important aspect of the Reggio Approach (see Chapter 12).

Daily routine

The HighScope typical day would comprise:

- greeting time
- large group time of 10–15 min
- small group time of 15–20 min
- planning time of 10–15 min
- work time of 45–60 min
- tidy-up time of 10 min
- recall time of 10–15 min
- outside time of 30–40 min.

Wiltshire (2012) comments on the importance of viewing these as maximum time periods for the various components listed above. She states that more than 15 minutes of large group time will result in fidgety children and that work time in excess of two hours will lose momentum. Compare this with the long hours that we expect 5-year-olds to be able to cope with in primary schools in the UK, particularly after lunch.

REFLECTIVE ACTIVITY

Carry out an audit within your setting over the period of one week:

- How long are children expected to 'sit still'?
- How long do children spend sitting on the floor in large group times?
- What is the motivation for this? Discuss with colleagues.

The role of the adult is clearly defined within the HighScope programme: to guide and scaffold learning and to engage the child in meaningful conversations at the planning stage. These will encourage the child to be able to articulate their own ideas and make choices and solve problems. All of this contributes to the child developing self-esteem and competence, but key to this is the relationship between the child and the adult. Knowing that your thoughts and opinions are valued and that you are being encouraged is an intrinsically motivating factor in taking control of your learning. Understandably, this is particularly important for children from disadvantaged backgrounds, where adult–child dialogue may be unlikely to promote this.

CASE STUDY

 This conversation between a mother and child, aged about 4, was overheard on a long train journey recently. There was also another child in the family, aged about 18 months.

Child: Mummy, I'm thirsty.
Mum (loudly): There's no more to drink. Sit down!
Child: Shoosh!
Mum: Look at me! Don't talk! Don't shoosh me! You talk too much!
Child: Mummy, when will we be there?
Mum: Come on, baby. Put your shoes on!
Child: Don't call me a baby!

This type of meaningless but ultimately stressful conversation had been continuing over the journey of about two hours. The mother was very apathetic and there were no games, toys, books or crayons for the children to entertain themselves with. All that was provided was food – muffins and sweets. The children's behaviour deteriorated over time and the 'conversation' consisted of comments from the child to which the mother responded with commands. Food was thrown around the table, on the aisle and at other passengers.

Analysing this snippet of conversation, the thought did occur that as the child was not in the least upset by the mother's response, this was very likely a normal state of communication between the mother and her children. Contrast this with the way in which HighScope teachers work with children, carefully supporting discussion and being able to promote higher thinking skills. This must surely contribute to the success of the programme as the children involved may be very used to a similar type of conversation at home as that detailed above.

REFLECTIVE ACTIVITY

Supermarket check-out queues and public transport are all excellent venues for being able to 'eavesdrop' anonymously on child–parent/adult dialogue. Be aware of this next time you are shopping or travelling, taking care not to be obvious or intrusive and later reflect on the interaction and try to analyse the conversation in terms of:

(Continued)

(Continued)

- the child making statements or asking questions
- the adult responding by issuing commands

OR

- the child making statements or asking questions
- the adult responding with language designed to support and extend the child's understanding.

Curriculum content

The adult role for HighScope teachers was to provide activities and experiences to meet the interests and needs of the child, but this was not at random. A range of 'key experiences', 58 of these, would be provided within five curriculum content areas:

- creative representations
- language and literature
- initiative and social relations
- movement and music
- logical reasoning.

Nowhere is the HighScope programme described as a 'preparation for school'. Although 'language and literature' is a clear heading above, activities were provided to promote a 'caught not taught' approach to learning. However, all the available literature does support this as a 'preparation for life'. Compare this with the formal approach to phonics and language 'training' that is prevalent today. What was important was being able to provide experiences and materials to help children 'develop the broad language and logical abilities that form the foundation of future learning' (OECD, 2004: 37).

An analysis of the programme (Wiltshire, 2012) would show that the key principles involve:

- children having active engagement with people, material and ideas
- children planning and carrying out activities of their own choosing and reflecting on them
- children's work being supported by adults who share control with the children.

Neaum and Tallack (2000) describe this as the adult having to be aware of the balance between encouraging, demonstrating and assisting, but not dominating, in order to establish a balance between instruction and children's initiatives so that their interests are reflected.

Staff were also encouraged to use a problem-solving approach to resolving social conflict from an early age, as by the time the children reached adulthood, they would have many of the necessary social skills, understand how to use them and the confidence to use them, gained from many years of practice and support (Wiltshire, 2012).

Qualifications of staff

One other very significant point to bear in mind concerns the staff employed to work with the children in the original project. According to Slaughter-Defoe (2005), not much is known about the personal attitudes and values of the original teachers, who would be concerned with educational attainment rather than future lifetime effects, but that an aim was 'concerned for children to come to appreciate, enjoy and love learning for its own sake, to value education as a vehicle for the development of critical thinking skills and to become the kind of person who is generally respectful and caring of others' well-being' (p. 233).

Weikart used graduate teachers to staff the project and, most importantly, all had to have a Certificate of Education. This is another significant aspect in terms of provision today, where in the UK we seem to be happy to allow our 3–5-year-olds to be supported by young staff with few, if any, academic qualifications. The necessity of the teaching qualification was justified by Schweinhart et al. (2005), as staff needed to be able to understand and support:

- children being intentional learners
- adults being able to introduce ideas whilst knowing that their role is to observe, support and extend learning
- in carefully setting out areas of interest
- by adding complex language and use of an appropriate questioning style, and being able to expand vocabulary
- children in making choices and solving problems
- by promoting an appropriate language model for adult–child and child–child inter-action as thinkers and doers rather than teacher initiating and child responding.

Overall research from the project has shown that children's language performance at age 7 improves as teachers' years of full-time schooling increase. In other words, children's language skills are better if they are taught by a more experienced teacher and yet in the UK we seem intent on removing qualified teachers from pre-school settings.

Cognitive performance improves for children as they spend less time in whole-group activities. This could also inform practice by planning for more individual activities rather than whole-class 'lessons'. Children's cognitive performance at age 7 improves as the number and variety of equipment and materials available to children in pre-school settings increase (Schweinhart et al., 2005). This highlights the longer term or cumulative benefits to the child of rich experiences in pre-school.

The long-term effects

Attitudes to education were significantly enhanced for the HighScope group and this effect continued throughout their school career. This also translated into employment statistics as a significantly higher percentage of the programme group were employed at the age of 27 (especially females) and at 40 (especially males). The same was also true for home ownership.

However, the statistic which has really caught the attention of politicians recently is the fact that the programme had strong evidence of a lifetime effect against being involved in criminal activities, with significantly fewer arrests for violence, property and drug crimes in adolescence, early adulthood and into mid-life, coupled with fewer criminal sentences: 52 per cent of the non-programme group but only 28 per cent of the programme group had served a prison sentence (Schweinhart et al., 2005).

The above has enormous implications for society. Many of the types of crime listed above are associated with a lack of impulse control, instant gratification and a lack of understanding of long-term consequences. It has been argued that the type of pre-school provision provided by the HighScope project with its focus on plan–do–review, and on adult–child dialogue which respects the child's views, provides children with opportunities to strengthen their ability to make decisions, plan intelligently and be aware of the consequences of their actions. It is, however, a very sobering thought that two years of the right kind of pre-school provision can apparently have the effect of dissuading children from a life of crime.

Evidence to reinforce this point comes from the fact that of the non-programme group, where crime rates in adulthood were higher, the group who performed least well in this respect were the children who experienced the didactic, teacher-led approach in pre-school. Blackwell (1994) noted that at age 15, there were twice as many acts of violence from children who attended the direct instructional programme as from the HighScope programme. This trend continued throughout later life.

My analysis of this would be in relation to the train conversation reported earlier. If children are spoken to in commands at home and are directed by adults in school, then this only reinforces what they already know. They are not being given opportunities to develop cognitive ability but grow up becoming reliant on other people to tell them what to do. This is echoed in the apparent shift in policy from 'behaviour management' to 'discipline' evidenced in the language used around encouraging Army personnel to fast-track as primary teachers in the hope that 'discipline' will improve in schools.

Children's behaviour might improve in schools if we provided appropriate activities and experiences for them in which they have a degree of choice and control.

From the point of view of a cost-benefit analysis, Schweinhart et al. (2005) state that the cost-benefit to society over the lifetime of the project represents 88 per cent in crime savings and 93 per cent of the public return due to males because of a reduction in male crime. Put simply, instead of being in prison and serving custodial sentences at an enormous cost to society, a much higher percentage of the programme group were in employment and contributing to society through payment of taxes.

Reasons for success

Allen and Whalley (2010) and Sylva et al. (1999) agree that the long-term success of the project was due to a combination of factors. First, children learn best through active learning processes which allow them to interact and engage with supportive adults, a variety of experiences, materials and events that are meaningful to them. Second, the processes involved should promote autonomy in children and encourage independence in the planning of their activities. The actual activities do not always have to result in a successful product as it is the learning processes which are of central importance and as such can be reflected upon, discussed, revisited and modified over time. These processes promote improved resilience in children, together with improved impulse control and anticipation of the consequences. It would appear that impulse control must be a behavioural trait that can be influenced by pre-school experience and then remain stable until onset for opportunities for criminal activity (Neaum and Tallack, 2000). The above authors state further that close contact between the family and pre-school mutually reinforce pathways for the behavioural complexity in which people's social and anti-social behaviours are embedded.

This type of learning environment reflects the social-constructivist approach to learning as promoted by Vygotsky's zone of proximal development (ZPD) in successfully achieving the balance between letting children discover for themselves and helping guide the course of learning, without being laissez-faire or directive (Wiltshire, 2012). By providing opportunities for sustained shared thinking, children learn to work through quite complex problems, including conflict resolution, employing a number of valuable skills in the process. Plan/do/review provides many opportunities for this type of collaborative approach (OECD, 2004).

Implications for early intervention today

There is much discussion currently amongst politicians of the importance of early intervention programmes and there is much about the HighScope programme which could be found in current high-quality pre-school provision. A pre-school programme that raises education and skill levels may be an important way to raise economic well-being through enhanced employment prospects for individuals. This must surely present compelling motivation for wider public investment in highly effective pre-school provision. There is a danger, however, that politicians might choose to cherry-pick certain aspects of the programme without fully understanding how interdependent all aspects of the programme are, and that cost-cutting or diluting certain aspects would be very likely to affect the desired outcomes. From this point of view, it would be worthwhile to highlight the significant features that are not currently typical of UK pre-school provision.

1   Qualifications of staff: The HighScope programme was staffed by teachers, all of whom held undergraduate degrees and a certificate of education. This is a very different situation from the UK today where teachers qualify to work in primary education but where the graduate specialist in early years education has been constantly eroded and in decline since the 1980s. The quality of personnel had a significant impact on the success of the project. In Scotland, in the interests of 'cost savings', teachers are being removed from pre-school provision whilst the initiative to raise the initial qualification for ECEC professionals has not yet been put in place and is stalling due to lack of funding. Initial Teacher Education in Scotland does not include an opportunity to obtain a specialist qualification in early years education.

2   Staff access to ongoing training and education: Caring is not enough, but must be informed care with staff awareness of child development. Current registration in the UK for childcare staff is through Social Services, not Education and the Standard for Childhood Practice in Scotland has a strong focus on the management aspects of settings. Weikart noted that methods of 'cascading' training in the workplace are often subject to declining quality as the strength of the original becomes diluted, yet this is the current practice in the UK through the provision of vocational qualifications and an environment which promotes 'caring guardianship' of children.

Blackwell (1994: 37) wrote:

> There is little use in young children leaving home for a few hours each day just to join another adult or group. High quality programmes, conducted by competent child development professionals who provide an environment to support learning, are the keys to effective provision.

Now Nutbrown (2012) sets out her vision in the final review report as one where:

* every child is able to experience high-quality care and education, whatever type of home or group setting they attend
* early years staff have a strong professional identity, take pride in their work, and are recognised and valued by parents, other professionals and society as a whole

- high-quality early education and care is led by well-qualified early years practitioners
- the importance of childhood is understood, respected and valued.

The interaction and communication between teachers and parents and the quality of the relationships that were built up, promoted a two-way partnership with information sharing in both directions between the home and the pre-school and encouraged the home to reinforce the learning processes for the child.

Questions have been asked as to why this programme, if so successful, has not been more widely copied in the UK. However, Blackwell (1994) states that in the main, because this was originally an academic research project, the evidence tended to remain within academic circles, and in the UK, in the same way as in the USA, there was the generally held belief at the time that early education could not possibly have this type of long-lasting effect. However, data collection over a sustained period of time has now shown the positive impacts from participation in the programme and the cost benefits to society from its provision. Together, the evidence offers a compelling motive for investment in this type of quality early intervention for at-risk children. The question is perhaps not concerned with whether we can afford to provide this type of support for these children, but whether society can afford not to.

Further reading

Epstein, A.S., Johnson, S. and Lafferty, P. (2011) 'The HighScope approach', in L. Miller and L. Pound (eds) *Theories and Approaches to Learning in the Early Years*. London: Sage.

Useful website

See http://www.highscope.org for all HighScope curriculum, training, research documentation and materials, or contact the HighScope Foundation, 600 North River Street, Ypsilante, MI 48198, USA. Tel: 734-485-200; fax: 734-485-0704.

References

Allen, S. and Whalley, M.E. (2010) *Supporting Pedagogy and Practice*. Exeter: Learning Matters.

Blackwell, F.F. (1994) *Highscope: The First 30 Years*. Hebburn: Highscope UK Publications.

Goswami, U. (2008) *Cognitive Development: The Learning Brain*. Hove: Psychology Press.

Heckman, J.J. (2005) Invited comments in Schweinhart et al. (eds) *Lifetime Effects: The High/Scope Perry Preschool Study Through Age 40*. Ypsilante, USA: HighScope Educational Research Foundation.

Neaum, S. and Tallack, J. (2000) *Good Practice in Implementing the Pre-School Curriculum*. Cheltenham: Nelson Thornes.

Nutbrown, C. (2012) *Foundations for Quality: The Independent Review of Early Education and Childcare Qualifications – Final Report*. London: Department for Education.

Organisation for Economic Co-operation and Development (OECD) (2004) *Starting Strong: Curricula and Pedagogies in Early Childhood Education and Care – Five Curriculum Outlines*. Paris: OECD.

Schweinhart, L.J., Montie, J., Xiang, Z., Barnett, W.S., Belfield, C.R. and Nores, M. (2005) *Lifetime Effects: The High/Scope Perry Preschool Study Through Age 40*. Ypsilante, USA: HighScope Educational Research Foundation.

Scottish Executive (2004) *Curriculum for Excellence*. Edinburgh: Scottish Executive.

Slaughter-Defoe, D.T. (2005) 'Life begins at 40', in L.J. Schweinhart et al. (eds) *Lifetime Effects: The High/Scope Perry Preschool Study Through Age 40*. Ypsilante, USA: HighScope Educational Research Foundation.

Smidt, S. (2011) *Introducing Bruner: A Guide for Practitioners and Students in Early Years Education*. London: Routledge.

Sylva, K., Melhuish, E., Sammons, P. and Siraj-Blatchford, I. (1999) *The Effective Provision of Pre-school Education (EPPE) Project: A Longitudinal Study funded by the DfEE (1997–2003)*. London: University of London, Institute of Education.

Wiltshire, M. (2012) *Understanding the HighScope Approach*. London: Routledge.

CHAPTER 15

AN APPROACH TO EXPERIENTIAL EDUCATION – FERRE LAEVERS

Key ideas explored in this chapter
• quality enhancement of practice through use of Laevers' approach
• supporting emotional well-being in children
• supporting involvement.

Introduction

Dr Ferre Laevers is a professor in Early Childhood Education and works at the University of Leuven in Belgium. In 1976, Professor Laevers embarked on a research project, which would encourage 12 Belgian (Flemish) pre-school teachers to take part in action research and reflect critically upon their own practice in relation to working with young children (OECD, 2004). This was an 'experiential' approach, involving a moment-by-moment description of what it means for a young child to live and take part in an educational environment. The model of experiential education (EXE) gradually emerged as a result of subsequent team analysis and discussion of what they had learned, the problems that had arisen and possible suggestions as to how these problems might be addressed. *The main finding of the project was that too many opportunities to sustain children's development remained unused.*

As a result of the project, an instrument was designed which could be used to measure two key aspects of children's experience – 'well-being' and 'involvement' – and is known as the Leuven Involvement Scale (LIS). Since its initial development, the use of the LIS has become an influential educational model throughout Europe and beyond, and Laevers' analysis of the child and its absorption in learning, where children are able to gain a deep, motivated, intense and long-term learning experience, at the very limit of their capabilities, is acknowledged worldwide (Allen and Whalley, 2010).

Taking an 'in-depth' look at the implications of using the Leuven Involvement Scale (LIS) in practice will, hopefully, allay some criticisms that this might just be yet another 'box to tick' to add to the existing repertoire of assessment methods that are already employed by ECEC professionals. In doing so, we shall consider some of the key features of the approach which support the role of the adult through:

- the 10 action points which can be used following initial observations
- the long-term effects of this type of child monitoring (which cannot be applied overnight)
- adoption of the system being equal to educational reform in itself
- enhancement of observation and reflection skills
- being more than merely an 'instrument' which can be added to an existing 'repertoire' for staff (Laevers et al., undated).

However, the main point in all of this is that we are looking at the educational experience from *the child's point of view.*

Quality

What constitutes 'quality' in childcare and education? According to the OECD (2004), two approaches constitute the norm. The first approach looks at the educational context, infrastructure, equipment and actions of the teacher, which might include the content of activities, teaching methods and teaching style. The second approach is to consider external forms of assessment, such as inspections, which might measure the extent to which 'desirable' goals are being met. We are all familiar with the use of performance indicators which measure these approaches.

The concept of 'quality' may mean very different things to different people. For example, the head teacher or manager may be concerned about improving 'performance' in relation to target-setting policies imposed by local authorities or other external regulators, including parents, usually to obtain better results or outcomes in some area. 'Quality' for parents of children in ECEC might be more related to the flexibility of the provision, homework, the uniform code, the cost and, for some in pre-school, the reputation of the setting in how well it prepares children for school.

One thing over which we can all be in agreement is that quality cannot be 'decreed': 'The design of a coherent framework is one thing – making it work in practice is another' (Rayna and Laevers, 2011: 161). In order to be able to assess situations, which are not equitable from the start, we have to take into account the context, environment and community, including the attitude and influence of parents in the setting, which is supported by Bronfenbrenner's Ecosystems Theory and discussed further in Chapter 8 of this book.

Such measures do not take account of the child's point of view, but this is precisely the central focus of Laevers' work. The LIS uses a quality indicator, expressed at the level of the child, where the approach mirrors 'engagement' and the 'emotional intensity' that define companionable learning; this requires a state of mutual respect between adult and child (Rayna and Laevers, 2011). Experiential education (EXE) can supply the 'missing link' between the two approaches described above and can help practitioners, who are in need of sensible guidelines, but who also realise that their actions need to be effective. This approach allows practitioners to assess the *context* and find out where it is leading (*outcomes*) by having a clear focus on the *processes* involved through observations of two dimensions: the degree of emotional well-being and the level of involvement observed in individual children. Pascal and Bertram (1995), having carried out a large-scale study on 28,000 children, endorsed this method as being able to provide good concepts (of well-being and involvement) for practitioners who wish to improve the quality of their work.

Emotional well-being

Laevers describes the indicators for emotional well-being in children as:

- feeling at ease
- being oneself
- feeling happy
- being able to act spontaneously
- showing vitality
- showing self-confidence.

The presence of these indicators will reveal to what extent the basic needs of children are being met: the physical need for tenderness and affection, for safety and clarity, for social recognition, the need to feel competent, the need for meaning in life and moral value (OECD, 2004).

REFLECTIVE ACTIVITY

This will form the start of a folio of observations designed to help you understand how the LIS scale can aid you in helping children reach their potential. You should choose a child within your setting, where you know that you will have ease of access to carry out a series of observations. By the end of this chapter, you will have a collection of data to support a detailed child study.

Ensure that you obtain any necessary permission from parents and/or the setting.

Observe the child for a period of about 15–20 minutes in any activity.

Make notes under the headings above (as you understand these concepts at present) to look for signs of well-being in the child.

Laevers discusses four domains of social activity in which the child can be observed and levels of well-being analysed:

- children of the same age group
- the adult in the setting
- family members
- the child's play within the class/within the wider school community.

REFLECTIVE ACTIVITY

Over the next few days, find opportunities to observe the same child in relation to the four domains of social activity listed above, using the well-being indicators as in the first activity in this chapter.

If you have contact with family members, it would be a good idea to ask them to carry out some short observations of the child in the home environment too and to share this with you.

These do not need to be lengthy observations.

According to Laevers (2005), the level of well-being in children gives a very good indication of how children are developing emotionally, and good emotional health is a prerequisite for full realisation of the child's potential. However, this does not just depend on what is observed in the immediate setting, but is interdependent with the level of well-being of parents/carers, within the family and the wider community. The adult role in the setting is to adopt a way of being which promotes an equal and reciprocal dialogue in learning between the adult and child. This way of being must demonstrate a deep sense of respect for the needs of the child, combined with acknowledgement of the capability of children to engage in these reciprocal relations. A further explanation of this type of adult–child interaction is described in Chapter 11 of this book.

Some aspects which indicate high levels of well-being that you might have recorded could include:

- openness and receptivity to ideas
- flexibility
- self-confidence
- self-esteem (does not dwell on failures)
- resilience
- the ability to handle life
- the ability to have fun
- the ability to enjoy what happens in the setting
- the ability to handle negative experiences
- assertiveness
- the ability to see self as competent.

REFLECTIVE ACTIVITY

Review the observations of the child, already carried out in the first two activities, in relation to the aspects above. Record any examples that you have observed which could illustrate these points. Make notes and record these in your folio.

You may have thought of other aspects which are not recorded above, but which are equally valid.

You will find from carrying out the above activities that it is possible to get immediate feedback in terms of the child's well-being. If this is deemed low, then as a responsible professional, you would wish to intervene with a clear aim to improve this state. This might involve improving the classroom atmosphere or perhaps being able to reduce the fear of failure or other pressures that the child is experiencing.

Laevers (2005) stresses the importance to the child of the adults in the setting being able to provide continuity, safety and clarity. In relation to this, it is extremely important to think about the background knowledge of the child to which we have access. How well do we know the parents? What sort of judgements do we make on family situations, for example because of our prior knowledge of the family?

CASE STUDY

I judged a child in one of my upper primary classes to be very articulate, bright and imaginative, with a positive outlook in general and to school. This was based on my contact with the child, but also with the parents, who were well educated and held professional posts which demanded responsibility. The family lived in very desirable, detached accommodation in a leafy suburb.

One day, the class was engaged in creative writing about 'A Perfect Day' and I looked forward to reading the ideas recorded. I was astonished to find that this child had written about a day when absolutely nothing 'out of the ordinary' happened. The story basically detailed a straightforward description of what one might expect of a normal day, with the family eating a meal together in the evening and then the child getting ready for and going to bed.

I discussed this unexpected response with other staff in the school and discovered, to my surprise, that, far from demonstrating writing that lacked imagination, this child had in fact projected 'a perfect day'. I was not aware of the home situation, where there was another child with special needs, who, at this point in time, was aged mid-teens, could be aggressive to the point of violence and regularly physically attacked the parents, with conflict situations often arising around mealtimes in the evening.

Reflecting on this, in the light of the new information, I realised that the school was in fact providing a level of continuity that allowed this child to feel safe and respected enough by adults, to be able to share these personal experiences.

Involvement

Involvement within EXE is not limited to particular stages of development or particular types of behaviour (OECD, 2004), but rather this is a 'state of being' that can be experienced by any individual at any age or stage. One of the key characteristics of involvement is concentration, together with strong (intrinsic) motivation, fascination and intensity of functioning. It is likely that the motivation will have been triggered by a strong exploratory drive and is likely to occur in the space known as the zone of proximal development (ZPD) (Smidt, 2009) where the activity matches the capability of the person. This contributes to the desirable state referred to by Laevers (2005) as 'deep-level learning'. This type of intense mental activity, he states, cannot happen without involvement and:

> a quality of human activity, characterised by concentration and persistence, a high level of motivation, intense perceptions and experiencing of meaning, a strong flow of energy,

a high degree of satisfaction, and based on the exploratory drive and basic development of schemes. (Laevers, 1993b: 61)

ECEC professionals are likely to be able to relate to this concept intuitively. We can all visualise the child 'involved' in activities, compared with the one who is wandering aimlessly around the room. Signs of involvement that we might observe include:

- concentration
- energy
- complexity and creativity
- facial expression and composure
- perseverance
- precision
- reaction time
- use of language
- satisfaction.

CASE STUDY

Oliver, 4 years and one month old, attended a nursery (in the voluntary sector) for five morning sessions each week. Staff were a little concerned that he appeared to 'flit' from one context to another. He would, for example, spend only a few minutes in the home corner, move to the writing table for a few more minutes, briefly return to the home corner and then move to the construction toys on the carpet. Staff had very little luck when encouraging him to participate in the adult-led art and craft activity arranged each day, for example making a mother's day card or making dough for bread. One nursery assistant felt it was important for him to make a card and managed to get him to the table but he quickly scribbled on the card, stuck on a flower and rushed off. They were concerned at his apparent lack of concentration and constant physical activity.

On carrying out formal observations over three sessions for 15 or 20 minutes each time, it became clear that Oliver was actually very engrossed in a game each time. On one occasion, this related to getting ready to go on holiday, going and coming back – something he had recently done with his family. His visit to each context was linked and he engaged other children in his game as he went along. One little girl appeared to be getting quite involved for a few minutes until he pushed her onto a chair and said 'Wait there!' and dashed back to the home corner. After a few moments, she gave up 'waiting' and went over to the computer. He however had not forgotten her and a good five minutes later went over to her, gave her some pieces of paper, said something unintelligible and carried on with his imaginary vacation.

REFLECTIVE ACTIVITY

Using the above suggestions for signs of involvement, carry out two short 10–15-minute observations on your chosen child:

1 Observe the child in a self-chosen activity.
2 Observe the child in an activity that has been imposed by an adult.

Compare the signs of involvement for the two activities. What can you learn from this?

It is likely that levels of involvement in children can and will vary, but, in general, the expectation would be that children are more likely to become involved in their learning where they have been able to exercise a certain amount of choice over the activities. For further discussion of this aspect, refer to Chapter 14 on the HighScope project in the USA. Laevers (1994) discovered that although levels of involvement in children can vary, levels of involvement within settings tend to remain relatively stable. He suggests that this is a result of the interaction between the context, including the way that teachers handle groups, and the characteristics of the children. From this, he draws the conclusion that the more competent the adult, the higher the level of involvement is likely to be on the part of the children. This, of course, raises the issue of what constitutes 'competence' in adults.

Applying the Leuven Involvement Scale (LIS)

So far in the observations carried out, you have looked 'in general' for signs of well-being and involvement. The LIS allows you to apply a process whereby you can make more accurate judgements about the depth of these states in children. This uses a 5-point graded scale:

Level 1

Here, there is low or no activity. The child can appear mentally absent. Any action can appear purely repetitive.

Level 2

The child is engaged in an activity but is open to many distractions and will not necessarily return to the activity voluntarily.

Level 3

The child is engaged in an activity but not really involved in it. Energy, enthusiasm and sustained concentration appear to be lacking.

Level 4

Moments of intense mental activity occur and the motivation is there to sustain this even after interruptions or distractions.

Level 5

There is total involvement expressed by concentration and absolute continuous and sustained involvement. Any interruption would be experienced as a frustrating rupture of a smoothly running activity. The child shows concentration, creativity, energy and perseverance.

In order to apply this scale to children's activities, it is necessary for the adult to 'become the child', that is to think oneself into the mind of the child, which is to 'empathise', in order to be able to assess the observed experience.

CASE STUDY

 To help you think about these different levels of involvement, it would be a good idea to consider your own levels of involvement in various activities and rate these against the LIS.

For example, when I have to engage with a writing task for work, initially I would rate myself at around Level 1 and if at home, can find lots of displacement tasks which would prevent me getting started, such as housework. At this point in time, the pressure to write would be an extrinsic one.

Then, I would acknowledge that I 'need to write' and would achieve an in-between stage, such as Level 3, where I am concentrating for some periods of time, but also would have BBC Radio 4 on in the background and be very capable of being distracted by that.

However, at some later point the energy, creativity and 'need' to write takes over and familiar music is switched on, rather than radio talk. This has to be familiar

(Continued)

(Continued)

music as this allows my brain to 'switch off' – unfamiliar music would not allow this state to be achieved. I am then not aware of what else is going on around me, I am totally absorbed in what I am doing, time passes quickly and the motivation to produce something satisfactory is intrinsic, rather than extrinsic. This would represent Level 5.

In the previous case study, 'Oliver' was totally absorbed in his play. Although it was not immediately obvious, he concentrated, was creative and energetic. He persevered to the point of resisting any interruption by adults.

REFLECTIVE ACTIVITY

Reflect on a similar experience from your own life. Break this down into different stages and analyse your perceived levels of involvement with the task.

State of flow

Laevers describes Level 5, the state of total concentration, as a 'state of flow' and based this on the work of Csikszentmihayli (1979) who describes this as where a great deal of mental energy is being used in an efficient way. These activities reflect the level of functioning that the individual has attained and cannot be represented in activities that are either too easy or beyond present capabilities. Signs of this high level of involvement include:

- no distance between the person and the activity
- an openness to relevant stimuli, and perceptual and cognitive functioning have an intensity lacking in other types of activity
- meanings of words and ideas are felt more strongly and deeply
- obvious satisfaction and a stream of energy felt through the body.

Many authors today agree that children are able to experience these qualities when they are engaged in quality play experiences (Bruce and Meggitt, 2002). Csikszentmihayli was interested in why some children did not seem to be able to develop and learn despite being provided with a stimulating environment and sensitive adult support. A study identified evidence to show that disengaged children usually scored low on measures of self-confidence and self-esteem (Basford and Hodgson, 2011). These authors note that levels of concentration and perseverance may well be different when the child is engaged in self-initiated rather than adult-initiated play.

Although it could be argued that the application of such a scale is subjective, it does place responsibility on the role of the adult in being able to make detailed observations to support these judgements. Critics might also say that this type of assessment is 'woolly' but Laevers (2005) argues that deep learning cannot be programmed and that the curriculum needs to be open enough to allow children to follow diverse routes to achieve their potential.

The following observation was part of a student assignment at undergraduate level.

CASE STUDY

Child F is 4 years and 5 months old. He is from The Netherlands and English is an additional language. He planned to do experiments and had drawn a diagram which was presented to the nursery staff. He brought his own science kit, linking home and school. He collected water in a test tube then placed a pipette into the water.

Observation

Child: Look at this! Watch what I can do! Oh, it's not drinking up the water!
Adult: Why not? (open-ended question)
Child: I don't know. (continues to simply place the pipette into the test tube of water)

Question

Adult: So – will the water go up if we sit the pipette in the water? (closed question)
Child: No.
Adult: What else can we do? (open-ended question)

As the pipette was handled, the child observes something happening which appeared to trigger his memory. At the same time, another child, watching, suggests, 'Press it!'

Test

F squeezes the pipette and the water goes up.

Result

Child: If I squeeze, the water will go up.

(Continued)

(Continued)

Analysis

The child approached this experiment confidently but was surprised by the initial result. It was clear that he had a prior knowledge of this experiment, but it also became clear that he needed more time to consolidate his practice. Providing the language to go with the action may also be a means to consolidating the learning further. Bee (2000) reminds us of Vygotsky's theory of ZPD and in particular the importance placed on the language used by the adult to describe or frame the task.

In carrying out observations of children, it is also very important to think through an analysis at the end of each of these, in order to consider what we have learned that might be of use in supporting or extending the child's learning. The role of the adult is extremely important in being able to make the difference between low and high levels of involvement for children. Laevers (2005) suggests that the more experienced adult is likely to be able to provide an environment which encourages autonomy for children, whilst in a sensitive manner can provide stimulating intervention to extend children's learning through, for example:

- suggesting activities for children who are wandering around
- offering materials to fit ongoing activities
- confronting children with thought-provoking questions but which demonstrate an empathic understanding of the basic needs of the child.

The same student, in an analysis of another observation of a different child, but which had involved issues around time and a visit to a forest, states:

As practitioners, it is our job to sustain the interest by making plans together with the children and to fuel the excitement by asking higher level questions. When child E asked when we could go back to the forest for our second attempt [to remove a rock] we planned to go at 11 am. Although I decided to go at 11 am, child E felt more in control because, at that time, he could tell me that it was time to go. [The adult had set a time on a whiteboard clock and Child E was asked to let the adult know when the two clocks matched.]

Having time between his first and second attempt allowed child E to formulate a plan. He used his time in the playground, between attempts, to come up with the idea of the digger in the sand pit as he was using it to dig, and the concept of time was introduced as we used the clock to inform our plan, extending thinking and observation skills further.

REFLECTIVE ACTIVITY

Using the LIS, carry out a short observation on your chosen child and analyse this in terms of well-being and involvement.
  Consider also the adult role, particularly in terms of:

- sensitivity and empathy
- stimulation
- autonomy for the child.

We have now considered the elements of emotional well-being and involvement in relation to one child in your setting. In order to build up a more comprehensive picture of the child, it would be a good idea to carry out further observations at different times of day and in different environments. For example, does the child react in the same way during outdoor activities? Many professionals base their judgements of children on what goes on within the four walls of their own classroom, but never take the opportunity to observe children at:

- break times
- lunchtimes supervised by other staff
- classes being taught by a specialist teacher.

It is also a very good idea to share some of these observations with other staff in your setting and to ask them to carry out some observations too as you may find that they notice different things about the child. It is unlikely that two observations would ever be identical.
  The next step is to think about initiatives that favour these states. We will now turn to the actual classroom environment and how this might support and encourage children to learn. Katz (in Laevers, 1993a) frames some questions:

- Are most of the activities interesting, rather than frivolous or boring?
- Are most of the activities meaningful, rather than trivial or mindless?
- Are most of the activities engaging and absorbing, rather than just amusing, fun, entertaining or exciting?

REFLECTIVE ACTIVITY

Using the questions above, designed by Katz, carry out an honest audit of your setting.
  Review the list that you have drawn up and answer the following questions:

(Continued)

(Continued)

- Which activities on offer would benefit learners?
- Which activities should be timetabled and decided by an adult?
- How much choice do children have?

Having completed the above, discuss your responses with others in your setting. Do some changes need to be made? Is there a way forward that you can agree on?

Laevers and Moons (1997, cited in OECD, 2004) have drawn up 10 action points which will support practice in creating an environment which is stimulating for children yet, at the same time, sensitive to their needs.

The 10 action points

1 Rearrange the classroom to include appealing corners or areas.
2 Check the content of the corners and replace unattractive materials with more appealing ones.
3 Introduce new and unconventional materials and activities.
4 Observe children, discover their interests and find activities that meet these orientations.
5 Support ongoing activities through stimulating impulses and enriching interventions.
6 Widen the possibilities for free initiative and provide support with sound rules and agreements.
7 Explore relations with each of the children and between children and try to improve them.
8 Introduce activities that help children to explore the world of behaviour, feelings and values.
9 Identify children with emotional problems and work out sustaining interventions.
10 Identify children with developmental needs and work out interventions that engender involvement within the problem area.

It can be clearly seen that action points 1–6 are mainly concerned with the environment, resources and matching activities to the perceived needs and interests of children. Action points 7 and 8 are more concerned with the field of human relations and how to support the emotional and social well-being of children. This, for me, is the crucial difference between the self-evaluation which is so prevalent in settings and Laevers' ideas which give credence to his claims for quality provision. Points 7 and 8 relate closely to the type of quality provision which is advocated by the HighScope approach (see Chapter 14) and facilitates the type of early intervention which we now know can have long-lasting, positive effects on children's development and learning, through a social-constructivist approach. Points 9 and 10 relate to provision for children with special needs.

REFLECTIVE ACTIVITY

You will have by now a substantial amount of data from your child observations.

Reflect now on the above action points and, in discussion with colleagues, draw up an action plan that will work towards meeting the child's needs or interests.

Use of the LIS, together with the 10 action points, provides an effective complement to other forms of external assessment and evaluation of provision. Together, they provide a holistic approach where the needs and interests of the child are placed firmly at the centre.

Processes to outcomes

EXE provides clear evidence to distinguish and explain the difference between superficial and deep-level learning for children and ways in which the adult can support this. Laevers (1993b: 56) argued that: 'Education can only be effective if it engenders changes at the level of fundamental schemas and goes beyond learning of specific information, skills or tricks.'

I find this statement very relevant today as the media is constantly reminding us that graduates and school leavers are not necessarily employable – for exactly those reasons. Even within universities, we are being asked to list 'graduate attributes' that apply to our taught courses – that is, the transferable skills or outcomes which they might acquire through study, in order to justify our stance. The UK has been good at providing content-based learning, with a measurable output, but perhaps at the expense of the emotional health and well-being of its children. The challenge for education today is, having provided quality and motivational experiences for children in the early years, being able to maintain this throughout compulsory education. This type of adult–child dialogue reciprocity should continue in a way that would allow the quality of intrinsic motivation to flourish. However, some areas of the UK show signs of taking this into consideration. The Curriculum for Excellence in Scotland (Scottish Government, 2004: 10) contains the statement: 'the curriculum should give opportunities for children to make appropriate choices to meet their individual interests and needs, while ensuring that these choices lead to successful outcomes'.

Perhaps this constitutes a start along the road to what Laevers (2005) describes as an open framework curriculum. If deep-level learning is our ultimate goal for children, then we have to realise that it cannot be programmed and that children follow a wide variety of routes along its path. Rather than continually looking at the end 'product' through testing and assessing children, we have the opportunity to develop a detailed child monitoring system which can allow children to perform at the limits of their capabilities.

The role of continuing professional development

Working with the LIS makes demands of professionals and requires a mindset which is open to reflection on experience. EXE relies greatly on the adult's style and also on personal interactions between the adult and child (OECD, 2004). However, this takes time to develop and will not happen as the result of a one-day training event. Using this approach requires the highest competence in adults, to ensure that children are learning. Rather than children being programmed by adults, the relationship is mutual: the child acts, the adult responds and this response, from the more knowledgeable 'other', shapes the next action of the child.

> It starts with standing close to children, sympathising with them, active listening and observation in order to understand how the environment is perceived by and impacts on children. It means asking oneself constantly how the organisation of the day, the materials and activities on offer, stimulating impulses and sensitive responses, can raise the quality of the life of the child and support its development. At the same time the adult engages in a shared learning experience, the exploration of the world and in wonder. (Laevers, 2005: 22)

Conclusion

Experiential education strives to promote the development of (future) adults who are self-confident, curious and able to explore and investigate, able to be creative and use their imagination. However, if a narrow curriculum is imposed by government with a focus on testing 'knowledge', then it is unlikely that we will be educating future adults to be able to cope with life and employment in the 21st century.

 ## Further reading

Laevers, F. (2005) 'The curriculum as a means to raise the quality of early childhood education: implications for policy', *European Early Childhood Education Research Journal*, 13(1): 17–29.
Ferre Laevers gave a keynote speech at the Scottish Learning Festival in Glasgow in 2009. It can be accessed at: http://www.educationscotland.gov.uk/video/f/video4565868.asp

References

Allen, S.F. and Whalley, M.E. (2010) *Supporting Pedagogy and Practice in Early Years Settings.* Exeter: Learning Matters.

Basford, J. and Hodgson, E. (eds) (2011) *Successful Placements in Early Years Settings.* Exeter: Learning Matters.

Bee, H. (2000) *The Developing Child*, 9th edition. New York: Allyn and Bacon.

Bruce, T. and Meggitt, C. (2002) *Child Care and Education.* London: Hodder and Stoughton.

Csikszentmihayli, M. (1979) 'The concept of flow', in B. Sutton-Smith (ed.) *Play and Learning* (pp. 257–73). New York: Gardner.

Laevers, F. (1993a) *The Project Experiential Education: Concepts and Experiences at the Level of Context, Process and Outcome.* Leuven: Leuven University Press.

Laevers, F. (1993b) 'Deep level learning: an exemplary application on the area of physical knowledge', *European Early Childhood Research Journal*, 1(1): 53–68.

Laevers, F. (ed.) (1994) *Defining and Assessing Quality in Early Childhood Education: Studia Pedagogica.* Leuven: Leuven University Press.

Laevers, F. (2005) *Deep Level Learning and the Experiential Approach in Early Childhood and Primary Education: Experiential Education.* Leuven: Katholieke Universiteit, Belgium.

Laevers, F., Vandenbussche, E., Kog, M. and Depondt, L. (undated) A process-oriented child monitoring system for young children, Experiential Education Series no. 2. Leuven: Centre for Experiential Education.

Organisation for Economic Co-operation and Development (OECD) (2004) *Starting Strong: Curricula and Pedagogies in Early Childhood Education and Care – Five Curriculum Outlines.* Paris: OECD.

Pascal, E. and Bertram, T. (1995) '"Involvement" and the Effective Early Learning Project: a collaborative venture', in F. Laevers (ed.) *An Exploration of the Concept of 'Involvement' as an Indicator of the Quality of Early Childhood Care and Education.* Dundee: CIDREE Report, Vol. 10, pp. 25–38.

Rayna, S. and Laevers, F. (2011) 'Understanding children from 0 to 3 years of age and its implications for education: What's new on the babies' side? Origins and evolutions', *European Early Childhood Education Research Journal*, 19(2): 161–72.

Scottish Government (2004) *Curriculum for Excellence.* Edinburgh: Scottish Executive.

Smidt, S. (2009) *Introducing Vygotsky: A Guide for Students and Practitioners in Early Years Education.* London: Routledge.

PART 4

THE DEVELOPING PROFESSIONAL

Introduction

This final part draws on many of the ideas explored in preceding chapters to discuss professionalism and continuing professional development (CPD) in the ECEC sector. Exploring and discussing the purpose of early education, the role of the ECEC professional and the nature of curriculum in early education has been an underlying theme throughout the book. In order to consider professionalism, purposes and the nature of curriculum, it is useful and indeed perhaps vital to first consider the specific body of knowledge that is peculiar to early childhood education and care.

In this last part, we will explore and discuss:

- concepts of professionalism in ECEC and the specific professional body of knowledge that might pertain to ECEC
- inter-professional practice and why it is an important aspect of the role of an ECEC professional
- how and why a practitioner can and should become involved in research
- teamwork within an ECEC setting
- issues around professional autonomy.

Chapter 16, 'Concepts and status of early years' professionalism', draws on research, particularly from Sweden, England and Scotland to explore and develop this complex debate. Part of the process of building our own personal as well as the public concept of ECEC professionalism revolves around the professional *status* of those involved in the care and education of very young children. The chapter looks at changes and proposed changes to training, qualifications and working conditions that may impact on personal and public concepts of professionalism, status and the impact on provision for children. A discussion is developed from a starting point of considering what professionalism is, through recent initiatives and drives to raise qualifications within the sector and changes to legislation to consider, 'What is the discrete and specific body of knowledge to which this group of professionals can/should lay claim?' The chapter concludes by considering the value ECEC professionals attribute to their work and therefore themselves, and argues the case for the 0–3 age range to come fully under the remit of 'education' rather than 'care', again drawing on comparisons with other EU countries.

Chapter 17, 'Inter-professional practice', considers what this really means, whether it does happen, how to make it happen and why we should be exploring different models and barriers to this way of working. There is a description of collaborative 'joint training' exercises. This includes an online activity with Robert Gordon University involving students across the different disciplines of Health, Social Work and Education. It is argued that policy documents such as Every Child Matters (ECM) and Getting it Right for Every Child (GIRFEC), as well as other 'drivers' towards inter-professionalism, are linked to the 'reconceptualisation' of a professional that accords with reflective practice and moves away from traditional constructs. This links to the other chapters in this part. In highlighting some of the many barriers to effective inter-professional working, some suggestions are made to overcome these by looking at interpersonal skills. This again links very specifically to Chapter 19, 'Working in a team'.

Chapter 18, 'The practising professional as researcher', seeks to clarify, first, what research is, and then goes on to discuss the role of the professional as researcher. It proposes that practitioner or 'action research' arises quite naturally from good reflective practice and takes the reader through the stages of beginning a research study. Key terms and aspects are defined and clarified, such as the difference between 'qualitative' and 'quantitative' research, 'methods' and 'methodology', but it is not intended as a comprehensive guide to carrying out research.

Chapter 19, 'Working in a team', examines what constitutes a 'team' in an ECEC setting which might include schools, private nurseries, children's/family centres or playgroups. The importance of good teamwork and what this means is established and theories of team building and leadership are explored. Through case studies, some examples are provided for exploration and to enable students to clarify their own understanding of teamwork, leadership and management roles. The definitions of 'leader' and 'manager' are examined so that the reader can reflect on and clarify their own understanding. Perhaps most importantly, the exploration of interpersonal skills mentioned in Chapter 17, with regard to inter-professional practice, is extended, and communication skills such as active listening and assertiveness are looked at in more detail.

Chapter 20, 'The issue of professional autonomy', examines whether it is being eroded by policy. It highlights the importance of professionals engaging with research and in debate about curriculum content, provision, practice and policy as a move towards greater autonomy. It discusses recent initiatives and developments in curriculum and other policy, and returns to the issue of an increasingly risk-averse society to explore the impact on professional autonomy. It draws together threads and emphases from Part 4, including:

- how and why concepts of professionalism have changed in recent years and the impact on status and the development of inter-disciplinary practice
- how professionals should respond to political pressures (including economic) and work around them – considering always what is in the best interests of children
- the suggestion that as professionals we have a duty to challenge compliance.

This last chapter also draws together some of the threads of the preceding discussion to explore this issue against:

- active and creative approaches to learning and teaching
- the socio-cultural context in which we work with children
- a comparison with other educational approaches
- present and changing concepts of professionalism
- inter-disciplinary practice
- the practitioner as researcher.

CHAPTER 16

CONCEPTS AND STATUS OF EARLY YEARS' PROFESSIONALISM

Key ideas explored in this chapter

- changes and proposed changes to the concept and status of the early years workforce
- what constitutes a professional body of knowledge
- the case for education and care coming together under education.

Professionalism

At the start of this chapter, it may be useful to take a few moments to consider what we mean by 'professionalism' for the ECEC workforce. Within the UK, although we do not like to admit to a distinction between 'care' and 'education', this division has been promoted historically and organisationally. Education authorities, as part of non-statutory provision, take responsibility for some 3–5 provision, but over recent decades a growing percentage of provision is regulated by Social Services and very much comes under the banner of 'care'.

An issue within the UK for ECEC workers is the multitude of job titles (Adams, 2008). This is partly historical as changes can be tracked showing a move from the concept of care of young children as being very much women's work. Forty years ago, the care of 0–3-year-olds was undertaken by mothers or 'nannies'. It was not professional and did not require academic skill or specific knowledge but only maternal qualities such as being kind and rather jolly. Job titles are moving towards Early Years Practitioner or Professional but the sector is still encumbered with a plethora of titles such as nursery nurse, nursery manager, nursery assistant, play worker, play leader, etc. Many, including those working in the sector, are confused about the level of qualification and the role of each.

REFLECTIVE ACTIVITY

Who do you consider to be a 'professional'?

From the following list of personnel involved in the care and education of young children, tick all those to whom you would attach the term 'professional'. Reflect on your list and discuss it with others.

Personnel	Professional	Not professional
Nursery teacher		
Class teacher P1–P3		
Head teacher		
Nursery nurse		
Nursery assistant		
Learning support assistant		
School nurse		
Family therapist		
Child psychologist		
Health visitor		
Childminder		
Play leader		
Playground supervisor		
Classroom assistant		
Nursery manager		

We would suggest that there might not appear to be a shared 'concept of professionalism' either within the workforce or within wider society. Qualifications for early years' practitioners are varied. Many teachers, across Scotland and the rest of the UK, working with children at the Early and First Level (ages 3–9) are doing so at the behest of head teachers, or for logistical reasons, and do not have any special qualifications or experience as these are not a requirement. Neither specialism in working with children aged 3–9, nor study and experience in working with 0–3s, is part of Initial Teacher Education (ITE) or a requirement to meet the Standard for Full Registration in Scotland. There has been little opportunity since the 1980s for specialism in early education in Scotland, either in ITE or as part of continuing professional development.

The greater part of teacher education in Scotland is still through undergraduate Bachelor of Education programmes which qualify teachers to teach from Nursery (3–5) through to P7 (rising 12), essentially ages 3–11, with no specific focus or specialisation. There are also full-time or part-time post-graduate routes through Postgraduate Diploma in Education (PGDE) provision. None of these routes offers a focus or specialisation in early years. Typically, a primary teaching qualification in England allows for a greater degree of specialisation. However, initiatives to raise the qualifications of ECEC professionals in England and Scotland have been instigated and have evolved against very much the same background. There are some important historical differences around ITE and qualifications for ECEC but the drivers towards greater professionalism, higher qualifications and specialisation come from the findings of the same sources, such as the Effective Provision of Preschool Education study and the Millennium Cohort Study and the subsequent reports (Sylva et al., 2004; DfES, 2007), and from findings of the OECD in their 'Starting Strong' reports (2001, 2006, 2009). Both Scotland and England are also influenced by EU strategies such as the Bologna Process and the European Qualifications Framework (Lund, 2008).

REFLECTIVE ACTIVITY

Which of the following definitions of 'professional' most closely correlate with your own?

a How you look, talk, write, act and work determines whether you are a professional or an amateur.
b Professionals are seen to base their practice on a body of technical or specialist knowledge that is beyond the reach of lay people.
c Professionals, through specialist and usually long periods of training, are taught to understand (this) research validated knowledge and apply it constructively and intelligently according to the technical rules governing the conduct of the profession.

(Continued)

(Continued)

d Professionals make judgements on behalf of their clients in uncertain and complex situations.

e Professionals commit to a set of principles that govern their practice and maintain a defined standard of practice.

f A professional is highly paid, has high status and a high degree of autonomy.

g A professional is dedicated, committed and highly skilled.

Do you have another definition of professionalism, not already mentioned above?

Discuss this with others in your setting. What conclusions can you draw?

Raising qualifications

In England, the Early Years Professional Status (EYPS) qualification was introduced by the government in 2007 as part of an ambitious plan to raise standards. The initial target was that all early years' children's centres (3,000) would have a 'graduate leader' by 2010 and then all full daycare settings by 2015. A number of ECEC workers have completed their Foundation degrees and gone on to achieve EYPS, whilst others have joined the workforce through initial training involving placement experience. However, it is unclear, or at least unproven, whether this process of raising the required level of qualification has had a positive impact on children or has established ECEC as a profession. It is surely far too early to tell. The impact on children will not be measurable for many years. It is only now, 40 years on, that the impact of the HighScope project (see Chapter 14) can really be assessed. Establishing ECEC as an accepted professional body of workers will also take many years, as has happened with teaching where the battle continues. A report by Aspect (2009) highlighted key problems in:

- the discontent and concern over pay and conditions for all early years' staff including EYPs
- the ongoing lack of status accorded to early years work and early years workers
- the general awareness of EYPs and what they do
- the issue of the huge range of roles and responsibilities undertaken by EYPs, with over 60 different job titles reported by those responding to the survey.

A similar situation confronting the same issues exists in Scotland. Non-teaching staff working with children aged 0–16 will have, or be working towards, vocational qualifications often starting with (N)SVQ3 in childcare and may need to be working towards degree-level qualifications, such as the BA Childhood Practice. In an attempt to 'professionalise the workforce', there is currently a perceived need to raise the standard of qualification of managers and lead practitioners in early years' settings, such as private nurseries. The Scottish Social Services Council (SSSC) has produced 'The Standard for Childhood Practice' (QAA, 2007) which provides a comprehensive set of benchmark statements.

The Scottish government is also concerned with a need for greater specialisation for those teaching in the early years (now referred to as Early and First Level under the new Curriculum for Excellence guidelines, for ages 3–9). This is supported by the Donaldson Review (2010) which proposes possibilities for further specialisation, particularly through continuing professional development (CPD) which would involve post-graduate study at Master's level.

It is interesting to consider these developments in terms of where they appear to work towards a common goal and where they diverge. On the one hand, the Scottish government appears to be set on a course to raise the level of qualification of all those in the ECEC sector, based on their understanding, as suggested by Sylva et al. (2004), that better qualified people educating and caring for children in the early years results in better outcomes for those children and society. On the other hand, very well qualified and experienced teachers are being withdrawn from school nursery provision across Scotland, either entirely, or more frequently assuming the role of 'cluster' teacher overseeing a number of nursery classes (sometimes geographically far apart), which results in less and less contact with children and families. A peripatetic role is hardly an encouragement to qualified teachers to specialise and undertake post-graduate study.

Yet the recommendations of a report from HMIe (2007: 20) state clearly and firmly that 'where services are being re-organised, care should be taken not to weaken existing, effective provision, such as that found most often in nursery schools with teacher involvement, which are providing high-quality nursery education'.

The developments taking place in Scotland correlate closely with those across the UK, particularly in England, that are influenced by the same research, reviews and reports, such as OECD (2006, 2009) and policy papers from the EU such as 'Improving the quality of teacher education' and 'Efficiency and equity of the European education and training systems', which emphasise the importance of pre-primary education 'because research shows that early learning secures better school results later on … member states, the EC recommends, should invest more in pre-primary education and the supply of specially trained pre-primary teachers will need to be improved' (Lund, 2008: 8).

The context in Sweden

There are marked differences between countries in their approach to the care and education of very young children, and within this to the qualifications and roles of staff. There are, however, commonalities. One is a developing and growing understanding of the importance of early childhood to later outcomes; the second is the economic argument for investing in early childhood care and education; and the third is the role of a qualified workforce. Urban (2010) concludes that 'there appears to be broad consensus that the workforce is central to achieving the ambitious policy goals, for example, of increasing both quantity and quality of provision' (citing Siraj-Blatchford et al., 2002; Dalli, 2003; MacNaughton, 2005; Oberhuemer, 2005; and OECD, 2006).

In their paper using data gathered from a study in Sweden, Kuisma and Sandberg (2008) state that 'over half of all pre-school employees have university degrees in early childhood education' and that 'in Sweden pre-school teachers work with children aged one to seven years' (p. 187). This is a very different picture in terms of qualifications of staff and provision for children to that in either Scotland or England. They go on to state that 'the public function of the pre-school in Swedish society is to be a first step in the education system and to influence lifelong learning' (p. 187), which again contrasts significantly with the view of society in the UK. Even so, the study found that 'pre-school teachers had a higher education and a wider pedagogical base of knowledge compared with day-care attendants' (p. 191), and the writers felt this was significant.

In an article in *Children in Europe* (issue 15), Annica Grimlund highlights very recent changes to the education and subsequent qualification of pre-school teachers in Sweden, with a return to the pre-2001 situation. They will be trained separately to school teachers and they will have a lower-level qualification (taking 3.5 years) at Bachelor degree level compared with five years at Master's degree level for teachers within the compulsory school system (Grimlund, 2008).

Change through legislation

Oberhuemer (2005) sees the introduction of frameworks for the early childhood curriculum as 'undermining the professional autonomy' of practitioners who 'need to be encouraged to see themselves as interpreters and not as mere implementers of curricular frameworks' (p. 12). She sees the raising of qualifications for ECEC workers as vital in the process of enabling them to be seen as professionals who interpret frameworks rather than technicians who implement them. She concludes her paper with: 'the quality of the early childhood workforce must necessarily be a major consideration in each country's aspirations for a high quality system of early education and care' (p. 14).

The strategy in use in Scotland is to raise the level of qualifications of ECEC workers and establish a degree-led workforce, through programmes incorporating the Standard for Childhood Practice combined with registration with SSSC. In both Scotland and England, this is part, perhaps the key part, of moves to reform the children's workforce, to integrate children's services and professionalise the workforce. Miller (2008: 255) states that 'the need to develop a professional workforce is generally agreed' and 'the reform of the children's workforce in England acknowledges that increasing the skills and competence of this workforce is critical to its success'. The very title of the new qualification in England (Early Years Professional Status) acknowledges this.

In Scotland, the establishment of this Standard (QAA, 2007) with the requirement for all 'lead practitioners' to be enrolled on a course of study that will lead to a recognised ordinary degree-level qualification mirrors the Early Years Professional Status degree-level qualification now required in England. Both initiatives stem from the same research, reviews and reports (OECD, 2001, 2006, 2009; Sylva et al., 2004; DfES, 2007). The 2001 report concludes that 'quality early childhood education and care depends on strong staff training and fair working conditions across the sector' (OECD, 2001: 11).

The EPPE report states: 'settings that have staff with higher qualifications have higher quality scores and their children make more progress' (Sylva et al., 2004: ii), which is a key finding. Under the same heading, it also states that 'quality indicators include warm interactive relationships with children, having a trained teacher as manager and a good proportion of trained teachers on the staff' (p. ii).

Adams (2008) has explored a number of issues around professionalism of ECEC professionals, including raising qualifications to degree level. Her article draws on 'two small-scale pieces of research' and explores perceptions, concepts and views of professionalism in the early years' context in Scotland. She examines 'how work with young children is perceived in Scottish society and value accorded to people who choose to work with young children' (p. 197). Against a background discussion of recent changes, particularly the initiative to engage lead practitioners in degree-level studies, the article highlights the barriers to moves to raise the professional status of ECEC workers and thereby increase their efficacy. She notes, for example, that the establishment of 'family centres' providing services for children from birth to age 5 and some after-school care where there was a 'policy decision not to appoint teachers … provided an unprecedented career opportunity for nursery nurses as they were now able to apply for management posts previously reserved for teachers' (p. 198).

However, Adams (2008) also suggests the many job titles (nursery nurse, nursery assistant, early years practitioner, play worker, out-of-school carer, etc.) 'provide fertile ground for a possible fragmentation of the concept of an early years profession' (p. 200). She draws comparisons with healthcare following the decision to raise nursing qualifications to degree level and the ensuing tension on the part of doctors not wishing to relinquish 'control'. She comments that 'in centres where teachers continue to be employed, teachers are less than willing to relinquish power to differently qualified personnel' (p. 201). Sandberg et al. (2007) discuss similar issues in Sweden between pre-school teachers and daycare attendants.

A discrete and specific body of knowledge

The concept of professionalism being centred on a specific body of knowledge recurs in all the literature from all countries. For example, Sandberg et al. (2007: 303) citing

Berntsson (1999) state: 'Today it is distinctive for a profession to have occupational group-specific knowledge, and that they have the sole right to that knowledge.' Webb et al. (2004: 85) state that professionalism has been 'a key contested term in the history of teaching' and argue that 'a specialised knowledge base' is a key trait of a professional occupation. This paper goes on to attest that other occupations seek the rewards of 'classic professions, such as law and medicine' through a process of 'professionalisation' which includes gaining higher qualifications. The process of establishing and gaining these higher qualifications is also about determining this specific body of knowledge. In their study into concepts of professionalism, Kuisma and Sandberg (2008: 192) found that 'results from both pre-school teachers and students strengthened the notion that the concept of professionalism stems from the possession of knowledge'. Importantly, with regard to this study, Kuisma and Sandberg (2008) also reported 'pre-school teachers' difficulties in claiming their professionalism and legitimacy in society … they do not receive proper acknowledgement for their responsibilities, **nor is their required education valued**' (p. 194, our emboldening). This does not augur well for the initiatives in the UK to raise qualifications for teachers and other ECEC workers!

Adams (2008: 200, citing Bernstein, 2000) says 'feeling "part of a profession" is more likely to be related to the inner dedication of a significant group of people who share a body of recognisable knowledge'. This must lie at the heart of the problem with regard to ECEC professionalism and the qualifications that justify their professional status; that is, 'what is the body of specific knowledge to which they lay claim?' Teachers and certainly teacher educators may feel quite certain what this body of knowledge is but politicians and the rest of society are far less so. The question is even more difficult to answer with regard to the ECEC worker. Most people believe that looking after *very* young children is a simple and natural task that any 'normal' person, and women in particular, can undertake. It is about caring and requires knowledge about hygiene and the right personality rather than academic qualifications (McGillivray, 2008).

CASE STUDY

Working as a teacher within the compulsory school system in Sweden brings with it some differences in terms of roles and responsibilities. One expectation, when working in a Grade 1–9 school (ages 7–16), is that staff should be willing to cover the short-term absences of others, which arise during non-contact time. This cover is not restricted to within one's own subject area. On one occasion, a male colleague, who was a modern languages teacher of English and German and therefore used to working with the 14–16 age group, volunteered to cover a PE class for Grade 1 (7-year-olds). I clearly remember the points in favour of this decision stated as:

- How difficult can this be?
- They are only 7-year-olds and I teach teenagers.
- I have children of my own.

At the end of the lesson, he returned to the staffroom, shaken and ashen-faced. The children had not behaved as he had expected and did not appear to like being told what to do; one child fell off the wall bars, another child vomited on the floor and a third was inconsolable as he was not 'her teacher'. Other learning for him emerged in discussion, such as: how do you get 25 7-year-olds across a main road (to the sports complex) without getting any children killed on the way there or on the way back?

The conclusion: he would never, ever volunteer to work with a Grade 1 class again, and from that moment on, displayed a much greater level of respect for the Early Stage teachers (*lågstadielärare*).

The point in the case study above is that the stated reason for confidence – being that 'anyone' can work with young children – is very common, and the fact that in the UK 'care' of children aged 0–3 has come under the auspices of Social Services and not Education departments does nothing to mitigate this stance. The emphasis is clearly on care rather than education. In Scandanavian countries, this is not the case (Utbildningsdepartementet, 2004/05, cited in Sandberg et al., 2007).

Interestingly, another Swedish study (Malm, 2009: 78), looking at professionalism for all teachers, refers to the McKinsey Report (2007), which emphasises the fact that 'students that do not progress quickly during their first years at school, because they are not exposed to teachers of sufficient calibre, stand very little chance of recovering the lost years'.

This supports the practice in other countries, such as Finland and South Korea, of recruiting the most highly qualified people to early years teaching and educating them to the highest standards. If the McKinsey Report is correct when it states that 'the available evidence suggests that the main driver of the variation in student learning in schools is the quality of the teachers' (p. 12), then this will be true of all teachers for all children at all ages, including those not given the job title of 'teacher', such as those working in ECEC. Layard and Dunn (2009), in their report for the Children's Society, 'A Good Childhood', find this message accords with experience within the English school system, stating that in primary schools, 'teachers account for up to 30 percent of the variance in their progress' (p. 87). Sandberg et al. (2007) note that 'in 2004 the

Swedish Government decided that pre-school teachers should have the overall responsibility for children's development and learning in pre-school in order to strengthen and guarantee quality' (p. 303), again citing Utbildningsdepartementet (2004/5). However, it is worth reinforcing at this point that the Swedish definition of 'pre-school teacher' means being qualified to work with children aged 1–6, but this is not a valid qualification for compulsory school (see Chapter 6).

Valuing the profession

Adams (2008: 202) also comments that 'the valuing of the work by the workers is a first essential step for an emergent profession', and this could be important in relation to raised qualifications. This is one way in which society recognises the value and should thus give ECEC workers greater confidence and belief in the value of what they are doing. We would argue that this could be very important for teachers working in the early years at the moment, as they are unlikely to have specialised during their ITE. They may be teaching in Nursery for the first time after 20 years' teaching at another level, or may have been placed with this age group but not as a result of their own choice.

A post-graduate specialism in Early Years Education at the University of Aberdeen has allowed teachers to experience working with very young children and also helped facilitate discussion and understanding around the staffing of 0–3 settings. A research study carried out with a pilot group of teachers posed the following question: In what way did the course reinforce your own values and beliefs or change any?

Subsequent analysis of the data identified a clear key theme centred on issues of professionalism, emerging from comments about working with other ECEC staff, understanding different roles, developing awareness of different qualifications, increased confidence in being able to justify practice and the development of professional practice.

Practice in a 0–3 setting was a steep learning curve for all participants, even for those who were parents themselves, as they experienced a very different role and dynamic. The students all acknowledged that the experience had pushed them out of their 'comfort zone', especially those who had 'no experience of children below the age of 3', that they had all been 'surprised' and some 'daunted' but had all 'really enjoyed it'.

The 'theme' around professionalism threaded through all aspects of the research data but dominated as participants spoke about differences in staffing structure, qualifications, adult-to-child ratios, roles and practices in the 0–3 settings. One student commented: 'The management were not necessarily directly involved with the children ... There seemed to be a lot of 16 year olds working with babies and those who did have the qualifications did not seem to be with the children so often.' Another student said: 'The manager was very keen to hear about what I was doing ... she has to eventually get her qualification up to a degree standard for registration and there was quite a mixture of different qualifications in the private nursery ... I have to say that I was really impressed by the private nursery – just the whole staff motivation.'

Students in general commented on their increased confidence in taking a step towards acquiring part of the 'professional body of knowledge':

- 'people used to get an extra qualification to teach in Nursery and I wanted to know what they were taught … So I want to be a little bit more of an expert and that was my main motivation'.
- 'I felt – it was my first year in Nursery – it would give me a deeper understanding of what I was doing as when I first came in I felt I didn't have a clue what I was doing so definitely it made me feel more confident'.
- 'it is nice to have the reading behind you and be able to make a professional argument … gave more assurance in what I thought myself and I can justify my decision making'.

REFLECTIVE ACTIVITY

The following strategies can develop professionalism. How helpful have you found them? Insert ticks under the relevant headings.

Strategies	Not very helpful	Quite helpful	Very helpful
Reflection-'in'-action			
Reflection-'on'-action			
Accredited courses of study			
Experience			
Observing others			
Being observed and receiving feedback			
Peer assessment			
Continuous assessment against a standard			

Reflection-in-action could be described as thinking about what you are doing whilst doing it, developing know-how' through repeated experience that you reflect on (Schön, 1983).

Reflection-on-action could be described as thinking about your actions after the event, a post-mortem or evaluation perhaps in discussion with others or written down (Tabachnick and Ziechner, 2002).

As stated at the beginning of this chapter, there has been a traditional division between care and education within the UK. Data from our recent research provides evidence that this still continues in Scotland despite some recent shifts in policy. Students discussed the divergence between what they learned from course materials, that reinforced their understanding of the importance of the very early years in terms of outcomes, and actual practice and provision. Many commented on the fact that staff involved with the youngest children were very young themselves and in possession of few, if any, qualifications. Those with higher-level qualifications spent little time actually with the children. Our students had become much more aware of the kind of training and qualifications required for working with children aged 0–3, but questioned the idea that higher academic qualifications for all would necessarily improve practice and provision, particularly if those with higher qualifications were less involved with the children day to day.

They felt this was contrary to the experience in schools but were also aware that the trend is to remove teachers from school nursery settings either altogether or in many cases with the provision of a 'cluster' teacher who oversees more than one nursery. This replicates the situation in 0–3 settings where the more highly qualified practitioner has less involvement with the children.

There was a consensus that the course of study had reinforced their already firmly held view that the first eight years of a child's life were the most important in terms of development and learning, and that they now felt more confident to 'justify' this stance and put together a 'professional argument'.

Most felt that 0–3 settings were about caring for children efficiently, economically and safely, whilst provision for 3–8-year-olds was about education: 'It was interesting to watch the (daycare) staff as I felt that most of the time they were caring for the children, nappy changing, teeth brushing, serving meals etc rather than interacting or playing with them.'

Another student summed up many of the comments made in one part of the conversation, saying:

> I do think it is *the* fundamentally most important stage and I think this really links to the question about professionalism in the early years because I think it is so often left to the least qualified – and I mean that in terms of experience as well … we leave the care of young children in our society to people who haven't had a chance to reflect, to research and look at other practice to find out what is the best way to approach really anything in these children's lives … the course made me feel *I* was becoming more professional … able to talk … and explain to people – parents – not in a patronising way because they know their children better than I do but to show that you are informed and for other staff and management.

In relation to the above, it is worth remembering that, coupled with a loss of teacher specialism over the past 30 years, particularly in Scotland, there has been a steady growth in managerialism and assessment-driven systems, particularly in England. There is evidence that staff cling to a professional integrity that is at odds with the current 'managerialist construction' that values masculine attributes (Osgood, 2006) and devalues 'emotional labour' (Taggart, 2011).

Sachs (2000) has identified two existing forms of professionalism as 'democratic' and 'managerial'. She suggests the latter has emerged from devolution and decentralisation, is rooted in private-sector practices that are inappropriate in education and has resulted in 'loss of morale among highly trained professionals'. She also suggests these two types are at loggerheads with each other, thus there is a need to establish another form between the two.

Sachs advocates a new professionalism for teachers, in talking about the 'activist professional'. Activist professionalism is founded on principles of mutual exchange, reciprocity and working together but also shared inquiry.

ECEC professionals are perhaps the least likely to become activist professionals as they are still establishing their shared concept of professionalism. Currently, they are the weakest group with the quietest 'voice' within education. There is discernable evidence of activist professionalism in responses from our EYPGCE students in terms of attempts to change their own practice, use learning from the course and share knowledge. Also, these teachers still clearly demonstrate that they share 'values, principles and strategies' more with other *teachers* than with others in the ECEC workforce.

Enhanced knowledge and understanding of who cares for very young children and how, enabled participants to reflect on the different roles, qualifications and practices across the sector and practice in their own setting (Alexandersson, 1994, cited in Sandberg et al., 2007). This led to further reflection on and questioning of both initial and continuing professional development for themselves and others in the ECEC sector.

Webb et al. (2004) state that professionalism has been 'a key contested term in the history of teaching' and argue that 'a specialised knowledge base' is a key trait of a professional occupation. This concept of professionalism is problematic for teachers and a greater problem for teachers and others working with very young children. The problem is that others do not recognise that they have 'occupational group-specific knowledge' and they certainly do not have a 'sole right to that knowledge'. Everyone has a view on education and most believe they know what is best for children, particularly very young children and particularly their own. As Ken Robinson (2006: unpaginated) says, whilst people at dinner parties may shy away from talking to teachers about their work, in general 'if you ask about their education they pin you to the wall … it goes deep with people like money and religion'.

REFLECTIVE ACTIVITY

Write down three things that you would include in a 'specific professional body of knowledge' for ECEC professionals:

1 ....
2 ....
3 ....

Write down three things that you would include in a 'specific professional body of knowledge' for doctors (General Practitioners).
    Which is easier? Why might this be?
    Compare and discuss your first list with other students/colleagues.

An important part of the ECEC professional role is to share and disseminate information, including knowledge and understanding both of individual children and childcare and education. This is not the case with all professionals. Doctors and lawyers fiercely protect their 'occupational group-specific knowledge' and even teachers in secondary education hold fast to their subject knowledge.

This is discussed by Adams (2008, citing Bernstein, 2000) who says 'feeling "part of a profession" is more likely to be related to the inner dedication of a significant group of people who share a body of recognisable knowledge' (p. 200).

In his discussion around the 'possibilities for re-envisioning the early childhood worker', Moss (2006) looks at some examples of re-structuring, notably in the Nordic states and particularly Denmark and Sweden. He notes that the integrated workforce in these Nordic states is based on two groups, one qualified at tertiary level and a second with a lower level of qualification. The re-structuring he discusses centres on the qualifications of the workforce. However, it is clear that, whilst all the evidence suggests that a better qualified workforce will provide better outcomes for children, it is also clear that in Scotland there is a split between 'childcare' and 'education', both conceptually and materially, that impacts on provision, outcomes for children, policy, funding – in fact every aspect. He suggests there are essentially two workforces and that there is 'a clear and deep fault line between the two' (Moss, 2006: 31).

REFLECTIVE ACTIVITY

Which of the following statements on the 'concept of professionalism' in the context of early years practice most closely correlate with your own?

a People working with very young children are not accepted as 'professionals' as they are not seen to possess a body of knowledge unavailable to the lay person, unlike doctors, lawyers or even secondary subject teachers.

b Early years workers need to be particularly strong to protect their developing professional values in the face of pervasive societal undervaluing of their work.

c There is a clear distinction and different professional role for teachers and other early years practitioners such as nursery nurses.

d Teachers or other practitioners in early years care and education are professional because they act professionally.

e Teachers or other practitioners in early years care and education are professional because they possess a 'unique set of skills, knowledge and values'.

f The professional competencies of those working with very young children are not articulated and communicated to service users.

g If none of the above correlate with your own view, try to suggest an alternative.

Again, discuss with colleagues and draw your conclusions.

Conclusion

There is still a split between 'care' and 'education', and there may be a danger that government policy to raise levels of qualifications, particularly through the adoption of a managerialist structure, will exacerbate the 'fault line'. There is a drive in Scotland and elsewhere to raise levels of qualification in 0–3 care settings but our research, supported by other large-scale studies, shows that highly qualified staff interact less with children.

There appears to be a tension between:

- government policy and actual practice
- the concept of professionalism held by staff undertaking accredited qualifications and the prevailing systems of managerialism and control.

Research tells us that the interests of young children are best served when they have regular contact with an ECEC professional who has early years' specialist training and experience. This training and ECEC professionalism need to be built around a common specific body of knowledge. These qualified professionals then need to remain in contact with children with a focus on education reflecting our better understanding, from research evidence, of the importance of the very early years in terms of lifelong learning and outcomes. Again, the UK might usefully learn from Sweden that 'the public function of the pre-school in Swedish society is to be a first step in the education system and to influence lifelong learning' (Kuisma and Sandberg, 2008: 187).

It seems likely that we will find, here in Scotland as in England, that despite changes to job titles and roles, pay and conditions remain the same, and this seems to be what impacts on practitioners' status as professionals (O'Keefe and Tait, 2004, cited in Miller, 2008). What remains unclear from the literature, that is reporting and reviewing usually very small-scale research studies, is whether the qualification impacts on practice and provision. This approach of setting a standard against which all are measured, has been criticised as merely a desire for control and consistency (Dahlberg and Moss, 2005). Critics suggest the raising of qualifications in this way has little to do with either raising professional status or attainment for children. It is merely a tool to enable those providing the care and education to be held accountable and a minimum standard to be consistently provided.

Further reading

The following three papers are readable and develop the discussion with reference to Scotland, England and Sweden:

Adams, K. (2008) 'What's in a name? Seeking professional status through degree studies within the Scottish early years context', *European Early Childhood Education Research Journal*, 16(2): 196–209.

Kuisma, M. and Sandberg, A. (2008) 'Preschool teachers' and student teachers' thoughts about professionalism in Sweden', *European Early Childhood Education Journal*, 16(2): 186–95.

McGillivray, G. (2008) 'Nannies, nursery nurses and early years professionals: constructions of professional identity in the early years workforce in England', *European Early Childhood Education Research Journal*, 16(2): 242–54.

 ## Useful websites

The Department of Education – http://www.education.gov.uk/

Education Scotland, Principles of Inspection and Review – http://www.hmie.gov.uk/documents/publication/ise09-02.html (accessed 03.03.11).

The Nursery Education Review Report sets out all the research relevant to Scotland on the impact of nursery education on young people before they enter primary school, at: http://www.eis.org.uk/images/nursery%20research%20review%20report%20291010.pdf (accessed 03.03.11).

References

Adams, K. (2008) 'What's in a name? Seeking professional status through degree studies within the Scottish early years context', *European Early Childhood Education Research Journal*, 16(2): 196–209.

Aspect (2009) 'In their own words: EYPs speak out', *Aspect's EYP Survey*. Available at: http://www.aspect.org.uk/eyp/wp-content/uploads/2009/04/eyp-p-survey-report.pdf

Dahlberg, G. and Moss, P. (2005) *Ethics and Politics in Early Education*. London and New York: Routledge.

Department for Education and Skills (DfES) (2007) *Quality of Childcare Settings in the Millennium Cohort Study*, Research Report. London: DfES.

Donaldson, G. (2010) *Teaching Scotland's Future: Report of a Review of Teacher Education in Scotland*. Edinburgh: Scottish Government.

Grimlund, A. (2008) 'Some items for an agenda of change', *Children in Europe*, issue 15.

HMIe (2007) The Key Role of Staff in Providing Quality Pre-school Education – Improving Scottish Education, Education Scotland, at: http://www.educationscotland.gov.uk/earlyyearsmatters/i/genericcontent_tcm4539278.asp (accessed 01.08.12).

Kuisma, M. and Sandberg, A. (2008) 'Preschool teachers' and student teachers' thoughts about professionalism in Sweden', *European Early Childhood Education Journal*, 16(2): 186–95.

Layard, R. and Dunn, J. (2009) *A Good Childhood: A Report for the Children's Society*. London: Penguin.

Lund, S.G. (2008) 'Education of a profession', *Children in Europe*, issue 15.

McGillivray, G. (2008) 'Nannies, nursery nurses and early years professionals: constructions of professional identity in the early years workforce in England', *European Early Childhood Education Research Journal*, 16(2): 242–54.

McKinsey Report (2007) *How the World's Best Performing School Systems Come Out on Top*. Available at: http://www.mckinsey.com/App_Media/Reports/SSO/Worlds_School_Systems_Final.pdf (accessed 23.03.11).

Malm, B. (2009) 'Towards a new professionalism: enhancing personal and professional development in teacher education', *Journal of Education for Teaching*, 35(1): 77–91.

Miller, L. (2008) 'Developing professionalism within a regulatory framework in England: challenges and possibilities', *European Early Childhood Education Research Journal*, 16(2): 255–68.

Moss, P. (2006) 'Structures, understandings and discourses: possibilities for re-envisioning the early childhood worker', *Contemporary Issues in Early Childhood*, 7(1).

Oberhuemer, P. (2005) 'Conceptualising the early childhood pedagogue: policy approaches and issues of professionalism', *European Early Childhood Education Research Journal*, 13(1): 5–16.

Organisation for Economic Co-operation and Development (OECD) (2001) *Starting Strong: Early Childhood Education and Care*. Paris: OECD.

Organisation for Economic Co-operation and Development (OECD) (2006) *Starting Strong II: Early Childhood Education and Care*. Paris: OECD.

Organisation for Economic Co-operation and Development (OECD) (2009) *Starting Strong III: Early Childhood Education and Care*. Paris: OECD.

Osgood, J. (2006) 'Professionalism and performativity: the feminist challenge facing early years practitioners', *Early Years*, 26(2): 187–99.

Quality Assurance Agency (QAA) (2007) *Scottish Subject Benchmark Statement: The Standard for Childhood Practice*. Edinburgh: Scottish Government.

Robinson, K. (2006) *Schools are Killing Creativity*. Available at: http://www.ted.com/talks/lang/eng/ken_robinson_says_schools_kill_creativity.html

Sachs, J. (2000) 'The activist professional', *Journal of Educational Change*, 1: 77–95.

Sandberg, A., Anstett, S. and Wahlgren, U. (2007) 'The value of in-service education for quality in pre-school', *Professional Development in Education*, 33(3): 301–19.

Schön, D.A. (1983) *The Reflective Practitioner: How Professionals Think in Action*. New York: Basic Books.

Sylva, K., Melhuish, E., Sammons, P., Siraj-Blatchford, I. and Taggart, B. (2004) *Effective Pre-School Education: A Longitudinal Study funded by the DfES 1997–2004 (EPPE Project)*. London: University of London, Institute of Education.

Tabachnick, R. and Ziechner, K. (2002) 'Reading 1.4: reflection on reflective teaching', in A. Pollard (ed.) *Readings for Reflective Teaching*. London: Continuum.

Taggart, G. (2011) 'Don't we care? The ethics and emotional labour of early years professionalism', *Early Years*, 31(1): 85–95.

Urban, M. (2010) 'Rethinking professionalism in early childhood: untested feasibilities and critical ecologies', *Contemporary Issues in Early Childhood*, 11(1).

Webb, R., Vulliamy, G., Hamalainen, S., Sarja A., Kimonen, E. and Nevalainen, R. (2004) 'A comparative analysis of primary teacher professionalism in England and Finland', *Comparative Education*, 40(1): 83–107.

CHAPTER 17

INTER-PROFESSIONAL PRACTICE

Key ideas explored in this chapter

- what inter-professional practice really means
- why inter-professional practice is important
- barriers to inter-professional practice and how to overcome them
- joint training.

What is 'inter-professional practice'?

The relatively new concept of inter-professional practice is complex and fraught with difficulty. One difficulty arises from, or is perhaps caused by, the language used to describe such practice. The list of terms includes:

- multi-professional/disciplinary
- inter-professional/disciplinary
- trans-professional/disciplinary
- integrated services
- multi-agency
- partnership working
- collaborative practice.

This is not an exhaustive list and you can no doubt add to it but it does provide a sense of the multiplicity of terms that can cause some confusion. It is helpful to define and consider the first three prefixes – 'multi', 'inter' and 'trans' – as a means to explore the meaning and purpose of the practice.

Multi-professional/disciplinary

A commonly used term that usually means individual disciplines assess the child and make recommendations, often without any consultation with other specialists. There may be a number of professionals involved with a child/family but they essentially remain within their own professional 'silo'. Meetings may not involve all professionals and be retrospectively sharing experiences, information and outcomes.

Inter-professional/disciplinary

This term implies specialists carry out their assessments but then share their results at team meetings. The hope is that this provides a more co-ordinated and individualised approach. Collaboration is implicit.

Trans-professional/disciplinary

This is a term largely used in the USA, in which there is a greater degree of shared responsibility and collaboration. A group of professionals form a team around a child, starting with a core team such as the class teacher and support assistant. We might call this 'collaborative working'.

Sanders (2004) explores the different terminology in some depth using a table sourced from Rawson (1994) that simplifies the terminology on one hand but also shows how there could be 75 permutations using different prefixes and suffixes. He concludes, citing Rawson (1994), Leathard (1990) and Ovreteit et al. (1997), that inter-professional working has the greatest utility. Inter-professional practice has been chosen here for the same reasons and simply because it is now the more commonly used term. It is used here to describe professionals from different disciplines, including education, health and social work, who may provide integrated services for children and families. Collaboration and partnership working between multiple agencies are understood to be intrinsic. The important elements that appear to be missing at the moment are shared responsibility and the concept of building a team around the child, starting with a core that might be a teacher and learning support assistant or teacher and nursery nurse. When working with numbers of students in training as classroom/ support assistants or nursery nurses, they often expressed their frustration that when a child they supported (sometimes one to one over a long period) was being assessed or discussed by 'specialists', such as educational psychologists or in a case conference with social workers, they were rarely if ever included. This may be as a result of their perceived status and reflects the approach taken in the past towards parents when 'specialists' did not consult parents but 'informed' them. The question of who is included in any 'multi' or 'inter' professional team is fundamental. It centres around concepts of professionalism, professional identity and status. Recent research and writing, particularly by Osgood (2012) and Lumsden (2010), highlights the key issues for the ECEC workforce in asserting their professionalism. It is vital for all in the ECEC workforce, including teachers, to be confident and assertive about their professionalism and their role. A group of professionals working together in a team need to perceive each other as having equal status in order to work well together (Ward, 2011).

Recent years have seen increasing pressure and desire for greater collaboration between professionals who provide services to children and families right across the UK. This has perhaps largely been due to 'an ambitious programme with the ultimate aim of eradicating child poverty by 2020' (Webster and Clouston, 2011: 83), by New Labour in England and Wales which led to Early Excellence Centres, Sure Start Local Programmes and national standards for centre leaders (DCSF, 2007). The practice of professionals working very closely together to support children and families has certainly arisen from the understanding that children such as those in high-profile child protection cases, but many others growing up in poverty in the 21st century, have been failed by the system. There has been 'starkly bleak' evidence that when professionals work in isolation, failing to collaborate effectively with agencies and individuals, failing to communicate and work together, children 'fall through the net' and the consequences can be dire (Gasper, 2010).

Sanders (2004) identifies two main dangers in terms of service delivery as *service gaps* and *duplication of service*. *Service gaps* may occur because the service provider does not know about the people who need their service or because they believe someone else is providing it. Similarly with *duplication of services*, the service provider does not know that this service, for example an assessment, has already been carried out. Certainly, the idea of professionals collaborating and agencies communicating and delivering integrated services is seen to be a more efficient and cost-effective model. It is seen by government 'as entailing more efficient use of staff, more effective service provision, and enabling professionals and lay people to achieve their objectives more fully and economically' (Sanders, 2004: 182). However, communicating and particularly meeting with numbers of people who may be geographically spread out can be very expensive. Administration can increase as numbers of people are 'copied in' to documents and even email – again, this is expensive in terms of time and money. Consider the cost implications of releasing a teacher, for example to attend a case conference about a child in their early years' class. The cost of supply cover even for half a day can often be prohibitive. It might be more sensible for government particularly to accept that inter-professional practice is not an answer to providing services in economically difficult times but is an effective method of providing quality services. The economic issues need to be addressed in order to make it happen.

Evidence for the benefits of inter-professional approaches as well as models and examples are found in other countries such as Sweden and Denmark but these have to be considered in the context of their culture. Funding made available for initiatives such as the children's centres in England and research studies have been critically driven by a political will, in turn driven by events such as the Victoria Climbié case and the subsequent Laming Report (2003). Policy and then practice have been shaped by Every Child Matters (DfES, 2004) in England and Getting it Right for Every Child (GIRFEC, 2006) in Scotland. The Every Child Matters document and related publications have now been 'archived'. However, essential elements are enshrined in legislation, including the focus on early intervention, a shared sense of responsibility, information sharing and integrated frontline services.

As Lumsden (2009: 152) states, citing DfES (2004): 'enshrined in legislation is the importance of integrated services and, by implication, the need for improved collaboration between professionals.'

The Common Assessment Framework (CAF) was put in place in England as part of the Every Child Matters policy agenda, to facilitate collaborative working to support children and families 'at risk'. 'The CAF is a standardised approach to conducting an assessment of a child's additional support needs and deciding how those needs should be met' (ECM, 2004, cited in Gasper, 2010: 7).

The Common Assessment Framework (CAF) process is simply designed as a four-step process to enable practitioners from across disciplines to identify a child's needs early, make a holistic assessment, deliver co-ordinated services and review progress. It is not designed as a risk assessment or to be used when a child is identified as being at risk but is a voluntary process that requires informed consent. As it was designed to be common to all disciplines, it can support inter-professional practice.

The aims of GIRFEC which is still current in Scotland can be summarised as follows:

- services are child-centred
- children get the help they need, when they need it
- responses are timely, appropriate and proportional
- action must improve outcomes for children
- the capacity of families and communities to meet the needs of children must be strengthened
- practitioners are enabled to spend more time with children and families.

GIRFEC contains eight goals that link to the Curriculum for Excellence (Scottish Government, 2004) and to the four capacities that these new curriculum guidelines aspire to for each child to become: successful learners, confident individuals, responsible citizens and effective contributors. These eight goals are known by another acronym, SHANARRI:

- **S**afe
- **H**ealthy
- **A**chieving
- **N**urtured
- **A**ctive
- **R**espected
- **R**esponsible
- **I**ncluded

It is easy to see how a number of professionals from different disciplines, such as health, social care and education, may need to be involved to achieve these aims.

Both these policy documents stress the importance of integrated children's services. The professionals providing these services range across education, health and social care. In many cases, these professionals come together more often and more 'naturally' in the early years' context. ECEC professionals managing centres necessarily draw on all these different disciplines in their own practice. As the requirement for higher qualifications impacts on practice, it can be argued that those qualified with Early Years Professional Status in England and with the BA Childhood Practice in Scotland are indeed a growing band of *inter*-professionals (Lumsden, 2010; Davis, 2011). Specifically in England the programme, now in its third revision, for the National Professional Qualification in Integrated Centre Leadership (NPQICL) that has been completed by individuals from various professional roots, embraces and promotes the concept of the inter-professional. Another 'driver' towards inter-professionalism may be found in the reconceptualisation of professional that accords with reflective practice and moves away from 'the received construct of the traditional "closed-shop" professional' (Trodd, 2011: 48).

The debate about 'what inter-professional practice is' and what it should 'look like' continues. There is increasing evidence to support it, despite perhaps an apparent 'stalling' from government. Davis (2011) draws on a range of literature to support the debate around whether the real goal should be a 'single children's services worker (which some refer to as a pedagogue)' (p. 21) or whether it is better to achieve a balance of 'different professional groupings with some core understandings' (p. 22). He suggests the 'utopia' of full partnership would 'balance the influence of different professions and their concepts' (p. 22) and achieve more through combined efforts. This sounds like good common sense but it is vital to find more hard research evidence on the outcomes for children of inter-agency working (Siraj-Blatchford and Siraj-Blatchford, 2009). It is the outcomes for children and families that are important here. There appears to be increasing evidence to support the benefits of the role of 'an inter-professional', such as the children's centre leader (CCL) in England, with the specific remit of bringing together practitioners from a range of disciplines as required (DfES, 2004).

Within child protection, the *jigsaw* metaphor has become established, particularly with regard to fatality inquiries such as the Victoria Climbié or Baby P cases (Sanders, 2004). This refers to the situation where many agencies or individuals had a piece of the 'jigsaw' or 'puzzle' but nobody had all the pieces or even enough pieces to realise what was happening to the child. This is a useful metaphor to highlight the need for good clear communication and the need for one identified person or agency to co-ordinate services. This would usually be referred to as the 'key worker' and is essentially the person who should collate and put together the information from other sources to complete the 'jigsaw'.

Barriers to inter-professional working and how to overcome them

Barriers include:

- not having a shared language, including terminology
- different understandings of 'client'
- workload and staff morale
- dissonance in cultures between agencies
- organisational priorities
- policies and procedures
- organisational structures
- training
- leadership or lack of it
- consent and confidentiality
- access to information, particularly via ICT
- lack of knowledge and/or understanding of the roles and responsibilities of other professionals
- lack of confidence in own professional identity
- increasing workloads
- limited resources
- values and attitudes.

The language barrier

This extends beyond the terminology used to describe this way of working. It can be seen again in the terms in which the 'service user' is described. A child or family may be referred to as the 'patient' by healthcare professionals, as the 'client' by legal or social work professionals, or as the 'victim' by police. The term 'service user' has been introduced as a catch-all but few appear comfortable with it. It is questionable whether forcing everyone to adopt the same terms is helpful when it has been found that 'staff from different disciplines need to feel sufficiently confident in their own roles and in their own professional identity, in order to feel safe enough to share and defer their professional autonomy to work effectively together' (Molyneux, 2001: 32). This is perhaps something that simply has to be acknowledged and accepted early on in any inter-professional engagement.

Another aspect of language use that causes particular problems is the use of acronyms or initials (first-letter abbreviations such as NHS for National Health Service). These are often used in documentation and more importantly at meetings where it can be very challenging to understanding and demand a high degree of assertiveness to ask for clarification. However, this is vital and any lack of knowledge about meaning of terms should be admitted to immediately, to prevent a whole conversation becoming a blur. All professionals need to clarify terms, particularly acronyms, to keep channels of communication open. Rawlings and Paliokosta (2011: 57) highlight how 'discourses and terminologies used by other professionals can be alienating due to lack of understanding of particular terms relating to expertise'. They see the particular linguistic repertoire used as an expression of power and important to professional identity. It is particularly important for the ECEC professional to establish and maintain their own professional identity and be clear and confident in their role and responsibilities to overcome this barrier.

REFLECTIVE ACTIVITY

Make a list of acronyms you use in your own setting or take any set of documents (for example, the Curriculum for Excellence documentation in Scotland) and list the acronyms used within it. You could do the same for almost any government report.

Personal qualities and interpersonal skills

Overcoming many of the barriers to inter-professional working depends upon individuals developing interpersonal skills such as communication and empathy and personal qualities that will support good effective teamwork and collaboration.

Important skills in developing inter-professional practice are exactly the same as those involved in developing teamwork (see Chapter 19) and these include:

- communication skills – creating rapport, active listening, body language, empathy, questioning, challenging
- assertiveness skills – giving/receiving criticism, saying no, expressing feelings appropriately, satisfying/defending needs whilst respecting others
- co-operation skills – team building, negotiation, conflict resolution, problem management, group work
- decision-making skills – gathering info, prioritising and focusing, summarising, setting goals, creating options for action.

Brookson (2010), writing about effective communication for teaching assistants, described as being 'at the heart of effective teaching and learning', lists the following skills:

- concentrating and listening attentively
- using appropriate non-verbal gestures
- using appropriate vocabulary whilst extending and providing new words and meaning
- asking open questions
- responding positively and with humour
- being receptive and open to new ideas and other ways of thinking, providing opportunities for meaningful dialogues with other children and adults
- encouraging turn-taking and respect for others' viewpoints.

Almost every word in the above list could apply to communication between professionals! It is just as important to:

- listen 'actively' by being attentive and showing that you are with your body language
- use words that everyone understands and clarify any 'jargon'
- make use of open questions to facilitate a full discussion
- be positive and maintain a sense of humour
- keep an open mind and engage in meaningful dialogue
- allow others to contribute and value their contributions.

Gasper (2010: 90) emphasises the value of dialogue that 'as a creative, dynamic medium has been demonstrated since Socrates' and how important it can be in the context of inter-professional practice to 'generate new ideas', and support everyone involved towards 'strategic planning and development'. He concludes that 'when the dialogue is between a variety of professional agencies motivated to contribute positively, the potential for creativity is even greater' (p. 90).

Assertiveness

The ability or the confidence to assert yourself is another key skill in becoming an effective member of any team (see Chapter 19). It is perhaps particularly pertinent in terms of working within an inter-professional team. It can be very challenging to assert yourself within a meeting of a group of professionals, for example, that you have only just met and who are likely to be highly qualified in their particular field. In this context, your ability to assert yourself appropriately and effectively will depend greatly on your continuing professional development and on building the confidence of a firm foundation of a strong professional identity. You need to know and understand your own role and responsibilities, and you need to find out about the roles and responsibilities of others so that you know what you can and cannot ask and expect from them.

REFLECTIVE ACTIVITY

Atkinson et al. (2005, cited in Ward, 2011) identify 'the lack of knowledge and understanding of other professionals' roles as one of the barriers to multi-agency working', and suggest this is exacerbated 'by real or perceived overlaps in areas of responsibility'. As has been stated above, it is vital for all participants in collaborative working to know their own role and responsibilities and that of others. One way to help you understand the role and responsibilities of others is to ask them. One method of doing this is to engage in 'learning conversations' with other professionals. This is a less formal and often more effective approach than conducting interviews or questionnaires.

The purpose of holding learning conversations with a range of other professionals throughout the community is to investigate their varying roles and responsibilities. You can also explore their beliefs and how these impact on children and their families.

You should share the purpose of the learning conversation and ask if they are comfortable with you taking notes. These notes should be confidential as all you need to record is the person's job title and not their name or workplace.

Rather than asking questions, which may restrict the answers given, you may find the following technique useful in supporting a free-flowing conversation. Sentence completion requires you to ask those you are conversing with to complete a sentence which you have begun. Try and test out the technique with friends or family before implementing it.

Possible sentence starters:

My role and responsibilities in working with children/families are …
Before I worked with children/families I used to think …
The key issue/s for supporting children and families today is/are …

I most enjoy ...
The one thing I would most like to change about my work is ...
I wish I could spend more time on ...

Alternatively, you could use 'open' questions such as:

I wonder if you could tell me about ...?
Can you describe your role in this setting?
You could explore the role of anyone involved with working with children and this might include:

- a community nurse/health visitor
- a family centre worker
- an educational psychologist
- a social worker
- a children's centre leader
- a community police officer
- an education/development officer
- a representative from voluntary agencies or charities.

You might share your learning from these conversations with other students or colleagues who have carried out the same process to gain a broader understanding of a range of roles.

Co-operation skills

Any group of people working together are effectively working in a team. Sometimes teams come together or are put together for short periods for explicit and very specific purposes. Sometimes teams are groups of people who work together over extended periods of time. You are likely to be involved in more than one team when working with children and families, and inter-professional practice is likely to involve you in teamwork with people you have not previously met and for short periods of time for a specific purpose. A team of professionals working together to support a child or children may be geographically widely spread, they may meet only occasionally over extended periods of time or they may meet frequently for a short time for one specific purpose and then disband. It may be that you work with an inter-professional team within a children's centre, but this is still far from being the norm across the UK. This is clearer when we consider when inter-professional working is more likely to happen and become important. This might be:

- when there are child protection issues
- when a child has Additional Support Needs
- for some children throughout their life
- for any child at some point.

These professionals still need to see themselves as part of a team and individually and collectively develop their team or co-operation skills.

Perhaps the most important factor in building and maintaining any team is in establishing shared goals and ensuring all members of the team know, understand and believe in those shared goals. It may appear that a shared goal between professionals supporting a child and their family would be self-evident but it is not. Each professional is likely to have a particular perspective and this gives rise to quite different goals. The case study below provides an example of a number of professionals supporting a child and his family with different concerns.

CASE STUDY

Robbie is 5 and has cerebral palsy and this means he has some difficulty walking, and some speech and visual impairment. He is in a local primary school class of 27 children and has a learning support assistant (LSA) to help him with physical skills, personal care and learning. He sees a speech therapist regularly and she has been into the school to work with him in class on one occasion. He has had two operations since starting school to help correct his vision and he has regular appointments at the hospital with a consultant. His mother is a single parent with another child, a daughter Leigh who is 5 months old, and so is unable to work and receives benefits. The family live in a high-rise flat and the mother has struggled to cope at times. A social worker has been assigned to the family and a health visitor has been visiting since shortly after the birth of Robbie's sister.

- Robbie's class teacher is particularly concerned to enable Robbie to keep pace with the rest of the class with the support of his LSA so that he is sufficiently included in all activities across the curriculum.
- The LSA is concerned that his physical disabilities are delaying his development of social skills and impacting on his ability to socialise with his peers.
- His speech therapist is focused on ensuring he can make himself understood as he becomes very frustrated when he can't, leading to tantrums.

- His consultant is focused on pacing corrective surgery so that it impacts as little as possible on his general health but is done at the optimum time.
- The family's social worker is focused on establishing routines that will help his mother cope and encouraging her to go to some group sessions at the community centre with other parents. She is also trying to ensure that the family receive the right benefit payments to which they are entitled.
- The health visitor is very concerned at the moment that Leigh is under-weight, has severe nappy rash and is not sleeping through the night.

REFLECTIVE ACTIVITY

How might these professionals work together to support Robbie?
Who might be well-placed to co-ordinate services?
Who is left to co-ordinate all these elements at the moment?

REFLECTIVE ACTIVITY

Think about any situation where you have been part of a team or group of people from different workforces, professions or 'walks of life', tasked to work together to achieve a shared goal. Did this group constitute a 'team' in your view? Was there a structure and, if so, what was the structure? Did people come together of their own accord or were they put together by some outside agency? How effective was the group? Was there a shared goal and was it clear? What would you identify as the 'enablers' or 'inhibitors' to the effectiveness of this group effort? Do these relate to the barriers identified here?

Joint training

Ultimately, inter-professional practice requires a 'mindset' that is actively looking for ways to work together, and to be effective all those providing services to a child and their family need to 'think, work and learn inter-professionally' (Trodd, 2011: 1). It seems that so far professionals have been expected to work together inter-professionally at times but have had little opportunity to learn together and therefore struggle to 'think inter-professionally'.

The School of Education at the University of Aberdeen (UoA) has been collaborating with the School of Health and Social Science at Robert Gordon University (RGU, also in Aberdeen) to develop and deliver a joint training programme for students from the three different disciplines. The programme began a few years ago with face-to-face sessions involving students of nursing, healthcare, social work, education, and on one occasion police cadets. The first session was a full day when, after some introductory input from tutors from across the disciplines and short activities in groups, the students watched a DVD that RGU made to constitute a case study. It was entirely fictional, but quite realistic, using actors to depict an extended family group dealing with some crises. In groups (mixed across the disciplines containing one tutor), the students discussed the DVD, responding to some specific questions. They watched part one followed by discussion and then part two followed by further discussion. The session concluded with a plenary session using a Personal Response System (PRS).

The programme continued with another face-to-face session the following year and for students on the Bachelor of Education degree programme at UoA this was in their third year of study. This was a morning session repeated in the afternoon for a second group and provided the students with an opportunity to role-play a case conference conducted by social work professionals. Students were furnished with 'case notes' shortly before the session so that they were familiar with the (fictional again) background. Prior to this, they were provided with information in a lecture by an RGU social work tutor, on the purpose and processes surrounding case conferences. At the start of the session, they were given roles to play.

Together, we have now created an online activity so that we can continue to involve students across disciplines, including more distance-learning students on work-based programmes such as the BA Childhood Practice, without the logistical difficulties of bringing them face to face. We have again used the fictional case study approach and this unfolds in three parts for the students, with steering questions for them to respond to and discuss online again in groups mixed across disciplines. Over the three years of development, we have added more 'life' to the case study with podcasts of conversations between characters and photographs within a virtual environment. As with face-to-face meetings, there are some barriers to engagement with this approach. First, some students struggle to get online due to technical difficulties; second, some are uncomfortable engaging with others they have never met; and lastly, it is easy to avoid as students are essentially on their own, usually in the evening or at weekends, and need to be self-motivated. It is particularly challenging when students are unable to log on at the start for any reason and then feel less inclined to come into the middle of a discussion already under way. However, there have been high levels of engagement from some students, and tutors have used the case study as part of assessment in some courses with or without the online activity. Tutors have summarised discussion for students, clarified particular issues and used extracts from the discussion site in face-to-face and online tutorials. This is providing rich experiential, though virtual, learning for different professionals in their initial training.

Students across all disciplines were positive in their evaluation of these sessions. They found both challenging in a number of ways. First, they felt the process highlighted gaps in their knowledge. Second, and perhaps most importantly, they felt challenged and rather exposed in front of students from other disciplines, people they didn't know well and in a new setting. Lastly, some found the content of the case studies, if not actually upsetting, at least uncomfortable. It seems it might be better for those entering these professions to engage with such challenges during their training rather than later in practice for real, or indeed to continue to avoid them altogether. We have not yet gathered sufficient data to evaluate the impact of this ongoing joint training initiative but anecdotally a number of education students reported, when in discussion following school experience, that they had found it 'very interesting' and that they were 'so glad they had the opportunity' (see Figure 17.1 showing the result of one evaluation of a group of 49 students). These responses are in line with research reported by the Department of Children, Schools and Families and the Department of Health that participants involved in opportunities to learn together about working together were very highly valued. Also, they valued the joint training more on reflection at the end than at the start (Carpenter et al., 2010).

A very similar approach to joint training has been used in Kingston University where the Schools of Health and Social Care Sciences and the School of Education are co-located on the same site. Joint training involved students from the three disciplines in small mixed groups, 'unravelling a case study involving complex issues in relation to a potential safeguarding and/or child protection matter' (Maisey, 2011: 110). Also, Lumsden (2009) recounts how two Midlands universities have taken this approach when Early Childhood Studies students participate in what is called the 'LIP project' which provides inter-professional learning opportunities over a three-year period. She explains that in Year 2 they 'participate in a role play of a child protection case conference' (p. 163), and also reports on research into the student experience which has found 'the experience challenges and changes their perception of families in child

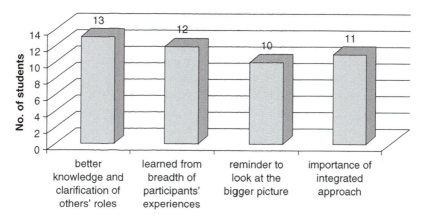

Figure 17.1 How will this enhance your future practice?

protection cases and that there is greater understanding of and commitment to multi-professional working'.

REFLECTIVE ACTIVITY

Consider a child and their family that you know. Write a short case study with a focus on the services, agencies and professionals they may engage with for support. You may need to engage in a 'learning conversation' with parents, carers or the child, and it is important to remember to maintain strict confidentiality when recording information. Change names of people and places in any documentation and be sure to gain permission from all participants at the outset. Reflect on this example from your own experience in terms of inter-professional practice.

Could you use a case study approach to engage with other professionals or students, either in face-to-face meetings or online?

Conclusion

There are many barriers to inter-professional working and probably only a few of them have been identified in this chapter. Perhaps the key to overcoming these is, first and foremost, motivation amongst professionals. This motivation is likely to come from an awareness of how bringing their skills together can benefit children and families. A child-centred approach, literally always keeping the child as the primary focus, will necessarily demand inter-professional practice, either at times or all the time, to fully meet their needs. In relation to safeguarding practices, Powell and Uppal (2012) cite a review by Munro (2010) which found that 'there is an overemphasis on processes and procedure rather than meaningful relationships between agencies'. They rightly stress the importance of recognising and understanding the differences between agencies but striving to overcome barriers in order to achieve the common goal of a 'healthy child who can thrive and achieve'.

Some of the ways the barriers to inter-professional practice might be overcome include:

- developing skills of communication
- regular dialogue and open lines of communication between professionals and agencies
- avoiding use of jargon and acronyms
- developing confidence in all members of any team
- strengthening professional identity and confidence

- increased knowledge and understanding of different roles and responsibilities
- developing interpersonal skills – including co-operation or team skills
- joint training – initial and ongoing.

Further reading

Davis, J.M. (2011) 'Defining integration: what are the different approaches?', in *Integrated Children's Services*. London: Sage. See Chapter 2.

Graham, S. and Jarvis, J. (2011) 'Leadership of uncertainty', in L. Trodd and L. Chivers (eds) *Inter-professional Working in Practice: Learning and Working Together for Children and Families*. Maidenhead: McGraw-Hill.

Lumsden, E. (2009) 'Joined-up thinking in practice: an exploration of professional collaboration', in T. Waller (ed.) *An Introduction to Early Childhood*. London: Sage. This is Chapter 11 in the book.

Powell, J. and Uppal, E.L. (2012) 'Teamwork and safeguarding', *Safeguarding Babies and Young Children: A Guide for Early Years Professionals*. Maidenhead: McGraw-Hill. This is Chapter 9 in the book.

Useful websites

The Common Assessment Framework (CAF) – http://www.education.gov.uk/childrenandyoungpeople/strategy/integratedworking/caf/a0068957/the-caf-process (accessed 01.08.12).

Confident minds – developing assertiveness skills, at: http://learnhowtobeconfident.net/assertiveness-skills (accessed 01.08.12).

References

Brookson, M. (2010) 'Working as a teaching assistant', in T. Bruce (ed.) *Early Childhood: A Guide for Students*, 2nd edition. London: Sage.

Carpenter, J., Hackett, S., Patsios, D. and Szilassy, E. (2010) *Outcomes of Interagency Training to Safeguard Children: Final Report to the Department for Children, Schools and Families and the Department of Health*. Bristol: DCSF.

Davis, J.M. (2011) *Integrated Children's Services*. London: Sage.

Department for Children, Schools and Families (DCSF) (2007) *Children's Workforce Development Council Report – Integrated Working: A Review of the Evidence*. Available at: http://dera.ioe.ac.uk/3674/1/Integrated_Working_A_Review_of_the_Evidence_report.pdf (accessed 12.11.2012).

Department for Education and Skills (DfES) (2004) *Every Child Matters: Change for Children*. London: HMSO. Available at: https://www.education.gov.uk/publications/eOrderingDownload/DfES10812004.pdf

Gasper, M. (2010) *Multi-agency Working in the Early Years: Challenges and Opportunities*. London: Sage.

GIRFEC (2006) *A Guide to Getting it Right for Every Child*. Available at: http://www.scotland.gov.uk/Resource/Doc/1141/0065063.pdf and the implementation plan at: http://www.scotland.gov.uk/Resource/Doc/131460/0031397.pdf

Laming, Lord (2003) *The Victoria Climbié Inquiry Report*. London: The Stationery Office.

Lumsden, E. (2009) 'Joined-up thinking in practice: an exploration of professional collaboration', in T. Waller (ed.) *An Introduction to Early Childhood*. London: Sage.

Lumsden, E. (2010) 'The new Early Years Professional in England', *International Journal for Cross-disciplinary Subjects in Education (IJCDSE)*, 1(3).

Maisey, D. (2011) 'Safeguarding, change and transitions', in L. Trodd and L. Chivers (eds) *Inter-professional Working in Practice: Learning and Working Together for Children and Families*. Maidenhead: McGraw-Hill.

Molyneux, J. (2001) 'Inter-professional teamworking: what makes teams work well?', *Journal of Inter-professional Care*, 15: 29–35.

Osgood, J. (2012) *Narratives from the Nursery: Negotiating Professional Identities in Early Childhood*. London: Routledge.

Powell, J. and Uppal, E.L. (2012) *Safeguarding Babies and Young Children: A Guide for Early Years Professionals*. Maidenhead: McGraw-Hill.

Rawlings, A. and Paliokosta, P. (2011) 'Learning for interprofessionalism: pedagogy for all', in L. Trodd and L. Chivers (eds) *Inter-professional Working in Practice: Learning and Working Together for Children and Families*. Maidenhead: McGraw-Hill.

Sanders, B. (2004) 'Inter-agency and multidisciplinary working', in T. Maynard and N. Thomas (eds) *An Introduction to Early Childhood Studies*. London: Sage.

Scottish Government (2004) *Curriculum for Excellence*. Edinburgh: Scottish Executive.

Siraj-Blatchford, I. and Siraj-Blatchford, J. (2009) *Improving Development Outcomes for Children through Effective Practice in Integrating Early Years Services*. Available at: http://www.c4eo.org.uk/themes/earlyyears/effectivepractice/files/c4eo_effective_practice_progress_map_summary_3.pdf (accessed 12.11.12).

Trodd, L. (2011) 'From a professional to an inter-professional', in L. Trodd and L. Chivers (eds) *Inter-professional Working in Practice: Learning and Working Together for Children and Families*. Maidenhead: McGraw-Hill.

Ward, U. (2011) 'Mentoring inter-professionally: a concept of practice for peer mentoring in children's centres', in L. Trodd and L. Chivers (eds) *Inter-professional Working in Practice: Learning and Working Together for Children and Families*. Maidenhead: McGraw-Hill.

Webster, S. and Clouston, A. (2011) 'Inter-professional learning and support: a case study of the Children's Centre Leaders' Network 2008–10', in L. Trodd and L. Chivers (eds) *Inter-professional Working in Practice: Learning and Working Together for Children and Families*. Maidenhead: McGraw-Hill.

CHAPTER 18

THE PRACTISING PROFESSIONAL AS RESEARCHER

Key ideas explored in this chapter
• how a practitioner becomes a researcher
• what research is and what it is for
• what 'action' or 'practitioner' research might look like
• an approach to carrying out an initial research project.

Introduction

Much has been written about research methods, methodology, ethical issues and analysis of findings. The idea of carrying out research can be daunting but in fact ECEC professionals are actually already doing so as part of their ongoing interactions, assessments and evaluations that inform their thinking and planning. Hopefully, this chapter will allow you to see that as a practitioner you have spent many hours observing and analysing how children learn and how you progress this learning. This chapter is intended to allow you to see how you can move from the stance of a practitioner to that of a researcher.

As an initial researcher, you will have a range of ideas and questions you want to address. Before embarking on any reading, consider the questions below and record your initial responses.

REFLECTIVE ACTIVITY

1 What is research?
2 What is action research?
3 What is the purpose of research?

What is research?

Research in its basic form is finding out something you didn't know beforehand. Sometimes, particularly in ECEC, we believe something to be true, for example that boys prefer certain toys and games, but we carry out research to evidence the truth of our assumptions. This can be confusing and challenging as others may not see the purpose so clearly, particularly when they hold very firm views and we, the researcher, have to be sure we remain objective. Lankshear and Knobel (2004) have defined research as a systematic process of searching again and again to answer questions.

Research can take different formats for different purposes. Verma and Mallick (1999) propose that research can be:

- **pure or basic research**: development of theory and discovery of fundamental facts to extend the boundaries of knowledge
- **applied or field research**: application of new knowledge to everyday problems
- **action research**: research on specific practical situations carried out by practitioners; its purpose is to solve clearly identified problems and it is continuous and cyclical; it is sometimes referred to as practitioner or teacher research
- **evaluation research**: carried out to assess the effectiveness of specific projects to see if the original aims have been achieved.

As an ECEC practitioner, you are most likely to undertake action research; this is the chosen format allowing us to solve identified problems and inform our own practice.

Those involved in education tend to want to make an overall difference to their practice, the learning experience or policy to inform practice. At the heart of our research is a desire to improve the learner's experience, leading to overall gains in whatever form this may be.

Research within the ECEC sector – social science research

In recent years, research has shifted focus from curriculum to pedagogy. Bruner (1996) discusses how pedagogy is shaped by teachers' intuitive assumptions about children's learning and argues for the importance of giving teachers deeper understanding of the learning process to take them beyond what he calls 'folk pedagogies'.

Educational research began to emerge in the 1990s, linked to the development of qualitative research. In those early days, if you were interested in teaching about or undertaking qualitative research you were often criticised (Lichtman, 2013). Research was seen in scientific terms, and this could not be science as you did not:

- test the hypothesis
- ensure it was objective
- have a large enough sample
- get someone else to interpret the data.

During the 1990s, a range of different qualitative approaches developed:

- postmodern
- structured
- case studies
- action research
- mixed methods.

And we will consider some of these approaches later in this chapter.

Are you already involved in research?

ECEC practitioners undervalue themselves as researchers. Through using reflective practice, they critically analyse real-life scenarios, drawing from years of practical engagement and reflection. Schön (1987) suggested the distinction between 'reflection in action' and 'reflection on action'. Reflection in action is about 'thinking on your feet' and 'reflection on action' is thinking after the event to evaluate what happened and why. Roberts-Holmes (2011) suggests reflective practice allows individuals to engage in research and to voice their opinions.

Reflection allows you to evaluate your practice and your professional development. Other chapters consider the 'professional role' and an important part of that is being accountable and should reflect upon practice to support the learning environment.

REFLECTIVE ACTIVITY

Keeping a research diary

You may have been involved in research previously or this may be your first sortie. As a support tool during this time, keep a research diary. This diary is a reflective log of your thoughts and feelings as they occur during the research process. Reflect upon your current practice and identify a critical incident which has been interesting, challenging and/or difficult for you to cope with:

a during the past two years
b more recently.

Extracts from your reflective diary can be used in your study in conjunction with additional pieces of data.

Making a start

The following is a systematic approach to the key aspects to consider when undertaking research.

Key processes for undertaking research:

1   Ideas, questions, theories to test
2   Reading literature, others' ideas
3   Clearly defining research questions
4   Identifying suitable approaches to data gathering
5   Gathering data
6   Analysing data
7   Interpreting data
8   Application, publication, alterations to practice.

Choosing a topic

It can be useful to ask yourself certain questions:

- Which aspects of care, education and the child are of particular interest to me?
- Which aspect would I like to study in greater depth?
- Why do I want to study them more closely?
- What do I know about each already?
- Which sources will help me find out more?
- Will I be able to carry out a practical investigation?
- Which topics will be of most benefit to me?
- Will I require parental or other permission and how do I organise this?

Effecting change

In the early stages of planning, it might be useful to spend some time thinking about your motive for selecting the topic of the project. What do you expect to get out of it? It could be about your own personal professional interest or to solve a personal professional problem. Perhaps you are interested in contributing to changing professional practice or policy. If this is the case then you will, even at this early stage, need to think about the eventual audience for your work and who, other than yourself, is likely to be affected by the outcome of your project. If you are to influence change to practices which are other than your own, then it would be foolish to attempt to plan and work through your project on your own. You will need to think carefully and strategically about how you might prepare those liable to be affected about the need for change. You will need to think carefully about the possible outcomes of your inquiry and any changes to which it might lead. If the change is to have the greatest chance of success, does it not also require involving from the outset those likely to be affected by the changes? So, it will be important to seek the co-operation of those likely to be affected both during the research/ development stage and also as a principal target audience for your findings at a later date. In bringing about change, there is often the need to balance 'development' and 'research'.

You have now thought about the possible topics, yourself and the children. You must now think about the 'setting' within which you work and the other people who work there.

REFLECTIVE ACTIVITY

The next set of questions you should ask yourself is:

- Have I discussed my suggested topics with the promoted staff/managers or lecturers?
- What was the initial reaction?
- Why do I think the suggested topics are relevant to my setting?
- Does my supervisor agree with my aspect of research?
- Was there one topic which interested me more than another? If so, why was this?
- When I talked to other colleagues about my possible topics, what was their reaction?
- Will they co-operate and show interest?
- What will these topics involve me doing – in other words, what investigations will I be making?
- What might the outcomes be?
- Will this topic give me what I most want for the setting and for myself?

Methods

Research methods include quantitative, qualitative and mixed method approaches. If you adopt a quantitative approach, you will need to use a large sample base and seek to prove the truth by experimentation and testing. This method relies on numerical data representing events that have been measured in some way and reflects regularities that might exist in an ECEC setting, for example attendance (Castle, 2012). If you adopt a qualitative approach, your focus will be on individuals or small groups and you will be concerned with understanding personal constructs, dealing with emotions, meanings and perspectives. You are likely to use a mix of these methods but tend towards largely qualitative research as you are unlikely to deal with large numbers of children or events. You are unlikely to need statistical analysis tools.

Mixed method is a third design and a more recent phenomenon that emerged during the 1980s combining quantitative and qualitative research designs. Mixed methods allow the researcher to take both a quantitative and qualitative approach. Creswell (2009, 2011) provides details on how to conduct a mixed methods study. Frequently, ECEC professionals engage with action/practitioner/reflective research in which mixed methods can be very useful. MacNaughton and Hughes (2008) state that at the heart of action research is the notion of instigating change in the institution, and such change might be in the form of practice, policy or culture within the institution. We sometimes refer to action research as 'practitioner research' because the practitioner is at the centre and in charge of the research as well as an active participant. Action research frequently focuses on collaboratively working with colleagues, parents and children. Action research is not, of course, limited to projects carried out by teachers in an educational setting. It is appropriate in any context when specific knowledge is required for a specific problem in a specific situation, or when a new approach is to be grafted on to an existing system (Cohen et al., 2000). Action research is not a method or technique. It is an approach which has proved to be particularly attractive to educators because of its practical, problem-solving emphasis, because practitioners carry out research and because the research is directed towards greater understanding and improvement of practice over time.

Methodology

Students frequently get confused between 'methodology' and 'methods'. Methodology considers wider issues around your research, the theoretical aspect of data collection and analysis. Methods are the actual data collection techniques you use – the questionnaires, interviews, etc.

Methodology will be a heading or chapter in any research study, and will answer the following questions:

- Who are the research participants?
- Have I obtained consent from all participants?
- How will data be collected, what is the reason for choosing this method and what was disregarded?
- Have I consider all the ethical issues, and will my research cause any harm?
- How will I record my data, interviews, questionnaires or pictures?
- What made me select these participants? Prior knowledge? Personal contacts?
- Is my research valid and reliable? How can I affirm this?
- What tools will I use to analyse the collected data?

The researcher needs to show why certain choices have been made and these aspects should be supported by referencing.

Literature review

Once you have identified an idea or topic to research and prior to constructing research questions, you should undertake a literature review. This allows you to ascertain if your research idea has been covered by other researchers who might be prominent in this field or whether you have identified a gap in the research. It is an opportunity to 'read around' your chosen topic. It may be that you have identified a 'gap' and you will need to access and read *related* literature.

One area where gaps can emerge is in research linked to how we use technology. As discussed in Chapter 10, technology moves so quickly and research linked to it needs to constantly catch up. A student recently offered a research proposal to consider how the children used i-pads. The student panicked as the literature review offered very little data. It was pointed out to the student that there were not yet many early years' settings offering children access to i-pads, so a gap had been identified in the context of research. There is, however, a good deal of *related* literature on the use of technology. Technology has also impacted upon how a literature review is carried out. Gone are the days of going to the library, looking at catalogues and trawling through research journals. The use of 'search engines' has made the task of identifying information so much easier. It can, however, have the disadvantage of delivering so much information the researcher has to be selective or the literature review would have no boundaries.

A traditional literature review has to be written in an impersonal and objective fashion (Lichtman, 2013). A review of the literature helps the researcher gain clarity as to the current state of research within their chosen area, what has gone before and what pieces are missing, as well as providing a framework for current research (Yin, 2011).

Walliman and Buckler (2008: 135) present the following literature review structure in Figure 18.1.

When conducting the literature review, read as much as time allows, be selective and avoid using literature just because it is there. Ensure that literature is up to date by referencing to recent research papers. When summarising the literature you have collated, you must be selective and ensure that all elements are relevant. The information collected will allow you to focus on constructing your research questions. The literature review will also help identify the differing methodologies. You might read (or at least access and scan) 30 or more texts and select four or five key sources for your literature review. You will refer back to these when you write up your findings and conclusions. You may refer to others at some point but even if you do not use them in this way, this reading 'around' the topic will clarify your thinking and inform your study.

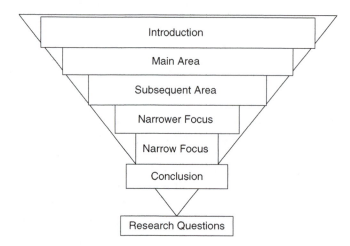

Figure 18.1   Walliman and Buckler's literature review structure

Research questions

When constructing research questions, you must ensure that they are specific and achievable. Your research questions will structure your research. Roberts-Holmes (2011) defines the importance of the overall research questions as:

- defining the limits and context of your study
- clarifying the purposes of the study
- helping to concentrate and focus your thinking, reading and writing upon the specific area
- helping to clarify the methods and identify what you actually need to do
- keeping your research going in the right direction for the duration of the study.

REFLECTIVE ACTIVITY

Try and write at least three specific questions linked to your chosen research topic. Ask a colleague or critical friend to analyse these questions – are they too narrow, or, if too broad, will they specifically address your topic?

Although the term research 'question' is usually used, you can narrow and focus your study without identifying or framing an actual question. In writing the main research question, you should identify an overall aim. An example might be as follows:

Example

Aim

An investigation of the problems of offering extended care for young children in a rural setting.
   You can then focus your study by identifying sub-questions or objectives.

Objectives

To systematically review the issues of extended care for young children by carrying out a literature review.
   To analyse the present needs of children and parents though interviews and a small focus group.
   To examine the availability of resources in terms of venue and staffing by interviewing staff.
   To synthesise all stakeholders' views to provide a feasible solution.

(Continued)

(Continued)

Collecting data

The collection of data can be through:

- case studies
- participant observation
- semi-structured interviews
- interviews with children/parents/colleagues
- sampling and surveys.

REFLECTIVE ACTIVITY

Imagine you are undertaking a piece of research within your own setting into family literacy and its impact on the development of children's language skills.

Design a questionnaire with six questions that is to be sent home for parents to complete. You will need to ask questions to elicit information about family life that might impact on language development, around whether parents read or read to their children; whether the family watches TV, eats together round the table, etc. Write down as many questions as you can.

Decide on the best six questions and then consider what you would need to do before distributing your questionnaire, such as seeking permission, and how you would introduce it and what other information would be essential – names, ages, gender, etc.

Questionnaires can be used for qualitative and quantitative methods. For qualitative studies, you are trying to gain an understanding from the participant's personal stance. Quantitative studies tend to be impersonal and gather data from a large identified participant base with a scaled questionnaire using a Lickert scale (see the example below) that is either numbered or on a continuum from 'agree' to 'disagree'. The data from these questionnaires can be collated and your analysis will be in a numerical format.

Example

Questionnaire

Please circle to indicate if you strongly agree (1), strongly disagree (5) or sit somewhere in between.

Q.1

I have enjoyed reading this book	1	2	3	4	5
I will recommend this book to others	1	2	3	4	5
I am motivated to begin research	1	2	3	4	5

Interviewing is the primary way that qualitative researchers gather data (Roulston, 2010). It can take the form of:

- **individual interviewing** – this allows the researcher to enter into a dialogue with the individual, and questions can range from being highly structured to having no structure (it could take the form of a learning conversation – see Chapter 17)
- **focus group interviewing** – this involves a group being interviewed at the same time. The benefits of a focus group interview are that individuals can bounce ideas off one another and often aspects that you may not have considered come to light. A disadvantage can be the difficulty in transcribing the interview as it can take more time and be more complex when participants talk together or interrupt
- **online interviewing** is relatively new and can take the format of chat rooms and webinars with interviews similar to the other formats.

The interview allows you to ascertain what the interviewee thinks or feels, or to gain or explore shared meanings. A structured interview format is often the choice of the novice researcher; this offers standardisation, especially if you are interviewing a range of participants. A structured interview can eliminate the role of the researcher and offer objectivity. However, most qualitative researchers would not advocate a structured interview. The favoured format would be a semi-structured interview offering flexibility where the interviewer can alter the questions as the situation demands. Rubin and Rubin (1995), when discussing qualitative interviewing, say that it is a great adventure and brings new information and opens windows into the experiences of the people you meet. Fontana and Prokos (2007) talk of in-depth interviewing providing greater breadth. One of the strengths of online interviewing is that it can be carried out at a time which is convenient for the interviewee and in surroundings which are familiar to them.

As the researcher, you will have identified your target individuals, and you will need to contact them. A key strength of qualitative inquiry is that participants are selected purposefully and we identify exactly who we want to interview. Within qualitative research, there are no rules as to how many interviews should be carried out. As qualitative research focuses on small numbers, we are looking for depth as we do not need to consider the degree of variation within the population which is required for quantitative research.

Interviews should be conducted in an environment where all parties feel comfortable. This is especially important when interviewing children (Roberts, 2008). As you are conducting the interview, also make general observations. This is important for a focus group approach as you may be witnessing aspects of power dynamics.

Ethical issues

If you are a student, your institution will have an ethics consent form that you will need to complete, indicating that you will do no harm during your research. Ethical behaviour is set by our individual moral principles, and rules which govern our profession. The collection of data should:

- cause no harm to the interviewee
- be confidential and stored in a secure manner (and data should be disposed of responsibly)
- provide informed consent (all participants will be informed of the nature of the study and are offered the opportunity to leave at any time without question).

As a researcher and when working with young children, you need to consider power dynamics which can act as a barrier. To overcome this, the child can become a researcher, whereby children interview other children (Gibbs et al., 2002). This could support the research in that children may ask questions you had not considered and children open up to their peers, particularly if your research involves children as respondents. In other words, you need to interview or complete questionnaires with them; you need to consider the ethics of what you are doing very carefully. Roberts (2008: 50) highlights how difficult it can be to gain informed consent as 'there are aspects of the adult/child relationship or practical issues concerning research in schools or youth settings, which may make non-participation difficult for a child or young person'. She is referring to older children and young people, and obviously this issue is even more difficult when it concerns very young children. Essentially, the researcher must do everything she can to ensure that the child has the opportunity to say 'no'.

Data can also be collected from case studies and observation of participants. As the focus of this book is children aged 0–8, the other key area for data collection is observation. As an ECEC practitioner, you will have experience of using observation to inform your daily practice. Observations can be used alongside other data collection techniques and the following are ones you may be familiar with:

- written records or narratives
- time and event sampling
- checklists
- diagrams such as tracking, graphs, flow charts, pie and bar charts or histograms
- use of a target child.

REFLECTIVE ACTIVITY

Identify a child and carry out two of the observation techniques listed, compare these and consider which technique offered the most data or which you were most confident in using.

Observations can be structured or unstructured. Carrying out observations within an early years setting can be problematic as there is so much happening. It can be difficult to record and maintain your focus. The volume of information means that recording the complete episode may be impossible so some form of anecdotal record will need to be designed that you can effectively reflect upon. Progressing to structured observations will require you to decide on the aim and focus. You should ask a colleague to cover your role whilst you carry out formal observations so that you can maintain your focus. Technology, especially video footage, offers the opportunity to revisit the experience, allowing a more in-depth analysis, but remember that transcribing is time-consuming and you must ensure you have permission.

Analysing qualitative data

You will inevitably begin to analyse, in the sense of engaging with the data from interviews and observations as it is gathered. When transcribing interviews, you will be revisiting the interview, and probably be unconsciously analysing the data. Qualitative data is inextricably bound up with human feelings, attitudes and judgements.

Initially, you will need to reduce the data into a manageable format, which could involve coding. Lofland (1971) came up with six classes which you could use to devise a coding scheme for 'social phenomena':

- acts
- activities
- meanings
- participation
- relationships
- settings.

The coding process allows you to select relevant data and identify emerging themes, categories or headings; these can be represented through the use of matrices and flow charts. You should try to relate the themes to the literature review.

Consider incorporating as many different forms of data to provide triangulation. This refers to the process of including multiple (at least three) data sources in your study (Castle, 2012). This increases the validity of your research and could be from observations, interviews, questionnaires, pictures and your research diary.

As you are analysing the data, refer back to your research questions. Does the collected data support these questions, and are the emerging themes similar to the findings identified in the literature review? Data analysis must also be supported by literature, justifying why you have identified these methods for analysis.

Discussion

As you analyse your results, you will offer some interpretation but you should discuss your findings with a focus on what the data actually means in terms of your work. In an action or practitioner research study, the impact of findings should link to impact on practice and recommendations for future practice. You should develop your discussion around what the findings mean to you; their significance to your future practice; the practice within your setting and the impact on others; whether there are implications for practice elsewhere; and how they relate to professional literature (particularly the literature you have already reviewed) and other research. You may also be able to identify opportunities for additional research, building on this initial study. Essentially, you need to provide as much in-depth analysis as you can. This can be a daunting task, particularly when you have collected quite a lot of data, and it will help to determine a structure for the discussion at the start. This may emerge from themes that you have identified from the analysis of data. Many student researchers find it helpful to return to their literature review and use the core sources from that to provide a structure.

Conclusions – your final part

Finally, you will want to draw some conclusions from your research and, as with your discussion, it will be important to structure this. Roberts-Holmes (2011) suggests the following questions to help with this:

- What tentative and cautious conclusions can you make from your small-scale research project?
- How does your study build upon/question/develop existing knowledge in this area?
- What reflections can you make about what worked well and what did not work well during the research process?
- What reflections can you make about your relationships with your research participants?
- What different and further questions would you ask if you were doing this project again?
- What could you do to improve your study?

A small-scale research study will not provide answers to any major questions within the complex field of early childhood education and care. You are likely to inform your own practice and may inform practice within your own setting. Each small piece of research may inform practice and provide answers in a wider context. You should not be disheartened if you find you are left with more questions than answers! This is an indication that you are developing as a researcher.

Conclusion

Starting research should not present enormous problems if you are realistic about the scale of the study you can undertake and take a step-by-step approach. It is important to explore some techniques, such as using questionnaires, before embarking on a full-scale research project. Perhaps the most useful technique in early childhood studies will be formal observations. Exploring and practising with a variety of techniques would be valuable to you as a researcher and as a practitioner. As with all research, it is vital to attend to ethical issues at the outset and throughout, and, again, when the research involves young children and their families this is particularly crucial.

Further reading

Harcourt, D. and Conroy, H. (2005) 'Informed assent: ethics and processes when researching with young children', *Early Child Development and Care*, 175(6): 567–77.

Lichtman, M. (2013) 'Designing your research: five popular research approaches', in *Qualitative Research in Education: A User's Guide*, 3rd edition. London: Sage. This is Chapter 4 in the book.

Roberts-Holmes, G. (2011) 'Ethical issues in early childhood research', in *Doing Your Early Years Research Project: A Step-by-Step Guide*, 2nd edition. London: Sage. This is Chapter 3 in the book.

References

Bruner, J. (1996) *The Culture of Education*. Cambridge, MA: Harvard University Press.

Castle, K. (2012) *Early Childhood Teacher Research: From Questions to Results*. London: Routledge.

Creswell, J. (2009) *Research Design: Qualitative, Quantitative and Mixed Methods Approaches*, 3rd edition. Thousand Oaks, CA: Sage.

Creswell, J. (2011) 'Controversies in mixed methods research', in N. Denzin and Y. Lincoln (eds) *The SAGE Handbook of Qualitative Research*. Thousand Oaks, CA: Sage, pp. 269–84.

Cohen, L., Manion, L. and Morrison, K. (2000) *Research Methods in Education*, 5th edition. London: Routledge.

Fontana, A. and Prokos, A. (2007) *The Interview: From Formal to Postmodern*. Walnut Creek, CA: Left Coast Press.

Gibbs, S., Mann, G. and Mathers, N. (2002) *Child to Child: A Practical Guide – Empowering Children as Active Citizens*. Available at: http://www.child-to-child.org/guide/index.html

Lankshear, C. and Knobel, M. (2004) *A Handbook for Teacher Research*. New York: Open University Press.

Lichtman, M. (2013) *Qualitative Research in Education: A User's Guide*, 3rd edition. London: Sage.

Lofland, J. (1971) *Analysing Social Settings: A Guide to Qualitative Observation and Analysis*. Belmont, CA: Wadsworth.

MacNaughton, G. and Hughes, P. (2008) *Doing Action Research in Early Childhood Studies*. Buckingham: Open University Press.

Roberts, H. (2008) 'Listening to children: and hearing them', in P. Christensen and A. James (eds) *Research with Children: Perspectives and Practices*, 2nd edition. London: Routledge.

Roberts-Holmes, G. (2011) *Doing Your Early Years Research Project: A Step-by-Step Guide*, 2nd edition. London: Sage.

Roulston, K. (2010) 'Considering quality in qualitative interviewing', *Qualitative Research*, 10(2): 199–228.

Rubin, H. and Rubin, J. (1995) *Qualitative Interviewing: The Art of Hearing Data*. Thousand Oaks, CA: Sage.

Schön, D. (1987) *Educating the Reflective Practitioner: Toward a New Design for Teaching and Learning in the Professions*. San Francisco, CA: Jossey-Bass.

Verma, G.K. and Mallick, K. (1999) *Researching Education: Perspectives and Techniques*. London: Falmer Press.

Walliman, N. and Buckler, S. (2008) *Your Dissertation in Education*. London: Sage.

Yin, R. (2011) *Qualitative Research from Start to Finish*. New York: Guilford Press.

CHAPTER 19

WORKING IN A TEAM

Key ideas explored in this chapter

- what 'teamwork' means within ECEC settings
- what constitutes 'good' teamwork, why it is important and how to be a good team member
- the role of team leader and manager.

What is a team?

A great deal is said and written about teams, teamwork and team building. Some of it is useful to an ECEC setting and some is best left in the business world for which it was first devised. In most cases, the internal team in an ECEC setting is small. Sometimes there is a very small team of 2–4 people operating within a larger team, for example in a school nursery class. The focus of this chapter is really on those small teams. Chapter 17 looks at inter-professional teams where the skills needed are essentially the same but the dynamics are very different. It is perhaps more difficult when there are only 2–4 people to perceive yourself as part of a team. Roles and responsibilities invariably overlap and the roles of leader and manager are not always clearly defined. It can be difficult sometimes on entering a nursery class, for example, to determine which person is the teacher, the nursery nurse and often even which person is the student. This is not a criticism as that is how a team should look, particularly to the children, when it is working well. A team can be any group of people of any size working towards a shared goal. In this context, we are concerned with the team immediately around the child when the child is attending an ECEC setting.

The team around the child within the setting must necessarily include the child and their parent/primary carer but the focus here is on the group of staff with the shared goal of supporting the child within the setting to achieve the most positive outcome. This is the definition of a team taken here, that is, 'a group of people working towards a shared goal'.

Why working in a team is important

Working in a team and working as a team help us reach our goals more quickly and efficiently. In an ECEC context, the ultimate goal is a positive outcome for every child or, in other words, enabling every child to reach their full potential. Every piece of recent policy documentation across the UK supports and promotes team working (see, for example, DfES, 2004a, 2004b; Scottish Government, 2008, 2010). However, it is often more helpful to go beyond policy directives to convince ourselves and others of the efficacy of working together as a team.

REFLECTIVE ACTIVITY

Think about the more obvious teams such as a football team, a team of soldiers or fire-fighters. The last is a good model to reflect on. Each group works together on a particular shift with each member of the team fulfilling a particular role, for example 'driver'. Each member is responsible for their own kit and specific jobs. Imagine if the alarm went and they stopped to argue over who was going to drive that day or if someone picked up another person's kit or had not stowed vital equipment after the last call-out.

There is a simple and quite fun activity that you can engage in with a group of people to highlight how much more effective you can be together. Form teams of 3–6 people. Give them 10 problem-solving quiz questions (the *SAS Survival Handbook* by Wiseman, 2009 is a good source). The questions should not pertain to their expertise so that they have a more equal chance of solving the problem. An example might be:

If you had to wade across a river in torrent where the water is chest high, would it be better to go across facing upstream, downstream or the other bank?

Each person should answer the questions individually first, writing down a response, then discuss and agree answers as a team. As a team, you will get more right answers and in the process identify strengths within the team.

Team working is important simply because it makes us more effective. In an ECEC setting, it will enable staff to achieve better outcomes for children, meaning each child can reach their full potential. Teamwork, developing and using the skills discussed later in this chapter, will also create a better working environment for ECEC professionals where they will feel less stressed. Identifying goals, working towards them together and achieving them is more rewarding as well as more efficient. Some of the important advantages for teamwork within an ECEC setting have been identified as:

- support, stimulation and a sense of belonging
- stress reduction and a pleasant working environment
- minimised conflicts and efficient achievement of goals
- the provision of a role model for children and parents (Rodd, 1998).

The last bullet point above is possibly the most important.

Team building

There is one model of team building that many are familiar with and this is Tuckman's (1965) team-formation model. This model is based on the principle that a team is like a living organism that goes through stages of development and continues to evolve; it is never static (Whalley, 2011). The model itself has evolved but remains useful, particularly the original four stages he identified, outlined as follows:

- **Stage 1: 'Forming'** – this is where the team first forms and begins to define roles and responsibilities and basically gets to know each other. There is a long way to go to build trust, set goals, sort out who is doing what and who can do what and generally gain clarity. Perhaps the most important thing at this stage is to establish and agree on leadership.
- **Stage 2: 'Storming'** – this is just as it sounds! A time where each team member begins to articulate their own understanding of their role and responsibilities and the goals. It can be competitive and anxious and cliques may form. Leadership can be tested but if team members listen and accept feedback, goals and roles can be modified, resources identified and trust built.

- **Stage 3: 'Norming'** – this is where the team starts to really get on with the job once the purpose, roles, responsibilities and resources are agreed on and identified. At this time, it is important to keep communicating, share and celebrate success, identify new goals, delegate more freely and perhaps select and induct new team members.
- **Stage 4: 'Performing'** – this is when the team is working well, is confident and effective. Confrontation can be risked as there is openness and trust between members. Perhaps most importantly, it is when individuals defer to team needs.

Pilcher (2009) suggests that it is in the 'storming' stage of team development that relationships within the team are at their most vulnerable, and consequently where relationships with parents are also at their most fragile. It can be the point where individuals or groups, in this case parents, can become isolated. Collaboration and partnership in the future can be compromised. This is why this model can be useful as it clearly identifies typical patterns of behaviour that are likely to occur in the development of any team. Most readers, I suspect, will be able to think of situations where they recognise these stages, particularly the 'storming' stage. Almost any group of people, however disparate, can manage to 'get on' for a short time, but also any group, no matter how well they 'get on' initially, will go through a degree of 'storming'. Sadly, not all groups establish 'norms' and start to 'perform'.

A final stage was added to the original four in Tuckman and Jensen (1977). Revisiting the theory, they suggested a final stage of 'transforming' or what is sometimes called 'adjourning'. The idea of completing a task, celebrating success, reviewing and moving on may seem less relevant in an ECEC setting. It may be easier to think about these stages simply as building and maintaining a team. In the sometimes stormy process of building a team or in the sometimes slow grinding process of maintaining a team for a long time, Edgington (2004) suggests three main types of team that can emerge in an ECEC setting. These are identified as:

- **a cosy team** where members have worked together for a long time and feel everything is working well for them, so will not welcome new members and will be averse to and ignore change; communication appears good but team members are merely affirming and maintaining the status quo
- **a turbulent team** where, although things may seem well in meetings where the decisions of the few are accepted, outside disagreement is strongly expressed and real change is resisted; communication appears to happen in formal settings (meetings) but there is no clear dialogue and no real shared decision making, and it is largely negative
- **a rigorous and challenging team** where members take a professional approach so that they can disagree but reach collective decisions; communication is good both formally and informally and the team are open to change and seek challenge and development.

REFLECTIVE ACTIVITY

Think about any 'team' you have been a part of:

- Can you identify which of the main types (above) your team was most similar to?
- How effective was the team?
- What were the key aspects that determined the level of effectiveness?
- On reflection, could you personally have changed the team and impacted upon its effectiveness?

Teamwork skills

It is clear from looking at the description of the types of team above that certain key skills impact on the building and maintenance of any team. Clearly, one is communication, and good communication might include:

- active and accurate listening
- setting aside time for talk, both informal conversations and formal dialogue in meetings
- allowing genuine discussion which must include disagreement at times
- making effective use of written communication.

Daly et al. (2004) identify characteristics of effective *workplace* communication, stating that it must be:

- clear, concise and easily understood
- presented objectively and in a manageable form
- regular and systematic
- relevant
- open to scrutiny
- a two-way process.

An important part of developing and establishing good communication lies in the development of supportive relationships and vice versa. Indeed, it is questionable whether one can exist without the other. Appropriate, supportive working relationships need to be based on:

- mutual respect
- empathy
- praise and encouragement
- team members being able to ask for help
- freedom to disagree.

It is important to stress that, whilst friendship between colleagues can meet all the above requirements, it is not a vital ingredient to good teamwork in any work environment. Close friendship between some team members can hinder cohesive teamwork by the whole group.

Personal qualities and interpersonal skills

The skills listed in Chapter 17 as being important to developing inter-professional practice are exactly the same as those required to develop a good team within a setting. These include:

- communication skills – creating rapport, active listening, body language, empathy, questioning, challenging
- assertiveness skills – giving/receiving criticism, saying no, expressing feelings appropriately, satisfying/defending needs whilst respecting others
- co-operation skills – team building, negotiation, conflict resolution, problem management, group work
- decision-making skills – gathering info, prioritising and focusing, summarising, setting goals, creating options for action.

All of the above skills would be called interpersonal skills. Although it could be argued that interpersonal skills that facilitate communication are humanity's greatest accomplishment, the average person does not communicate well. In our society, it is rare for people to share what really matters. It is equally rare for people to listen intently enough to really understand what another person is saying. Sometimes people fix their gaze on a friend who is talking and allow their minds to wander off to other matters. Sometimes they pretend to listen but are merely marking time, formulating what they will say as soon as they can begin talking.

REFLECTIVE ACTIVITY

Here is a list of personal qualities:

- reliability
- flexibility
- even-temperedness
- patience
- having a sense of humour
- being a good communicator
- trustworthiness

- empathy
- tolerance
- being a good listener
- practicality.

First, consider each of these and rate them in terms of how important these qualities are to building good working relationships in your workplace and with other professionals.

Now consider these qualities again – *in terms of how you rate yourself!*

Now consider whether the above list is of qualities or skills. *If they are qualities, does that mean you either possess them or you don't and there is nothing you can do about it? If they are skills, can you develop them and, if so, how?*

You might want to discuss this with other students and/or colleagues – but you do not have to share your own rating!

Whether the list above refers to qualities or skills, they can be developed and improved in any individual – but only if the need to do so is identified and accepted by the individual. It is rather like an addict who has to recognise his addiction and desire to beat it. Sadly, many of us continue through life firmly believing we are patient, flexible, empathic good listeners and that problems are caused by others. This is more comfortable because we cannot do anything about that and it lets us off the hook.

Ineffective communication causes an interpersonal gap that is experienced in all facets of life and in all sectors of society. However, research studies indicate that, despite a tendency towards defensiveness, people of all ages can learn specific communication skills that lead to improved relationships and increased vocational competence.

REFLECTIVE ACTIVITY

What specific barriers are apt to hinder a conversation? Experts in interpersonal communication have identified responses that tend to block conversations. These include:

- **criticising** – making negative evaluations of the other person, their actions or attitudes
- **stereotyping**, name calling, generalisations or 'put-downs' – such as 'you're always doing silly things like that' or 'she's hopeless, just silly'
- **analysing and making a diagnosis** – supplying explanations and reasons for why a person behaves as they do (sometimes called 'psychobabble')

(Continued)

(Continued)

- **giving orders** – issuing instructions or commands to do what you want done
- **moralising** – telling another person what is the right thing to do
- **repeated closed questions** – these only allow one correct answer
- **advising** – giving the solutions to any problem without room for discussion or dissent
- **diverting** – distracting by introducing other topics that push aside another person's problem or issue
- **logical argument** – introducing facts or figures to convince the other of your argument without consideration of the emotional factors
- **reassuring** – trying to stop the other person from feeling or expressing their negative emotions.

These ways of responding may block conversation because they thwart the person's problem-solving efficiency and increase the emotional distance between people.

Thinking back over a conversation you've had recently, can you identify any of these roadblocks?

Active listening

Much of our time, whatever occupation we are in, is spent in communication. Studies have shown that this is about 70 per cent for most people, and nearly half of that time is spent listening. Learning to be an effective listener can be difficult but is important because of the amount of it that we do each day. It can be helpful to define the difference between hearing and listening:

Hearing	is a word used to describe the physiological sensory processes by which auditory sensations are received by the ears and transmitted to the brain.
Listening	refers to a more complex psychological procedure involving interpreting and understanding the significance of the sensory experience.

Listening is a complex skill that takes what we hear and makes sense of it. It is really a collection of skills that include hearing and can be clustered as follows:

- attending skills – these are about giving your physical attention to someone; these non-verbal signals that indicate you are paying attention include eye contact, posture and movement
- following skills – these are about allowing and encouraging the other person to talk and include appropriate questions, encouraging brief comments or sounds, sentence starters and attentive silence

- reflecting skills – these are about being able to demonstrate that you have understood properly and giving an opportunity for clarification, and include restating salient points or paraphrasing and making summative reflective statements.

Using this collection of skills effectively is often referred to as active listening, an important part of this complex lexicon of communication. Effective listening which will be active listening is vital to support dialogue. 'Active listening focuses attention on the speaker. It means withstanding the inner urge to talk about yourself. It requires concentration and a genuine willingness to hear what is being said' (Walker and Gibson, 2011: 12).

Assertiveness

Another important communication skill is assertiveness. Each individual has a unique personal space which is physical, psychological and values territory which is theirs. This space varies in size and in many other ways from one person to another. To learn to successfully defend one's space is important but assertiveness is more than this. Assertive people reach out to other people. They are honest with themselves and others. They can say directly what it is they want, need or feel, but not at the expense of others. They are confident and positive but can see another point of view. Being assertive requires self-respect and respect for other people (Daly et al., 2004).

One way of understanding assertion is to see it as a way of defending one's space and impacting on other people and society in non-destructive ways. The assertive person utilises methods of communication which enable them to maintain self-respect, pursue happiness and satisfaction of their needs, and defend their rights and personal space without abusing or dominating other people. Assertiveness is a way of being in the world which confirms one's own individual worth and dignity, whilst simultaneously confirming and maintaining the worth of others.

A useful way of defining assertion is to place it on a continuum between submission and aggression and to contrast it with them. One route to developing the confidence to assert yourself without negative impact on others in the workplace is continued professional development. Confidence needs the foundation of knowledge and understanding and a strong professional identity.

Teamwork skills would include the interpersonal skills outlined above, but more specifically can be identified as:

1 **Listening:** there is a time to talk and a time to listen and the time to listen comes twice as often as the time to talk.
2 **Sacrifice:** each team member may need to make a sacrifice. It could be time, resources or positions of power.
3 **Sharing:** what one person knows may be the key to another person's problem. We have to be willing to share those keys, even when it will make someone else look better.

4   **Communication:** when there are problems or successes, a team has to be willing to communicate effectively what went right and wrong. It is just as important to analyse and celebrate your successes as to focus on your problems or failures.

5   **Language:** it is important to use positive language. If you are at all demeaning, domineering or insulting, the team will grind to a halt and just consist of rivals.

6   **Hard work:** team members have to be willing to work hard on an individual basis and then turn that hard work over to the team and achieve a shared goal.

7   **Persuasion:** everyone should be encouraged to exchange, defend and then eventually rethink their ideas. You have to love your idea but be open to persuasion. (Adapted from: http://www.tips4teamwork.com/top-7-teamwork-skills.htm)

As stated in Chapter 17, perhaps the most important factor in building and maintaining any team is establishing shared goals and ensuring all members of the team know, understand and believe in these shared goals. It may appear even more self-evident that a team *within* a setting should share goals around supporting a child and their family. The case study in Chapter 17 illustrated how a team of professionals from different disciplines might have had different perspectives giving rise to slightly different goals, at least in the short term. The case study below provides an example of how professionals supporting a child and her family within a setting might have different concerns or different levels of concern, as well as different approaches to dealing with them.

CASE STUDY

Linzi is 2 years and 5 months old. She attends a local authority nursery every day from 9.00 to 11.30. Her mother is a young (aged 19) single parent who is struggling to cope both financially and emotionally. Most days, Linzi's gran, who is herself not yet 50 and still working full-time in a local supermarket, brings Linzi to nursery and sometimes collects her depending on her shift pattern. Jenna is the key person assigned to Linzi – she is only 17 and six months into her training. Stacey is the more senior member of staff in the room with Linzi, and Phyllis is the manager of the centre. A number of other members of staff have contact with Linzi and her family throughout the week.

Linzi developed quite severe eczema at about 18 months old. She is often tearful, particularly in the morning after Gran has left, and this seems to be getting worse. She has sometimes been quite aggressive towards other children, although she is very keen and determined to play with others, seldom settling to anything on her own even for a moment. Jenna and Stacey have both found it difficult to communicate their concerns to Linzi's mother. She is unwilling to talk to Jenna who feels this is because they are close in age. She appears to listen to Stacey on the few occasions where Stacey has forced a conversation but does not act on advice. Linzi's gran is very friendly towards Jenna but when feeling the need to raise any concerns will only talk to Stacey. She has made it clear to Stacey that she feels she is 'on top of things' and 'quite capable of supporting her own daughter to bring up Linzi'. Stacey knows Gran as she is a neighbour. Neither Mum nor Gran are keen to talk to the manager.

Jenna would like more support from Stacey and the manager to help her establish a better relationship with both Mum and Gran and feels that her concerns, arising from working closely with Linzi and seeing her day to day, are not being heard and addressed. She is concerned about the management of her eczema, her crying and her aggression towards other children which she feels are all connected. Stacey feels that as long as Linzi is attending regularly, these concerns are being monitored. She believes she has met her responsibilities as she has spoken to both Mum and Gran and has asked them to meet with the manager. She has made it clear to Jenna that she does not want her to 'go over her head' to enlist more support from the manager. The manager is currently preparing for an inspection coming up in the next six weeks and is spending a good deal of time on paperwork.

Meanwhile, another member of staff, who is responsible for preparing food and cleaning on a part-time basis, is a friend of Linzi's mum. She constantly 'chats' to Jenna, telling her about how her mum leaves her with her gran, ignores advice about how to treat the eczema, buys her sweets and toys to 'keep her quiet' and quite a lot of detail about nights out and boyfriends. When Jenna repeats some of the information to Stacey, she is told very brusquely that this is just gossip and it is thoroughly unprofessional for Jenna to engage in any such conversation.

The team members around Linzi, in the case study above, are not communicating very well with each other. They are not communicating well with the primary carers for Linzi. There is a dynamic set-up between all parties due to their respective roles and responsibilities, age and experience, and their individual understanding of people and situations. There are many factors impacting upon how they perform as a team, not least their understanding that they are a team and should act as one.

REFLECTIVE ACTIVITY

Consider the situation in the case study of Linzi. Do you think Stacey and Jenna see themselves as a team? Do you think they consider the manager, Phyllis, as part of their team? They are a team but what is stopping them from acting as one?

(Continued)

(Continued)

What can you imagine happening in this scenario?

Different events might cause a crisis for Linzi, such as Gran becoming ill and being unable to offer support, or Linzi needing a stay in hospital because of skin infection or asthma. Even a small change in circumstances, such as Gran changing jobs and no longer working hours that enable her to pick up and drop off at Nursery, could be stressful for Linzi. Who is most likely to become aware of such a crisis and how could it be averted or mitigated?

What would you do if you were Jenna?

What would you do if you were Stacey?

What would you do if you were the manager?

Leadership and management

The terms leader and manager are often used interchangeably and it is a moot point whether there is a definable difference. It is worth consideration and it is suggested here that there is. Consider for a moment whether it is possible for a team to be led (perhaps strongly and well) but not managed, or alternatively well managed but lack leadership. The words we use and the labels we apply can be emotive. The word 'leadership' suggests power, charisma, inspiration – someone with ideas and influence. The word 'manager' suggests order, efficiency and generally more pragmatic and less exciting skills. Perhaps we should think carefully about what it is we want in an ECEC setting and what is realistic – ideally, of course, leadership and management but, on balance, skilled and effective management alone might be preferable to charismatic leadership without good management skills. It is possible for many to learn and develop the skills of good management but surely only those with innate talent will emerge as leaders?

REFLECTIVE ACTIVITY

Reflect on this as you read through the chapter. Is there a clear difference between management and leadership? Can you have one without the other? Is one more important than the other in this context? Can you learn skills for both?

As with team building, there are many theories of management and leadership style. Again, many of these are more suited to the world of business but it can be helpful to explore these and the key factors they identify. McCauley et al. (1998, cited in

Whalley, 2011) identified five 'S' factors that can critically affect the cohesion of any team, including:

- **stability** – in other words, teams can work better with the same members over time
- **similarity** – it helps if members are similar in respect of age, gender, skills, etc.
- **size** – large teams are more difficult to maintain
- **support** – teams need good leadership and management (it is interesting that both terms are used)
- **satisfaction** – teams that do not perform well or experience success and have the opportunity to celebrate it are likely to fall apart.

It is clear in the case study above that there are problems due to the disparity in age and experience, and perhaps a lack of leadership and management. A good inspection report might give the team a boost but only if it is acknowledged and celebrated in terms of a *team* success.

Theorists have identified different leadership styles such as the democratic leader, the authoritarian leader and the laissez-faire leader. This is not always helpful, particularly in the context of an ECEC setting where roles often overlap, are often thrust upon team members and, as in any context styles, are difficult to define. A nursery manager may strive to be democratic but be perceived as laissez-faire and sometimes be forced to adopt an authoritarian style. Daly et al. (2004) have drawn on various management and leadership theories to identify some key characteristics of effective early years' management. These include:

- the ability to define a mission, a vision for the future or a strategy and communicate to the team and all stakeholders (parents, local authority, etc.)
- being a good communicator
- the ability to create an atmosphere of trust and confidence by respecting confidentiality
- being prepared to delegate by identifying skills and strengths in other team members and using them
- respecting the views of the team by being open to new ideas and able to take calculated risks and review of old ones
- finding out what motivates or makes the team 'tick'
- supporting all team members by listening, offering training, etc.
- being a good role model, or in other words leading from the front
- encouraging a 'can do' attitude by being positive and sharing success
- ensuring optimum use of resources, particularly human resources
- maintaining a sense of humour!

One theory of leadership that is often referred to and can prove useful in furthering our understanding of the dynamics involved, is MacGregor's X and Y theory (MacGregor, 1960). Simply explained, in this theory he identifies two kinds of leader or 'boss'. The 'X' boss believes employees dislike work and try to avoid it so assume they have to bully people into working and doing what they want. The 'Y' boss thinks employees like their work and see it as an important part of their life. MacGregor suggests people behave as the boss expects, so those working for a 'Y' boss would value and enjoy their work. There is some merit in this theory when viewed alongside theories of learning and studies of behaviour management. We understand the importance of positive role models, motivation and reward for successful learning for children. Why would it be any different for adults in the workplace? A positive attitude, the ability to persuade and inspire others to follow rather than push, and the ability to delegate and empower others appear in every list of key attributes for leaders and managers. Perhaps the ultimate goal in an ECEC setting, as Canning (2009: 42) suggests, is 'letting go' of staff, 'empowering them to grow as practitioners and to support them in gaining ownership of their roles and responsibilities'.

Conclusion

Working as a team can create the best environment for children in an ECEC setting as well as staff. There is no identifiable negative outcome from working as a team whilst there are many that arise from failing to do so effectively. Some of the barriers to building and maintaining a team can be exacerbated by working in a very small team. Initially, people working with very few others and often on a part-time basis may not see themselves as part of a team. Disparity in age, experience and qualifications can create challenges but there are steps to take to overcome these and motivation is certainly a key factor in doing so. The leader or manager plays a vital role in motivating the team.

Neugebauer and Neugebauer (1998) have identified a useful five-step framework for team building as:

- set achievable goals – ideally all team members together
- clarify roles – to themselves and others
- build supportive relationships – this should include all team members with identified opportunities to give and receive feedback and develop trust
- encourage active participation – use individual skills and knowledge and accept and value all ideas and inputs
- monitor team effectiveness – ensure goals are achieved and celebrated, acknowledging each contribution.

Further reading

Pilcher, M. (2009) 'Making a positive contribution', in A. Robins and S. Callan (eds) *Managing an Early Years Setting*. London: Sage. This is Chapter 5 in the book.

Rodd, J. (2012) 'Building and leading a team', in L. Miller, R. Drury and C. Cable (eds) *Extending Professional Practice in the Early Years*. London: Sage. This is Chapter 21 in the book.

Whalley, M. (2011) *Leading Practice in Early Years Settings*, 2nd edition. Exeter: Learning Matters. See Chapters 2 and 7.

Useful website

Useful handouts showing Tuckman's Team Development Model can be found at: http://salvos.org.au/scribe/sites/2020/files/Resources/Transitions/HANDOUT_-_Tuckmans_Team_Development_Model.pdf

References

Canning, N. (2009) 'Empowering communities through inspirational leadership', in A. Robins and S. Callan (eds) *Managing an Early Years Setting*. London: Sage.

Daly, M., Byers, E. and Taylor, W. (2004) *Early Years Management in Practice*. London: Heinemann.

DfES (2004a) *Children Act 2004*. London: HMSO.

DfES (2004b) *Every Child Matters: Change for Children*. London: HMSO.

Edgington, M. (2004) *The Foundation Stage Teacher in Action: Teaching 3, 4 and 5 Year Olds*. London: Paul Chapman Publishing.

MacGregor, D. (1960) *The Human Side of Enterprise*. New York: McGraw-Hill.

Neugebauer, B. and Neugebauer, R. (eds) (1998) *The Art of Leadership: Managing Early Childhood Organisations*, Vol. 2. Perth: Childcare Information Exchange.

Pilcher, M. (2009) 'Making a positive contribution', in A. Robins and S. Callan (eds) *Managing an Early Years Setting*. London: Sage.

Rodd, J. (1998) *Leadership in Early Childhood*, 2nd edition. Buckingham: Open University Press.

Scottish Government (2008) *The Early Years Framework*. Edinburgh: Scottish Government.

Scottish Government (2010) *Getting it Right for Every Child*. Edinburgh: Scottish Government.

Tuckman, B. (1965) 'Developmental sequence in small groups', *Psychological Bulletin*, 63: 384–99.

Tuckman, B.W. and Jensen, M.A.C. (1977) 'Stages of small group development revisited', *Group and Organization Studies*, 2: 419–27.

Walker, F. and Gibson, J. (2011) *The Art of Active Listening* (eBook). Available at: http://www.amazon.co.uk/The-Active-Listening-Communication-ebook/dp/B005MSOIVM#reader_B005MSOIVM

Whalley, M. (2011) *Leading Practice in Early Years Settings*, 2nd edition. Exeter: Learning Matters.

Wiseman, J. (2009) *SAS Survival Handbook: The Ultimate Guide to Surviving Anywhere*. London: HarperCollins.

CHAPTER 20

THE ISSUE OF PROFESSIONAL AUTONOMY

Key ideas explored in this chapter

- what we mean by professional autonomy
- why it is important
- how it is being eroded and how this can be reversed
- the possible impact of quality continuous professional development on challenging compliance.

Defining professional autonomy in ECEC

Autonomy could be defined as freedom, choice or self-regulation for the individual. An accepted definition of professional autonomy would be one where individuals within that profession were encouraged and enabled to apply their own professional judgement to situations and are able to act accordingly. However, in order to be able to do this within a profession, some limits or boundaries as to what is acceptable must be agreed. This could be defined as the 'specific body of knowledge', and this aspect is developed further in Chapter 16 of this book.

Any publication concerned with good practice in ECEC could be guaranteed to stress the importance of allowing maximum opportunities for autonomy of the child. Yet, this characteristic which we are so keen to promote in children, is one that has been consistently eroded in the ECEC staff who work with these children. The OECD (2004) raises the important question of what freedom exists at the setting level, the ECEC professional level and the child level, and states that there should be a commitment that 'all curricula should give centres, teachers and children the largest possible freedom' (p. 26), but still retain the direction of overall common goals.

Raya (2007) asserts that professional autonomy is a necessary and complementary concept of learner autonomy. Anderson (1987: 368, cited in Raya, 2007: 33) describes autonomy as a point along a continuum which provides a balance between standardisation and uniqueness: 'Unbridled it becomes license; excessively controlled it becomes standardised; and somewhere in between, it provides the freedom needed by teachers to function professionally and effectively in their classrooms.'

Although Raya was referring specifically to teachers in secondary schools, the above quote is equally appropriate for the ECEC workforce. Osgood (2006) refers to the current professional context for ECEC workers in the UK as providing a 'hot topic for debate and contention'. She asserts that all practitioners within this area have experienced an intensification of workload where the preoccupation is with 'meeting standards' rather than with wrestling with the meaning of professional identity. She would assert that this could not only be used as 'a means of control and increased domination to those in power' (p. 5), but that it is in fact a deliberate strategy on the part of government.

Possible reasons for this state are suggested. One is that the workforce is predominantly feminine but also mostly made up of working-class women, where the power issues exerted by government policy contribute to a loss of identity and ensuing marginalisation of the workforce. This is analysed and explained in terms of Foucault's theory (1980) where workers become 'fashioned' through government discourse in certain ways to ensure that political and societal goals are met. These issues of power, domination and top-down control of the workforce lead to a situation where the 'power of discourse and the role of agency … suggests that government policy is both text and discourse and that through policy, governments seek to establish a "correct reading" or to promote certain discursive "truths", for example, about what it means to be a professional in ECEC' (Osgood, 2006: 7).

As a result, groups such as the ECEC workforce, then become marginalised by the manifestation of this power, which is interpreted and subsequently accepted as the truth around an issue, so that it becomes increasingly difficult to challenge accepted authority, and a simultaneous loss of professional autonomy ensues, as described by Foucault (1980: 27):

Knowledge linked to power, not only assumes the authority of 'the truth' but has the power to make itself true. All knowledge, once applied in the real world, has effects, and in that sense at least, 'becomes true.' Knowledge, once used to regulate the conduct of others, entails constraint, regulation and the disciplining of practice.

In the case of ECEC, the effects of this have been to increase and monitor performativity through the use of reductionist systems such as audits, checklists and other tasks imposed to provide 'evidence' of quality and accountability. These measures actively work against the promotion and development of higher-order thinking skills, such as creative and critical thinking, analysis, problem solving and visualisation, for children and staff. Such measures also work against a social-constructivist approach to professionalism, meaning the ways in which our 'world view' is shaped not only by our own efforts, but by the opinions and ideas of others. A social-constructivist approach to learning that encourages children to learn through social interaction, to learn with support from peers as well as adults, and to take ownership of their own learning underpins what is seen as best practice in ECEC and yet it is not modelled in the approach to learning for ECEC professionals. Sandberg et al. (2007) writing about continuing professional development (CPD) for pre-school professionals in Sweden, stress the importance of the socio-cultural aspects of learning for ECEC workers and point out that these aspects are central to promoting successful developmental pedagogy.

The erosion of professional autonomy

Osgood (2012) has problematised the situation as being one where, at government level, a 'crisis in care' is admitted, with the ensuing directives being engaged with a reform of the childcare workforce. We should also remember that the main reason for expansion of daycare in the UK was not for altruistic reasons in terms of the benefits to children, but rather to allow more mothers to join the workforce. Since that time, the childcare workforce has been viewed as 'lacking', in order words conforming to a deficit model, further aggravated by persistent low pay and poor working conditions.

Many directives about the 'appropriate' level of qualification for ECEC workers have been declared by, for example the Scottish Social Services Council (SSSC), the regulatory body for care in Scotland. These qualifications, as in the rest of the UK, can be obtained by a variety of means, through Further Education colleges, on-the-job training or universities. However, the most important factor is that the goalposts for these qualifications keep shifting and ECEC workers are faced with a myriad of choices and progression routes, yet few people in authority appear to have any overarching understanding of the situation. How is this helping children?

Evidence from workforce development meetings demonstrates that currently the situation is no better than it was 10 years ago. Staffing of daycare still remains a problem, wages are still extremely low and working conditions unimproved for the majority of the ECEC workforce. Currently, around the area in which our university is situated, many ECEC workers are de-registering themselves from 'lead practitioner' roles, in order to avoid having to work towards further qualifications. The government aim of having 'a professional' working in every setting, or in the case of Scotland, the SSSC requirement to have every setting managed by a graduate in Childhood Practice, or with a Professional Development Award at SQA Level 9 in Childhood Practice, is perhaps admirable. However, evidence from action research carried out by teachers on our post-graduate courses in Early Education and substantiated by students on the BA Childhood Practice programme, is showing that the people achieving or working towards the degree are not necessarily in daily contact with children. This may be because the clear focus of both of these qualifications, as promoted by the regulatory body, is on 'management' and the focus on the 'child at the centre' seems to have become somewhat more diffuse. How is this helping children?

Funding of these 'necessary' qualifications is also another issue. Osgood (2012) discusses the economic rationale behind policy reform in ECEC, which she considers to have a masculine profile within a feminised profession. Sandberg et al. (2007) state that in Sweden it is the local authorities who are directly responsible for staff training and development, similar to Scotland where local authorities, at least for early years development, delegate funding procedures to Childcare Partnerships. Burchell et al. (2002) also discuss the relative costs of training. 'In-house' training within local authorities can be significantly cheaper than buying into university provision. Davies and Preston (2002) point out that government policy which has supported the move to 'marketplace provision' has also had the effect of placing universities in direct competition with one another and with 'partner' local authorities. Marketplace provision is not necessarily synonymous with quality. How is this helping children?

Osgood (2006) discusses this aspect further by referring to the local authority 'in-house' CPD provision which was designed largely to meet changes in government policy but bring with it increased accountability, performativity and standardised approaches to practice – all of which can be 'measured' against set targets. This, she states, can contribute to certain professional groups becoming more marginalised and devalued as potential counter-discourses are effectively suppressed. However, Davies and Preston (2002) argue that CPD can take the ECEC professional, including teachers, beyond the observable behaviours required for registration or Initial Teacher Education (ITE) by setting up situations which allow them time to reflect on and analyse their own practice and to re-evaluate their existing knowledge in the light of new information. This possibility of evaluating work within a theoretical framework is not a category addressed by inspections.

Osgood (2012) rightly points out that the ECEC workforce is being made to take the blame for government policy which is patently not working. It is not, after all, sensible for governments to blame themselves or the service user (in this case, children and families) for any failures. The results of good practice in ECEC will really be seen when children complete their education and move into adulthood. HighScope (see Chapter 14) is the only substantial research project extending over a long enough term to deliver useful data. There has been much more discussion and apparent emphasis on the importance of ECEC and particularly early intervention, in recent years. There is greater understanding that 'dollar for dollar' the best returns occur in the earliest years (Heckman, 2008). This means that putting time and money into ECEC ensures better outcomes for more people, and therefore fewer people end up without qualifications or skills, in prison, unemployed, etc. The HighScope research bears this out (Schweinhart et al., 2005). However, the desire to intervene early or provide education and care for all children at an earlier age has translated into a plethora of standardisation, target setting and paper chasing that has little to do with raising the *quality* of provision.

Hargreaves and Hopkins (2002, cited in Walsh, undated) believe that deep pedagogical changes will not be driven by centralised government policy. These authors agree that 'informed prescription' needs to be replaced with 'informed professionalism' but are concerned that in the past 20 years many staff have lost some of the ability to have confidence in their own thoughts and ideas. The authors here are referring to schools, but the statements are equally appropriate for the ECEC workforce:

> The too lengthy period of informed prescription has actually reduced the capabilities of the teaching profession to respond to change creatively. Teachers now expect change to be required of them, but change that is centrally prescribed, governed by the rule book and by constant assessment of content and a narrow range of skills. (p. 16)

Implementation of the Curriculum for Excellence has been under way in Scotland for some years now. One of the implications of the values, purposes and principles of this new curriculum, encompassing ages 3–18, and so for teachers, schools, early years centres and colleges, was to:

> clarify about what education is seeking to achieve for each child; flexibility to apply professional judgement in planning programmes and activities to respond to the needs of individual children; a curriculum which is not overcrowded because of too much content; more teaching across and beyond traditional subject boundaries; time and space for innovative and creative teaching and learning. (Scottish Executive, 2004: 16)

Evidence from visits to many schools would substantiate the comments made by Walsh, Hopkins and Hargreaves above. The space for creativity, innovation and professional judgement has been given to staff, but in many cases staff are uncertain and feel de-skilled in knowing how to go about making use of this freedom in ways that are beneficial to children, particularly in early years. Guidance, which was given around possible experiences and outcomes, is often and increasingly being interpreted by school managements and local authorities as 'targets'. There are, of course, some schools with enlightened leadership and strong and relevant support from local authorities, where there are clear examples of excellent and innovative practice.

An example of this, which should indeed be interpreted as good practice, is the merging of pre-school (nursery, 3–5-year-olds) and Primary 1 (5–6-year-olds) into 'Early

Level', with encouragement to use play-based approaches to ease the transition into school. There are some excellent examples of doors being opened, literally, between the nursery and P1, with children having freedom of access across both areas, with a restricted amount of whole-class teaching taking place in any one school day, allowing a much clearer focus on individual needs. However, there are many other examples of a 'token' approach to these play-based approaches, with 'soft start' being typically around 30 minutes of 'free play' when children come into class in the morning. This suggests that active learning is not really valued, but that the 'real work' will start at 9.30 instead of 9.00. Or perhaps that 'real school' will start in Primary 2 instead of Primary 1?

CASE STUDY

One child on starting Primary 1 (5–6-year-olds) was obviously experiencing separation anxiety from his parents. The child was tearful and unable to settle each day and at times through the day.

The child had previously attended the nursery class in the same school, without any problems.

The explanation from the class teacher was that:

- the child was spoiled and used to getting his own way
- the child would have to get used to the routine of 'real' school
- the child would have to grow up – and quickly.

How would you have dealt with this situation in your setting?

With reference to the Leuven Involvement Scale (LIS) discussed in Chapter 15, how would you rate:

- the involvement of the adult?
- the well-being of the child?

This reaction from a teacher may reflect the fact that there is currently no requirement for teachers to develop and extend their expertise in working with young children beyond the basic teaching qualification. Many teaching in nursery or Primary 1 (now the Early Level in Scotland) have no specialist training. In many authorities in Scotland, teachers are being withdrawn altogether from nursery classes which are being run by Early Years Practitioners (EYPs). This contradicts evidence from research that supports properly and more highly qualified ECEC professionals working with very young children (Sylva et al., 2004). As is clearly demonstrated by the HighScope programme in Chapter 14, the positive effects of early intervention can be long lasting, with appropriate staffing. The presence of the most able people educated to a high standard initially and engaging in ongoing specialist professional development is supported by practice in Sweden and in Finland that is justified by results reported in OECD (2004) and is also reported on in the UK (Layard and Dunn, 2009), based on research (Sylva et al., 2004) referred to above. A high standard of entry to begin qualifications to work in ECEC, followed by a high standard of qualification to enter the profession and again followed by a requirement for continued professional development, will have an impact on professional status and professional autonomy. For the latter, it is vital to establish a 'specific body of knowledge' or 'occupational specific knowledge' and it is hard to see how this can happen in the present climate.

There is a two-tier system at present within the ECEC workforce, in terms of status, and we are not suggesting that teachers are 'better' than other staff employed in pre-school settings. Teachers have a different role to play. However, for early intervention to be of benefit to children in the long term, we must be able to harness all professional roles within ECEC in a way that enables people to work together. Children in Europe (2008) suggests that rather than a fixation on outcomes, in asking whether services have achieved specific targets, the question should be re-phrased to ask, 'What has this service for children achieved?' This could be re-phrased again, as above, to 'How is this helping children?' Surely this is *always* the question.

The qualifications minefield

During a recent workforce development meeting, where ECEC workers were interpreting presentations by a regulatory body as yet another demand being made of them, a question was posed: 'Which other professions have to compete constantly with regulatory bodies moving the goalposts in terms of their perceived competence to do the job that they are employed to do?'

After considerable reflection on this question, the only satisfactory answer that can be suggested is the fact that other professions insist on the entrance qualification being gained before the person is employed. Perhaps this is something that we should strive for again in the UK? The Nutbrown Review, Interim Report (2012a) states that many respondents have suggested a return to the type of taught qualification, such as NNEB, which existed previously. However, perhaps the significant word here is 'taught', in contrast with the work-based routes for vocational qualifications. There may be criticism for developing a 'one size fits all' approach, but it could also be suggested that it would in fact help strengthen the voice of the sector. An unsolicited contact from a recent BA graduate sums up the current situation:

> It occurred to me yesterday that 21 years on from my previous post in the same school, under different leadership, despite gaining an NC, HNC in Childcare and Education, achieving the BA Childhood Practice, self funding and undertaking high quality CPD on an annual basis, my working conditions have deteriorated beyond recognition and employment prospects are no better.

Anecdotal evidence from student cohorts on the BA Childhood Practice at our university would provide further evidence in support of the above statement. Many students view the degree as a transferable qualification and a one-way ticket out of a poorly paid and undervalued profession. How is this helping children?

We are aware of the significance of recent research around brain development of babies and young children and the importance of positive experiences within the early years for future development, yet we also appear to be happy to continue to leave the care of young babies to those with the lowest of all academic qualifications, often themselves challenged by demands of literacy and numeracy. Work-based routes into various professions were introduced to 'professionalise' the workforce and provide a way of formalising experiential learning gained over a number of years. However, this has now become a seemingly acceptable route for school leavers. Nutbrown (2012a, section 3.14) states:

> Several people have ... expressed concern that the work-based learning route – originally conceived as a way of recognising the skills and knowledge that experienced members of the workforce possess – lacks the rigour and depth of knowledge necessary to train new entrants to the workforce.

Is this really in the best interests of our very young children? OECD (2004: 28) states clearly that 'staff meeting children every day must have high standards of training, since it is the daily interactions between the adult and the child that make the difference in children's well-being and learning'.

The Nutbrown Review, Interim Report (2012a: 10) also states:

> The status of the profession is intrinsically linked to the qualifications market. The demands we place on those on award bearing routes leading to work in the sector reflect the aspirations we have of them. Raising the bar on entry requirements, and demanding high levels of qualification, can help to demonstrate a commitment to a high status profession. Introducing more teachers into early years settings – with specialist early years training – will also likely contribute to better outcomes for children and a higher status profession.

We would agree with the above statements, and from those points of view perhaps we should look at the 'standards' which apply to the ECEC workforce, including standards for Initial Teacher Education, as being the minimum requirement.

These findings reported by Nutbrown in the Interim Report (2012a) have translated, in the final report, to a call for Level 2 English and maths as 'more stringent entry requirements' to address the poor standards of literacy and numeracy found among many who have achieved the Level 3 early years qualification (Nutbrown, 2012b). This is in the hope that it will help to 'put an end to the view that early years is an option for those who are "not bright enough" to do other jobs, or a "last resort" for those who have left school unqualified' (section 3.14). This seems to be a rather 'watered down' version of 'raising the bar' and steers away from introducing more teachers with specialist early years training.

Undertaking high-quality CPD provision, where all could take part together, thus strengthening inter-professional approaches, would provide a mechanism for all staff working with young children to find their 'voice' and start to bring about changes from inside the sector. If we take the undergraduate teaching qualification as an example, we can clearly see that throughout their time at university (four years in Scotland), the student has input from suitably qualified staff concerning educational theory and practice. The student goes out on school experience and in most cases the quality of the student experience is determined by the quality of the classroom experience observed, together with the level of interest and support provided by the class teacher. Throughout all of this, the student is working towards being able to achieve the Standard for Registration with the General Teaching Council for Scotland. No student at this point is going to consider themselves an 'expert' in their role, certainly not an expert in early years education, merely a beginner, continuing along the pathway of lifelong learning. For the new teacher, autonomy is also likely to be a daunting prospect and they are very likely to be caught up with the current preoccupation with assessment, accreditation, target setting and accountability.

The impact of quality continuing professional development (CPD)

We can enable the ECEC workforce to develop a collective voice and professional autonomy, through the provision of quality CPD. Working with babies and under-3s is not part of initial teacher education programmes. However, the importance of knowing about a pupil's prior learning and experience is understood. It might, therefore, be sensible for anyone involved in teaching, particularly in the early level of primary school, to be required to undertake quality CPD which involves theory and practice in child development and learning, from conception. Development of expertise within this area, together with a basic qualification, would provide professionals with the underpinning theory, the evidence and the justification to be able to challenge, from the standpoint of a knowledge base, some of the top-down directives that are prevalent today.

This type of CPD, which is founded on a social-constructivist approach, is an extremely important contribution to providing an impact on practice. Burchell et al. (2002) state that the impact of one person's CPD can be significant for others within that context, by informal means of disseminating information through low-level chat in the staffroom. This was reinforced by a student on the Post Graduate Certificate (PGC) in Early Years who contacted me by email to say: 'I have found my time at ... to be inspirational. It is so different from anything I've ever seen before. It's hard to get me to stop talking to colleagues at work about what can be achieved!'

One inspired member of staff can make a difference! Sandberg et al. (2007) would agree with this statement but take this a step further by stating that for the practice of an individual to change, it has to be challenged in a different context. This implies actual practice in another context, not just observing.

Laevers (2005) is very clear that autonomy requires an experienced 'teacher' style. Burchell et al. (2002), Davies and Preston (2002) and Sandberg et al. (2007) all identify increased self-confidence, self-esteem, motivation and competence as positive charac-teristics which are strengthened through participation in CPD. Both Burchell et al. (2002) and Sandberg et al. (2007) also discuss the emerging 'changed view of the child', which encourages teachers to view the child as a competent person and thereby to move the teacher/child relationship further along the axis of mutual respect. Sandberg et al. (2007) also point out that this facilitates changes in practice in the ways of working with young children, as engagement with underpinning theory during CPD provides greater pedagogical security upon which to base decisions and justify actions. Davies and Preston (2002) also agree with this point of view and state that it is not enough to be able to relate theory to practice; the theory has to be inte-grated and demonstrated in practice, which takes time, as learning must be internalised before being embedded in practice.

Many authors, including those mentioned above, are widely in agreement concern-ing the importance of quality CPD for ECEC staff and also concerning the desirable characteristics that might emerge. Osgood (2006: 11) sums up this possible impact on practice by stating:

> In summary, I am proposing that education and training that goes beyond the demonstra-tion of 'technical competence' to provide an opportunity for critical reflection and con-sciousness raising will enable practitioners to assess how they are positioned and the ways in which they might actively reposition themselves in competing and alternative discourses of professionalism.

In order to benefit from this type of deep-level learning, Laevers (2005) suggests that teachers or other ECEC staff need to have first acquired a certain degree of compe-tence and experience. This would be supported by Sandberg et al. (2007) through the need for having 'distance from the training'. Staff do need to have distance from their initial qualification to allow the learning from that to be practised and internalised before undertaking this type of CPD.

If these conditions are met, then undertaking this type of CPD can make a radical impact on practice, and in particular on the ways in which the child is viewed. Sandberg et al. (2007: 317) state, in relation to CPD for pre-school staff in Sweden: 'Pre-school teachers take part in the latest educational research into children's play, learning and development. Such research influences teachers' fundamental views and attitudes, and therefore their professional identity.'

Evidence from student assignments as part of the PGC Early Years would certainly substantiate these statements:

- 'It has made me a lot more confident in fighting my own corner in the early stages back in school.'
- 'It is nice to have the reading behind you and to be able to make a professional judgement ... it gave more assurance in what I thought myself and I can justify my decision making.'
- 'I was able to be a lot more articulate about ... [and] justify what I was doing.'

Conclusion

All the curricula and pedagogies that we have reviewed throughout previous chapters: experiential education (EXE) (Laevers), the HighScope curriculum, the Reggio Emilia approach, Te Whāriki, the Swedish curriculum, start from the premise that the child is a competent individual, and encourage the development of a mutual respect between adults and children (OECD, 2004). It is clear from extensive studies, including more recent research highlighted in Chapter 1, that children learn much through observation and imitation. It seems important then that if our aim is for children to learn how to learn, develop positive dispositions towards learning and become lifelong learners that the adults educating and caring for them should be models.

One further point is worth noting. At the same time that Sweden simplified its qualifications system for ECEC, it also brought all the pre-school and daycare services under the umbrella of Education, rather than Social Services. Likewise in New Zealand with the introduction of Te Whāriki, one body, the Ministry of Education, governs services for children. Professional autonomy and a stronger voice for the ECEC workforce might be promoted in the UK more easily if services were also to be firmly united under Education. The fact that services and provision for babies and toddlers are wholly or partly governed by 'care' authorities sends out a strong message that this is the important aspect in the first years of life – when in fact this is also the most important time for *learning*. Perhaps in this way, we will be able to build a strong and equal partnership between 'care' and 'education', where both sides can be 'treated as equal parts of the educational system' (Children in Europe, 2008: 9).

Professional autonomy is built on the possession of a body of knowledge that is specific to the profession. In ECEC, the specific knowledge must be concerned with theories around how children develop and learn. By grasping the concept of professional autonomy, we have the possibility to allow the ECEC workforce to develop from mere 'technicians' to 'active professionals', able to take decisions based on professional judgement and justified by a solid knowledge base.

Here is a final quote from a former head teacher of a primary school in Scotland (TESS, 2012: unpaginated) regarding the implementation of the Curriculum for Excellence:

> [There is a] problem with educational initiatives like Curriculum for Excellence. Someone starts off with a very good idea and then everyone else steps in with their tuppence worth. It seems as if it is necessary to add and add until the originality and freshness disappears. The straitjacket is firmly clamped on. What was initially intended as CfE starts to get buried alive ... In my brief encounter with the education system of the US, with its over-reliance on tests and grade scores and general stifling of creativity, I would conclude that CfE is a gift to Scottish education. It is about engaging with children's learning and allows a professional freedom that many Americans would die for.

There is scope for professional autonomy to flourish within this type of curriculum, but we must be able to support ECEC staff in developing this.

Further reading

Children in Europe (2008) *Young Children and their Services: Developing a European Approach*. Available at: www.childrenineurope.org

Nutbrown, C. (2012) *Review of Education and Childcare Qualifications: Interim Report*. London: Department for Education.

Organisation for Economic Co-operation and Development (OECD) (2004) *Starting Strong: Curricula and Pedagogies in Early Childhood Education and Care – Five Curriculum Outlines*. Paris: OECD.

The Times Educational Supplement Scotland (2012) 'Take an ex-pat's word for it: Scotland's CfE is to die for!', 25 May.

References

Burchell, H., Dyson, J. and Rees, M. (2002) 'Making a difference: a study of the impact of continuing professional development on professional practice', *Journal of In-Service Education*, 28(2): 219–30.

Children in Europe (2008) *Young Children and their Services: Developing a European Approach*. Available at: www.childrenineurope.org

Davies, R. and Preston, M. (2002) 'An evaluation of the impact of continuing professional development on personal and professional lives', *Journal of In-Service Education*, 28(2): 231–54.

Foucault, M. (1980) *Power/Knowledge: Selected Interviews and Other Writings, 1972–1977* (C. Gordon trans.). New York: Pantheon.

Heckman, J.J. (2008) *Return on Investment: Cost vs. Benefits*. University of Chicago. Available at: http://www.childandfamilypolicy.duke.edu/pdfs/10yranniversary_Heckmanhandout.pdf

Laevers, F. (2005) *Deep Level Learning and the Experiential Approach in Early Childhood and Primary Education: Experiential Education*. Leuven: Katholieke Universiteit, Belgium.

Layard, R. and Dunn, J. with the panel of The Good Childhood Inquiry (2009) 'Conclusions', in The Landmark Report for The Children's Society: *A Good Childhood: Searching for Values in a Competitive Age*. London: Penguin.

Nutbrown, C. (2012a) *Review of Education and Childcare Qualifications: Interim Report*. London: Department for Education.

Nutbrown, C. (2012b) *Foundations for Quality: The Independent Review of Early Education and Childcare Qualifications – Final Report*. London: Department for Education.

Organisation for Economic Co-operation and Development (OECD) (2004) *Starting Strong: Curricula and Pedagogies in Early Childhood Education and Care – Five Curriculum Outlines*. Paris: OECD.

Osgood, J. (2006) 'Deconstructing professionalism in early childhood education: resisting the regulatory gaze', *Contemporary Issues in Early Childhood*, 7(1): 5–14.

Osgood, J. (2012) *Narratives from the Nursery: Negotiating Professional Identities in Early Childhood*. London: Routledge.

Raya, M.J. (2007) 'Developing professional autonomy: a balance between license and responsibility', *Independence*, 40.

Sandberg, A., Anstett, S. and Wahlgren, U. (2007) 'The value of in-service education for quality in pre-school', *Professional Development in Education*, 33(3): 301–19.

Schweinhart, L.J., Montie, J., Xiang, Z., Barnett, W.S., Belfield, C.R. and Nores, M. (2005) *Lifetime Effects – The High/Scope Perry Preschool Study Through Age 40*. Ypsilante, USA: High/Scope Educational Research Foundation.

Scottish Executive (2004) *Curriculum for Excellence*. Edinburgh: Scottish Executive.

Sylva, K., Melhuish, E., Sammons, P., Siraj-Blatchford, I. and Taggart, B. (2004) *Effective Pre-School Education: A Longitudinal Study funded by the DfES 1997–2004 (EPPE Project)*. London: University of London, Institute of Education.

The Times Educational Supplement Scotland (TESS) (2012) 'Take an ex-pat's word for it: Scotland's CfE is to die for!', 25 May.

Walsh, K. (undated) *Leading and Managing the Future School: Developing Organisational and Management Structure in Secondary Schools*. National College for School Leadership. Available at: http://www.rtuni.org/uploads/docs/Leading%20and%20Managing%20the%20Future%20School.pdf (accessed 23.05.12).

INDEX

THE GOOD WRITING GUIDE FOR EDUCATION STUDENTS

Third Edition

Dominic Wyse *Institute of Education, University of London*

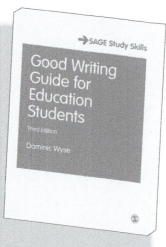

This accessible guide to writing academically is based on the author's many years of experience helping students to improve their writing and get better marks in assignments. The advice works because it uses real examples of students' work to explain what tutors look for, and shows you how to get there.

New to this **Third Edition**:

- Increased coverage of plagiarism (and how to avoid it)
- How to show critical reflection and judgment
- Turning useful notes from lectures and readings into powerful written arguments
- Updated material on citations and references
- New examples of students' work
- Developing an academic 'voice'.

The book is packed with practical advice on how to read widely, search for reading materials, structure your writing and use language effectively. With plenty of dos and don'ts, this is a perfect guide for students studying at all levels.

Dominic Wyse is Professor of Early Years and Primary Education at the Institute of Education, University of London.

CONTENTS

Reading Widely \ Searching for Reading Materials \ Planning for Writing \ Small-Scale Research Projects \ Referencing \ Structuring Your Writing \ Grammar and Punctuation \ Spelling \ Presentation and Proof-Reading \ Assessment and Learning from Feedback \ Further Reading \ Glossary \ Index

READERSHIP

Education students studying at all levels

SAGE STUDY SKILLS SERIES

2012 • 168 pages
Cloth (978-1-4462-0709-3) • £60.00
Paper (978-1-4462-0710-9) • £16.99

ALSO FROM SAGE

UNDERSTANDING EARLY YEARS POLICY

Third Edition

Peter Baldock *Education Consultant, Sheffield*, **Damien Fitzgerald** and **Janet Kay** *both at Sheffield Hallam University*

'Baldock et al is a core text for undergraduates and postgraduates interested in the complex and broad implications of Early Years policy and policy-making. This new edition offers insights into domestic and international perspectives on Early Years, and opportunities to increase understandings of how policy is shaped and applied through case studies and reflective exercises'

-Dr. Richard Race, *Department of Education, University of Roehampton*

Fully updated to include all the latest developments in early years policy such as the revised Early Years Foundation Stage (EYFS) this book explores how policy is made, implemented, analysed and developed over time. There is a complete overview of early years policy, and an evaluation of its ongoing impact on practice. Case studies, points for reflection and activities encourage discussion and critical thinking.

This **Third Edition** has been significantly updated to include:

- A new chapter on international early years policy
- Discussion of the impact of the recession and the Coalition Government's policies
- Material on how ordinary practitioners can influence policy
- A revised timeline of early years legislation.

This text is an essential read for early years students at all levels, and early years practitioners.

CONTENTS

READERSHIP

Early years students at all levels; also early years practitioners

January 2013 • 208 pages
Cloth (978-1-4462-0705-5) • £70.00
Paper (978-1-4462-0706-2) • £23.99

ALSO FROM SAGE